Aesthetics of Music

Volume 7

Books by David Whitwell

Philosophic Foundations of Education
Foundations of Music Education
Music Education of the Future
The Sousa Oral History Project
The Art of Musical Conducting
The Longy Club: 1900–1917
A Concise History of the Wind Band
Wagner on Bands
Berlioz on Bands
Chopin: A Self-Portrait
Schumann: A Self-Portrait In His Own Words
Mendelssohn: A Self-Portrait In His Own Words
Liszt: A Self-Portrait In His Own Words
La Téléphonie and the Universal Musical Language
Extraordinary Women

Aesthetics of Music Series

Aesthetics of Music in Ancient Civilizations
Aesthetics of Music in the Middle Ages
Aesthetics of Music in the Early Renaissance
Aesthetics of Music in Sixteenth-Century Italy, France and Spain
Aesthetics of Music in Sixteenth-Century Germany, the Low Countries and England
Aesthetics of Baroque Music in Italy, Spain, the German-Speaking Countries and the Low Countries

The History and Literature of the Wind Band and Wind Ensemble Series

Volume 1 The Wind Band and Wind Ensemble Before 1500
Volume 2 The Renaissance Wind Band and Wind Ensemble
Volume 3 The Baroque Wind Band and Wind Ensemble
Volume 4 The Classical Period Wind Band and Wind Ensemble
Volume 5 The Nineteenth-Century Wind Band and Wind Ensemble
Volume 6 A Catalog of Multi-Part Repertoire for Wind Instruments or for Undesignated Instrumentation before 1600
Volume 7 Baroque Wind Band and Wind Ensemble Repertoire
Volume 8 Classic Period Wind Band and Wind Ensemble Repertoire
Volume 9 Nineteenth-Century Wind Band and Wind Ensemble Repertoire
Volume 10 A Supplementary Catalog of Wind Band and Wind Ensemble Repertoire
Volume 11 A Catalog of Wind Repertoire before the Twentieth Century for One to Five Players
Volume 12 A Second Supplementary Catalog of Early Wind Band and Wind Ensemble Repertoire
Volume 13 Name Index, Volumes 1–12, The History and Literature of the Wind Band and Wind Ensemble

www.whitwellbooks.com

David Whitwell

Aesthetics of Music

VOLUME 7

AESTHETICS OF BAROQUE MUSIC IN FRANCE

Edited by Craig Dabelstein

Whitwell Publishing • Austin, Texas, USA

Whitwell Publishing, Austin 78701
www.whitwellbooks.com

© 1996, 2013 by David Whitwell
All rights reserved. First edition 1996.
Second edition 2013

Printed in the United States of America

Paperback
ISBN-13: 978-1-936512-64-5
ISBN-10: 1936512645

Composed in Minion Pro

CONTENTS

	Foreword	vii
	Acknowledgements	xi
1	*The Musical Scene in France*	1
2	*Aesthetic Views of French Musicians*	19
3	*Mersenne*	37
4	*French Philosophers, I*	83
5	*French Philosophers, II*	119
6	*Descartes*	163
7	*French Drama*	183
8	*French Fiction*	213
9	*On French Manners*	227
10	*Voltaire, as Philosopher*	243
11	*Voltaire, as Playwright*	283
12	*Voltaire, as Poet*	301
13	*Voltaire's Fiction*	317
	Bibliography	327
	Index	331
	About the Author	335
	About the Editor	337

FOREWORD

WE DEFINE MUSIC to be that form of music performed live before listeners. We define Aesthetics in Music to be a study of the nature of the perception of music by the listener.

We believe the performance of music in actual practice falls naturally into four classes. These are Art Music, Educational Music, Functional Music and Entertainment Music.

I. ART MUSIC

Art Music we believe is defined by four conditions, *all* of which *must always be present*. These are:

1. *Art music is inspired.* Art music is music in which it seems evident that the composer has made an honest attempt to communicate genuine feelings. Feelings, which may range from lofty and noble to superficial and vulgar, must be presumed to be generally recognizable in music, as they are in any other art form, including painting, sculpture, dance, and architecture. In Art Music, lofty and noble feelings are paramount.

    Due to the common genetically understood nature of emotions, it must also be understood that in music emotions or feelings cannot be 'faked.' They will always be recognized as such by any contemplative listener.

2. *Art Music has no purpose other than the communication of its own aesthetic content.* Art Music is free of any purpose or function, save the spiritual communication of pure beauty.

3. *Art Music is that which enjoys a performance faithful to the intent of the composer.*

4. *Art Music must have a listener capable of contemplation.*

If any of these conditions are missing, the performance must result in a lesser aesthetic experience. For example, the *Ninth Symphony* of Beethoven played in a stadium, during the half-time of a professional football game, would fail for the lack of the presence of Condition Number Four. The same Symphony heard in a concert hall, but in a poor performance, not faithful to the intent of the composer, would fail for the lack of the presence of Condition Number Three.

II. Educational Music

Educational Music may or may not have the same conditions as Art Music, excepting Condition Number Two; it may or may not occur within an educational institution. Educational Music is didactic music, music which has the specific and *additional* aim to educate. In the strictest sense, if the *primary purpose* of Music is to educate, it cannot be Art Music—for Art Music has no purpose.

III. Functional Music

Functional Music is music put at the service of something else. We include here, for example, all kinds of religious music, music for weddings, music for the military, and occupational music. Functional Music may share the same conditions as Art Music, excepting Condition Number Two.

One may ask, How can a Mozart Mass be called Functional Music, and not Art Music? If the observer were not contemplatively listening to the music, but were rather contemplating religious thoughts, then the Mozart Mass becomes merely a very high level of Functional Music. If, on the other hand, the observer is a contemplative listener of music, forgetting about religion, then the Mozart Mass is Art Music, but has failed in its purpose as church music.

Military and wedding music are examples of music in which the contemplative listener is missing entirely. How about airport, supermarket and elevator music where there is no listener at all? According to the definition we have given above, recorded music without listeners is not to be considered music at all.

IV. Entertainment Music

Entertainment Music is music with no object other than to please. It will always be missing Condition Four, the contemplative listener. For this reason, Entertainment Music may be inspired music, but the composer is unlikely to be inspired by lofty and noble emotions, knowing there will be no contemplative listener. Entertainment Music and Art Music can never be the same thing because of Condition Number Two: Art Music has no purpose other than the communication of its own aesthetic content. It is inconsistent with the nature of great art to have any extrinsic purpose, including the purpose to entertain.

The first philosopher to address the impact which Art has on an observer was Aristotle, in his *Poetics*, as part of a discussion of Tragedy, which like music has both a material, written form and a live performance form. In this treatise, Aristotle first considers the nature and contribution of each of the specific components of the written form of the Tragedy in his typically methodical style. His great contribution, however, comes when he has completed this discussion, for he then goes beyond the material form of the play itself to discuss the observer. He makes it clear that not only is the end purpose of the elements of the play to produce a specific experience in the observer, but that the nature of this experience is what distinguishes Tragedy from other dramatic forms, such as Spectacle. It was in this moment that he created a new branch of Philosophy which we call 'Aesthetics.'

Our purpose is to provide a source book of representative descriptions of actual performances, observations by philosophers, poets and other commentators which contribute insights to our understanding of what music meant to listeners during the early Renaissance. It is for this reason that when discussing contemporary treatises on music that we concentrate on those passages which offer insights relative to the aesthetics of music and musical performance rather than the usual technical subjects such as scales, modes and counterpoint which fill most books on Renaissance music.

Since traditional musicology has focused almost exclusively on sacred and secular vocal music of the Renaissance, we have also included numerous references which we hope will reveal a much wider world of music during this period.

We are also interested in contemporary views on the physiology of knowing, especially with regard to the relationship of the senses and Reason, and related psychological ideas, such as Pleasure and Pain and the Emotions, which might offer a frame of reference for their perspective on the perception of music.

This is the seventh volume in a series of eight, ranging from the music of the ancient civilizations through the Baroque Period.

David Whitwell
Austin, Texas

ACKNOWLEDGMENTS

This new edition would not have been possible without the encouragement and help of Craig Dabelstein of Brisbane, Australia. His experience as a musician and educator himself has contributed greatly to his expertise as editor of this volume.

                                    David Whitwell
                                      Austin, 2013

1 THE MUSICAL SCENE IN FRANCE

France began the seventeenth century on the fast track to a modern society.[1] Under Henry IV's minister, Sully, an honest, intelligent Calvinist, the privileges of the nobility were restricted and worthy members of the middle class were given important new opportunities. Tax abuses were ended, the economy was restored, industries were strengthened, civil engineering projects modernized France while explorers claimed new colonies in Canada. All this ended with the assassination of Henry IV in 1610.

Control now returned to Catholic kings and although the two chief ministers, Richelieu and Mazarin, were effective administrators, the state reverted in many ways to an old fashioned monarchy.

MUSIC OF THE COURT

The Baroque arrived in France under the reign of Louis XIII, a weak man who suffered in equal measure from physical problems and doctors.[2] Inclined toward the male sex, when the worried government officials pointed out that he had not visited the bed of his wife in thirteen years, he relented and produced his greatest contribution to France—Louis XIV.

Louis XIII was remembered by his contemporaries as being very fond of music, for sometimes joining his singers and for having actually composed a *ballet de cour*.[3] Under his Chapelle there were only fourteen singers, two choirboys, a cornettist and a lute instructor was engaged for the education of the choirboys. The musicians of the Chambre included another five singers, two lutanists, a spinet player and a flautist.

The larger instrumental ensembles were organized under the Écurie,[4] the most important of which were the *24 Violins du Roi* and the distinguished *Les Grands Hautbois*. The latter ensemble had been formed under François I and consisted of an expanded Hautboisten

---

1. Our purpose here is not an attempt to summarize the technical development of Baroque music itself in France, and its composers, but rather to present a brief overview of the environment in which the music was performed and its general aesthetic nature. At the same time, we take the opportunity to include important material not found in general music history texts.
2. In a single year they bled him forty-seven times and gave him two hundred and fifteen enemas!
3. Catherine Massip, 'Paris, 1600-61,' in *The Early Baroque Era* (Englewood Cliffs: Prentice Hall, 1994), 225.
4. This was an ancient title meaning 'stable,' but now included not only musicians, but riding masters, heralds of arms, sword bearers and officers of the royal household. It might have been better named the Department of Ceremony.

ensemble of two shawm and two cornett players playing dessus (treble), four alto or tenor shawms playing haute-contre and taille parts, two trombones playing basse-taille, and the bass shawms playing a basse part.[5] These larger ensembles provided the music for the *ballet de cour*, the principal large-scale musical entertainment of the early seventeenth century and a form similar to the English masque, and for Italian Opera when it reached the court in 1645.

Louis XIV developed a court bigger and richer than any in the history of modern Europe. Many German dukes sent their eldest son on a sabbatical to Versailles to learn how to do it right! When Frederick the Great in Potsdam once wondered why he was sitting on French furniture, in a French-styled palace, speaking French and eating French food, the answer was the influence of the court of Louis XIV.

Louis XIV himself was also an extraordinary man, as kings go. He was an effective and hard-working administrator, in addition to having strong personal qualities. He created the most extensive musical establishment known until his time, organized under four separate administrative branches: the Écurie, the Chapelle, the Chambre and the Maison Militaire.

The musicians of the Écurie enjoyed high prestige, having the right of *commensaux* (meal companions of the king), exemption from many taxes and obligations to church-wardens and civic officials. They received gifts of food, clothing and financial bonuses and they were allowed to live and do extra work in Paris. At this time the members appear to have been hired more on the basis of recommendation, than by audition. It follows that study with a current member was the most promising route to success for a young musician. The importance of such teacher–pupil relationships can be seen in a typical contract drawn up between Jean Baptiste Desjardins, a member of the *Les Grands Hautbois*, and a student named François Gillotot. The modern teacher might feel reluctant to assume some of the responsibilities expected of the seventeenth-century teacher.

> Today it has appeared in front of the notary of Paris that the undersigned Jean B. Desjardins … is obligated to François Gillotot, a servant of M. the Abbey Bouchart … to show him how to play the oboe, flute and instrumental music which this entails. Gillotot may be free to obtain this goal and do his profession without being obligated. Mr. Desjardins will furnish him with instruments. This contract entails the sum of 185 livres … [The final payment] is made when Mr. Desjardins succeeds in placing Gillotot in a quality position as an oboist. Desjardins must try to place Gillotot … Gillotot must go precisely all the days to take his lessons with Desjardins.[6]

Although the *Les Grands Hautbois* consisted of musicians who were primarily wind players, it is clear that by this date they were actively doubling on other instruments as well. In the case of one member, Jacques Danican Philidor, the inventory taken after his death in 1708 revealed that he owned fourteen oboes [shawms] (dessus, quintes and tailles), twenty-one

---

[5] Jules Écorchville, 'Quelques Documents sur la Musique de la Grand-Écurie du Roi,' in *Sammelbande des Internationalen Musikgesellschaft* (1903), III, 608ff.

[6] Dated October 3, 1701, quoted in 'Documents du Minutier Central,' in *Recherches sur la Musique francaise classique* (Paris: Picard, 1968), 245.

flutes (dessus, quintes, tailles and bass), two bassoons, two flageolets, a violin, a tambour and a pair of timpani.[7]

It was this ensemble which introduced the modern oboe during the second half of the seventeenth century. A fascinating report by one listener, who heard the ensemble in about 1665, appears to have heard the players at the time they were still struggling with learning to control the new instrument.

> The oboes, whom one can now hear at the king's palace and in Paris, have stately repertoire and style. Their cadences are correct, their vibrato is sweet, their ornaments are just as correct as the more educated vocal ones and those of the most perfect instruments. We have seen their success in the theater, especially in certain entrées. They had a marvelous effect in one Pastorale. But one can never be confident of the air; the shortness of breath, the thickening of the lungs, the fatigue of the stomach and finally, one is conscious of a notable difference in beginnings and endings; here one could discover more exactness.[8]

For the larger productions, such as those by Lully, these wind players often joined the strings, doubling their parts. The famous Jean-Jacques Rousseau, who had once been a professional music copyist, recalled this tradition and reveals further details of the modern oboe in its first generation.

> The parts for the oboe that one extracts from the violin of the grand orchestra can not be exactly copied as they are in the original, since the tessitura is less than the violin and there are soft notes it can not produce; it is also not as agile at slow speeds: the force of the oboe must be handled gently so as not to obscure the accents of the music. If I had to judge a symphonic copyist … I would give him the task of extracting an oboe part from the violin. Every copyist should know how to do it.[9]

Another separate ensemble under the Écurie was the six-member *Musettes et Hautbois du Poitou*.[10] The musette was a small, highly decorated, bagpipe, but what was the 'Hautbois du Poitou?' The instrument was used in three sizes in this ensemble (alto, tenor and bass), but as there no surviving specimens, no one is quite sure how the instrument differed from either the old shawm or the new oboe.[11] There is one contemporary reference which recalled,

> … and the oboes from Poitou were called upon to dispel the despondent mood of the king.[12]

---

7   Marcelle Benoit, *Versailles et les Musiciens du Roi* (Paris: Picard, 1971), 360.

8   Abbé des Pures, quoted in J. Écorcheville, *Vignt suites d'orchestre* (Paris, 1906), I, 92.

9   Jean-Jacques Rousseau, 'Copiste,' in *Dictionnaire de Musique* (Paris, 1767), 130.

10 Marcelle Benoit, in 'Paris, 1661-87: the Age of Lully,' in *The Early Baroque Era* (Englewood Cliffs: Prentice Hall, 1994), 253, curiously reduces this to 'Poitevin bagpipes,' which neither describes accurately the musette, nor is reflected in court documents in the National Archives.

11 Trichet and Furetière, in their treatises on instruments, and Diderot, in the *Encyclopédie*, all mention the instrument but fail to provide details. Mersenne, in his *Treatise, on Instruments* [V, xxxiv], includes an illustration which pictures this instrument as differing with the oboe primarily in having a capped reed.

12 *Commentaires of Philippe de Commines*, quoted on the jacket of the LP Turnabout Vox TV-S 34376.

Similarly, another ensemble in the Écurie, *Les Cromornes*, consisted of an instrument for which there are no survivors. While it is tempting to think of this as a crumhorn ensemble,[13] the evidence points rather to some member of the bassoon family.[14]

Finally, there were two ensembles, the *Les Fifres et Tambours* and *Les Trompettes*, which supplied ceremonial duties and accompanied the king everywhere he went.

Another administrative wing, the Musique de la Chambre, was organized under two *surintendants*, one of whom was the famous Jean-Baptiste Lully. Lully's success in organizing the large-scale musical entertainments of the king was the source of his eventual control of the musical activities at Versailles, as well as over the stage productions in Paris. It was under this administrative unit that Couperin begrudgingly made his trips to the palace. Speaking of one of his publications, he says,

> I have composed them for the little chamber concerts where Louis Quatorze made me come every Sunday in the year.[15]

Under this wing also was a Master in charge of the education, in both music and grammar, of the children of the court as well as the vocal teacher, Michel Lambert. The quality of singing greatly improved at this time and led to the performance of art songs, in addition to the ballets du cour. Women singers begin to appear during the reign of Louis XIV and their role in singing art songs seems to have followed the king's preference. A court document of 1661 observes,

> When, having withdrawn privately into his Closet, [the king] wishes to hear French or Italian *airs*, no one else can please him more agreeably than [Anna Bergerotti].[16]

Also employed in the Chambre were a number of lute, theorbo and wind players, as well as keyboard performers. The positions for string players were expanded to now include both the *24 Violins du Roi* and a separate *21 Petits Violins*.

The Chapelle was administered by a *sous-maître*, who organized and rehearsed the daily services and supervised the education of the children of the choirs. This area was also greatly expanded under Louis XIV and by the 1670s there were some sixty singers. To these were added cornett, bassoon, sackbut and serpent players independent of the other administrative areas.

Finally the administrative section called Maison Militaire, which was the military guard protecting the king, maintained not only the usual fifes, trumpets and drums, but also two four-member Hautboisten bands, which is to say oboes and bassoons. These two often com-

---

13   A mistake made by Benoit, 'Paris'.
14   As a matter of fact, in Walther's *Musikalisches Lexikon* (Leipzig, 1732), 193, one finds,
     Cromorne (gall.) s.m. bedeutet (1) einen Basson.
15   François Couperin, *Concerts Royaux* (Paris, 1722), Preface.
16   Quoted in Benoit, in 'Paris,' 250.

bined and are found in pay records as '8 hautbois des Mousquetaires.' We have pointed out above the practice of such players doubling the string parts when needed. On one interesting occasion, in 1698, the king and much of his musical establishment were in Fontainebleau. For some reason, the king and the string players had to make an early return to Versailles and the final performance of the comedy, *Bourgeois gentilhomme*, in Fontainebleau was performed by the Hautboisten of the Mousquetaires alone![17]

These various ensembles performed, often combined as larger groups, for every kind of state occasion. Foremost among these state events were national celebrations honoring the birth of royal children. Since these celebrations lasted one year, often a new child was born before the year was concluded and everything had to begin all over again.

One separate administrative staff existed solely to organize every moment of Louis XIV's day. The king was not permitted to even take a walk through the formal gardens behind Versailles without elaborate organization in advance. The walk would, of course, be scheduled for a specific time and the royal trumpets would be positioned by the door through which the king exited the palace. As the king took his walk, he heard constant music. An Hautboisten ensemble may have been placed in some bushes, for example, and played until the king passed. Then this ensemble ran ahead to a new hiding place, while perhaps a string ensemble hiding behind trees played in the interval, before it also repositioned itself, and so it continued.

But the entire court lived at Versailles—hundreds of people—and some entertainment had to be offered them all. This often took the form of carrousels, relics of the age of armed tournaments, or *divertissements*, which were allegorical in character.[18] The largest of the latter were known as *grands divertissement*. One of these, given in 1664 in honor of Anne of Austria and Marie-Thérèse, was called 'Les plaisirs de l'île enchantée,' the principal events of which lasted three days before six hundred official guests. We may imagine that many of the noble guests also came with their own ceremonial musicians. The Duke of Noaille, for example, brought four trumpeters and two timpani players 'dressed in flame colored satin and silver, their plumes of the same livery.'[19]

On the first day the king appeared in a carrousel as the character, Roger. Other allegorical figures included the Centuries, the Twelve Hours, the Signs of the Zodiac. After an allegorical presentation of the Brass Age, the Silver Age, the Golden Age and the Iron Age, and before another pageant with the theme of the Four Seasons, there was a concert under the direction of Lully.

> Thirty-four musicians very well dressed, who were to precede the Seasons, and made the most agreeable Consort in the World.

---

17 National Archives, Paris (MS.Bundle 01/2830, Nr. 86, 88).

18 Benoit, 'Paris,' 240ff, gives a nice summary of a number of these performances.

19 Much of the official speeches, lyrics for songs, and translations of contemporary newspaper articles which described these events are reprinted in John Ozell, *The Works of Mr. de Moliere* (New York: Benjamin Blom, 1967), Volumes I and II.

Another allegorical pageant on a pastoral theme, and also before the four Seasons, included more rural music.

> Fourteen musicians of Pan and Diana preceded those two Deities, with an agreeable Harmony of flutes and bag-pipes.

Following a dance by the Four Seasons (riding a horse, an elephant, a camel and a bear!), one account indicates that Lully conducted a concert of Hautboisten with flutes. Next, a machine-operated forest of artificial trees lifted twenty-four dancers into the air. This day ended with a great banquet with music by 'thirty-six violins, very well dressed, behind on a little stage.'

The second day featured a play by Molière, *La princesse d'Élide*. However, before the play, and between the Acts, there was an independent Intermezzo with music by Lully. The text was no doubt also by Molière, for he personally played a role in these intermezzi. Apparently everything began with some kind of overture, for we read, 'So soon as the curtain was drawn, a great Consort of Instrumental Music was heard.'

Scene One of the Intermezzo consisted of a song by Aurora. Scene Two is entitled 'Huntsmen and Musicians.' Here were four Huntsmen asleep on the grass, who were three singers of the king's chapel, with Molière himself playing Lyciscas. After some dialogue,

> several horns are heard, and in Consort with violins begin a Tune, to which six Huntsmen dance with a great deal of Exactness and Order.

Now the play itself begins, with another Intermezzo between each Act. In the Intermezzo before Act Three, the character Moron, who was also played by Molière, begs for a singing lesson. He proves to be a poor student, for in the Intermezzo before Act Four he complains,

> Why can't I sing? Damn'd Step-mother Nature, why did you not give me wherewithal to Sing like another? ... Why is it that I can't Sing? Have I not a stomach, a throat, and a tongue like another? Yes, yes; come then, I too will Sing, and show you that Love enables one to perform all things.

And this character played by Molière then did sing! Following the play, a final Intermezzo was given, consisting of some of the noble guests disguised as shepherds and shepherdesses who sang and danced. It was during this Intermezzo that we find the following extraordinary description:

> While these amiable persons are dancing, there rises from under the stage the machine of a great tree, on which are sixteen fauns, eight of whom play on the flute, and the rest on the violin, with the most agreeable consort in the world. Thirty violins answer them from the pit, with six other instruments of harpsichords and theorbos.

The third day's activities were given by the artificial lakes behind the palace. Behind the lakes was a sizable artificial palace built for this performance.

> Their Majesties being arrived, had no sooner taken their places, than one of the two Islands that were by the sides of the first, was all covered with violins very well dressed. The other that was opposite to it was at the same time covered with trumpets and timpani, whose habits were no less rich.
> But what was more surprising, was to see *Alcina* issue from behind a rock, borne by a sea-monster of a prodigious bigness.

After a song of welcome by Alcina,

> A consort of violins is heard, while the frontispiece of the palace opens with wonderful art, and towers rise.

Now comes a ballet battle between dwarfs and giants. The day ended with the artificial palace disappearing in a blaze of fireworks.

> Then claps of thunder followed by several flares of lightning, portend the destruction of the palace, which is presently reduced to ashes by an artificial fire, which puts an end to this adventure, and to the diversions of the *Enchanted Island*.

A newspaper said nothing so magnificent had been seen for several centuries.
The formal three-day presentation of the 'Les plaisirs de l'île enchantée' was concluded, but not the entertainments. The following two days, Saturday and Sunday, there were several more horse tournaments. On Sunday evening Molière's comedy, *Impertinents*, was given, 'intermixed with dancing.'
On Monday, the king gave a lottery, through which all the noble ladies won 'precious stones, furniture, plate and other like things.' In the afternoon there was another tournament and in the evening another Molière play, *Tartuffe*.

> Although the king thought it very diverting, yet … his extreme scrupulosity in point of religion could hardly bear that resemblance of Vice and Virtue; and though he did not doubt the good intentions of the author, yet he forbade the acting of the comedy before the public, until it was entirely finished and examined by competent judges, that it might not deceive others, who were less capable to make a just discernment of it.

On Tuesday there were more tournaments and another play, *The Forced Marriage*, by Molière in the evening. Finally, on Wednesday, the festivities ended as the king left for Fontainebleau.
A contemporary account of another of these divertissements, the 'Les fêtes de l'Amour et de Bacchus' of 1668, leaves the impression that the music one heard might have been of a much higher aesthetic level than the allegorical themes might otherwise suggest.

> If one takes the Music, there is nothing which does not perfectly express all the passions, delighting the spirit of the Hearers. But what was never before seen is that pleasing harmony of voices, that symphony of instruments, that delightful union of different choruses, those sweet songs, those tender and amorous dialogues, those echoes, in short, that admirable conduct in every part, in which it might always be seen from the first words that the Music was increasing, and having begun with a single voice, it concluded with a concert of over one hundred persons, seen all at once upon the same Stage, uniting their instruments, their voices and their steps in a harmony and cadence that brings the Play to an end, leaving everyone in a state of admiration that cannot be adequately expressed.[20]

The central figure in attempts to develop authentic French opera was Jean-Baptiste Lully, composer of ballet and instrumental music to the king, who had, from 1663 to 1671, collaborated with Molière. When Cardinal Mazarin, as part of his desire to bring Italian culture to Paris, sought to establish Italian opera, he turned to the famous Cavalli to stage a revival of *Xerse* for the wedding of Louis XIV. For *Xerse*, Lully was engaged to compose a number of *entrés de ballet* (featuring Spaniards, Basques, Iberian peasants, Scaramouche, Negroes, sailors, buffoons, satyrs, etc.) to be inserted into an opera which now required eight hours to perform. A following work by Cavalli, *Ercole amante*, had eighteen *entrèes* by Lully. These works were described not as operas, but 'royal ballet, intertwined with a tragic poem sung to music.' None of this resulted in popularizing Italian opera, but it appears to have popularized Lully, who was given the responsibility of creating genuine French opera, *tragédie lyrique*.

The king's instructions in 1672 to Lully acknowledge that 'music occupies one of the foremost positions among the liberal arts, with the aim of encouraging its favorable development.' Lully, 'who has given, and continues to give, daily—and pleasurable—proof of his abilities,' is instructed to establish a Royal Academy of Music for the establishment of 'public performance of theatrical dramas in the manner of Italy, Germany and England.' Lully was not only appointed for life, but after him one of his sons would be assigned to continue his duties. The following text indicates the extent of Lully's control, the reservation that aristocratic persons must be allowed to sing[21] and the interesting suggestion that Lully apparently desired to establish an affiliated school of music.

> And as compensation for the notable expenses which M. Lully shall inevitably be required to sustain in connection with the aforesaid representations (with regard to the scenes, costumes, machines, theater and all other necessities), We hereby grant him permission to give public performances of all his compositions, including those represented in Our presence, save that he shall not be permitted to make use of those musicians in Our personal employ for performances of the said dramas; he shall also be authorized to request such sums as he shall retain necessary and to station guards or other officials at the entrances of the venues where the aforesaid performances shall be given. At the same time, all persons of whatsoever quality or condition

---

20 Quoted in Ibid., 243.

21 This stipulation reflects the change taking place everywhere since the Renaissance, by which it was becoming the custom for the servants, and no longer the gentlemen themselves, to perform music.

(including Our own court officials) are expressly forbidden to enter the venues in question without having paid; likewise, no person whatever may organize the performance of any wholly musical drama (in French or any other language) without the written consent of M. Lully, upon pain of a fine of ten thousand *livres* and confiscation of theaters, scenes, machines, costumes and other things—a third for Our own direct benefit, a third for the *hôpital-général*, and a third for M. Lully, who shall also be empowered to establish private schools of music in Our city of Paris and wherever else he deems necessary for the good and well-being of the aforesaid *Académie royale*. And since the said Academy shall be modeled upon these already in existence in Italy, where gentlemen may sing in public without contravening aristocratic decorum, We desire and hereby command that all gentlemen and *Mademoiselles* be permitted to sing in the aforesaid dramas and other entertainments in Our Royal Academy without prejudice to their titles of nobility, privileges, offices, rights and immunities.[22]

Upon the death of Louis XIV, Philippe, Duke of Orléans became regent until the young Louis XV came of age, thus much court activity was that designed for a child. Although all the court ensembles continued under the reign of Louis XV, his preference was for private concerts and the court no longer saw the great *divertissements*. Although he came from a musical family, Louis XV himself seemed little interested in art music of any kind. Perhaps, as one of the most famous womanizers in history, his mind was elsewhere.

Neither was the cultural climate surrounding Louis XV conducive to the serious development of art forms such as opera. The fact that Louis XV preferred the French styles of the older Lully and the contemporary Rameau, while his queen was more inclined to Italian comic opera, led to entertaining reading in the press, but little important music.

The singers who traversed the stage in Paris may have been more interesting than the characters they played, if we can judge by the French soprano known as La Maupin. We first hear of her as being married to a young businessman and living in Paris. Soon after her marriage, she began an affair with a fencing master, with whom she also studied the art of the large and small sword. Upon the occasion of her husband being offered a position in Provence, La Maupin, not wishing to give up her life in Paris, moved in with the fencing master. When her husband began legal action against the lovers, they fled to Marseilles where they both apparently had sufficient voices to be employed by the local Opera.

Soon tiring of this lover, La Maupin developed a passion for, and seduced, a young woman. Alarmed friends of the young woman captured her and for her safety hid her in a convent in Avignon. La Maupin, however, soon discovered her location and, presenting herself as a novice, gained admission to the convent. La Maupin set fire to the convent and in the confusion carried off her young female lover. The young woman's friends rescued her once again and at this time La Maupin apparently lost interest and turned her attention toward Paris.

In 1695 she joined the Paris Opera, attracting immediate attention in the role of Pallas in *Cadmus*. Following this success she apparently enjoyed several years of extraordinary

---

22 Quoted in Lorenzo Bianconi, *Music in the Seventeenth Century*, trans. David Bryant (Cambridge: Cambridge University Press, 1989), 240.

popularity. When a male singer in the Opera, named Dumesnil, managed in some fashion to slight her, La Maupin dressed in male attire and waited for him after the opera one evening in the Place des Victoires. When Dumesnil appeared, she insisted that he draw his sword and fight. When he refused, she gave him a sound beating and took from him his watch and snuffbox. The next day Dumesnil boasted to his friends of the Opera company that he successfully defended himself upon being attacked by three thieves. La Maupin, of course, humiliated him by immediately revealing that it was she alone who had beat him for his cowardice, producing his watch and snuffbox as evidence. On another occasion, a member of the company who similarly became the object of her wrath, hid from her for three weeks in the Palais Royal before finally making a public request for her pardon.

On the occasion of a great ball given by Monsieur, brother to Louis XIV, La Maupin appeared again dressed in a man's clothing. During the course of the ball she insulted a young lady, whereupon three of the lady's friends, supposing La Maupin to be a man, demanded that she follow them outside where they proposed to defend the young lady's honor. While she could have easily avoided the fight by revealing herself to be a woman, she instead drew her sword and killed all three. She returned to the ball as if nothing had happened and explained the situation to Monsieur. He apparently found her story amusing and extended his pardon.

Some time later La Maupin turns up in Brussels, where she became the mistress of the Elector of Bavaria, who was in residence there. After a period of time the Elector tired of her and his passions turned to the Countess of Arcos. To rid himself of La Maupin, the Elector gave this lady's husband a large sum of money to deliver to La Maupin with an order to leave Brussels. La Maupin declared this a gesture worthy of a scoundrel, threw the purse in the Count's face and left for Paris.

Upon her arrival in Paris she resumed her success on the stage. In 1705 she announced her retirement from the Opera, surprised her friends by declaring her devotion to her husband and left Paris to join him in Provence. It is here with her husband that we last find mention of La Maupin, living out the rest of her life in a most pious manner, until her death at age thirty-four!

CIVIC MUSIC

By the middle of the seventeenth century all the important academies which would have such significant influence on French culture before the French Revolution were established. The *Académie Française*, founded by Cardinal Richelieu in 1635, was the first to be chartered.[23] It was soon followed by the *Académie Royale de Peinture et de Sculpture* (1648), the *Académie*

---

23 One of the early members, Valentin Conrart, was interested in the study of setting the Psalms to music, but the academy restricted itself to matters of language.

de Danse (1661),[24] the *Académie des Inscriptions et Belles Lettres* (1663),[25] the *Académie des Sciences* (1666), the *Académie Royale de Musique* (1669)[26] and the *Académie d'Architeture* (1671).

It would make nice history if one could say that these academies were the direct development of the brief-lived academies of the sixteenth century, in particular that of Baïf, but in fact there was a distinct break due to the civil disruptions at the end of the century. One brief attempt to recreate the earlier academies was made by David de Flurance Rivault, a teacher who had been appointed as the chief tutor to the young Louis XIII. He submitted a design for the establishment of an academy offering a broad range of studies, but nothing came of it.[27]

The *Académie Royale de Musique* became the sponsor for the long series of dramatic works with music by Lully and after his death in 1687 it was the scene of debates over the principles of his music and the future of French music. After the long period of Lully's domination of the artistic choices before the French upper class, the period after his death saw an international expansion of the repertoire, with Italian and even German works achieving popularity. Additional international influence must have been present in the form of the great number of musically educated foreign nobles who came to experience the Versailles court.

For the middle and upper middle class, the large number of publishers and instrument makers suggest an active musical scene. Private concerts began to flourish in the late seventeenth century, ranging from those organized by individual professional players to the famous *concerts spirituels* begun by the king's organist, La Barre. By the early eighteenth century these concerts had become much like modern ones, with ordinary citizens buying tickets to attend.

Perhaps the most extraordinary story of non-aristocratic sponsorship of music is that of the wealthy financier, Alexandre-Jean-Joseph Le Riche de la Pouplinière (1693–1762). An amateur musician, he maintained his own orchestra led by three extraordinary music directors: Rameau, J. W. A. Stamitz and Gossec. His example may not have been unique, for a character in Molière's *Le Bourgeois gentilhomme* (II, i) observes that to be a person of quality, one must 'have a concert in his home every Wednesday or Thursday.'

In general, little research has been done with respect to the activities of the seventeenth-century French civic musical organizations, but there is extant a by-laws of 1606 for a civic musicians guild in Strasbourg which contributes much information. The references here to a 'king' refer not to the aristocratic king, but a member of the guild elected to be the leader. The title 'king' was used in imitation of the only form of government known at the time.

---

24 The *Académie de Danse* had to do battle with the chief violin representative of the Parisian musicians guild, who believed the control of dance was their business. See Frances Yates, *The French Academies of the Sixteenth Century* (Nendeln: Kraus, 1968), 300.

25 This academy had among its duties the organization of fêtes and royal entertainments, thus touching on musical activities to some degree. Quinault, who was writing librettos for Lully, was expressly commanded by the king to consult with the Academy. See Frances Yates, Ibid., 301.

26 This academy was concerned only with opera.

27 Some information on his plans is given by Frances Yates, Ibid., 277. We are happy to read that he was criticized for teaching young Louis XIII too much about mathematics and fortifications and not enough about *belles lettres*. [Ibid., 281]

1. No wind player, string player or other musician may play by day or night, in the street or in a house for dances or dinners, nor may he receive money or gifts, unless he is first admitted to the guild of musicians of Alsace, under penalty of confiscation of his instrument; the same is true for minstrels.
2. Each new member must swear to be obedient to the king and the brotherhood statutes.
3. Each member when in uniform must wear a silver medal showing the Queen Mother of God.
4. Upon entering the guild he must show his birth certificate and have a signed authorization by the noble of the area he comes from.
5. To be admitted a player in the city, a minstrel must have served two years apprenticeship.
6. The right to join as an apprentice, or to resign an apprenticeship, costs 12 Strasbourg *schellings*.
7. To become a guild member, or to resign, costs two '*écus d'Empire*'.
8. All the members will assist with the annual Musicians Day festival and are exempt from annual taxes.
9. On the day of this celebration, the entire guild must meet at the church, then to the castle to give homage to the noble. Each of them has to take part in the guild meal and take his turn at the dance which the king will have arranged with the host.
10. If a member, through illness or by order of the noble, cannot take part in this festival, he must justify it with good evidence and send his annual tax.
11. Each member has to pay the sergeant who announces him.
12. Each year, at the time of this festival, the members must renew their certification that they are on the roles of the guild. Without this certificate they are prevented from playing their instruments.
13. If a member leaves the guild and wishes to return he must pay one '*écu d'Empire*'.
14. Upon the death of a member, his best musical instrument and his medal belong to the king of the guild.
15. A member does not have to have apprentices.
16. None will play instruments at dinners, dances, festivals, day or night, indoors or out, without being contracted through the guild.
17. If someone makes a contract with a musician after he has made a contract with a first one, the former does not have to play unless the latter receives a salary equal as if he had played.
18. No musician has to play with a musician who is not a member of the guild.
19. One does not play instruments for the wedding of a Jew who has not paid a golden *guilden*, which must be given to the king.
20. All difficulties relative to the profession, contracts contrary to the statutes and injuries between members, etc., are settled by a tribunal of the guild and the king.[28]

The tastes of the lower classes was centered on popular songs, which were often parodies on popular stage works or comments on the life of the upper classes. One of the most exciting forms of entertainment for the lower classes must have been the popular street fairs where one could see farces and plays, street entertainers, animal shows, and hear music. One of the most famous of these fairs is described in Scarron's poem, 'La Foire St Germain,' of 1643.

---

28 M.B. Bernhard, 'Notice sur la Confrèrie des Jouers d'Instruments d'Alsace,' in *La Revue historique de la Noblesse* (Paris, 1844), 8ff.

The noise of the penetrating whistles,
The flutes and the flageolets,
The cornetts, oboes and musettes,
The sellers and the buyers,
These mingle with the acrobats,
And the tambours with bells,
Marionette players,
That the people cry singers![29]

The Mémoires of the abbé de Marolles, which includes extensive description of the Touraine countryside during the first years of the seventeenth century, describes the music of a peasant wedding.

Then there was a concert with bagpipes, flutes and hautboys and, after a sumptuous banquet, country dancing.[30]

The reader may be surprised to learn that slave galleys were still common in Southern Europe in the seventeenth century. Musicians among these slaves were sometimes allowed to perform when the ship was in port and the touring Englishman, John Evelyn, heard some of these musicians in 1644 in Marseilles.

The Captaine of the Gally royal gave us most courteous entertainment in his Cabin, the Slaves in the interim playing both on loud & soft musique very rarely: Then he shew'd us how he commanded their motions with a nod, & his Wistle, making them row out; which was to me the newest spectacle I could imagine, beholding so many hundreds of miserably naked Persons, having their heads shaven close ... a payre of Course canvas drawers, their whole backs & leggs starke naked, doubly chained about their middle, & leggs, in Cupples, & made fast to their seates: and all Commanded ... by an imperious and cruel seaman ... Their rising forwards, & falling back at their Oare, is a miserable spectacle, and the noyse of their Chaines with the roaring of the beaten Waters has something of strange & fearful in it, to one unaccustomed. They are ruled & chastiz'd with a bullspizle dry's upon their backs & soles of their feet upon the least disorder, & without the least humanity ... after we had bestow'd something amongst the Slaves, the Cap: sent a band of them to give us musique at dinner where we lodged.[31]

---

29 Quoted in Clifford Barnes, 'Instruments and Instrumental Music at the Théatres de la Foire,' in *Recherches sur la Musique francaise Classique* (Paris: Picard, 1965), V, 142.
30 M. de Marolles, *Les Mémoires de Michel de Marolles, abbé de Villeloin* (Paris, 1656).
31 John Evelyn, *The Diary of John Evelyn* (Oxford, 1955), II, 164ff, for October 7, 1644.

CHURCH MUSIC

The conservative clergy of Paris issued the *Ceremoniale parisiense* in 1662, a document based on the discussions of the Council of Trent, which warned against using any instrument but the organ in the church. This seems to have retarded somewhat the introduction of string instruments in French church music, as one does not find violins introduced at Notre Dame in Paris until the end of the seventeenth century or in the case of Chartres and Nantes, the early years of the eighteenth century.[32]

Nevertheless, wind instruments seem to have continued to some degree, either for choral support or in special ceremonies. During the seventeenth century the clergy themselves in Nantes played the serpent, cornett and crumhorns. The music master at the Chartres Cathedral taught his dozen or so boys not only singing and composition, but also bassoon and serpent. In Paris a serpent had been heard accompanying the plainsong at Sainte-Chapelle since 1651.

The court of Louis XIV probably was above the rulings of the clergy, for there the use of instruments continued to support the numerous Te Deums for military or political purposes, but more creative experimentation existed as well. In the *Messe pour plusieurs instruments au lieu des orgues* of Marc-Antoine Charpentier, for example, one finds a 'Kyrie,' 'Domine Deus Agnus,' and 'Quoniam' with four-part wind ensembles and two other movements for two oboes and continuo. The 'Offerte' is for two ensembles, one of strings and the other a wind band [*Choeur des instruments à vent*].[33]

Some of the larger cathedrals of Paris also appear to have ignored the *Ceremoniale parisiense*, for one finds complaints such as that of Le Cerf de la Viéville,

> Very many people no longer go to High Mass or Vespers in the Cathedrals unless the Bishop is officiating there with additional Musical forces; nor to Tenebrae unless the lessons are set by the hand of a famous composer.[34]

He complains that for the past twenty-five years even trumpets and drums have been heard in the church.

---

[32] George Grove, *The New Grove Dictionary of Music and Musicians* (London: Macmillan, 1980), XIV, 194; IV, 177; XIII, 21.

[33] H. Wiley Hitchcock, 'The Instrumental Music of Marc-Antoine Charpentier,' *The Musical Quarterly* 47, no. 1 (January 1961), http://www.jstor.org/740542. The autograph is in F:Pn (MS.Rés. Vm 1.259/I, 67ff). The wind ensemble is scored in four different clefs, including the so-called 'French Violin Clef,' as was the custom for French court wind band compositions.

[34] Benoit, in 'Paris,' 257.

MILITARY MUSIC

During the first part of the seventeenth century, military music in France centered on the trumpet, of which most companies had two but those with more than two hundred soldiers being assigned a third.[35] Each regiment also maintained a Trumpet-major, who was necessary to train new trumpeters in a repertoire which was not yet notated. During parades the trumpets rode before the commander in front of the troops. In battle, however, both the trumpets and the commander were placed safely in the rear.[36] Mersenne commented on the psychological value of the trumpet.

> But its principal usage is destined for war ... It is easy to conclude ... how they would prepare the heart and mind of the soldier for going to war, for attacking, and engaging in combat.[37]

Mersenne describes a number of specific trumpet signals and concludes with some interesting details.

> Thus two or more trumpets are easily heard a quarter league away and make many discourses which can take the place of speech. Still there is nothing particular in that, except that they can be heard from further away than the other instruments, which can be similarly used to hold some desired discourse.[38]

Several sources mention a trumpet signal called 'la sourdine,' which Kastner says was used to march 'with little noise,'[39] and of which a treatise of 1631 adds,

> the mute is used when there is a risk of being discovered by the enemy or when it is wished to surprise them, as also when it is desired to decamp or secretly withdraw.[40]

The importance of these signals in the field necessitated some care in the selection of the man assigned this responsibility. One French treatise commented on the character needed in the trumpeter as follows:

> The trumpet must be a man of patience and vigilance, to be ready at all hours to execute the orders of the calls ... The trumpet must be a discreet man, primarily when he is used in the negotiations, where he must never use other terms than those he is instructed with, never

---

35 Paris, National Archives (MS 01/715, vol. 171, 173, 179, 181ff).
36 Georges Kastner, *Manuel Général de Musique Militaire* (Paris, 1838), 107ff.
37 Marin Mersenne, *Harmonie Universelle* (Paris, 1636), 331.
38 Ibid., 332.
39 Kastner, *Manuel Générale*, 107.
40 Pierre Trichet, *Traité des instruments de Musique* (Bourdelois, 1631). A copy can be found in F:Psy [MS.1070].

interfere by giving counsel, in order that in conferences and treaties there will be no ambiguity or statements contrary to those proposed.[41]

Another contemporary treatise adds an interesting comment on the relationship of the trumpeter and his horse.

> The trumpets are the instruments best to use of horse dancing because they [the horses] can learn to breathe when the trumpets breathe. There is no instrument more agreeable to the horse, because it is martial, and the horse which is naturally generous, likes to be animated by its sound.[42]

The timpani appears for the first time in the French cavalry at the time of Louis XIV, although the first instruments were those captured from German troops and only those French units which had achieved such an acquisition were permitted to use them. Thus the timpani became prized emblems of a regiment's honor and when abroad the timpanist was preceded by four Cavaliers for protection. In the end, however, it was the responsibility of the player to prevent the capture of his instruments.

> The timpanist must be a man of heart, preferring to perish in combat rather than surrendering his timpani. He must have good arm movement and an accurate ear, and be able to divert his master with agreeable tunes. There is no other instrument which gives a more martial sound than the timpani, especially when it is accompanied by trumpets.[43]

Finally, one observer maintained that the timpani had a positive effect on the character of the horse.

> The beating of the timpani, which controls the stamping and the marching of the horses, also insures that these animals march with the most noble pride.[44]

Militarily and musically, the most important development in military movement was the reintroduction of coordinated marching, a practice which had been lost since the ancient Romans. In France this seems to have begun with an attempt to march to drums[45] during the sixteenth century, as suggested by Arbeau.

---

41   Alain Mallet, *Les Travaux de Mars ou l'Art de la guerre* (Paris, 1691), III, 96.

42   Claude Ménestrier, *Des Ballets anciens et modernes, selon les règles du Théâtre* (Paris, 1682), 238.

43   Mallet, *Les Travaux de Mars*, III, 98. The comment on the need of a good ear refers to the role of the timpani in supplying the bass of the trumpet choir.

44   Claude Ménestrier, *Des représentations en musique, anciennes et modernes* (Paris, 1681), 124.

45   The French drum signals of the seventeenth century are discussed in detail by René François, *Essay des Merveilles de Nature, et des Plus Nobles Artifices* (Rouen, 1626), 140ff and by Mersenne, *Harmonie Universelle*, 556.

Were it not for these, the men would march confusedly and without order, which would cause them to be in danger of being overthrown and defeated.[46]

But for the ordinary soldier, marching precisely to complex drum cadences must have proved difficult. Consider, for example, this description from a seventeenth-century French treatise.

> A company of soldiers marches to the beating of the drums who give seven beats; some are given by the drums and others are rests. They pick up one foot on one, suspend it on two; on three they put that foot down and begin to lift the other. On four they suspend it, on five they put it down and on six they affirm it. The seventh is a rest, after which they begin again.[47]

One French military leader who argued strongly for coordinated marching was the general, Maurice de Saxe (1696–1750).[48] He was also one who reminded his colleagues of the forgotten tradition of the ancient armies.

> I begin with the marche; the necessity to discuss this may seem extravagant to the ignorant.
> No one knows what the ancients understood by the word *Tactique*; many soldiers use it and believe it to mean (only) the movement of troops in battle. The whole world beats a march without knowing its tradition and everyone thinks this noise is nothing but an ornament of the military.
> We should have a better opinion of the ancients and the Romans, who should be our teachers. It is absurd to believe that this war noise served no more unique purpose than to deafen their ears!

The general pictures the army without the beat of the drum: 'Every soldier walks according to his own ease, some slow and some fast.'

> If one is marching and orders the front to quicken the pace, the rear unavoidably loses ground before they perceive the order. Then, the rear runs to catch up, whereupon the front also begins to run, throwing everything into disorder.

In addition to solving these problems, the use of a beat helps prevent the troops from getting tired. The general offers his readers what he calls 'extraordinary' proof of this fact.

> There isn't anyone who has not seen people dance all night with continuous energy. But if you have someone dance even two hours *without* music, he will protest! This proves that music [*les tons*] have a secret power over us which disposes us to exercise our bodies and makes it easy at the same time.

---

46 Thoitot Arbeau, *Orchésographie* (1588), trans. Peter Warlock (New York, 1925), 26.
47 Ménestrier, *Des représentations*, 124.
48 Maurice, comte de Saxe, *Les Rêveries ou Mémoires sur l'art de guerre* (Hague, 1756), I, vi, 23ff.

It was this secret, the general suggests, that enabled the Roman armies to cover such great areas of Europe. He contends that they could march twenty-four miles in five hours, by marching to a cadence!

The real progress came in the seventeenth century with the establishment of standing armies, in place of the long European tradition of calling up troops only as the need presented itself. The presence of standing armies made feasible the creation of standing musical groups and so the appearance of the Hautboisten band (oboes and bassoons) marks the beginning of true coordinated marching to music as it had been known to the ancient Greeks and Romans. The most knowledgeable authority suggests that the Hautboisten band were added to companies of the Mousquetaires in the year 1665.[49] By 1683 the Hautboisten bands were becoming so popular with the officers that the king had to attempt to curtail the practice for reasons of economy.

The military Hautboisten bands accompanied the troops to battle, but, judging by an account from the Battle of Mons in 1691, they also must have performed music beyond that required by marching troops.

> One day, during the siege of Mons, after the tragic spectacle which had offered murderous hostilities, the artillery became silent suddenly around 11 a.m. and the frightful sound of bombs was replaced by an oboe concert which the officers of the King's regiment were giving for the women of the city. The musicians had installed themselves on the still burning remains of the city which our troops had just taken possession of. It seems that the women of the city were sensitive to this homage, because they rushed up to the ramparts to hear the concert, and returned only after it had ceased.[50]

A French newspaper[51] preserves an account of another military concert, held in a tent during the Siege of Namur in 1692.

> The king having invited the ladies to dinner the next day treated them to a war-like concert, composed of 120 tambours of the Gardes, 40 tambours of the Swiss Guards, with trumpets and timpani of the Gardes du Corps, the Light-Guard, to the number of 36, and all the oboes of the Mousquetaires and the Regiment of the king. Altogether they played a French march, and then the Swiss march. The trumpets and timpani gave separately the pleasure of a march on horseback. Mr. Philidor, whom the king had put in charge of the concert, had arranged a great finale for the entire ensemble. The oboes played airs form *La Grotte de Versailles* and Mr. Philidor played with them. The trumpets and timpani then gave a divertimento of the old *airs de guerre*, which they did in two choirs, interspersed with menuets played by the oboes. All the tambours, timpani and trumpets then played 'la charge' at the same time and the king had them repeat it three times. After that one heard the three last arias from *Psiché* ... All of these airs were well played, nicely orchestrated, and played by all of these excellent men, each outstanding in his profession.

---

49 Benoit, *Versailles et les Musiciens du Roi*, 236.
50 Quoted in Kastner, *Manuel Générale*, 103, fn 1.
51 *Mercure Galant* for May, 1692.

2 AESTHETIC VIEWS OF FRENCH MUSICIANS

ON THE AESTHETICS OF MUSIC

On the Definition of Music

Nothing sets in better perspective the significance of the contributions of Rameau than the writings of Marc-Antoine Charpentier (1634–1704), who was actually a gifted composer. What he writes under the subtitle 'The Definition of Music,' reads like some medieval Scholastic pronouncement at the University of Paris.

> Music is a harmonious combination of high, medium, and low sounds. The third either against the bass or among the parts creates all the harmony.
>
> Diversity alone causes all perfection, just as uniformity creates all staleness and disagreement. Changes of motion and of mode aptly done contribute marvelously to the diversity which music demands.[1]

In Jean-Philippe Rameau (1683–1764) we have one of the most brilliant men among all early musicians. Born not only a prodigy, but with profound instinctive feelings about music, he also had such an inquisitive and penetrating intellect that he found correct answers in the area of harmony which had eluded the best minds for a thousand years. With this balance, we might say of left and right hemispheres of the brain, and living in the stimulating first years of the Enlightenment, we believe he might well be thought of as the first *modern* thinker in music.

One can see this sense of balance in his definition of a musician. In the following, written in 1727, he first refers to the long medieval Scholastic tradition which esteemed music only from the perspective of rules and mathematics. Such a musician he clearly rejects. Then, in the second paragraph, he refers to the opposite kind of musician, one who operates purely from instinct, responding to his own emotions. He points as well to the limitations of this kind of musician. Finally, perhaps reflecting his view of himself, he reserves his praise for the balanced musician, one who engages both left and right brains.

---

1 Quoted in Jon Kuyper, 'Marc-Antoine Charpentier's *Règles de Composition*' (University of Iowa, Unpublished dissertation, 1971), 53.

> A learned musician is generally understood to be a man who understands everything about the various combinations of sounds. At the same time, however, he is so engrossed in these combinations that he sacrifices everything: good sense, feeling, imagination, and reason. Such a musician is an academician, of a school that is concerned with notes alone and nothing further. We are right to prefer to him a musician who prides himself less on learning than taste.
>
> The latter, however, whose taste is limited by the range of his sensations alone, can excel only in certain types of music that are natural to his character. If he is naturally tender, he will express tenderness. If his temperament is witty, lively, playful, his music will correspond accordingly. Moreover, since he draws on his imagination for everything, without the assistance of art, by this means of expression he soon burns himself out. In his first fire he was all brilliance, but this fire consumes itself as he tries to rekindle it, and nothing remains but banality and repetitions.
>
> Therefore we should like to find for the theater a musician who would study nature before painting it; not only his taste, then, but his learning and judgment would enable him to select the coloring and shading appropriate to the desired expression.[2]

Rameau, with his balance of the intellect and native instincts, and perhaps following the fashion of wide-ranging investigation which characterized the Enlightenment, was by nature a keen observer. A few passages in his writing reveal that he had given considerable thought to the physiology of the perception of music. In the following he touches on a very significant topic and yet one which still has not received more than preliminary research. We know that the overtone series is a natural law of physics.[3] It follows that our species has heard, no matter how unconsciously, the overtone series in all sounds since its very beginning. Is it possible, through adaption, that our species has an internal genetic tonal system? In 1734, Rameau was clearly pondering observations which he had made along these lines.

> In music the ear obeys only nature. It takes account of neither measure nor range. Instinct alone leads it.
>
> Whether a novice or the most experienced person in music, the moment one sings an improvisation, one ordinarily places the first tone in the middle register of the voice and then continues up, even though the voice range above or below this first tone is about equal; this is completely consistent with the resonance of any sounding body from which all emanating overtones are above its fundamental tone which one thinks one is hearing alone.
>
> On the other hand, inexperienced as one may be, one hardly ever fails, when improvising on an instrument, immediately to play, ever ascending, the perfect chord made up of the overtones of the sounding body, the major form of which is always preferred to the minor, unless the latter is suggested by some reminiscence.[4]

---

[2] Letter to Houdart de la Motte, October 25, 1727, quoted in Gertrude Norman and Miriam Shrifte, *Letters of Composers* (New York: Knopf, 1946), 18ff.

[3] After the initial discovery, it took two thousand years for theorists to understand it correctly!

[4] Jean Philippe Rameau, *Observations sur notre instinct pour la musique et sur son principe* (1734), quoted in Sam Morgenstern, *Composers on Music* (New York: Pantheon, 1956), 44.

Twenty-five years later he was still struggling with this idea. He begins by discounting the ancient explanations based on faith and wonders why these early philosophers did not pursue natural rules, that is understanding based on Nature.

> [The ancient writers] found the relationships between sounds in divinely inspired order; they discoursed a great deal on that subject, and every reason they were able to advance evaporated like a wisp of smoke. Finally the geometricians and the philosophers became disheartened. Can it be true that up to the present time man has always been so enthralled by this single inspiration that it never occurred to anyone to seek the reason why, despite ourselves, we should be compelled to prefer certain intervals to others after certain sounds, especially after the first sound? Allow your natural feelings to operate in yourself with no preconceived expectation and then try to see if you can ever ascend a semitone after a given semitone, and whether you can do the same thing after two successive tones. Why was this suggested to me in this way? Whence this sensation? What could have given rise to this sensation in me, if it was not in the moment itself? It was necessary to test the effect of the sound, and from it three sounds would have been distinguished which form that enchanting harmony, and from there one would have proceeded with certainty, as I believe I have done.
>
> The principle is inexhaustible and holds true for theology as well as geometry and physics. Anyone more enlightened than myself should be able to draw the most far-reaching conclusions from this and already I can envision the origin of that final knowledge which cannot be denied without denying the phenomenon from which it is derived.[5]

We presume that it was from this observation of the natural aspects of music, the overtone series, that Rameau concluded that it was harmony, and not melody, which was the fundamental element of music. From the perspective of the listener, this is a conclusion which is not substantiated by modern clinical research in psychology.

> Music is generally divided into harmony and melody, but we shall show in the following that melody is merely a part of harmony and that a knowledge of harmony is sufficient for a complete understanding of all the properties of music.[6]

Later Rameau elaborates on this contention, beginning with the admission, 'it would seem at first that harmony arises from melody.'[7] However, he suggests, whatever logic one might discern in a melody, it all becomes unintelligible as soon as other voices are added, for they will have their own, and therefore conflicting logic. All this is avoided, he proposes, if one builds melodies solely from the harmony.

> It is harmony then that guides us, and not melody. Certainly a knowledgeable musician can compose a beautiful melodic line suitable to the harmony, but from where does this happy ability come? May nature be responsible? Doubtless. But if, on the contrary, she has refused her gift, how can he succeed? Only by means of the rules.

---

5   Letter to A. M. Beguillet, October 6, 1762, quoted in Gertrude Norman and Miriam Shrifte, *Letters of Composers*, 20.
6   Jean-Philippe Rameau, *Treatise on Harmony*, trans. Philip Gossett (New York: Dover, 1971), 3.
7   Ibid., 152.

Since it was the reflections on ancient Greek music by the sixteenth-century humanists which initiated the whole Baroque movement in music, and since interest in Greek philosophy remained strong, Rameau realized he was in need of further explanation. Because the humanists understood ancient Greek music to be unaccompanied, and therefore consisting of melody only, Rameau's harmony-based philosophy denied, in effect, everything admired in ancient Greek testimony on music. He deals with this by simply saying the ancient Greeks did not know what they were doing.

> The Ancients defined the properties of the modes perfectly well, in terms of the different effects they produce and the way in which they control harmony and melody. But the Ancients were always ignorant of their true nature, for they attributed all the power of these modes to melody. They assumed that melody had to be derived from the seven diatonic notes of the perfect system, without distinguishing among them further. As they thought that by using each note of the system as the principal one they would be able to create as many different effects as there are notes in the system, they simultaneously lost sight of what should have been their model.[8]

On Taste in Music

The most important accomplishment of the Baroque in music was the freeing of music from the old Scholastic understanding that music was a branch of mathematics. It was this fact which made the question of taste immediately important, for in the past 'good taste' was tied to 'following the rules.' Therefore, when Jean Rousseau (not to be confused with Jean-Jacques Rousseau) considered this question in 1687, it was the proper role of the rules which had to be addressed.

> But genius and fine taste are gifts of nature, which cannot be learnt by rules, and it is with the help of these that the rules should be applied, and that liberties may be taken so fittingly as always to give pleasure, for to give pleasure means to have genius and fine taste.[9]

Similarly, when Couperin, in 1717, mentions the 'old' style, it was the rules-dominated polyphonic style he was thinking of.

> Let the style of playing be directed by the good taste [*bon-goût*] of today, which is incomparably purer than the old.[10]

---

8   Ibid., 159. We must point out that Rameau was quite mistaken in his interpretation of Greek modes here.

9   Jean Rousseau, *Traité de la Viole* (Paris, 1687), quoted in Robert Donnington, *The Interpretation of Early Music* (New York: Farber and Farber, 1964), 425.

10 François Couperin, *L'Art de toucher* (Paris, 1717, reprinted Wiesbaden: Breitkopf & Härtel, 1933), 33.

Rameau, writing in 1726, makes the same point.

> It is often by seeing and hearing musical works (operas and other good musical compositions), rather than by rules, that taste is formed.[11]

The following year Rameau views the question in a more practical perspective. Perhaps more significant is the fact that he does not include the theorists, the 'learned,' among those with 'good taste.'

> You will then see that I am not a novice in the art and that it is not obvious that I make a great display of learning in my compositions, where I seek to hide art by very art; for I consider only people of taste and not at all the learned, since there are many of the former and hardly any of the latter.[12]

It follows that during the Baroque it was therefore 'taste' and not rules alone which governed the elements of performance. As Michel de Saint-Lambert, writing in 1702, states, in the questions of inequality[13] in rhythm and of tempo, 'taste judges.'[14]

The interest among French philosophers in *Goût*, or taste, led to much discussion regarding taste, or style, in the music of the various national peoples. The French composer, Sébastien de Brossard, in his *Dictionaire de musique* (1703), defined style as follows.

> Style is understood in music as the form and method that each person has especially for himself to compose, perform and to communicate. And all of these [forms and methods] are quite different, according to the measure of the genius of the composer, the country, and the people according to which the material, the place, the time, the subject, the expression etc. are rendered. Thus one says: the style of Carissimi, Lully, Lambert etc. ... The style of joyful and merry music is very different from that of the serious; the church style is very different from the theatrical or chamber styles; the Italian style is sharp, colorful, expressive; the French in contrast, natural, flowing, tender. From these facts result various descriptive phrases in order to stress all of these different characteristics: the old and new style; the Italian, French, German styles; the Church, Opera, Chamber styles; the joyful, merry, colorful, sharp, moderate, expressive, tender, excited styles; the grand, sublime, galant styles; the normal, common, vulgar, fawning styles.[15]

---

11 Rameau, *Le Nouveau Système de musique théorique* (1726), quoted in Morgenstern, *Composers on Music*, 43.

12 Letter of Rameau to La Motte (1727), quoted in Julie Anne Sadie, 'Paris and Versailles,' in *The Late Baroque Era* (Englewood Cliffs: Prentice Hall, 1994), 182.

13 De Bacilly, in *L'Art de bien chanter* (Paris, 1668), 232ff, suggests that the practice of performing with inequality came about because composers were reluctant to write dotted rhythms for fear they would become in performance jerky.

14 Michel de Saint-Lambert, *Principes du Clavecin* (Paris, 1702), quoted in Donnington, *The Interpretation of Early Music*, 452.

15 Quoted in George J. Buelow, 'Music and Society in the Late Baroque Era,' in *The Late Baroque Era* (Englewood Cliffs: Prentice Hall, 1994), 15ff.

François Couperin, in thinking of the difference between French and Italian style, observed in 1717,

> The French gladly swallow what is novel, at the expense of losing what is fit and proper, which they believe they understand better than other nations.[16]

On the Purpose of Music

As we have remarked, the hallmark of the Baroque style is a new appreciation of the communication of feelings through music. Relatively little was written on this subject by the musicians themselves in France during the seventeenth century. One exception was Charpentier, who wrote at length at this time on the subject of expressing the feelings in music. He first mentions this subject in a brief discussion of modulation. The first virtue of modulation, for Charpentier, was a rather practical one, to facilitate the range of singers.

> The second and principal reason is for the expression of the different emotions for which the differing power of the modes is most appropriate.[17]

We see how literally he meant this, in the lists of keys and associated emotions, 'The Power of the Modes,' which he immediately supplies. It is an interesting list, although the reader may be surprised to find the key of Eb major, home to so much pleasing music of the Classic Period, described here as 'Cruel and harsh.'

C major	Gay and martial
C minor	Somber and sad
D minor	Serious and devout
D major	Joyous and very martial
E minor	Effeminate, amorous, and plaintive
E major	Quarrelsome and crude
Eb major	Cruel and harsh
Eb minor	Horrible, hideous
F major	Furious and fiery
F minor	Gloomy and plaintive
G major	Sweetly joyous
G minor	Austere and magnificent
A minor	Tender and plaintive
A major	Joyous and rustic
Bb major	Magnificent and joyous

---

16 Couperin, *L'Art de toucher*, 22.
17 Quoted in Kuyper, 'Marc-Antoine Charpentier's *Règles de Composition*,' 54ff.

Bb minor	Gloomy and terrible
B minor	Lonely and melancholy
B major	Harsh and plaintive

Charpentier does not elaborate on this list, but he evidently took the subject seriously. He does not forget to include 'good choice of meters and of modes which suitably make the passion which one wants to represent,' when he later sums up the elements which 'can not fail to make music as beautiful as it is good.'[18]

For Couperin, the first obstacles to the communication of feelings lay in notation and tradition.

> In my opinion, there are faults in our way of writing music, which correspond to the way in which we write our language. The fact is we write a thing differently from the way in which we execute it; and it is this which causes foreigners to play our music less well than we do theirs. The Italians, on the contrary, write their music in the true time-values in which they have intended them to be played. For instance, we dot several consecutive eighth-notes in diatonic succession, and yet we write them as equal; our custom has enslaved us, and we hold fast to it.[19]

For Rameau, as he points out in 1726, a greater concern for the composer was to find a deeper meaning of feeling in the musical materials.

> We may note that the semi-skilled generally use a chord because it is familiar to them or pleases them, but the expert uses it only to the extent that he feels its power.[20]

For Rameau, the 'rules' now take second place.

> While composing music is not the time to recall the rules which might hold our genius in bondage. We must have recourse to the rules only when our genius and our ear seem to deny what we are seeking.[21]

The following year he observed that it is Nature which, for him, precedes rules.

> Nature has not completely deprived me of her gifts and I have not surrendered myself to mere combinations of notes so far as to forget their intimate relationship with that beautiful Nature which by itself suffices to give pleasure.[22]

Regarding the role of the performer, we have two points of perspective. There is the discussion of this question in the literature, but then there are also descriptions of performers

---

18 Ibid., 62.

19 Couperin, *L'Art de toucher*, 23.

20 Rameau, *Le Nouveau Système de musique théorique*, 42.

21 Ibid., 41.

22 Letter to Houdart de la Motte, October 25, 1727, quoted in Norman and Shrifte, *Letters of Composers*, 19.

themselves. Early comments on the role of the performer in communicating feeling focus on the voice, for which this question first emerged in the discussions of the Camerata. For example, Pierre Trichet discussing string technique in 1631 observed,

> After the human voices, there is nothing so captivating as the affecting vibrato [*les mignards tremblements*] which can be produced on the fingerboard, and nothing so ravishing as the sobbing bow strokes [*les coups mourants de l'archet*].[23]

Among French commentators, the question of communicating feeling soon became identified with time, or the movement of music through time. Charles Masson writing in 1699 finds,

> Measure is the soul of music, since it excites with such truthfulness of emotion [*fait agir avec tant de justesse*] a great many people, and by the variety of its *mouvmens* [spirit, character?] can again stimulate so many different feelings, being able to calm these and arise those, as has always been observed.[24]

Couperin was one who gave great significance to the role of time in relationship with the expression of feelings. In the following he makes several important points. First, in addition to his distinction between 'Measure' and 'Time,' he reminds us that the Italian terms familiar to us as 'tempo' designations had earlier a strong mood or character connotation as well. It is also a significant point, which Couperin mentions here, that the notation system has no symbols whatsoever for feeling.

> I find we confuse Measure or Time [the number of beats in a bar] with what is called Cadence or Movement [tempo, together with accent phrasing, or expression or feeling]. Measure defines the number and quality of the beats; and Cadence is literally the intelligence and the soul which must be added to it. The sonatas of the Italians hardly admit of this Cadence, this expression or feeling. But all our airs for the violin, our pièces for the harpsichord, for the viols, etc., describe and seem to be trying to express some feeling. Thus, not having devised signs or characters for communicating our specific ideas, we try to remedy this by indicating at the beginning of our pieces, by some such word as Tenderly, Quickly, etc., as far as possible the idea we want to convey. I hope that someone will take the trouble to translate us for the benefit of foreigners; and may it procure for them the possibility of judging of the excellence of our instrumental music.[25]

This seems also to be what was intended in Jean Rousseau's viole treatise of 1687.

> There are people who imagine that imparting the movement is to follow and keep time; but these are very different matters, for it is possible to keep time without entering into the movement, since time depends on the music, but the movement depends on genius and fine taste.[26]

---

23 Quoted in Peter Walls, 'Strings,' in *Performance Practice: Music after 1600* (New York: Norton, 1989), 71.
24 Charles Masson, *Nouveau Traité* (Paris, 1699), quoted in Donnington, *The Interpretation of Early Music*, 412.
25 Couperin, *L'Art de toucher*, 24.
26 Quoted in Donnington, *The Interpretation of Early Music*, 425.

In another place, Couperin considers the relationship of time and expression on a much lower, although no less important, level.

> As the sounds of the harpsichord are determined, each one specifically, and consequently incapable of increase or diminution, it has hitherto appeared almost impossible to maintain that one could give any 'soul' to this instrument. However, by investigations which have lent assistance to what little native talent Heaven has granted to me, I shall endeavor to show by what means I have managed to gain the happiness of touching the hearts of people of good taste, who have done me the honor of listening to me …
>
> The feeling or soul, the expressive effect, which I mean, is due to the cessation and suspension of the notes, made at the right moment, and in accordance with the character required by the melodies of the preludes and pieces. These two *agrémens*, by their contrast, leave the ear in suspense, so that in such cases where string instruments would increase their volume of sound, the suspension [slight retardation] of the sounds on the harpsichord seems (by a contrary effect) to produce on the ear the result expected and desired …
>
> With regard to the expressive affect of the aspiration, the note over which it is placed must be detached less abruptly in passages which are tender and slow than in those which are light and quick. As for the suspension, it is hardly employed at all except in slow and tender pieces. The duration of the rest which precedes the note over which it is marked must be left to the taste of the performer.[27]

Sébastien de Brossard, in an early dictionary of music (1703), considered time from a different perspective with regard to the recitative. Writing of *rubato* in *Largo* tempo, he observes,

> In Italian recitatives we often do not make the beats very equal, because this is a kind of declamation where the Actor ought to follow the movement of the passion which inspires him or which he wants to express, rather than that of an equal and regulated measure.[28]

Similarly, under 'Recitativo,' Brossard comments on the importance of adjusting tempo to the emotions of the words.

> This is a manner of singing which holds as much of declamation as of song, as if one declaimed in singing, or as if one sang in declaiming, hence where one has more attention to expressing the passion than to following exactly a timed measure.[29]

It seems clear that all of Couperin's contemporaries would have at least agreed with him when he observed,

> Just as there is a difference between grammar and declamation, so there is an infinitely greater one between musical theory and the art of fine playing.[30]

---

27   Couperin, *L'Art de toucher*, 14ff.
28   Sébastien de Brossard, *Dictionaire de Musique* (Paris, 1703), 'Largo.'
29   Ibid., 'Recitativo.'
30   Couperin, *L'Art de toucher*, Preface.

These have been theoretical comments, written observations on the role of the performer with respect to the communication of emotions. They seem almost disinterested in comparison with descriptions of actual performance. A manuscript by Diderot, purporting to describe the nephew of Rameau, seems, among other things, to have been inspired by performers which Diderot had actually observed. The nephew is in a cafe and is singing tunes from opera.

> While singing fragments of Jomelli's *Lamentations*, he reproduced with incredible precision, fidelity, and warmth the most beautiful passages of each scene. In that magnificent recitative in which Jeremiah describes the desolation of Jerusalem he was drenched in tears, which drew their like from every onlooker. His art was complete—delicacy of voice, expressive strength, true sorrow ...
>
> Worn out, exhausted, like a man emerging from a deep sleep or a prolonged reverie, he stood motionless, dumb, petrified. He kept looking around him like a man who has lost his way and wants to know where he is. He waited for returning strength and wits, wiping his face with an absent-minded gesture. Just as a man who on waking should see a large number of people around his bed and not remember or be able to conceive what he had done, he began by asking: 'What is it, gentlemen? Why do you laugh? You look surprised—what is it?' Then he added: 'This, this merits the name of music. There is your true musician.'[31]

The possibility that there were French singers so lost in their feelings seems evident in the reaction of a French critic in 1702, when he similarly described a violinist as,

> an ecstatic who was so carried away with the piece that he was playing that he not only martyred his instrument but also himself. No longer master of his own being, he became so transported that he gyrated and hopped around like someone overcome by a demon.[32]

An account of a singer finds her to be not a demon, but an Italian!

> She caused a great sensation, but it was short-lived: several people concluded that she could not even sing properly, for this *is quite in the Italian tradition*, and she pulled the most horrible faces. She seemed to be suffering from convulsions.[33]

One can find many earlier references by French composers and theorists to the role of the listener, with respect to music's ability to soothe, or to affect character, etc. In the eighteenth century, however, there is something new added: the reference to listening to music as music. This is what Couperin had in mind when he observed,

---

31 Quoted in Denis Diderot, *Rameau's Nephew and Other Works*, trans. Jacques Barzun (Garden City: Doubleday, 1956), 69.

32 Quoted in Hans-Peter Schmitz, *Die Kunst der Verzierung im 18. Jahrhundert* (Kassel: Bärenreiter, 1955), 12.

33 Quoted in David Maland, *Culture and Society in Seventeenth-Century France* (New York: Scribner's, 1970), 80ff.

There is no doubt that a certain song or melody, a certain passage, if executed in a certain way produces a different effect on the ear of a person of taste.[34]

It is in this sense, the modern concept of a completely non-utilitarian art music, that Rameau writes in 1726: don't think, don't put academic rules first, just let yourself be carried away.

> To enjoy the effects of music fully, we must completely lose ourselves in it; to judge it, we must relate it to the source through which we are affected by it. This source is nature. Nature endows us with the feeling that moves us in all our musical experiences; we might call her gift *instinct*. Let us allow instinct to inform our judgments, let us see what mysteries it unfolds to us before we pronounce our verdicts, and if there are still men sufficiently self-assured to dare make judgments on their own authority, there is reason to hope that none will be found weak enough to listen to them.[35]

In a remarkable passage eight years later, which represents a dramatic departure from the contentions of the sixteenth-century French philosophers who placed all meaning in the words, Rameau makes the same point even with regard to listening to music with words. He says find your meaning in the music, don't force your impressions of the music to fit the accepted meaning of the words. He might as well say, listen with the right brain, not the left. He concludes here with a reference to the dawn of the Enlightenment.

> Often we think we hear in music only what exists in the words, or in the interpretation we wish to give them. We try to subject music to forced inflections, but that is not the way to be able to judge it. On the contrary, we must not think but let ourselves be carried away by the feeling which the music inspires; without our thinking at all, this feeling will become the basis of our judgment. As for reason, everybody possesses it nowadays; we have just discovered it in the bosom of nature itself. We have even proved that instinct constantly recalls it to us, both in our actions and in our speech. When reason and instinct are reconciled, there will be no higher appeal.[36]

In a more extended passage from this same treatise, Rameau's reasoning is only flawed by his error that 'harmony alone can stir the emotions.' We know today, from clinical research in the perception of music, that it is primarily melody which carries emotional meaning for the listener, and furthermore it is genetic, as is demonstrated in part by the fact that it also holds true for lower species.

> A mind preoccupied, while listening to music, is never free enough to judge it. For instance, if we think to attribute the essential beauty of this art to changes from high to low, from fast to slow, soft to loud—means which do give variety to sounds—we will judge everything according to this prejudice, without considering how weak these means are, or what scant merit there is

---

34 Couperin, *L'Art de toucher*, 13.
35 Rameau, *Le Nouveau Système de musique théorique*, 43.
36 Rameau, *Observations sur notre instinct pour la musique et sur son principe*, 44.

in making use of them; we will fail to perceive that they are foreign to harmony, which is the sole basis of music and the true source of its glorious effects.

A truly sensitive spirit must judge quite differently! If the spirit is not moved by the power of the expression, by the vivid colors of which the harmonist alone is capable, then it is not absolutely satisfied. The spirit may, of course, lend itself to whatever may entertain it, but it must evaluate things in proportion to the impact the given experience exerts.

Harmony alone can stir the emotions. It is the one source from which melody directly emanates, and draws its power. Contrasts between high and low, etc., make only superficial modifications in a melody; they add almost nothing …

If the imitation of noise and motion is not used as frequently in our music as in Italian music, it is because with us the main object is feeling. Feeling has no predetermined rhythms, and consequently cannot be everywhere reduced to a regular measure without losing that verity which is its charm. The musical expression of the physical lies in beat and rhythm; that which touches the emotions comes, on the contrary, from harmony and its inflections, a fact which we must carefully weigh before deciding what should carry the balance.

The comic genre almost never aims to express emotion and consequently is the one genre that lends itself to those cadenced rhythms by which we do honor to Italian music. We do not always notice, however, how our own musicians have made felicitous use of them. Our enjoyment of the few attempts which the delicacy of French taste has permitted our composers to risk, has proved how easily we can excel in this genre.[37]

On Performance Practice

At the end of the seventeenth century, we are attracted to two observations by Charpentier on the subject of 'practical music.' First, he concludes his book on the rules of composition by admitting,

Practice teaches more about this than all the rules.

Charpentier also addresses a word to the accompanist:

Those who make too much of a disturbance, who raise their hands in order to overpower their clavier, are incapable of accompanying well.
What can be said about one instrument can be said and has to be true about all the others.
When the voice rests, the brilliance of the hands may appear without destroying good taste.[38]

Couperin, in 1717, offers some interesting and self-explanatory advice to players. It is also worthy of note that this is one of the earliest documentations of performers playing (written music) from memory.

---

37 Ibid.
38 Quoted in Kuyper, 'Marc-Antoine Charpentier's *Règles de Composition*,' 65ff.

With regard to making grimaces, it is possible to break oneself of this habit by placing a mirror on the reading-desk of the Spinet or Harpsichord …

It is better and more seemly not to beat time with the head, the body, nor with the feet. One should have an air of ease at one's harpsichord; not gazing too fixedly at one object, nor yet looking too vague; in short, look at the assembled company, if there be one, as if not occupied with anything else. This advice is only for those who play without the help of their books.[39]

The most interesting topic discussed by these musicians is improvisation, by which we mean both true improvisaion [ornamentation] and the simple addition of ornaments. As with other countries, it is quite clear that improvisation was assumed, as we can see in Michel de Saint-Lambert's *Les Principes du Clavecin* of 1702.

If the choice of the fingering is arbitrary in playing the clavecin, that of adornment is no less so. Good taste is the only rule to be followed. There are ornaments that are essential in the music and that it would be hard to do without. The most important of these is the trill; the others are the mordant, the arpeggio, and the falling tone. But though those we shall talk about later are not so necessary nor so much used, they lend much grace to compositions and one would be wrong to neglect them.[40]

This same writer also gives two general rules for ornamentation. First, he advises against taking too many liberties for fear that 'you will spoil that which you are trying to embellish.' Second,

The ornaments should never alter the melody nor the pace of the piece. Thus in the pieces with gay movements the runs and arpeggios should go faster than in slow movements. You must never hurry in making an ornament, however fast it should be played. You must take your time, prepare your fingers, then execute it boldly and freely.[41]

François Couperin also clearly implies an expectation of improvisation.

Although these preludes are written in measured time, there is nevertheless, a style, dictated by custom, which must be observed. I will explain what I mean. A prelude is a free composition, in which the imagination gives rein to any fancy that may present itself. But as it is rather rare to find geniuses capable of production on the spur of the moment, those who have recourse to these non-improvised preludes should play them in a free, easy style, not sticking too closely to the exact time, unless I have expressly indicated this by the word *Measuré*. Thus one may venture to say that in many things, Music (as compared with Poetry) has its prose, and its verse.

---

39 Couperin, *L'Art de toucher*, 11.

40 Michel de Saint-Lambert, *Les Principes du Clavecin* (1702), quoted in Carol MacClintock, *Readings in the History of Music in Performance* (Bloomington: Indiana University Press, 1979), 218.

41 Ibid., 224.

> One of the reasons why I have written these preludes in measured time was to make them easier, as will be found to be the case, whether in teaching them, or in learning them.[42]

A rather extraordinary comment by Bénigne de Bacilly, urges singers to slow down the beat in order to have more time to improvise, especially in dance forms such as the gavotte.

> It is completely unfair to criticize this style of performing by saying that the melodies [are then no longer] danceable, as thousands of ignoramuses have done. If this were to be the intention of the performing singer, then his function would be no more than that of a viol.[43]

We are also given several aesthetic goals for improvisation. One is that the end must still be to please the listener, as Bacilly writes in 1668.

> A piece of music can be beautiful and please not, for want of being performed with the necessary embellishments, of which embellishments the most part are not marked at all on paper, whether because in fact they cannot be marked for lack of signs for that purpose, or whether it has been considered that too many marks encumber and take away the clearness of a melody, and would bring a kind of confusion; besides, it is useless to mark things, if you do not know how to fashion them with the appropriate refinements [*avec les circonstances necessaires*], which makes all the difficulty.[44]

Another goal was that the end must be natural to the performer. But, Louis Bollioud de Mermet, in 1746, complained that now all sonatas sounded the same as performers had begun to standardize types of improvisation.

> One could easily persuade oneself that he who plays music in such a complicated and unnatural manner is an evil-doer on whom this labor was imposed for punishment.[45]

Because this aspect of performance was so much a part of the very understanding of music itself, from the perspective of the player, even in those cases where composers were beginning to 'write out' or to realize the ornamentation, their wishes were ignored. Couperin complains in 1722 that the information in his prefaces is being ignored and pleas that his music,

> will make a certain impression on people of good taste only if everything which I have marked is observed to the letter, without addition or subtraction.[46]

---

42 Ibid., 33.

43 Quoted in Ellen Harris, 'Voices,' in *Performance Practice: Music after 1600* (New York: Norton, 1989), 108.

44 Bénigne de Bacilly, *L'Art de bien chanter* (Paris, 1668), quoted in Donnington, *The Interpretation of Early Music*, 155.

45 Louis Bollioud de Mermet, *De la corruption* (Lyon, 1746), quoted in Ibid., 156.

46 François Couperin, *Pièces*, Liv. III (Paris, 1722), Preface.

EDUCATIONAL MUSIC

Saint-Lambert in his treatise of 1702 discusses music education, which he specifies should begin at five or six.[47] He also observed that regardless of the aptitude of the student, his final achievement was often made possible, or prevented, by the quality of his teacher. He then provides the most remarkable portrait of a good music teacher to be found in early literature.

> A teacher to be good must have two qualities: *knowledge* and *probity*; because to make a good pupil the master must absolutely have two rules: *he can* and *he will*.
>
> By the 'knowledge' of a teacher is not meant simply that he is a very expert player on the clavecin and an excellent composer of music; it must be demonstrated that he joins to those two advantages the talent of expounding clearly, which is a quality completely apart from that of being a celebrated musician.
>
> A good teacher knows to the bottom the abilities of those who put themselves in his hands, and accommodating himself to the range and capacity of each of them, he teaches each in the way that suits their talent. He devises as many methods as he has different talents to bring along. He speaks childishly to children, reasonably to reasonable persons: to both he speaks intelligently and tersely. He expounds his principles in an orderly way and always presents them as simple and separate ideas. He does not embarrass the memory of those he is teaching with useless fine distinctions. He teaches a general rule as if it had no exceptions, waiting for the time when this exception arises to talk about it, because he knows that it is better understood at this point, and he knows that if he had talked about it earlier it would have confused the general rule. He gives his first rule as if it were the only one he would ever have to talk about, and when he passes to the second he never mentions those which are about to follow.
>
> Passing from theory to practice, the good teacher is able to choose for each pupil the pieces best suited to the abilities of their hands. He even composes some expressly for those who may need them. But after having given some easy piece to his pupils to assure them at the beginning, he then gives them some that are directly opposed to the abilities of their hands in order to correct the faults.
>
> The good teacher brings far along the road to perfection the student who has much facility in this practice and even further the one who has more facility. He causes the male and female students who may have more talent than he has to play better than he does. And because he knows that one cannot profit unless one really likes playing, he has a special secret to cause his pupils to like learning. This talent is the most necessary when he has children to teach, for the natural fickleness of young children often, after having desired ardently to play the clavecin, makes them take a distaste for it after the third or fourth lesson because of the difficulty they have found; and their distaste goes so far at times that an exercise which is really a game, and should really be learned as a game, becomes for them a cause for sadness and tears. So it is up to the teacher to relieve his young pupils of the difficulties that annoy them and to act so that they give themselves over to their exercises, if not with pleasure at least with courage and perseverance.[48]

---

47 Michel de Saint-Lambert, *Le Principes du Clavecin*, 213.
48 Ibid., 213ff.

We also have a number of interesting observations on music education by François Couperin. First, he specifies that the proper age at which children should begin is from six to seven years.[49] Then, regarding the actual pedagogy,

> During the first lessons given to children, it is better not to advise them to practice in the absence of the person who is teaching them; little people are too easily distracted ... For myself, when giving children their first lessons, as a precaution I take away the key of the instrument on which I have been giving them instruction, so that, during my absence, they cannot spoil in one instant all that I have most careful taught them in three quarters of an hour.[50]
>
> ......
>
> One should not begin teaching the tablature, or musical notation to children until after they have a certain number of pieces in the fingers [from memory]. It is almost impossible for them while looking at their book, not to let their fingers get out of proper position, and not to make contortions with them; and even the *agrémens* themselves might be spoilt by it; moreover, the memory improves greatly in learning by heart.[51]
>
> ......
>
> Those who instruct young people would do well to instill into them gradually a knowledge of the intervals, of the modes; of their cadences, both perfect and imperfect; of chords, of chords by supposition. This develops in them a sort of 'local memory,' which makes them surer, and helps them to put themselves right again, with understanding, when they have broken down.[52]
>
> ......
>
> It would be well if parents, or those who have the care of children, showed less impatience, and more confidence in the teacher: (being sure of having made a good choice) and if the able Master, on his side, showed less condescension.[53]

And regarding the physical problems of older students:

> People who begin late, or who have been badly taught must be careful; for as the sinews may have become hardened, or they may have got into bad habits, they should make their fingers flexible, or get someone else to do it for them ... that is to say, they should pull, or get someone to pull their fingers in all directions; that, moreover, will stir up their minds, and they will have a feeling of greater freedom.[54]
>
> ......

---

49 Couperin, *L'Art de toucher*, 10.

50 Ibid., 12.

51 Ibid., 13.

52 Ibid., 22.

53 Ibid., 18.

54 Ibid., 12.

> Men, who wish to attain a certain degree of perfection, should never do any rough work with their hands. Women's hands, on the contrary, are generally better ... A man's left hand, which he uses less in this work, is usually the more supple at the harpsichord.[55]

Finally, Rameau, in 1744, gives advice for a young composer on the developmental stages of composing.

> It would be necessary, before undertaking so great a work [as an opera], to have written small compositions, cantatas, divertissements, and a thousand trifles of the kind that nourish the spirit, fire its imagination, and make one imperceptibly capable of greater things. I have followed the theater since the age of twelve; I did not work for the Opéra before I was fifty years old, even then doubting my capacity to do so.[56]

---

55 Ibid., 13.

56 Jean-Philippe Rameau, letter to Mongeot, 1744, quoted in Piero Weiss, *Letters of Composers Through Six Centuries* (Philadelphia: Chilton, 1967), 81.

3 MERSENNE

Marin Mersenne (1588–1648) studied mathematics, physics, the classics and metaphysics at the Jesuit College of Le Mans and later at the college at La Flèche, where one of his classmates, and life-long friend, was René Descartes. After becoming a Jesuit priest, and a member of the Minorite friars, Mersenne began teaching Hebrew, philosophy and theology at the Sorbonne in Paris in 1619. His residence became a required stopping place for every intellectual visiting Paris, which, together with his correspondence with persons throughout Europe, including Galilei, Huygens and Descartes, made him a virtual one-man academy.

His studies and experimentation in music resulted in his *Harmonie universelle* (1636), a work of encyclopedic proportion organized in five treatises:

I   *Traitez de la nature des sons, et des mouvements de toutes sortes de corps.*
II *Traité de mechanique.*
III *Traitez de la voix, et des chants.*
IV *Traitez des consonances, des dissonances, des genres, des modes, et de la composition.*
V   *Traité des instruments.*

The first two treatises deal with mathematics-based music theory and acoustics. The final three deal with vocal production, composition and instruments.

Reflecting his background, the perspective of Mersenne is as thoroughly mathematics-based and theologically oriented as any late medieval Scholastic university theorist. Nowhere is this more evident than in the second treatise, *Traité de mechanique*, which, in addition to subjects such as the soul and relationship of the senses to man, deals with pure science, which he attempts to correlate with music. His discussion in this treatise reflects clearly his twin centers of gravity, mathematics and theology, as well as his very impressive breadth of knowledge of earlier treatises. His purpose was an attempt to prove mathematically the ancient Greek thought that music must be related to a great harmony of nature created by God. While the treatise's value as science is weakened by errors in mathematics and by his acceptance of contemporary deductions, especially in astronomy, which are now understood to be incorrect, it is nevertheless an interesting and very valuable reflection of seventeenth-century French intellectual thought.

The entire thrust of philosophical thought in music beginning with the late sixteenth century was centered on the understanding that the central purpose of music is to express feelings, the vital concept which was to carry musical development into the future. Since these ideas were synonymous with the specific rejection of the old Scholastic mathematics-based explanations of music, it is curious to read Mersenne's extensive attempts to base explanations of music on mathematics in his *Traité de mechanique*. In great mathematical detail, he attempts to relate consonance and dissonance to solid geometry, physics and mechanics. For Mersenne, this mathematical knowledge was central to the 'theory' of music and like a medieval academic this, in turn, was central to the definition of 'musician'.

> Those who know only singing and the manner of composing, as well as singers and those who play instruments, do not merit the name of musician, just as bricklayers do not deserve to be called architects, since the former do not know the ratio of the harmonics which they make or in which they assist, as the latter do not know why palaces and other edifices have one figure rather than another. Thus the practice of music is like a body without a soul if one does not know the theory, which surpasses practice as much as the spirit surpasses the body and the heavens surpass the Earth.[1]

In his fourth treatise, Mersenne seems to suggest that goodness in a composition is a matter of mathematics. Can we find here the birth of the rationale for modern analysis?

> Since the goodness of composition consists in the natural order of the consonances, in their succession, and in the harmony which they make, we can say that the examination of this order is the idea of all the examinations which can be made of all the other kinds of compositions.[2]

In this same treatise Mersenne presents a detailed theory on voice leading and intervals, as the basis for composition.[3] It is entirely mathematics-based, resulting in musical examples expressed in a kind of tablature-notation consisting entirely of numbers.

> This manner of composing can be used by learned theoreticians, who wish to compare and send their compositions to each other, or who wish to have their compositions printed without using the [normal musical] notes of practice, which not every printer has.[4]

For the modern reader, perhaps the most interesting pages within the maze of mathematics in the *Traité de mechanique* are those which discuss the ancient theory of the 'music of the spheres.' To understand this subject, observes Mersenne, is a natural thing for musicians who wish to 'contemplate celestial things while playing' or for the admiration of God, 'who

---

1 Marin Mersenne, *Harmonie Universelle*, II, ii. The English translation is taken from John Egan (Bloomington: Indiana University, unpublished dissertation, 1962). [All translations from the Second Treatise are taken from this source.]

2 Marin Mersenne, *Fourth Treatise of the Harmonie Universelle*, ed. Robert Williams (Rochester: Eastman School of Music, unpublished dissertation, 1972), IV, iv, 24. As hereafter, these numbers represent: Treatise, Book, and Proposition. [All translations from the Fourth Treatise are taken from this source.]

3 IV, iv, 5ff.

4 IV, iv, 17.

has preserved such beautiful proportion in the order which he has placed in all parts of the universe."[5]

Mersenne begins his discussion with the statement that he will not attempt to prove the existence of the music of the spheres and then devotes many pages to doing precisely that.

> Of course, we shall not be able to show whether the planets and stars make any sound. If the air extends as far as the firmament or infinity, as some people believe, having no doubt that God created it infinite, since it is an opinion fairly well received in the [ancient] schools that God was able and is still able to create an infinite air, and since we have neither known nor revealed principles which oblige us to believe that God did not create it infinite, then it is probable that the stars and planets make some sound, inasmuch as they do move in the air. We do not hear the sound, for we are accustomed to it from the wombs of our mothers. Sometimes the sound is too far from us, too low, too high, or too great to be heard, as happens with certain other phenomena. We are, for example, unable to hear the sound or noise which ants and other little animals make when they walk, run, crawl, or fly, inasmuch as the sound is too little and too feeble.
>
> It may be concluded that sound has too imperceptible extremities. It may be too strong or too violent. It may be too feeble or too small. It may be made by too slow movement or too small movement. It may be made by a too swift, too large, or too precipitous movement. Both extremities exceed the sphere which the ear has for its activity and understanding.
>
> Now, if the celestial bodies do make sounds, one may ascertain what their qualities are by considering the size and movement of the celestial bodies.[6]

Mersenne next paraphrases the conclusions of the ancient Greek Pythagorean school of philosophy, not a single word of which by the way, is extant in the writings of Pythagoras himself.

> The seven planets contain not only the consonances, but also the dissonances. Orpheus invented his heptachord or lyre of seven strings, each of which represented one of the planets, but the Pythagoreans added the *Proslambanomenos* from the Earth up to the Moon in order to create their lyre with eight strings. There was a whole-tone from the first acquired string up to the principal, which they called *Hypate*; there was a semitone from *Hypate* to *Parhypate*, which represented the distance from the Moon to Mercury. From *Hypate* up to *Lichanos* there was a whole-tone, which represented the distance from Mercury to Venus. From *Lichanos* to *Mese*, or from Venus to the Sun, there was another whole-tone. From there to Mars, or from *Mese* to *Paramese*, there was a semitone. Finally, from the *Paranete* or from Jupiter there was a whole-tone, and from Jupiter to *Nete* or Saturn there was another whole-tone. Consequently they placed the octave from the Earth to Saturn, the perfect fifth from the Earth to the Sun, the perfect fourth from the Moon to the Sun, the perfect fifth from Venus to Saturn, and the perfect fourth from the Sun to Saturn. Thus they based their music on planetary movement from east to west, for the movement of the lowest planets is the slowest, and that of the highest planets is the quickest, since the latter make a greater journey in the same time.

---

5 II, viii.

6 II, v.

If, however, we tune a lute according to planetary movement from west to east, it is necessary to change the order of the names and give the *Proslambanomenos* to Saturn, the *Hypate* to Mars, etc.[7]

Mersenne quotes at length another contemporary who believed in the music of the spheres, the German astronomer Johann Kepler (1571–1630). Kepler, who concentrated on planetary motion, speculated on combinations of sounds, chords, which might be created by the passing of the planets.[8] Mersenne suggested that if the planets produce harmony, 'it would be necessary to make Saturn and Jupiter the bass, Mars the tenor, the Earth and Venus the alto, and Mercury the soprano, because Mercury has a greater range and is livelier than the others.'[9] If there really is music of the spheres, Mersenne recommends that musical instruments should be tuned to these pitches. Unfortunately, he adds, there will always be something missing in this celestial harmony because of the great time intervals involved—Saturn and Jupiter, for example, only coinciding every eight hundred years.

In another treatise, Mersenne cites Gosselin and Guy Aretin relative to their theories that the musical intervals and the voice can be related to the planets, concluding that Jupiter is the root, Saturn is the second, the Moon is the third, Mercury is the fourth, Venus is the fifth, the Sun is the sixth, Mars is the seventh and Jupiter again the octave. Mersenne, however, finds this knowledge not necessary for practical musicianship.

> But it is not necessary that the musician know the properties of the planets in order to compose good songs. For all kinds of music can be composed without knowing the planets, which have no particular influence on the voice.[10]

ON THE PHYSIOLOGY OF AESTHETICS

Mersenne, in his *Harmonie universelle*, does not devote much attention to speculation on the workings of the brain. There is only one important passage which has some relevance to his later comments on music, especially with respect to the emotions.

> But it must be noted that there are two motivating qualities in the animal, one of which is called *natural* because it does not depend at all on knowledge, and consequently it performs its func-

---

7 II, v.

8 Kepler's treatise on the 'music of the spheres' is reviewed in Volume Six of this series. Kepler, in view of the recent discovery that the planets revolve around the Sun, and not the Earth, concluded that a listener could only hear these chords if he resided on the Sun!

9 II, viii.

10 Marin Mersenne, Treatise Three, Book One, *Traitez de la Voix, et des Chants.*, trans. Edmund LeRoy (New York: Julliard School, unpublished dissertation, 1978), III, i, 7. [All translations from Treatise Three, Book One, are from this source.]

tions without knowing them, as is seen in the movement of the heart and arteries, and in that of respiration.

This quality is no different from the vital force in oysters and in other fish and animal with shells. The other quality is sensual, which we have in common with all sorts of animals and which is subdivided into three others, namely into that which directs, that which thrusts, and that which performs by way of execution. These things can be called *direction*, *impetus*, and *execution*.

The imagination is that which directs by the knowledge it has of the object. That which excites or disposes more particularly to action is called *appetite*. And the motivating force, named *execution*, brings our desires to fruition and is the efficient cause of all our movements.

As for the imagination and appetite, they are moral motives rather than physical and natural, and have another cause than the motivating force, for the imagination is in the brain; and the sensitive appetite, of which we speak, is in the heart.[11]

Mersenne briefly, and unfortunately without elaboration, touches on a basic aspect of the left and right hemispheres of the brain, namely with respect to the distinctions between speech and singing. He wonders what would be the nature of speech if a child were reared in an environment which it never heard another human talk, although he doubts such an experiment could ever be made.[12] After much speculation he concludes that the different voices which express 'the passions of the soul' in men and animals are natural, but language itself is artificial.[13] This eventually leads him, in Proposition 12, to wonder if 'the musician can invent the best language of all those by which the conceptions of the mind can be expressed.'[14]

On the Senses

In his second treatise, *Traité de mechanique*, following an attempt to equate the metric system to consonances in music and the meter of poetry, Mersenne proposes to demonstrate the correspondence between the senses and music.

> We shall commence with tastes, the most agreeable of which must correspond to the octave. These are the sweet tastes which are found in honey, sugar, flowers of honeysuckle …
>
> The fatty or greasy taste corresponds to the perfect fifth, since, with the exception of the sweet, it is the most agreeable taste.
>
> The perfect fourth is comparable to the salty taste, for the salty taste is disagreeable in combination with the sweet, as is the perfect fourth when it is joined with the octave. If the perfect fourth is joined with the perfect fifth, however, it is agreeable, as is the salty taste with the fatty …
>
> The astringent taste corresponds to the major third, and the insipid taste to the minor third. These two consonances combine well with the octave, as do the astringent and insipid tastes

---

11 III, i, 1.

12 Now such examples have been found, and such children cannot utter intelligible sounds.

13 III, i, 10.

14 In III, i, 20, Mersenne discusses how the study of singing can improve pronunciation in speech.

with the sweet. The gentle impression which the astringent and insipid tastes make on the gustatory sense is similar to that which the major or minor third takes on the ears. Although they can be mixed with the salty, the astringent and insipid tastes do not combine so well with the fatty. Similarly the major or minor third combines better with the perfect fourth than with the perfect fifth. When the major or minor third combines with the perfect fourth, it forms the major or minor sixth. The sixths, however, are less agreeable than the thirds. Just as the thirds do not contain the octave or the perfect fifth, so the astringent and insipid tastes do not partake of the sweet or the fatty.

The major sixth corresponds to the sour taste, and the minor sixth with the acid taste. Just as the major sixth combines well with the minor third and the minor sixth with the major third, so the sour can be joined with the insipid and the acid with the astringent. Such taste combinations ought to result in the sweet taste, just as the major sixth combines with the minor third to form the octave and the minor sixth combines with the major third to form the octave. The octave thus formed, however, lacks the perfect fifth, just as the corresponding taste combinations lack the fatty taste.

The sharp taste can be combined with the sour, such as wine with pepper, and that the sharp and sour agree with the tasteless and the sweet. Just as the two sixths agree with the octave and the perfect fifth. The two sixths can not be joined with the perfect fourth, just as the two aforesaid tastes can not be agreeably combined with the salty.

The bitter taste is like the whole-tone. It is always disagreeable. The tastes of all fruits begin with bitterness, as one experiences with unripe fruits. So, too, songs often begin with the whole-tone. The whole-tone is never more disagreeable than in combination with the octave, and the bitter is never more disagreeable than in combination with the sweet.

On the other hand, the bitter is never more agreeable than in combination with the salty, just as the whole-tone is never more agreeable than in combination with the perfect fourth so as to create the perfect fifth. For this reason certain people prefer the taste of salty olives to that of pheasants.[15]

Mersenne next suggests that colors correspond with music in a similar manner. He cites a few examples taken from the sixteenth-century Italian philosopher, Girolamo Cardano (1501–1576), beginning with white and black corresponding to the major and minor sixth. Cardano's theories of colors in their harmonic ratios, says Mersenne,

> will enable one to judge how the splendor and light of colors may be compared with the splendor of music or with that which heightens harmonies and consonances. Music is like perspective. Harmonies are like paintings which artists enhance with shading just as musicians set off consonances with a silence and dissonances. Silence can be compared with darkness, and vocal or instrumental sounds with diverse lines or the traces of the brush, colors, light, and shadows which ameliorate painting. Some sounds and intervals wound the ear, just as some colors offend the eye. Perhaps bulls and elephants really are terrified when they see red, and there are also certain sounds and intervals by which bulls and other animals can be enraged.

---

15 Mersenne, *Harmonie Universelle*, II, ii. English translation is taken from John Egan (Bloomington: Indiana University, unpublished dissertation, 1962).

As green refreshes the spirit primarily, and blue the eye, even so the perfect octave and the perfect fifth delight the ear more than do the other intervals.

Everyone will be able to judge the consonances and sounds most agreeable to himself and compare them with colors, tastes, smells, paintings, qualities of touch, and all other things which give him pleasure.[16]

In his third book, Mersenne attempts to make similar correspondence between music and 'Isorropics, weights, machines of war and peace, the beating of the pulse, and the health of body and soul.' Regarding the soul, he paraphrases Ptolemy in saying,

The octave is similar to the reasonable or intellectual spirit because of its uniformity and equality … He compares the perfect fifth with the sensitive spirit and the perfect fourth with the vegetal, inasmuch as the perfect fifth approaches the octave more closely than does the perfect fourth, just as the sensitive spirit is closer to the intellectual than is the vegetal. The vegetal spirit contains three parts, namely, growth, strength, and decline of life, just as the perfect fourth contains three intervals. The sensitive has four faculties [although he lists five], namely, sight, hearing, smell, taste and touch, just as the perfect fifth has four divisions. The intellectual spirit has seven faculties, namely, imagination, thought, memory, ratiocination, opinion, reason, and science, just as there are seven divisions of the octave.[17]

The position of the Church had long designated the eye as the most important of the five senses, for its obvious relationship to the intellect. Mersenne presents an interesting, and more balanced, comparison of the importance of eye and ear.

If the eye discovers a greater array of things present, the ear discovers a greater array of things absent … If the eye enjoys light and colors, the ear enjoys harmony of sounds and discourse that surpasses all that is comprehended by the eye … If the eye is more prompt in its actions, the ear hears in recompense all that is said in front, behind, and to the sides, [while] the eye sees only what is in front.[18]

---

16 Ibid., II, ii.

17 II, iii.

18 III, i, 53.

ON THE AESTHETICS OF MUSIC

On the Definition of Music

In the first proposition of the second book of his third treatise, Mersenne provides his most concise definition of music, in the context of a discussion of song.

> The song, or air, is a derivation of the voice, or of other sounds, by certain intervals either natural or artificial, which are agreeable to the ear and to the spirit, and which signify joy, or sadness, or some other passion by their movements.[19]

Having written this, it is interesting that he seems compelled to clarify the distinction between song and the vocal qualities of speakers and actors. It is especially interesting that he heard preachers whose regular tessitura encompassed a fifth.

> An objection can be made here, saying that the definition of this first theorem pertains to harangues, or discourse, and to the recitation of tragedies and comedies, for an orator, or someone representing a personage of the theater can observe all the intervals; diatonic, chromatic, or enharmonic within the octave. Experience has shown us how preachers use the half tone, the tone, the major third, the minor third, the fourth and the fifth, according to their accents or movements which they employ. From this it can be seen that several excellent musicians state that the discourse made by such men form a *Faux-Bordon*. This is verified by the preachers who speak as if they sang. That is why their discourse is less agreeable, and less profitable.

Later in this book he adds a few comments on the aesthetic qualities of song.

> I say that the song which is best proportioned will be best of all. It will have all parts which correspond exactly to the letter and subject chosen, and this will never be better than when it describes the grandeur and praise of God, and the love and ardor which we must eternally consider.
>
> It is easy to conclude that all the chansons of the court which have only profane subjects, and contain the praises of men, or flattery, and vanity and lies, cannot be perfect since truth is lacking in them …
>
> As for the note and song that must be given the chanson, I say first that it must have the range of a 19th, in order that it is not without the number which is employed to celebrate the grandeur of Him who has used the six days of creation to make the Universe … Secondly, the chanson must contain all the beautiful and ravishing passages which can be imagined, and all the sweet consonances, for if it lacks these things it will not be the most perfect possible. In the third place, it must be sung by an excellent voice.[20]

---

19 Marin Mersenne, *Treatise Three, Book Two ('Second Book of Songs') of the Traitez de la Voix et des Chants* …, trans. Wilbur F. Russell (Princeton: Westminster Choir College, unpublished dissertation, 1952), III, ii, 1. [All translations from Treatise Three, Book Two, are from this source.]

20 III, ii, 22.

Mersenne makes only a few references to the actual elements of music with respect to their aesthetic qualities. In one passage where he is arguing for the importance of the triad, it is interesting that he knows no explanation for its absence in medieval and early renaissance music.

> Composers maintain as a certain rule that thirds or their replicas should never be lacking in compositions in three or more parts, since they do not have charm without them … Thus we have reason to be astonished that the ancient Greeks and Latins rejected the third from the category of the consonances, since without them music in several parts has almost no charm at all.[21]

He seems to revert to his perspective as a priest with respect to dissonance, finding that it has the same effect among chords as 'the vices do among the virtues.'[22] A dissonance resolved, he says, is like a pardon.

The remainder of Mersenne's attention to the definition of music is focused on the problem of the classification of the many kinds of music. Almost as if he were not quite sure which type of classification would be most functional, he proposes several means by which one can organize and discuss types of song.[23] One can organize them according to 'Diatonic, Chromatic and Enharmonic,' by the twelve modes or by their emotional character.

> In the third place, the songs divide into as many types as there are passions, for there are sad and languishing; there are joyful ones; ones fit for war, and others for peace.

They can be further divided into 'Dactylic, Anapestic, Iambic, etc.'

Mersenne then proposes the division of songs into one of three genres: the Vaudeville or Chanson, the Motet or Fantasie and the third being all kinds of dances. Or,

> If one wishes even a more definite division, he can consider twelve types of compositions of music practiced in France; Motets, Chansons, Airs, Passamezzi, Pavanes, Allemandes, Gaillards, Voltes, Courantes, Sarabandes, Canaris, Branles, and Ballets.

Before continuing his discussion on classification, in particular before his discussion of dance forms, Mersenne makes the interesting observation that he understood that 'the chanson and dances accompany each other ordinarily.'[24] Following are some of the more revealing comments he makes relative to the nature of the basic musical forms.[25]

> The *Vaudeville* is the most simple of all the Airs, and can be applied to any kind of poetry sung note against note, without being [notated], according to the longs and breves found in the verse …

---

21   IV, iv, 28.
22   IV, v, 2.
23   III, ii, 4.
24   III, ii, 22.
25   III, ii, 23.

> The Vaudevilles are simple indeed, because the least artisans are capable of singing them, since the author is content with presenting something which is agreeable to the ear, rather than making counterpoint, fugues, syncopes, or other formal arrangements.
>
> The *Motet* is so called because it is used in a short period of time, as if one had only a few words to say, and is used to present some brief idea in music …
>
> When the musician takes the liberty of using everything which comes into his spirit without expressing passion in words, the resultant composition is called *Fantasie*, or *Recherche* …
>
> The *Passemezze* is an Italian song for dancing. It was used in former times as an entrée to the basse danses. It is danced by making several turns around the room with certain posed steps, and then crossing the middle, as the word bears …
>
> The *Pavane* comes from Spain, and is called thus because those who dance it make wheels in front of each other as the Pagans do, and with such seriousness that the cap and sword are not awkward at all, but necessary to better perform the step …
>
> The *Allemande* is a dance of Germany, which is measured like the Pavane, but it is not used in France as much as the others … Today it is usually played without being danced …
>
> The *Sarabande* was invented by the Saracens, or Moors, and took its name from them … It is danced to the sound of guitar, or castanets … Its steps are composed of stretches or slides.
>
> The *Volte* shows by its name (meaning to turn) that it comes from Italy, and is a turning dance …
>
> The *Courante* is the most practiced of any dance in France, and is performed by two people at a time, who run in time to the Iambic foot …
>
> The *Galliard* is a dance which took its name from the liveliness, or *Gaillardise* used in dancing, and the liberty which allows the dancers to go on the bias, across, or the length of the hall. Some say that it comes from Rome.

On the Perception of Music

Mersenne is one of very few early writers who ventured beyond the mathematics-based discussion of the theory of music to speculate about the psychological perception of music. He begins by observing that the brain is capable of processing sounds beyond those used in music, indeed capable of hearing musical sounds in the forces of Nature.

> The brain, which is more universal than the will, can contemplate the natural noises, and examine whether the different thunderings, roarings, and rumblings of the sea form consonances and dissonances.[26]

He wonders if the pitches used in music, specifically in singing, are somehow innate, provided by Nature, or if they are entirely taught by man. It is a question of Art versus Nature in

---

26 Marin Mersenne, Treatise Five, *Traité des instruments*, trans. Roger Chapman (The Hague: Nijhoff, 1957), V, i, 5. [All translations from Treatise Five are from this source.]

terms of pitch. While Mersenne concludes on the basis of his experience that pitch is artificial, taught by man, some studies today suggest man may carry a genetic, natural pitch template.

> Now there is no doubt that the degrees and intervals of voices take after Art … for if they do not depend on Art, those who teach singing to children would have no trouble at all in making them intone and sing exactly; and all men would make the exact intervals without having learn them. This is against experience.[27]

Mersenne now turns to the perception of pitch in terms of high and low. From his experience he concludes that it is the highest voice which is most prominently perceived, something which has also been confirmed by modern clinical research to be a specific function of the brain. Mersenne finds a 'natural' example in the peasant.

> Experience shows us that nature without artistry does not ordinarily use a bass at all, for peasants and shepherds sing only the treble or the tenor whenever they sing.[28]

He has also found this principle demonstrated by the performances of trained musicians in the concert hall.[29]

> We experience that the trebles in concerts, as much vocal as instrumental, awaken the attention best and are very much more agreeable, as if approaching more nearly to heaven and life, than the basses. Now we take more pleasure in drawing to us those who are more perfect and more full of life than those who are more imperfect and nearer to death. Thus it happens that we love and caress infants more than old people who are like great and weighty sounds and like winter, just as children are like spring and summer and heat or fire. Bass voices are like gloom, sought after only by owls and goblins; but high voices are like light and day, serving as ornaments to nature as high sounds do to music which loses all her charm when she does not have good trebles. Bass voices serve almost as nothing more than to make the high sounds perceptible, and to make them enter the ear and the mind with more diversity and pleasure.[30]

He does, however, offer one aesthetic objection.

> Although the high may be more agreeable, nevertheless the intensity and the work necessary to produce this voice withdraws and diminishes the pleasures of the ear, for when the pleasure does not surpass the pain, it cannot be great.

---

27 V, i, 3.

28 IV, iv, 3.

29 In III, i, 23, Mersenne discusses the construction of concert halls relative to acoustics, concluding that an ellipse shape produces the best results.

30 III, i, 17. The final line refers to what we call today the 'pyramid principle,' by which lower tones must be played louder, and higher ones softer, to counterbalance the action of the brain which makes us imagine we hear higher pitches louder than we do.

From this experience Mersenne appears to jump to the conclusion that the perception of Beauty in music is therefore found in music consisting of a single part, as opposed to multi-part sounds. His argument is that the essential Beauty is found in the succession of pitches, not in the vertical accumulation of pitches.[31]

> Just as the beauty of the universe arises from the fine order which it preserves in all its parts, and the beauty of the face arises from the position and the relationship of all the parts which compose it, likewise, the pleasantness and the goodness of music arise from the order which is observed among the consonances, which serve as the principal material for composition, which is more agreeable as the succession of these consonances is better and more carefully observed.[32]

Mersenne contends that in everything we experience, 'we receive more pleasure in knowing one thing distinctly and perfectly, than in knowing several things indistinctly and imperfectly.' After giving several illustrations of 'simpler is better,'[33] Mersenne advances the contention that a simple unaccompanied melody is 'more agreeable' to the listener than multi-part music.[34] He finds this idea opposed not only by composers, who are afraid their works will be discredited, but by Nature, where nothing is simple, but rather composed of elements. Nevertheless, for Mersenne, experience still taught that simple solos brought more delight than music in several parts. He curiously fails to distinguish the separateness of the senses in his discussion here, as he advances the argument that *smelling* a single flower produces a more distinct pleasure than *seeing* a bouquet of mixed flowers. Musically, he focuses on the observation that hearing *fa, me* sequentially, as in a melody, is pleasurable, but hearing them together is not.

For the sake of discussion, however, Mersenne considers the perception of multi-part music with respect to aesthetics. If pleasure comes from hearing distinctly, he asks, does it not follow that duos should be more pleasing than trios? Can this not be considered, Mersenne wonders, as an analogy to the difficulty in following a single soldier in battle [a single line in multi-part music] as opposed to watching a duel [two-part music]? Here, he interrupts himself to tell a rather extraordinary anecdote about the great composer Claude Le Jeune.

> It is believed that when Claude Le Jeune showed his musical pieces in five, six, and seven voices to the masters of Flanders and Italy, they did not even want to look at them, and he had no

---

31 Modern clinical research in the perception of music seems to suggest that meaning in music is conveyed almost entirely by genetic preference for melodic patterns.

32 IV, iv, 1.

33 For example,

> Even the sweat and the other excrements, of men as well as of animals, who subsist more simply, for example, of those who eat only bread or plants, and who drink only water, do not have as bad an odor as those who subsist on meat and who drink wine.

34 Behind his pronouncements, however, is his personal preference for the performance of chant in the church, the aesthetics for which we shall see him argue for at length below, under Functional Music.

audience at all, and that after having composed in two parts, in which he succeeded so poorly, he acknowledged to himself that he did not understand the true composition of music.[35]

Mersenne continues with arguments pro and con, in judging the virtues of two- versus three-part music, including analogies from Nature and theology. His consideration of why three or more parts are more agreeable than two, includes analogies with geometry and another detailed attempt to correlate color and musical tones.[36]

In the end, he concludes that the greater number of voices the better, so long as each sings in perfection.[37] Indeed, in another place he mentions in passing,

> The third part increases the pleasure of duos so perceptibly that it is almost not possible to express it.[38]

If he finds himself admitting that 'songs in several voices have a great number of beauties of which the simple solos are deprived,' he acknowledges as well his realization that others will disagree with him. Thus, he says, 'this distinction will remain problematical.'[39]

On the Purposes of Music

It is evident that Mersenne considered that the essential purpose of music was closely tied to the expression of emotions. This, in turn, was inseparable from the natural 'passions' in man, a subject to which he devoted considerable attention. Before we follow his arguments on the passions, it might be appropriate to first read his observations on the role of the composer, performer and listener regarding the general question of the communication of emotions in music.

With regard to the role of the composer, Mersenne seems, as he often is, torn between opposing values. First, he had a certain loyalty to the ideas put forward by Baïf during the attempts of his famous Academy to reproduce Greek song. In spite of the strong support for Baïf's ideas here, we must point out that Baïf's concept was not carried forward. His assumption that Greek music proceeded on a basis of one note for each syllable had no basis in actual knowledge of Greek music and, in any case, resulted in songs which were staid, lifeless and without feeling.

---

35 IV, iv, 2.
36 IV, iv, 4.
37 IV, iv, 2.
38 IV, iv, 24.
39 IV, iv, 3.

We must place each note with each syllable in such a way that we never make a barbarism, which consists in lengthening a short syllable, or in making short that which is long. This makes the composer ridiculous, and makes him pass as a dunce or a dunderhead.[40]

Mersenne, when discussing the role of the composer in 'writing good songs,' retains the general view of the sixteenth-century humanists that the source of all emotion in song lies in the words.

The art of writing good songs on all kinds of subjects does not depend solely upon the genius, the caprice, and the inclination of those who write them, but also upon the judgment, which should serve as guide for composers, as for other craftsmen …

With regard to melody, there is no need to explain its degrees and intervals [having done this in an earlier book, thus] nothing more can be desired except a good judgment to use them suitably, according to the different subjects which are presented. For example, sorrowful and amorous things are quite well represented by major, mean, and minor semitones, and still better by enharmonic dieses, if we wished to accustom the voice to them, and similarly, by the minor third, which follows the nature of the semitone, and by the minor sixth, which is suitable for representing the greatest moans and pains. Things which possess something great and arduous, or rustic, such as martial and vigorous actions, are better represented by the tones and by the major thirds and sixths, or by the perfect or augmented fourth …

We must consider the entire text, and the purpose or intent of that which it contains, and where it inclines the mind, so that we might accommodate to it an inflection and movements so suitable, that when sung, they have at least as much force on the listeners as if it were recited by an excellent orator. Thus the composer, or rather the singer, bends and inclines his mind to all that he wishes. For this purpose, the composer should indicate all the places of the song in which the voice must be strengthened or weakened, and where the accents of the passions … should be made, so that the singer might follow the intent of the composer punctually.

He must also indicate the tone on which the voice should begin, for experience shows that songs recited on certain tones are much more agreeable and have more effect upon listeners than when they are sung a tone higher or lower …

There is still something else in airs, however, which is more difficult to indicate and execute when singing than all that of which we have spoken up until here, namely, a certain grandeur, which accompanies the agreeableness of singing in the harmoniousness of the voice, and gives a single song something great and beautiful. This occurs with almost all other things which can be executed by the skill of man, which consists in action, as happens with dances, with the manner of bearing oneself on horseback, which has given the name of *fine and handsome man on horseback* in the academy of Pluvinel. This is noted also in perspectives, in scenes, in buildings, and everywhere else where there are things which partake of greatness and beauty. Hence the simplest clothes appear better on a well-formed body than the most handsome in the world on a badly formed body …

---

40 IV, v, 10. In IV, vi, 29, Mersenne seems to approve of this, on the basis of his belief that this was the principle of the practice of song by the ancient Greeks.

> We must acknowledge that the accents of the passions are lacking most often in French airs, since our singers are content with tickling the ear and with pleasing by their affectations, without concerning themselves with exciting the passions of their listeners, according to the subject and the intention of the text. They also do not have this grandeur, which arises from beauty and greatness of which I have spoken, and the song does not always express the significance of the words, for which we should have quite a particular care.[41]

Aside from this emphasis on the words as the source for the emotions communicated in music, Mersenne also recognized that there was something else, something which he associated with the importance of the composer being himself inspired.

> We should consider well, understand, and express the meaning and intent of the words and the subject, in order to accentuate and animate it in such a way that each part makes all the effect of which it is capable. This happens particularly when the composer himself is struck by the feeling which he desires to impress upon the minds of his listeners when writing and singing his airs, just as it happens that the orator has more power upon his audience when he is moved and completely convinced of his reasons.[42]

And beyond this, there was something which had to be supplied by Nature. Composers, he concluded, are born and not made through 'Art.'

> Whatever rules we could give for composing fine and beautiful airs on all kinds of subjects and texts, it appears that they cannot bring this to pass until we are induced by the favorable genius and natural inclination of those who write excellent ones without having learned or established any other rules than those which their imagination furnishes …
> I shall be of the opinion of those who say that the genius of music is like that of the poet, the painter, the orator, and of several other craftsmen, to whom nature, or rather the Master of Nature, has dispensed certain gifts to which art cannot attain.[43]

In another treatise, Mersenne, while still identifying the source of 'passion' in the text, now appears to place more emphasis on the 'passions' themselves. We also find here an interesting discussion of the correspondence of music and color.

> If we can find and establish infallible rules for making songs, we shall have accomplished one of the most difficult things in music … And if one demands why it is [more] difficult to make a good song, [than] it is to add parts to a song already composed, and to compose in two, or several parts, I reply that one must be more learned to recognize good songs, than to compose in several parts.

……

---

41 IV, vi, 8.

42 IV, vi, 9.

43 Ibid.

> I say now first that the infallible rule for songs is that they follow and imitate the movement of passion which they wish to excite in their hearers. For example, if one wishes to arouse war passion, or color, the Iambic or Anapestic movement should be used ... He who knows the real movements, knows the best part of music, and the rules which are most necessary in singing.
>
> The second part pertains to intervals, and the degrees used in chansons, for here also the same degrees must be used according to the passions which are to be aroused. For example, if anger rises or falls by degrees, it is necessary that the song does the same, [for] it is certain that songs were invented to arouse the passions. For example rejoicing pertains to the passions, and it is their beginning, foundation, and the end, for pleasure is nothing other than perfect love. I do not believe that other rules are necessary for making good songs on all types of subjects ...
>
> ......
>
> It should be noticed here that songs are similar to the nuances of colors, which follows the idea of not being able to pass from one extremity to another without passing through a central shade. That is why one can be instructed in making good songs by the consideration of the nuances, for as one has seven intervals, or eight sounds in the octave, so one takes seven or eight colors for each shade, as is seen in the shade of purple, blue, and chartreuse, or lemon yellow. In this way one can compare each song to each color ...
>
> One can add that if songs are made of the twelve tones in the octave, one has also twelve colors, and that a shade may have as many colors as the octaves do sounds, or intervals, for each may be divided into an infinity of degrees.
>
> One can be instructed by an analogy to other things. Simple tones compare to simple colors. Intervals of sounds compare to mixtures of the colors, and the songs to paintings.[44]

Regarding color, it is interesting that Mersenne thought it might be helpful if the composer arranged to have his music actually printed in color to help identify the emotions he had in mind. Therefore, the diatonic, a joyful set of intervals, might be printed in black; the chromatic, whose half-steps arouse sad, amorous, and ravishing feelings, could be printed in red; and the enharmonic, since it is particularly fitting 'for ravishing the mind in the contemplation of heavenly things,' could be reproduced in blue.[45]

Mersenne also assigned significant responsibility to the performer for the communication of the emotions in music to the listener. Since Mersenne was primarily interested in song, his discussion centers on the singer.

> The Italian [singers] observe several things in their solos of which ours are deprived, since they represent as much as they can the passions and the affections of the soul and the mind, for example, choler, wrath, spite, rage, lapses of the heart, and several passions, with a violence so peculiar that one would almost judge that they felt the same affections which they represent when singing, whereas we French are content with charming the ear, and use a constant mildness in our songs, which hinders their vigor ...

---

44 III, ii, 6.

45 'Embellissement des chants,' according to David Duncan, 'Persuading the Affections: Rhetorical Theory and Mersenne's Advice to Harmonic Orators,' in *French Musical Thought, 1600–1800* (Ann Arbor: UMI Research Press, 1989), 156.

Our singers imagine that the exclamations and the accents which the Italians use in singing, however, possess too much tragedy or comedy. This is why they do not wish to make them, although they ought to imitate what they have of goodness and excellence. For it is easy to moderate the exclamations and to accommodate them to the French mildness, in order to add that which they have that is more moving to the beauty, the distinctness, and the softening of cadences, which our musicians make with good grace when, having a good voice, they have learned the method of singing well from good masters.[46]

We find the most interesting comments by Mersenne on the subject of the performer those which deal with the problem of the emotions and their actual notation symbols. He wishes for a notational system which was more helpful and he is correct: we do not have a single written symbol which is addressed to feeling!

There are a number of passions which we can make appear in singing, for which we have not yet devised symbols, such as the great *exclamations* of Italian airs, and the representations of lapses of the heart. It appears that if the circumflex accent had not been used for the double-flagged notes … it would be suitable for representing these great cries and excesses of the voice, since it is composed of the acute and the grave accent, just as the exclamation of despair and of pain is composed of a cry of the voice and a small rest which descends to the third, the fourth, the minor sixth, or other intervals, according to its magnitude and the strength of the voice which sings …

We lack symbols to represent the notes or syllables which we should sing more strongly, as we have some bowing strokes much stronger than others. Since the voice has as many degrees of force as of intervals, we can divide this force into eight degrees, as we divide heat and the other qualities, so that the first degree is suitable for expressing very weak echoes, and the other seven degrees designate the different degrees of the most vehement passions up to the eighth, which will represent the greatest exclamation which can be made, such as that of despair and of any great pain of the mind or the body, such as we can imagine that of Esau when he roared and cried when demanding the benediction of his father Isaac. These different degrees of force can be designated by numbers, or by as many dots or accents. Since, however, they have already been used for other purposes, there would be need to add new symbols, although if we retain the ordinary usage of notes, which carry the value of time with them, numbers can serve to indicate the differences of force of the voice.[47]

If we wish to regulate and write airs so that we understand perfectly all that is required for their perfect execution, we must indicate the time of the beat. If the composer has the intent that one or more notes and beats should be longer or shorter than they are ordinarily, he should indicate this with specific signs. Otherwise, the air cannot be recited according to his intention, as we experience with Italian airs, which are never sung according to the intent of the composer, unless one has first heard them recited according to his method and his spirit. This can in some way be accommodated to speeches, for we could use certain characters to designate the manner of reciting them perfectly.[48]

---

46 IV, vi, 6.

47 Marcel Tabuteau, the legendary Principal Oboe of the Philadelphia Orchestra, devised such a system of numbers for teaching expression which he taught his students at the Curtis Institute of Music.

48 IV, vi, 7. An error in Mersenne's original publication misnumbers the propositions from this point on, beginning with 8, instead of 7.

Regarding the listener, Mersenne makes an error which is frequently made even today. Mersenne assumed that music produced its impact on man in a process similar to painting. But here he is mistaken, painting is a representation, but music is not—it is a *direct* communication between its source and the listener.

> Music is an imitation or representation, as is Poetry, Tragedy, or Painting ... for it does with sounds or with the articulated voice what the Poet does with verses, the Comedian with gestures, and the Painter with light, shade, and colors.[49]

Mersenne did recognize that to some degree taste is an individual matter. This has more than ordinary significance, for in a series of treatises so highly dependent on mathematics, it is an admission that mathematics and science cannot account for everything in music.

> Since the rules have been formulated only upon the different observations of the mixture of sounds, some of which have been more agreeable to those who formulated the rules than others were, it is free to those who are as capable, or more so, than they, to observe that which pleases them, since their ear is as good and as well trained, and since that which is offensive to some can be pleasing to others. For the rules of harmony are not like those of geometry, which force the mind of all those who have common sense to adopt them. They depend upon the ear and upon custom.[50]

But a Church philosopher cannot long leave Reason behind. Judgment of the good is partly Reason, not just the ear, Mersenne maintains. Speaking of the interval of the fourth, he observes,

> If perchance someone finds it a little harsh in certain places, he will judge it quite good when his ear is accustomed to it. The same thing will happen to him as to the disciples of Pythagoras who did not wish to approve of thirds and sixths until time and their use, based upon Reason, made them understand the excellence of these consonances, so that he will judge that the fourth is an excellent chord.[51]

Finally, Mersenne does make one very important point: one can only judge music by hearing it. He reminds us that before the advent of recordings, persons heard much less music than we hear today. Perhaps more than anything else this helps explain the emphasis on theory over practice in earlier periods, for they had to work from imagination rather than from direct, live experience.

> If we wished to have all the pleasure which can result from music, it would be necessary to have all the ways of singing and make them appear one after the other, in order to judge how

---

49 II, 97.

50 IV, iv, 21.

51 IV, v, 5.

one surpassed the other. For example, it would be necessary to have one or two madrigals or other Italian airs sung by a dozen fine Italian voices, as well as sarabandes by the Spanish, and courantes and airs by French; and then to have the best pieces of music written for instruments played by each of them … Since, however, no book can furnish the practice of this music, and since it is not easy to encounter it, it is sufficient to show what our France has invented, or what it has added to music, or at least its attempts, which can only be praiseworthy, even though they have not attained perfection.[52]

It is clear that the subject relative to the communication of emotions in music which was of most interest to Mersenne was that which has been labeled by many modern writers as the 'doctrine of the affections.' In general, this describes the contemplation by many seventeenth-century philosophers on how the emotions in music correspond with the psuedo-sciences of the 'temperaments' and the 'humors,' substances such as bile, or various organs, which supposedly affect the personality, or describe the personality. For these writers, this doctrine offered a possible vehicle for explaining the affect on the body by the obvious experience of emotions in music and vice versa.

Prior to this discussion in the seventeenth century, there was a long period of theorizing by Church philosophers on the relationship of these same 'humors,' as well as the emotions, to the soul. It seems clear that at least part of Mersenne's introduction to this subject came from the writings of Pontus de Tyard (1521–1605), who was the 'theorist in residence' of Baïf's Academy, for he specifically quotes from his writings on this subject.

> Pontus de Tyard also speaks thereof in his second *Solitaire*, in which he says that the agreement of the four humors is called health and the discord thereof is called sickness. The changeability of the pulse attests to this; it is like the master of the music of the human body. Philosophers have considered three kinds of movement in the spirit, namely, desire or concupiscence, ire, and reason, which produce an intellectual harmony in man when they accord with the will of God. Otherwise they yield a very disagreeable dissonance.
>
> Desire has three divisions. Ire has four, and reason has seven. The divisions are called virtues. The first division of desire is Temperance, which despises the voluptuous. The second division is Continence, which suffers failure and poverty without tiring. The third division of desire is Shame, which rejects any rejoicing over the voluptuous.
>
> Ire has four divisions, namely, Clemency, Courage or Assurance, Fortitude, and Constancy.
>
> Reason has seven divisions, namely, Understanding, Perspicacity, Curiosity, Counsel or Consideration, Wisdom, Prudence, and Experience.
>
> Temperance taken from the ternary of the perfect fourth, Fortitude drawn from the quaternary of the perfect fifth, Prudence drawn from the septenary of the octave, and Justice taken from the perfect consonance (inasmuch as it unites the powers of body and soul) make the perfect quaternary of the Pythagoreans, in which all the perfect consonances can be found.[53]

---

52 IV, vi, 24.

53 II, iii.

In this same place, Mersenne also paraphrases Ptolemy, concluding,

> There are certain sounds which excite some to voluptuousness, others to pity and mercy, and still others to rage and ecstasy. The passions of the soul are changed according to the sounds, songs, and modes which are used.[54]

Mersenne begins the discussion of his own theories on the relationship of music and the temperaments with a number of general observations on the nature of the emotions and music. He begins by considering the 'voices of animals,' which he finds serve to 'signify the passions of the soul, but does not always signify the temperament of the body.'

> Experience points out [that] … birds, dogs, and other animals make another sound when angered than when complaining, or when sick than when well again and in good health. For bile makes the voice high, melancholy and phlegm make it low, and the bloody humor renders it tempestuous. Thus the height is compared to fire, depth to earth and water and tempestuousness to air.[55]

Mersenne concludes that pitch itself is not an infallible indication of temperament, in either man or animal. However,

> As for the other qualities of the voice, such as sharpness, sweetness and agility, they seem to be able to give us more certain indications of temperament. For those who speak swiftly and brusquely are ordinarily testy, and those who speak slowly are melancholy. But those who speak moderately are cheerful and of a good temperament.

This line of thought leads him to speculate on the origin of speech.[56] Did Adam teach 'such voices as he wanted to each kind of animal to express its passions?' Or, did God differentiate 'their languages so that the different species could be distinguished by the voice just as they are by their exterior shape?' Without attempting to answer these questions, he returns to the temperaments.

> One can say in general the hardest and roughest voices are the most appropriate for signifying the passions, and griefs and displeasure; and the the sweetest voices are most appropriate for the amorous passions, and that the great cries best represent the great sorrows and sadnesses.

Now Mersenne begins to wonder if it might be more effective in expressing our feelings, if we substituted singing for speech. In fact, he concludes that 'song seemingly is more appropriate and natural for expressing the passions.'

---

54 II, iii.
55 III, i, 7.
56 III, i, 14.

For the song of a[n interval of a] second is appropriate for expressing sadness and that of a third is appropriate for expressing joy. And if one were to examine the nature of all intervals, one would find the conformity they have with each thing, such that he could enjoy them in place of our ordinary [speech] for making us understand and for expressing the nature of things.[57]

But, he admits, that persons with limited vocal resources would thus have trouble expressing themselves.[58]

It would seem a given conclusion to a seventeenth-century philosopher such as Mersenne that 'happy' songs should be more agreeable to the listener than sad ones. But to his astonishment, he found the opposite was sometimes the case! This led him to formulate the proposition, 'To determine if chansons which are sad and languishing are more agreeable and pleasant than those which are gay.'

> This proposition is not useless, for being well explained it will give us insight into the nature of man, and of music. It seems that one cannot doubt that gay chansons are not more agreeable than sad ones, since all men desire to rejoice and disperse sadness which ruins health and state of the body.
>
> One sees that the Ballet airs, and the violins arouse men of their gaiety, derived from the quick movements, and high-pitched sounds, rather than those airs played on the lute, or bass viols, which are ordinarily more serious and languishing.
>
> The trumpets are another proof of this when they use the first mode, which is the gayest of all, and arouses all sorts of emotion in men. We know from experiences that the movements of heart and imagination follow the sounds and movements of the trumpet.
>
> To which one can add that sounds, and rhythms of gay songs approach life, rather than the sad airs, since life consists of perpetual movement. The vibrations of air which make the high sounds, and rhythmic movements which are quicker approach nearer this continuity than those which are serious, or weighty and slow sad songs. They represent broken and dying life. One experiences that gay songs are proper for dancing, and even those who have never learned to dance derive some pleasure from these chansons. This does not happen in the case of sad airs, or lugubrious melodies, which are only proper for making their auditors weep and die, rather than for laughing or life. These airs are composed of rhythms suitable for engendering sadness, and consequently for making the inactivity fall upon the limbs which cause them to become paralytic and incapable of movement.
>
> Nevertheless all musicians are of contrary opinion, and the listeners who sing confess that they receive more pleasure from sad and languishing songs, than from gay ones ...

---

57 III, i, 33. Duncan, 'Persuading the Affections,' 156, cites 'Embellissement des chants,' for a passage we have not found, in which Mersenne makes further associations between specific intervals and emotions.

> Mersenne thought the major modes evince joy, and 'masculine and courageous actions,' such as war. Impelled upward toward the fourth, the major third has a vigorous character, whereas the minor third is a lethargic interval, either remaining inert or collapsing toward the second.

58 In III, i, 36, Mersene offers a remedy for clearing the throat, a potion of the 'grain of ground cole-wort mixed with sugar, or with Spanish licorice, or with tobacco syrup.' He adds, 'I leave out all the extraordinary remedies and many ways that actors and preachers use to preserve their voices.'

However one can first consider that men have much more melancholy and phlegm than bile, and they embrace the earth more than air, or the skies, and the gay airs being of an aerial nature, representing fire, are not so suitable to the nature of men as the sad and languishing songs which represent the earth, melancholy, and phlegm. I have proved in the 31 propositions of the 'Book of Sounds' that the high sounds are more agreeable than the low ones, because they partake more of the nature of air and fire. This does not mean however that sad songs must be less agreeable than gay ones. But the reason is not enough, since one meets bilious men, who are pleased with sad songs, as well as melancholy ones, in a way that it is necessary to take the nature of the sad songs in mind, since some listeners differ in their opinion.

It is necessary to consider the nature of sad airs, which consist of several things, for the melody of sad airs represents languor and sadness by its continuation, by its weakness and its trembling. The half-tones and sharps represent the tears and complaining because of their small intervals which mean weakness. The small intervals which are made in rising or falling are similar to children, to the old, and to those who arise from a long illness, who cannot walk in large steps ...

And then when one takes a long time to shift from interval to interval that shows a great weakness, which makes its impression in the soul of the listener ... Gay songs are so rapid, that one has not as much time to notice them, since they do not remain long enough in one place to make an impression on the soul. I do not wish to speak here of the text which augments sadness, when it makes us review the unhappy accidents of life with which we have been tormented, since sad airs can exist without words.

However, it is necessary to notice that all men are more subject to sadness than to joy, for if each one could reflect on the actions that he does, or on his thoughts, he would find a dozen of the sad ones for each gay one. Sadness fell upon us after the original sin, and is natural to us. In contrast, joy comes to us by accident, as happens in joyous gatherings, where each one forces himself to give pleasure to his companion (which he does not always succeed) and there are many who have laughed while the heart was sad. But it seems that often one lets himself follow the common opinion that there are sad songs, and that one should say they are gay, since they bring contentment to the listeners. Many times musicians call songs sad when in reality they are not, but rather they fit the voice of those who lament, particularly well.

What is this pleasure derived from sad things? How is it engendered in listeners? I would say only that there are two types of sadness, one moral, because its motifs are drawn from deprivation, the other is natural, and comes from the melancholic humor, or from the phlegmatic, when one has sinned to excess. Sad songs do not engender either, but leave the listener in whatever humor he was previously in. If we use reason, we see that the melancholiacs derive more pleasure from gay songs than from sad ones, since the brusque and lively movements of the chansons are more suitable for dissipating excessive humor of melancholy, rather than the slow and languishing movements of lamentations. One is cured by the contrary of his ailments, if we believe Hippocrates rather than Paracelsus, who believed that people are cured by similar things.[59]

Mersenne also wonders which is the most effective means of determining the emotions of men. He notes in passing that some believe the emotions can be read in the face and others in the lines of the hand. He rejects the opinion of Aristotle that a strong voice can necessar-

---

59 III, ii, 26.

ily be associated with a hot temper. The most interesting discussion here is on the subject of laughter, based on a book on this subject by Prosper Aldorise. First the interesting observation is made that all laughter uses one or other of the five vowels (Ha Ha Ha; Hee Hee Hee, etc). From this the following discussion ensues.

> Now since a greater ardor is necessary for moving the wings of the lungs when the laugh is made on *a*, it can be said that those who form *a* while laughing have more ardor than those who form *o* and *i*, and that *e* signifies a greater ardor than *u*. A shows the moistness and facility that the glottis has in opening, and, consequently, that one is full-blooded. But *e*, *o*, and *i* show its dryness and that those who form these letters while laughing are of a cold and dry temperament. Just as the vowel *u* signifies that one is cold and moist, the vowels *i* and *o* show that one is hot, dry, and bilious. *E* signifies melancholy, and *u* signifies phlegm, and those who form the said letters while laughing are subject to the maladies deriving from these humors, or are appropriate to the virtues that these same humors favor. This is why I conclude that *a* and *o* signify audacity and liberality when they are made by a quick movement, and that *e* and *u* signify avarice; that those who form *a* and *o* are loved by those who form *e* and *i*, who look for ardor to be perfected and conserved; and that those who form the same letter are loved reciprocally because of the resemblance; that those who form *a* and *o* have a quicker and sharper mind; and that those who form *e* have better memory and less imagination, and that they are more opinionated; that the vowels *i* and *u* show a short life and the others a long life; such that the spring of his life who forms *a* lasts 25 years, which he similarly confers to the summer, autumn, and winter of life.[60]

Mersenne's own special area of interest, within the general topic of music and the emotions, was the relationship of the vocal accents of speech and the melodic accents he heard musicians add to the music and how these might be related to the 'temperaments' and the 'humors.' He begins by considering the use of accent in general.

> With regard to the ordinary accents of which the Greeks, the Latins, and the other nations speak, they admit only three, namely, the grave, the acute, and the circumflex, or the accents of grammar, rhetoric, and music.[61]

Mersenne now wonders if the individual use of these accents may identify 'the temperament and humor.' First, he points out that one can easily identify persons from different parts of France merely by their accents. To him it followed that,

> Experience teaches that those who are hasty and abrupt in their actions and who are easily upset have an abrupt and high accent, and that those who are gloomy have a low, slow, and heavy one. Just as there are quite as many temperaments and different humors as there are men, likewise there are just as many different accents and different manners of speaking … This can apparently arise only from the difference of their humors and the diversity of their organs, which arises from the difference of their temperaments.[62]

---

60   III, i, 46.

61   IV, vi, 10.

62   IV, vi, 11.

Mersenne now offers the proposition: 'The accent of which we speak here is an inflection or modification of the voice or the word with which we express the passions and the affections naturally or artificially.' He finds this a natural expression in speech, but he is suspect of singing for through the study of the art of singing, singers may learn, like actors, to only imitate an emotion.

> The difference of this definition is explained in the words *with which we express*, etc. For nature itself teaches us which accents we must use to show and designate our passions and affections, which are expressed solely artificially with the simple word or with singing. For the song and discourse depend upon art and instruction. We cry, shout, and give certain accents to the voice and the words, without having learned to make them. These accents of passion are common to men and animals, who cry differently to show their joy than to show their sorrow.[63]

Mersenne now sets forth in some detail his own theory that 'Each passion and affection of the soul has its proper accents by which its different degrees are explained.'

> Every day we experience that choler is expressed by an accent different from that of admiration or sorrow. If we follow the division which philosophers make of the passions of the soul, we shall establish eleven kinds of accents. For they admit eleven passions, namely, six in the concupiscible appetite, which resides on the right side of the heart, or in the liver, as the Plationists wish, and five in the irascible appetite, which is on the left side of the heart, or in the gall, or in other places according to this Latin distich,
>
> > *The heart savors and the lung speaks, the gall awakens wrath,*
> > *The spleen causes laughter, the liver urges love.*[64]
>
> The first passion of the concupiscible appetite, or of concupiscence, is love, which is the root of all the passions. For we do not hate anything except when we believe that it is opposed and is contrary to that which we love. Thus all the disorder of the passions arises from love, which is divided into desire and joy, according to the different movements which it gives to the soul.
> Hatred is opposed to love, and has its advancement in flight and in sorrow. Thus the six passions can be reduced to these two capital ones, since they are an advancement of love and of hatred, and since we do not desire anything, or rejoice in anything other than those we love, just as we shun nothing and grieve at no things other than those we hate.
> Hope, boldness or daring, choler, fear, and despair belong to the irascible appetite …
> We can conclude from this that the ancients established these four passions, namely, joy, pain, fear, and hope, as the four elements, or the four humors, of the appetite which we have in common with the animals. We can, however, admit love and hatred instead of joy and pain. We must see in what the movement of these passions consists before establishing certain accents for them.

---

63 IV, vi, 12. Mersenne adds,

> If we had observed the different accents which the animals make use of to express their passions, we could perhaps have some knowledge of their temperaments and their humors, but it would be necessary to make a great number of observations on this subject.

64 *Cor sapit, et pulmo loquitur, sel commovet iras, Splen ridere facit, cogit amare iecur.*

In the first place, the heart enlarges, blossoms out, and opens in joy and hope, just as heliotrope, roses, and lilies do in the presence of the sun. It is from this that the complexion of the face is rosy, because of the vital spirits which the heart sends above. Thus if joy is so great that the heart remains without a great enough quantity of these spirits, we faint, and sometimes die laughing.

On the contrary, when sorrow is excessive, the same spirits withdraw to the heart in too great a multitude, and smother it, since it can no longer move nor open. Thus these two passions are like the ebb and flow of the sea. For joy is like the flow which brings a great quantity of stones, shells, and fish to the shore of the sea, and joy brings a quantity of blood and spirits to the face and the other parts of the body. Fear and pain, however, are like the ebb, which withdraws that which was gathered. For fear and terror render the face pale and the countenance bleak and hideous by withdrawing the blood and the spirits, and cause melancholy to corrupt the little blood which remains in the veins, and fills the imagination with frightful dreams. It is necessary, therefore, that the accents with which we express the different affections and passions of the soul be different, and that some of them imitate and represent the flow of spirits and blood, and others the ebb, that the former be quick, lively, cheerful, and similar to the flowers and odors of spring, and the latter be similar to rain, snow, winter, and all that is disagreeable, that the former be similar to consonances and ensemble pieces, and the latter to dissonances and disturbing noises, and finally, that the former have as many perfections as the latter have imperfections.

We must see whether it is possible to establish four principal accents according to these four different passions. For the accents of which we speak here can be called the word or discourse of the passions, just as words and ordinary discourse are called the discourse of the mind, which partakes more of artificial means than of nature, just as that of the passions partakes more of nature than of artificial means. Consequently, the latter is less subject to concealment than the former. With regard to the accent of joy, it is certain that it is different from that of sorrow. That of joy, however, includes that of desire and love, just as the triangle includes two right angles, and just as the rational soul includes the sensitive and the vegetative. This accent is cheerful, pleasant, and quite agreeable, and can be divided into as many other accents as there are different degrees of joy and love.

The accent of sorrow is slow, gloomy, and troublesome. That of hatred is more violent, and approaches that of indignation, which is contained in that of choler. With regard to the accent of flight, it is related to that of fear, and that of desire is like that of hope. The accent of despair follows that of sorrow, just as that of boldness follows that of hope and desire. It is difficult, however, to express all these accents.[65]

The final sentence, above, reflects the fact that Mersenne realized that his ideas were far too complex to be notated in either speech or music. He therefore urges that the time has come to invent new symbols for the 'passions.'

Up until the present we have not had signs at all by which we could indicate and signify the accents of the passions, and the accents left us only the grave, acute, and circumflex accents, with that of admiration and interrogation. This is why we must find symbols suitable to signify and express love, hatred, sorrow, choler, indignation, and the other affections of the soul.

---
65 IV, vi, 13.

I recall that physicians have devised new names to designate the six muscles which move the eye, and that they have called the one which raises it haughty, and the one which lowers it humble. The two which move it toward the nose have been called amorous, and those which move it to the left are called the muscles of indignation. We can add to this the one or ones which make the tonic movement, whether it is made by a seventh muscle or by the mutual assistance of the six others.

Astronomers also have made use of new symbols to explain the twelve signs of the zodiac, the seven planets, and their aspects. Chemists, Egyptians, Chinese, and all kinds of craftsmen are not admonished at all when they invent new symbols to explain the specific remarks and difficulties of their art …

We must, therefore, take this same liberty to indicate the accents of the passions. For this I divide each passion into three degrees, just as physicians divide the degrees of the primary qualities into four degrees, and philosophers into eight. In order to keep it short, I shall relate all the passions to the three principal ones, namely, to choler, joy, and sorrow. For envy, jealousy, and hatred are mixed and composed of sorrow and cholera. Love is a joy which has begun, and if the absence of that which we love afflicts us, it is a sorrowful love, or an amorous sorrow.[66]

To be sufficient to express the necessary range of emotions, Mersenne finds the need for nine new symbols. He expresses this in the proposition, 'All the accents which we use to express the three passions to which we have related the others have need of nine different characters to be explained and understood, namely, three for the three degrees of choler, and just as many for the degrees of love and of sorrow.'

The first degree of choler is noted in the voice when it rises a little higher and when we speak with more vehemence. If we touch the pulse, we shall quickly judge that the heart beats more swiftly or more strongly. We must observe, however, whether this pulsation is sesquialtera that of the natural pulsation, or whether it observes some other proportion, in order to establish the first degree of choler and to have its internal character by the movements of the pulse or by that of the respiration, and its external character by the height or force and speed of the voice.

Since this accent originates from the bile, we could represent this first degree of choler by one dot of flame or of fire, or by some other symbol which designates how many degrees it must raise or strengthen and hasten the word to the first degree of choler. This could perhaps be done with flagged notes and the *fredons* of music.

The second degree of choler gives a stronger blow to the reason, which begins to yield to passion. It can be explained by two dots of flame. If the pulse of the first degree of choler is sesquialtera that of the natural, the pulse of the second degree will be double in swiftness the natural, and consequently, sesquiteria that of the pulsation which the second degree makes, for the double ratio is composed of the sesquialtera and the sesquitertia. We must, nevertheless, note that the natural pulsation does not pass at once to the second degree, nor does that of the second degree to that of the third. It is enough, however, to have established the final point of these degrees, which we can reach either all at once, or by several intervals, just as we can go from the lower sound to the fifth without using degrees, or with the ordinary degrees.

---

66 IV, vi, 14.

The third degree of choler which ascends to wrath, can be represented by a flame with three dots. The pulsation of the heart will be triple that of the natural, either in speed or force, or in both. We can relate to this the range of the voice which in pain rises more than a twelfth from the tone of the ordinary word which is used without passion, to the cry of wrath and despair. For if the voice ascends higher, it becomes raucous and disagreeable, and should be called a squeal rather than a human voice. Thus those who have arrived at this degree no longer say a word, or if they talk or cry out, they lower the tone. Moreover, it is difficult, and perhaps naturally impossible, for the pulse to beat more than three times more swiftly in choler than outside of it. Since, however, we must avoid as much as possible the innovation of symbols, an acute accent can designate the first degree of choler, two the second, and three the third. If we wished to use specific letters, they can carry with them any point or sign we wish, by which those who read the discourse will be warned that it is necessary to pronounce the end or some other part of the sentence with the first, the second, or the third accent of choler.

The same thing must be said of the accents of the passion, of joy, and of sorrow, which have their beginnings, advancements and endings, as do choler, illnesses, and the other things of this world, although the pulse and the voice of these two passions are not as easy to explain as those of choler. We can, nevertheless, establish accents and symbols for them in proportion of those of choler.

Some have believed that the passions change the weight of the body, and that the man in choler is lighter by eight pounds per hundred than when he is sorrowful, by a thirteenth when he is in the final degree of choler, and by a twenty-fifth when he is extremely joyous. These remarks, or rather these imaginations, however, are quite false, for inflammation and death bring a greater alternation to beasts and the human body than do all the passions of the soul of the body. Nevertheless, the living body is not lighter than the dead one, nor the warm and inflamed breast than the cold one, as we have experimented quite exactly.[67]

Next he considers to what degree the various 'passions' he has been discussing can be expressed in musical notation and he finds the problem much more difficult than in the case of speech.

This is quite difficult to explain, so much so because it appears that music desires a certain delicacy and agreeableness which cannot be compatible with the vehemence and severity of the passions, particularly with choler. For with regard to the accents of sorrow and pain, it is easy to make them by means of the semitone which the voice forms when yearning. This is almost the only accent in French airs, in which we sometimes mix also the accents of joy, love, and hope, appropriately enough. The Italians, however, have more vehemence than we do for expressing the strongest passions of choler with their accents, particularly when they sing their verses for the theater to imitate the scenic music of the ancients. The accent of choler is made by rushing the final syllables, and by strengthening the last sounds. If we reflect upon the elevation of the voice, we shall note that it is often raised an entire tone, a third, and a fourth, when pronouncing the final syllable of words which are used in choler and sometimes by the same intervals or by the diapente when sustaining the voice on the antepenultimate syllable. The manners in which

---

67 IV, vi, 15.

choler is expressed, however, are so diverse that there is almost no interval at all which it does not use, according to its different degrees and the other passions which accompany it. Thus the musician should consider the time, the place, the characters, and the subject for which the accent should be made, in order that he indicate it on the syllable which the voice should sustain, and which it should raise and strengthen.

I have noted that the tone of voice of choler often ascends an entire octave or more all at once. This is difficult to perceive, unless we try to place these intervals into music by forming the same intervals slowly, and little by little, so that the imagination might have the time to understand the interval of choler. The same thing must be said of the accent of spite, displeasure, and the other passions, which will often be found on a tone of voice much higher than we believe, although it is also made sometimes on the same pitch by striking it more strongly and more quickly.

I leave the investigation of symbols necessary to indicate this passion and the others, to composers who desire to write songs in which nothing is lacking, and particularly, who have the intent to accent them in all kinds of ways. This will give such a charm and such an air to the songs and the solos, that all who hear them will acknowledge that they are animated and full of vigor and spirit, of which they are devoid without these accents. Composers can be instructed in this by considering the striking of chamades, charges on the drum, and those of trumpets, whose last sounds of each beat represent choler by the promptness and the force of the blow of the stick or the tongue. With regard to the promptness, we have flagged or double-flagged and triple-flagged notes, which are quick enough to indicate the speed of all the degrees of the most rapid passions, just as we have those of sixteen, twelve, eight, six, four, three, and two beats, which are slow enough to indicate the listlessness of the greatest sorrows. Thus we are only lacking symbols which designate the impetuosity, the vigor, and the force of these passions. For example, we can designate the first degree with the same mark by which we indicate the first minutes, namely, by this small straight line, ', by the second by the sign of the seconds, ', the third by the sign of the thirds, ", etc. Those who teach singing, however, should show all these different degrees of the passions to children, just as they teach them cadences and various passages and trills, so that they might be lacking in nothing to accent all the syllables and the notes indicated by the composer, who should strive for a knowledge of the movements and degrees of each passion, in order to represent them as simply as possible.

If the composer of airs judges that he cannot form the accents of the passions with the ordinary intervals of the diatonic and chromatic, that is, with the music which we ordinarily use, it is easy for him to use the enharmonic dieses which I have explained in Book Three, and in those on lutes and the organ. For example, if he finds that the major third is too small to express some passion and its accent, he can increase it by any diesis he wishes, that is, by the one which makes only a quarter tone, or by that which makes a third of a tone, or by any other interval he judges suitable for his intent. I have wished to add to this so that we might not think that the Greeks have had, or were able to have, any other degrees or intervals than those which we can use just as well as they did in all kinds of situations, without there remaining any reason for us to doubt that they were able to write better songs than ours, particularly if we accommodate to them all which we have said.[68]

---

68 IV, vi, 16.

Mersenne now turns to the role of rhythm in the communication of emotions in music. In the following proposition, the word 'movement' is used to refer to emotional character, not tempo or as a term to distinguish part of a larger form as we use the term today.

> Rhythmics is an art which considers movements and which regulates their succession and their mixture to excite the passions and to maintain them, and to increase, decrease, or calm them.[69]

He begins here a discussion of the application of the Greek rhythmic modes to composition. His aim in his discussion under this proposition was apparently to justify and encourage the continuation of the ideas of Baïf, which he discusses in another place.[70]

> This description contains the principal effects and the highest intent of rhythmics, whether we consider it speculatively, or insofar as practice is concerned. For those who use it on drums and trumpets, in dances and ballets, in songs and in lines, etc., have no other intent than to please the listeners and the spectators, or to excite them to some passion or affection, either of joy or of sorrow, and of love or hatred, etc. Thus fine poets, such as Virgil, use quick movements, represented by short syllables, by dactyls, anapests, and other similar feet, to give a similar impulse or a similar imagination to the reader or the listener ... It is certain that when these movements are well-regulated and arranged they have a great power over the mind or over the blood and the other humors, since some feel inclined to sing and dance in rhythm when they see this practice, even though they had no intention, and that just as we often yawn when seeing others yawn, we also find ourselves singing, leaping, or dancing without any preceding deliberation, which the imitative nature anticipates in several of its movements. From this it is easy to conclude that he who gives beautiful movements to his airs and who expresses better for listeners the passion of the text, should be preferred to all the others.[71]

Mersenne admits it is difficult 'to prescribe what the succession of these movements should be to excite the listeners to the given passion.' It is equally difficult to persuade composers to observe these, not only because they find the application of these modes result in tedious rhythms, but because they would prefer to write what comes to them solely from their imagination.

No doubt following the ideas of Baïf and his sixteenth-century Academy, Mersenne now discusses the Greek term, 'rhythmopoeia,' which he defines as 'the art of making beautiful movements on all kinds of subjects.' Again, the word 'movement' here refers to emotional character.

> We have explained all these species of feet and of lines, so that it is only necessary to add to their properties, so that composers might use them and so that before beginning a fantasy or

---

69 IV, vi, 18.

70 IV, vi, 24.

71 IV, vi, 18.

any other musical piece which can be imagined, they might know the movements which must be used, if they desire that their music make some impression upon the minds of the listeners ...

For example, he should choose the genus and the mode of music so that if it is more appropriate to use the degrees of the diatonic [*genus*] and the Phrygian mode, he avoids the chromatic degrees and the pitches of the Lydian, and if the song should be made in the first or lowest pitches of the system, which are called by the Greeks *hypatoides*, he does not touch at all those in the middle, nor above, which they call *mesoids* and *netoids*, according to the passions which he wishes to excite ...

After having chosen the melody, it is necessary to join to it the proper movement ...

Secondly, we should choose the species of movement and times necessary to execute the required effect. Since equal movement is suitable for minds which love tranquility and peace and which are favorable to repose and solitude, if we wish to induce this affection, or if we wish to maintain it, it is necessary to use the Dorian mode of the ancients and their hesychastic with spondaic movement, which admits all feet whose lowering is equal to the lifting ...

When, however, we wish to change this affection to enter into more turbulent passion, it is necessary to use the Phrygian mode and the double movement and feet whose lowering or *thesis* is double the lifting or *arsis*.[72]

In relating these ideas to instrumental music, Mersenne adds,

Those who are not tied down to words, however, and who are content to write branles and other species of fantasies and dances for ballets, can apparently use more kinds of movements, since they subject themselves neither to prose nor to verse. If it is permitted to philosophize in this matter, we can say that the iamb is suitable for expressing choler, since it imitates the quickness and lightness of fire at its beginning, and it doubles its force in the second part of its movement, which is double the first which the Greeks make in lifting, as is that of the *pyrrhic*. Practitioners call this iambic and trochaic movement *ternary beat*, although it is actually *double*. Those who desire to pass beyond this to find the reason for the effects of each movement, foot, or line, can endeavor to know the movements of the passions, the blood, and the other humors, which ordinarily follow and accompany. For it appears that there is no more powerful means for exciting the passions of listeners than to use the same times and movements which the same passions make use of in those who are touched by them.

Thirdly, we can pass from one genus of movement to another as well as from one mode to another ... It is good, however, to return to the first kind of movement before ending, just as we return to the mode ...

Fourthly, we must choose good words to make good effects, and must use the vowels *a* and *o* several times when we wish to represent great and magnificent things, and the feminine *e* and the short *i* and *u* several times to express sorrowful, abject, and small things. This is portrayed quite well by the word *petite*.

We should also choose words full of harsh consonances, such as *r*, to express troublesome things, and those which have more pleasant consonants, such as *d*, *l*, and *z*, to represent that which is pleasant and agreeable.

---

72   IV, vi, 27.

Beyond this focus on the communication of emotions, Mersenne found other important purposes in music. First, of course, as a priest, an important purpose in music was to bring man to God. In particular, Mersenne found in the strings, which never fail to sound when played, a metaphor for how man should respond always to the will of God.

> For since there is no movement that does not lead the way to the first Motive Power, it is reasonable that the movements from which one receives so great contentment and whence one draws so great a harmony, lead us to that, of which Providence incessantly beats the measure of the harmony of the universe and governs the grand concert of everything, lest it be said in Eternity that the musicians were more stupid and irrational than the inanimate creatures.[73]

Another purpose of music, which he mentions in a letter to the great Dutch mathematician and physicist, Huygens, is to offer delight.

> Similarly airs are not made to excite anger, and some of the other passions, but to delight the minds of listeners, and sometimes carry them to devotion … I do not want to deny that certain songs carefully joined to the text, cannot move one to pity, to compassion, to regret, and to other passions, but only that this is not their principal goal, but rather to delight, or even to fill knowledgeable listeners with admiration, which will make them investigate the causes of so signal an effect.[74]

Mersenne mentions the important purpose of music therapy in only one place, making clear he lacked the personal experience to judge the validity of the claims of this practice.

> Some believe that the ancients practiced certain well regulated dances, which cured men of certain maladies, when they were sick. If one could put this art into practice, one would save great sums of money now used in medicine. But we have no knowledge of the movements necessary to cure or to prevent sickness, and when we shall have, there would be few people who would be willing to undergo such a test.
>
> ……
>
> As for the perfection of these dances, it consists in perfecting the spirit and body, and putting them in the best possible condition. The best perfection of nature consists in knowing and contemplating the works of nature; the movements of the stars, the elements, their greatness, light, and perfection, and to elevate one's self, by means of them to the Author of the Universe, who is the great master of the Ballet which all creatures dance by well-regulated movements, and which ravish the sages and savants, and bring pleasure to the angels, and to all the blessed.[75]

Finally, Mersenne also mentions as a purpose of music the concept of ethos of which the ancient Greeks were so enthusiastic. In only one place does he suggest that he may have

---

73 V, iii, 17 (Collary 8).
74 Letter to Constantin Huygens [November 14, 1640], quoted in Duncan, 'Persuading the Affections,' 165.
75 III, ii, 22.

believed music can affect the manners of men. This comes at the end of an interesting discussion in which he contends that since all voices are unique, it might be possible to create a *phtongonomie* or *phoniscopie* to identify individual voices. While he does not further describe these terms he has invented, he adds that 'the face and the voice are mirrors of the soul.' In another place, Mersenne wonders why man was made with the ability to make only one sound at a time.[76] He doubts that man would be able to accomplish anything he cannot do with one voice and concludes that God made it necessary for man to need another man to make harmony, 'so that the harmony of voices might invite men to the harmony of manners.'[77]

However, in a letter to Huygens, he privately confessed great doubt whether music can in fact have significant influence on the actions of man.

> Now to begin this examination, it is first necessary to assume that music, and consequently airs, are made particularly and principally to charm the mind and ear and to make us pass our lives with a little sweetness among the bitter things encountered in it. For to think that music serves to persuade us of the intention of the musician as perfectly as could a good orator, and that it has as much power to conduct us to virtue and to make us hate vice as much as the voice of a good preacher, even though the same things are sung as he recites in the pulpit, and to believe that singing can be used as easily for instruction as can speaking and lecturing, it is this that it is difficult for us to accept.[78]

On Performance Practice

Since Mersenne's primary interest in music was in song, he comments in several places on the essential qualities of a good singer. In a brief outline of the principles of teaching sight-singing, the focus of which is the ear, Mersenne also makes a brief appeal for the importance of quality of voice, one that is,

> beautiful, full, pleasant and mellow, borne and guided in a beautiful way ... [created by the] rollings of air in the canal or pipe of the throat, without the pit of the stomach, the nose, the roof of the mouth, nor the movement of the jaws ... It seems, however, that the present fashion is only to delicacy and affectation.[79]

Additional qualities of a good voice are the ability to hold a steady tone and 'pleasantness and a certain harmoniousness upon which depend the charms which delight the listeners,'

---

76 III, i, 21. In III, i, 22, Mersenne mentions that the 'son of Pierre d'Avignon' astonished everyone by singing one part and whistling another simultaneously.

77 III, i, 6.

78 Letter to Constantin Huygens [November 14, 1640], quoted in Duncan, 'Persuading the Affections.'

79 IV, vi, 1.

which is encountered quite rarely. Still another quality needed is that it be 'full and solid, which increases its harmoniousness.'

> This can be explained by the comparison with a canal which is always full of water when it flows, or by that of a body and a face well filled-out and in good condition, whereas voices which are deprived of this quality are like a thin trickle of water which runs in a large canal, or a lean and gaunt face.[80]

Donnington cites additional vocal qualities mentioned by Mersenne.

> A solid sostenuto without pitch wobble; flexibility in passage work; accurate intonation; sweetness and a certain harmoniousness, on which depends the charms with ravish the hearers, for voices which are hard do not please, however accurate they may be, and possessed of the other qualities I have mentioned, for they have too much sharpness [*aigreur*] and glitter [*esclat*], which hurts sensitive ears, and which hinders their gliding pleasantly enough into their hearers' spirit to win them, and to carry them whither so ever you desire.[81]

As with his views on composers, Mersenne concludes that to some degree the beautiful singer is born and not made.

> This should be ascribed to the order of Divine Providence, which makes use of all kinds of conditions, as it does of as many voices, to compose the great concert of this universe, whose beauties and charms we will never understand except in Heaven.[82]

With regard to that which could be taught, Mersenne was critical of most singing teachers for not having good enough voices to demonstrate well for their students. Also, he notes,

> In addition, they should have traveled in foreign countries, particularly in Italy, where they pride themselves on singing well, and on knowing music much better than the French. For although all which they do is perhaps not to be approved of, nevertheless, it is certain that they have something excellent in their solos, which they animate much more powerfully than do our singers, who surpass them in affectation, but not in vigor.[83]

This reference to Italian singers reflects the fact that the spreading popularity of Italian opera was making Italian singers an inevitable model for all of Europe. Above all, the Italian singers were known for their emotional delivery.

> As to the Italians, they ... represent as much as they can the passions and the feelings of the soul and spirit; for example, anger, fury, spleen, rage, faintheartedness, and many other passions,

---

80 IV, vi, 5.
81 Quoted in Donnington, *The Interpretation of Early Music*, 517.
82 IV, vi, 6.
83 Ibid.

with a violence so strange, that one judges them as if they were touched with the same affects as they represent in singing; in place of which our Frenchmen are content to caress the ear, and use nothing but a perpetual sweetness in their songs; which hinders their energy.[84]

Mersenne also admired the freedom of interpretation enjoyed by the Italian singers.

> Italian musicians do not make as many difficulties as we do, however, for they are given much more freedom than the French are, as much in the inflection and intervals of simple solos, as in duos and ensemble pieces. I do not find fault with them for this, since they find it good, and there is no legislator who forbids them the opposite, or who forces them to our customs and our imaginations.[85]

In another place he mentions these qualities but now adds the characteristics he admires in the French tradition.

> Therefore I am able to speak to our advantage, since we in many things, particularly politeness, delicacy, and in the way in which we perform them. For as to the quality of the voice, or its force, the Italians can dispute with all other nations, since they have many fine traits, and many inventions in which our songs are destitute.[86]

Having said here that French singers are destitute in their improvisation, in another place Mersenne seems to hold the opposite view. It is the kind of discrepancy which makes him difficult to read.

> Every nation imparting a knowledge of singing, and that makes passages in the throat, and the Italians themselves who make a particular profession of music, avow that the French perform the best passages, whose beauty and sweetness it is not possible to explain, whether with the eye or ear, for the trickling and murmuring of waters and the singing of nightingales is not as agreeable. And I find nothing in nature whose analogy can make us understand these passages, being more ravishing than divisions, for they are the quintessence of music.[87]

At a time when the opportunity to actually hear music was much more rare than today, Mersenne concluded that it was impossible to judge, regarding the best voice, unless one could hear singers from all countries, including Asia.

> If one wants to judge what the best method of singing is and in what the best quality of the voice consists, it is necessary to establish the rules that are accepted by all singers and proven by reason. And then he who executes them the best in singing surpasses all other voices ... will be the best.[88]

---

84 II, vi, 356.

85 IV, iv, 23.

86 III, ii, 3.

87 III, i, 32. Mersenne makes the interesting observation that the ancient Greek writers never mention ornaments.

88 III, i, 34.

In the meantime, however, he concludes that French singers are the best.

Mersenne wrote an entire treatise on instrumental music, much of which is, again, mathematically based. He goes into considerable detail, finding, for example, that a harpsichord has more than 1500 separate parts.[89] He also discusses problems in pitch and especially the need for some means of establishing a standardized pitch. His recommendation for a solution to this problem was to write next to the bass part in every composition the number of vibrations of the first pitch in the bass. Thus, musicians in all countries would perform the work at the same pitch![90]

As he progressed, writing about each of the families of instruments, Mersenne was frustrated at his inability to find factual information regarding the history of the development of the instruments and their manufacture.

> One almost always has trouble and difficulty in noting the primary inventors of artifices and things used for pleasure or the usefulness to man, whether our predecessors were so negligent that they have left us no clue or they were ignorant of letters and did not know how to read or write, as is experienced now among the Canadians and other savages.[91]

Mersenne includes among his general comments on instruments some discussion of the aesthetic qualities of the various families of instruments.[92] How does one establish which instruments have the most agreeable sound? This, says Mersenne, is a very difficult question and he finds professional musicians have a great diversity of opinion. For one thing, no one has heard all the instruments, especially those in foreign countries. Another reason has to do with the temperament of the observer.

> The difference of temperaments which are found in men similarly causes the sound of some to seem more agreeable to that one than the others, so that these reasons ... can hinder the sincerity of the judgment.

Familiarity also affects the judgment, thus,

> soldiers and those who have a warlike temperament and stirring blood find the sound of the trumpet more agreeable than that of the lute or the other instruments, and hunters are more fond of the sound the horn makes than of the others, because they are accustomed to hear it; for what is familiar to us often pleases us more.

Well, says Mersenne, these kinds of difficulties are found in all worldly things, but man must exercise his Reason and make judgments. Therefore he generalizes that the sound of the lute is most charming; the German flute is more agreeable than other flutes and that the

---

89 V, iii, 20.
90 V, iii, 18.
91 V, vii, 2.
92 V, i, 4.

violin is the most ravishing of the strings. More interesting to us are some of his comments which reflect on ensemble quality.

> As to those which are produced by the wind, one can say in general that all the tones which are made by interrupted air alone are sweeter than the tone of the other wind instruments and any other which could be produced by the string, but they are not so agreeable as those which are made by the vibration of a reed, for although they seem rough, they have a natural gaiety which makes them preferable to the dismal and somber sweetness of the flute, although the gloomy sounds produce a concert of many parts more agreeable than that which is made of gayer tones …
>
> Now in speaking of sounds more generally, we can say that the sweet ones are gloomy, choked and shut up, like those of the stopped flutes, and that the gay ones are more open, like those of the reeds and of flutes that the organ makers call in resonance. The tones are almost all the same provided that they are not so weak that the ear cannot perceive them or so violent that it would be offensive. What makes them more pleasant is the variety with which one embellishes them, either successively or simultaneously with other sounds.

In conclusion, Mersenne offers three additional aesthetic principles with regard to judging the various instruments. First, he concludes that variety is an important factor for the listener.

> Choose whatever tone you wish and listen continually: it will put you to sleep or give you a headache. The tone of a flute, placed on a windchest, being continued is amazingly tiresome and displeasing, and that of a lute will be even more … Then it is the variety that makes the tone agreeable; and if it is not varied, it deserves mostly to be called noise rather than harmonic sound.

Second, he concludes the judgment of individual instruments will depend in part on the 'temperament' of the listener.

> If the sound of the flutes, among which can be placed the trumpet, has more power over the mind, it is because of the greater impression it makes in the air, or because of its particular quality. And actually in addition to that reason, experience shows that those who have a more delicate ear and more refined and subtle minds, are pleased more in the sounds of the string instruments. And those with grosser and heavier spirits take a greater pleasure in the sound of the trumpet and flutes, although this may not perhaps be so general that the contrary cannot occur.

Finally, Mersenne recognizes an analogy with color, with the single instrument being like a simple color such as black or white and a concert being like a colored painting. This, in turn, has a relationship with acoustics.

> Some [paintings] are made of such skill that they must be seen in the distance and the others close by, since the pictures which have the thickest colors which are cracked, as the painters say, who have much more skill, demand to be seen from the distance, are loved, cherished, and esteemed by the sons of Art. The others on the contrary, which are very much softened and finished, require to be viewed from very close, and are much esteemed by those who are near-

sighted and who are unable to consider of what skill consists. In the same way, the music of the lutes is for those who do not wish to hear the music so much as the voice, and that of the viols is for those who by pushing farther away prefer to hear rather than to see. Now this resemblance will make us note in passing that the low tone, which approaches silence is comparable to black, and the higher to white.

Turning to the string instrument family, Mersenne finds the violin has the greatest 'effect on the passions and affections of the body and soul' of any string instrument, for reasons of 'the great tension of their strings and their high sounds.'

> Those who have heard the Twenty-four Violins of the King avow that they have never heard anything more ravishing or more powerful. Thus it comes that this instrument is the most proper of all for playing for dancing as is experienced in the ballet and everywhere else.[93]

Later, he observes,

> Now the violin has this above all the other instruments aside from the song of animals, both winged and terrestrial, that it imitates and counterfeits all sorts of instruments, such as the voice, the organ, the hurdy-gurdy, the bagpipe, the fife, etc., so that it can suggest the sadness, as the lute does, and can become animated like the trumpet.[94]

Above all, Mersenne seems to place a high aesthetic value on the string instruments in part because of the ease with which one can hear their overtones. While he could not offer the correct explanation of what the overtones were, physically,[95] he could find in them a metaphor for moral action.

> If the tone of each string is more harmonious and agreeable as it makes a greater number of different tones heard in the same time, and if one may be permitted to compare moral actions to natural, and to translate Physics into human actions, one can say that each action is as much more agreeable and harmonious to God, as it is accompanied by a greater number of motives, provided that they all be good.[96]

Regarding the brass instrument family, Mersenne was most fascinated by the trumpet, in part by its range, which in his time exceeded even the organ!

---

93 V, iv, 1, replacing the wind band of the sixteenth century. In IV, iv, he gives the instrumentation of the famous Twenty-Four Violins of the King as 6 treble, 6 bass, 4 contratenors, 4 alto and 4 'of a fifth part.'

94 IV, iv.

95 Even though Mersenne understood the tones of the natural trumpet corresponded to the overtone principle, he did not understand that the sounds heard above a string tone were based on the same principle. His best guess: 'It is more probable that these different sounds come from the different movements of the exterior air.'

96 V, iv, 10.

> As to the range of the trumpet, it is marvelously great ... It surpasses all the keyboards of the spinets and organs.[97]

His most interesting comment relative to the trumpet is with regard to its tone, especially if one remembers that in nearly all early literature the trumpet tone is described as 'harsh' or 'powerful.'

> [Those who play well can] imitate the softest echo and take away boredom and the desire to hear the softness of the lute and other instruments in those who love harmony.[98]

We also find interesting Mersenne's comments on the fact that this instrument, being limited to the overtone series, could not play all the notes. In the following he offers his charming natural explanation for a familiar problem, the out of tune B/Bb in the third octave and the subsequent gap from G to the C above.

> But because it is neither consonance nor difference of consonances, Nature rejects it and prefers to break the course of its intervals and its melodies, rather than to pass through an interval which is only of value to wound the ear and mind ... It can still be said that Nature, having given the [first] six tones, as the six days on which she rests, that she imitates her Author Who reposed at the end of the six days.[99]

Among the other brass instruments, we find particularly interesting his comment that the trombone performed the same diminutions as the other wind instruments.[100]

Related by the type of mouthpiece was the cornett family, a family of instruments which reached its artistic highpoint in the sixteenth century. A gap in the handed-down oral tradition of teaching has left us with insufficient information regarding the performance practice of this instrument, especially with regard to the embouchure on the side of the mouth and how the latter and syllabification created articulation. No modern player can exemplify this famous description of the cornett by Mersenne.

> As to the characteristic quality of sound that they produce, it is similar to the brilliance of a sun's ray, which appears in the shadow or in the darkness, when one hears it among the voices in the cathedrals or chapels.[101]

There were astonishing virtuosi of the cornett known to Mersenne, including one who could play eighty measures, and another one hundred measures, in one breath.

---

97 V, v, 11.
98 V, v, 18.
99 V, v, 13.
100 V, v, 22.
101 V, v, 23.

> Still this seems to surpass all credence, since one cannot live without very often drawing a breath, even if he uses no part of the breath for singing or for making any instrument sound …
>
> From this it can be concluded that the cornett helps in conserving the wind, and in dispensing less at a time than one would do with the mouth in ordinary respiration.[102]

The bass of the cornett family was the serpent, which Mersenne characterizes in another often quoted sentence.

> The true bass of the cornett is performed with the serpent, so that one can say that one without the other is a body without soul.[103]

In a different treatise, Mersenne says a serpent is capable of sustaining twenty of the most powerful voices or can be so sweet as to play chamber music. The instrument, he says, is so easy a child of fifteen can master it.[104]

The most surprising comments by Mersenne regarding the familiar wind instruments are associated with the oboe [shawm]. Whereas today we think of a conical bore instrument as being more moderate in sound than a cylinder bore instrument, Mersenne, astonishingly enough, found the opposite. Of conical bores in general he explains,

> This renders their tones more violent than those of the instruments which are drilled with a single thickness from the beginning to the end.[105]

Thus, he finds the oboe also 'violent' and nearly as powerful as a trumpet!

> As to their music, it is suitable for the large ensemble, such as the Ballets, although the violins are now used in their place, for weddings, for village festivals, and for other public celebrations, because of the great noise that they make and the great harmony that they render, for they have the strongest and most violent tone of all the instruments, except for the trumpet.[106]

One also finds in Mersenne's fifth treatise an engraving of the Hautbois du Poitou,[107] an instrument active in the court of Louis XIV, but for which little technical information is known. Mersenne pictures it as an oboe-type instrument with a capped reed.

Another instrument popular in the court was the musette. While actually a bagpipe, the court oboists regarded this instrument as a part of the oboe family, because the chanter is in

---

102 Ibid.

103 Ibid.

104 II, v, 278.

105 V, v, 32.

106 V, v, 33. Raguenet in 1702 speaks of the new oboe as being as mellow as a violin. See Donnington, *The Interpretation of Early Music*, 557ff.

107 V, v, 34.

fact a little oboe and sometimes was played as such, without the air bag. The court oboists were the performers of the musette at court, as Mersenne confirms.

> When one has heard the musette in the hands of those who play it perfectly, as does Mr. des Touches, one of the Royal oboists, it must be admitted that it yields to none of the other instruments, and that there is a singular pleasure in hearing it.[108]

As a churchman, Mersenne gives special attention to the organ. Two of his observations are particularly interesting in terms of aesthetics. First, Mersenne endorses, Giovanni Doni's[109] suggestions of a correspondence between the modes and the color of specific organ pipes.

> The organ can be used to express each mode because of the great number of its stops, of which the one of tin is proper for the Dorian, and the others composed of pipes more or less large at the top than at the bottom, closed and open, for example, the narrow ones are suitable for the Phrygian, and the wider ones for the Lydian; and then he says that the pipes which imitate the block flutes are good to express the Dorian; those which imitate the fife and the flageolet for the Phrygian; and the cornett and the pipes which make the German flute for the Lydian. The boxwood is proper to make the Dorian pipes; the regals are good for the Lydian, and the brass pipes for the Phrygian.[110]

We also find enlightening Mersenne's personal criteria for what makes a good organist. Of particular interest here is his documentation of the practice of improvisation by organists.

> One can observe that the organist is best who makes the plain chant or subject heard better, who makes the other parts of the counterpoint sing, and performs the cadences best.
> Some make a great fact of those who can make three or four hundred measures of good counterpoint figured against an organ point; the others of those who have a great velocity and dexterity, as happens when they make thirty-second notes in the binary measure, which lasts only a second; and still others of those who make a very great number of passages, of diminutions, and variations against some subject given them. To this can be added that those who play with a beautiful movement and good grace, and who are exact in their measure are the most perfect of all.[111]

Mersenne included under percussion instruments which were to be considered musical, only those which produced a pitch—pitch, but not 'noise,' being describable by mathematics.

> All the bodies which make noise and which produce a sensible sound when they are struck can be placed in the rank of percussion instruments.[112]

---

108 V, v, 28.

109 Giovanni Battista Doni, *Compendio del trattato de' generi e de' modi* (Rome, 1635).

110 V, vii, 30.

111 V, vi, 41.

112 V, vii, 1.

The most interesting discussion which Mersenne engages in on this subject is relative to popular myths associated with church bells. He relates a number of superstitions believed by the public regarding the disturbances in the air caused by the ringing of the great cathedral bells. Among these, some believed it could cause the death of the fetus in the womb. Mersenne adds,

> Since it is experienced that the drum, the thunder, and the trumpet make more effect on the mind or the senses than the sound of other instruments, it is easy to conclude that the great effects of music or other sounds can happen only through great movements, which are made of a lot of air, or that the violence must make up for the size of the air when there is little air which serves the noise.[113]

Mersenne does not concern himself with the rules of performing ornaments in his treatises. Occasionally he mentions them in passing, as for example that the trill must begin on the upper note and this note must be more elongated than the principal note.[114] One comment we find of particular interest with regard to aesthetics.

> Trilled cadences are the most difficult part of all that has to be done in singing, because it is necessary simply to beat the air in the throat [*battre l'air de la gorge*] which must make a series of repercussions [*tremblemens*] without the help of the tongue. But they are as much more pleasing as they are more difficult, for if the other progressions are the colors and the shadings, the cadences can be called the rays and the light.[115]

Finally, Mersenne makes two interesting observations on the subject of conducting. First, in his mathematical style he defines the 'beat.'

> The *beat* is the space of time used to lift and lower the hand. Since we can make these two opposing movements swifter or slower, he who conducts the ensemble determines the swiftness according to the kind of music and the material it employs, or according to his wish. I shall, however, henceforth take one beat, whether it is binary or ternary, for one second, that is, for 1/3600 of an hour, inasmuch as the slowest vibration of the pulse of the heart which I have been able to encounter lasts exactly one second and beats 3600 times in an hour. Thus the systole, or the contraction of the heart, will correspond to the lifting, and the diastole, or the dilation, to the lowering of the hand, so that the masters of music speak truly when singing the praises of God, *My heart and my body will rejoice in the living God.*[116]

---

113 V, vii, 28.

114 IV, vi, 7.

115 II, vi, 355. Mersenne adds,

> As for ornaments from the lips, they are not agreeable, nor permitted, any more than those which seem to be drawn from the stomach.

116 IV, iv, 20.

Second, he offers a few comments on conducting technique.

> The semibrevis ordinarily lasts one lifting and one lowering of the hand, which can be made as well with the foot.[117]

In the case of a ternary beat, Mersenne recommends 'two white notes in striking, and a single one in lifting.' Those accompanying singers can also conduct with the fingerboard of a lute, etc. And he notices that where there are those singers who 'have a delicate and exact ears and a well-ruled imagination' they can keep the beat even without a conductor.

EDUCATIONAL MUSIC

A document discovered by Frances Yates, and written early in the seventeenth century by Mersenne, reviews the goals of the famous Baïf Academy in Paris in the late sixteenth century. It is apparently based on personal information given Mersenne by an older man who had been a member of the academy.

> [The Academicians] did not wish to bring in a new kind of music, unless you call that new when something is restored to wholeness, but wished to recover those effects which, as we read, were once produced by the Greeks, by joining Gallic verses to our carefully cultivated music. For they hoped to exhilarate the depressed spirit, to reduce the over-elated spirit to modesty, and to stir themselves to other feelings by their own music …
>
> When Jean Antoine de Baïf and Joachim Thibault de Courville labored together to drive barbarism from Gaul, they considered that nothing would be of more potency for forming the manners of youth to everything honorable than if they were to recover the effects of ancient music and compose all their songs on the models of the fixed rules of the Greeks.

Mersenne makes a comment on the state of aesthetics in music at the beginning of the seventeenth century, when he wishes that an academy like Baïf's might be reestablished.

> Would that that Academy might drive its roots into this our time and put forth flowers and fruits, never ceasing from divine praises and bringing forth musical persons, each of whom should make music which his whole heart …
>
> Would God that that Academy were started which should praise God with continual praises, hymns, and psalms by day and night: in which young men might be so imbued with musical discipline that the best singers of churches, cathedrals, and other places should be taken from thence, and the whole of Gaul, in fact the whole world, should ring to the greater glory of God, and the hearts of all be inflamed with divine love.[118]

---

117 IV, v, 11.

118 Quoted in Yates, *The French Academies of the Sixteenth Century*, 24ff.

Well read himself in the ancient philosopher's theories of music, he argued that every musician attending such an academy should study philosophy.[119] Sounding very much like an ancient philosopher, he writes,

> Everything in the world can be represented by means of sounds, for since all things consist in weight, in number, and in measure, and sounds represent these three properties, they can signify anything that one wishes.[120]

It follows, therefore, that the kind of academy he envisioned was one that studied ancient music, as we can see in his comments in the preface to his *Quaestiones in Genesim* (1623). He begs the archbishop to found an academy, bringing together men from throughout Europe, to restore 'ancient music,' which will have the goal, among others, of restoring virtue and refuting deists and atheists. His discussion here indicates he was, like the Greeks, still thinking of music as a branch of mathematics. Nothing came of this and thirteen years later he bemoaned that there was still,

> no academy for the theoretical study of music, although it is well known that good music of the Dorian mode is so necessary for the good of the state and the good of religion.[121]

Mersenne makes one further observation on the nature of musical study, or as he calls it, the 'science' of learning an instrument. He points out that all the arts and sciences are governed by three conditions for acquiring perfection. These are *Nature*,

> which must be understood to be the inclination and the natural disposition that we have toward certain sciences, and toward the particular arts, as happens when some are attracted to painting or sculpture, and others to architecture, to geometry, etc.[122]

The second condition is *Discipline*, which refers to the study with 'good masters,' and the third is *Exercise*, which means practice.

FUNCTIONAL MUSIC

Mersenne mentions in passing, and unfortunately without details, the practice of improvisation in the performance of chant, something which is mentioned in a number of other sources. He says only,

---

119 I, 'De la nature et propriétés du son,' 6.
120 I, 43.
121 I, 'Préface au Lecteur.'
122 V, ii, 91.

> I reserve several other examples for the song book of the church, which can be enriched with a thousand wonderful inventions.[123]

In a brief discussion of the church modes here, Mersenne concludes,

> I add only that the fifth, sixth, and the twelfth seem most beautiful to me, but each one can choose that which pleases him most for his particular consolation, and even add as much new as he wishes.
> But it is certain that when several songs of the church are sung, with attention and required devotion, one will receive a great contentment, for there are few more beautiful.

In his most interesting discussion of Church music, Mersenne presents a lengthy argument which attempts to establish the aesthetic superiority of the unison,[124] the point of which was a thinly disguised defense of traditional Church chant. It is appropriate to conclude this chapter with this discussion, for it also characterizes the struggle which a seventeenth-century Church philosopher such as Mersenne faced. His education and perspective was rather narrow, being defined at every turn by the Catholic Church and its traditional tenets. And yet, all around him knowledge was making rapid strides in every field, surging toward the Enlightenment. How was such a traditional Church philosopher to respond to this new environment? One response was literary productions such as this one of Mersenne which are virtual encyclopedias in their field, like modern equivalents of the massive medieval *summa* of Thomas Aquinas. It was as if there was a desire to expand the Church's message to encompass every new idea. We can also see Mersenne, although he argues for the aesthetic value of the unison, making a final attempt to argue for the aesthetic value of the old unison Church music in preference to baroque polyphony. Thus we find here a personal involvement, even a passion, expressed in his language that we did not find in much of his earlier commentary. First he argues that the unison is,

> more pleasing than the octave because it flatters the ear more, and it is understood more easily by the imagination, which is the principal seat of pleasure.[125]

He adds that he finds in the unison, but not the octave, an equality that one also finds in many equations of science and in the equilibrium which characterizes the science of mechanics.

Next, he finds virtue in the fact that 'experiment shows that all the consonances tend towards the unison.' One reason for the powerful impression which Church chant makes is that 'the mind is not distracted by the variety of the consonances and dissonances.' Another argument for the unison, over the octave, reminds the reader how much longer the church services were in the seventeenth century.

---

[123] III, ii, 4ff.

[124] II, ii, 4.

[125] The English translations for this Proposition are taken from Edward Lippman, *Musical Aesthetics: A Historical Reader* (New York: Pendragon Press, 1986), 107ff.

Now one of the strongest reasons that persuade us that the unison is more pleasing and more natural than the octave is drawn from the experience that shows that we become bored much more in hearing singing at the octave than in unison, which one hears in churches with pleasure for a period of several hours: and although children sing naturally at the octave with men, nevertheless their intention [!] is to sing in unison.

Why, then, he asks 'since all music exists only for the sake of the unison which is its end, do we not value it more highly than all the other harmonies?' Clearly describing himself, he answers,

As to those who have risen above all that is created, and who have experienced a thousand times the aversion that one has towards all the truths of mathematics and of physics when they have been discovered, from which one receives almost no contentment except in the labor one undergoes in searching for them, they receive no contentment from concerts, and love to hear singing at the unison more than in several parts, as much as the unison represents to them the abode of the blessed, and the perfect union of the three divine persons who are in the unison of a perfect equality.

Some people, intent on contemplation, would rather hear no singing at all than be distracted. Those who do not understand all this must be extended pity.

I estimate then that the unison is more pleasing than the consonances, and that we must show compassion for the fragility and inconstancy of men who do not have this feeling, and who think more highly of diversity and inequality than of unity and equality, inasmuch as they do not judge things because they possess more simplicity and more excellence, but by what contributes best to their appetite and to their phantasy.

Now Mersenne borrows from geometry the notion that lines, figures and bodies derive all meaning from the point. Thus, consonances depend on the unison, like lines on the point,

and that is why they are the sweeter the more they approach it, for they have nothing sweet nor pleasing except what they borrow from the unison of their tones.

But does not the need for variety speak against the aesthetic virtue of the unison? Mersenne agrees we cannot be content for a long time without the variety of 'different actions and passions, of which each tires us, and at once displeases us.' For example, he says, if we are weary, we desire to sit. But after sitting 'two or three hours,' one is as weary as before. From this he concludes,

Now that state of variety in which we are, is the reason that we avoid the unison as much as we can, because it is too sweet and too excellent for this life. Thence it comes that we prefer to finish music with the octave, the fifth, the third …

And does not the diversity we find in Nature argue against the aesthetic primacy of the unison? After a long discussion, he concludes it is the imperfect state of men that blinds them from seeing clearly 'the great union of all creatures.' And in a flash of eloquence, Mersenne suggests it is all a matter of perspective.

> As to the greater knowledge that comes from the other consonances, one may compare it to the light of several little candles, or to that of glow-worms: but that of unity and the unison is similar to the light of the sun, which obscures all the others by its presence, as the grace and the excellence of the unison makes that of the other consonances vanish.

After still another attempt to prove that 'the unison is more excellent than the other consonances,' by astrology, Mersenne offers his final conclusion on this subject.

> Now all these considerations bring us to recognize that the unison is the most perfect and the most pleasing consonance of music, since it participates more abundantly in that which renders it sweet and pleasing; and since there is only a single imperfection of the variety that preoccupies us, and that makes us prefer what is more similar to our frailty and our misery, which is not able to subsist here without diversity, which is the mother of corruption, although we would aspire to the unison and to unity.

From all this, Mersenne is moved to make a final observation on the educational and moral purpose of music.

> Now if music serves for something in this world, one should particularly make use of it to recall the memory of one part of these considerations, so that it not be said in eternity that men who make a profession of reason, and who should make use of recreations and of speculations for the end to which God destined them, have abused the chaste and rational pleasure of music, and have imitated some musicians, who do not at all raise themselves higher than to the passion and the action of the senses, and to the pleasure of the ear, which should serve solely as a channel to provide free entrance to the contemplation of eternal things, and to the pleasure that comes from the thought of the final end, of which true philosophers should converse incessantly.

4 FRENCH PHILOSOPHERS, I

IT MIGHT BE APPROPRIATE TO BEGIN with a brief summary of the development of theories of aesthetics during the seventeenth century. The *Académie Française* had been founded in 1635 and was originally dedicated 'to the giving of certain rules to our language, to rendering it pure, eloquent, and capable of treating the arts and sciences,' a function it claims even today. But it was the founding, in 1648, of the *Académie Royale de Peinture et de Sculpture* which would lead to serious discussions regarding aesthetics in the arts. Its pronouncements were doomed to failure for two reasons. Not only did its 'rules' set a standard too high to encompass many artists, but 'rules' in aesthetics can never contain the breadth of artistic talent. As a result, during the seventeenth century there was a debate on aesthetics in the arts which far surpassed similar discussions in other countries. While these debates, at least within the Academy, were centered on painting, the general principles discussed clearly framed similar discussions which included music.

While 'la belle nature' had been duly recognized by the Academy, a very important philosopher, the Abbé Batteux (1713–1780), came forward to make nature the very core of aesthetics and, at the same time, to plant the first seeds of Romanticism. He believed the ancient Greeks had already discovered that it was not enough to imitate nature, but that the artist had to be selective, imitating the best of nature. This had a certain didactic end as well, for in the viewing of the beautiful and the good the observer is also stimulated to ideas which are more beautiful and good.

The question of imitating nature became more complex following the influence of the German philosopher, Leibnitz, who advanced the idea that nature consists of distinct and individual beings, for which he coined the term 'monads.' No leaf, no blade of grass, he pointed out, is like another. These views helped move aesthetics based on nature toward a more narrow concept of realism. Thus Roger de Piles contended that in landscape painting the viewer should not just recognize trees, but specific trees, oaks, elms, firs, etc. Realism was inseparable from Truth, thus De Piles could exclaim,

> I love the several celebrated schools, I love Raphael, Titian and Rubens, and I seek always to discern the rare qualities of those great painters; but whatever qualities they may have, I love truth more![1]

---

1   Quoted in Frank Chambers, *The History of Taste* (New York: Columbia University Press, 1932), 115.

The concepts of Truth and Nature destroyed many ancient foundations, including Church dogma. The recognition of individuality in Nature greatly weakened any concept of aesthetic 'rules' and it followed that Reason must be questioned by Feeling. One can see manifested here not only the Enlightenment, but important ideas underlying the distant Revolution.

Everywhere attention turned to the expression of feeling. When the distinguished archaeologist, Count Caylus, established a prize at the Academy for 'expression,' he meant the expression of the passions. He stipulated, 'This study is to be made through nature and not otherwise.' Pascal was writing, 'All our Reason is reduced to sentiment.' It was in this environment that the writings of Abbé Du Bos (1670–1742) appear. Du Bos, taking for granted the importance of Nature and Truth, adds important new arguments. He brought back the Aristotelian concept of catharsis; the viewer must be moved. More important, he made pleasure the aesthetic goal of art. The greatest painter, he says, is 'he whose works give us the greatest pleasure.' Implicit here was another attack on the 'rules,' which do not always account for what gives pleasure.

> The greatest versifiers are not the greatest poets, nor are the most correct draftsmen the greatest painters.[2]

Equally important, Du Bos introduced, even if through the back door, the important question of Universality. He approached this by way of dealing with pleasure and catharsis. What pleases one man, he notes, or one man's taste, is dependent on habit, age and nationality. Therefore, in painting it is useless to discuss aesthetics in terms of line, color and composition. Taste becomes *personal* taste.

> The predilection, which causes us to prefer one part of painting to another part, does not depend upon our reason, any more than does the predilection, which causes us to prefer one kind of poetry to another kind. The predilection depends on our taste, depends on our organization, our present inclinations and the situation of our spirit.[3]

If taste is an individual matter, the question follows, Is the best art that which appeals to the most individuals?

One can see how the very foundations of an Academy dedicated to formulating the 'correct rules' were severely shaken. Because of the loss of effective control by the Academy, together with the general decay of central authority under Louis XV, criticism was taken up by the public, by the amateurs. 'Everyone,' wrote La Font de Saint Yenne, 'has the right to form his own opinion.'[4]

The right of the individual to judge, explains as nothing else can the environment which made possible the explosion of popularity enjoyed by Italian opera. In France, the undeniable

---

[2] Ibid., 121.

[3] Ibid., 120.

[4] La Font de Saint-Yenne, '*Réflexions sur quelques Causes de l'État présent de la Peinture en France*' (1746).

popularity of Italian opera with the public led to another round of debates on the distinction between French and Italian styles in music. It is among the writings of the contributors to this debate that we find the most interesting comments on aesthetics in music in France.

The debate between modern aesthetic virtues and those of ancient Greece continued throughout the Baroque in France. In this book the reader will find this question raised in regard to a number of individual art mediums. Among those who addressed this issue in more general terms was Jean de La Bruyère (1645–1696), who saw not so much a problem of choice, but of chronological common sense.

> We brought back the Doric, Ionic and Corinthian orders: that which had been seen only in the ruins of ancient Greece and Rome became modern, and is now displayed in our porticoes and peristyles. In the same way, in our writings we can only reach perfection and, if possible, surpass the ancients, by imitating them …
>
> There is in art a point of perfection, just as there is in nature a point of excellence or of ripeness. The man who feels it and loves it has perfect taste; the man who does not feel it, and who loves what falls short of it or is in excess of it, has defective taste.
>
> How many centuries elapsed before men, in the arts and sciences, were able to return to the taste of antiquity and, at long last, become simple and natural once more![5]

Quite extraordinary is the fact that La Bruyère could also see this in retrospect from some point far in the future.

> Even if the world is only to last for a hundred million years, it is still in its first freshness and has barely begun; we ourselves are close to primitive man and the patriarchs, and are likely to be confused with them in the remote future. But if one can judge of the future by the past, how much is still unknown to us in the arts, in the sciences, in nature and indeed in history![6]

For François La Mothe-Fénelon (1651–1715) the ancient-modern question was as much psychological as artistic. His explanation is one of few given for the continued presence of pastoral themes throughout this period.[7]

> When poets wish to charm men's imaginations, they lead them far from great cities and cause them to forget the extravagance of their century. They put them back into the golden age and, rather than portraying turbulent courts and great men unhappy in their greatness, they show us shepherds dancing on flowery grass under the shade of a grove in a delightful season …

---

5   Jean de La Bruyère, *Characters*, trans. Jean Stewart (Baltimore: Penguin Books, 1970), 26ff. Jean de La Bruyère (1645–1696) was born to a bourgeois family, studied law and in 1673 became Treasurer-General of Finance in Caen.

6   La Bruyère, Ibid., 240.

7   During the reign of Louis XIV one of the forms of entertainment by the wealthy nobles was to pretend they were poor peasants. Louis had a miniature peasant village constructed behind Versailles where his wife would dress in peasant clothes and spend hours feeding the ducks, etc.

> Nothing more plainly marks a spoiled nation than our disdainful luxury which rejects the ancients' frugal simplicity. It was depravity such as this which overthrew Rome.[8]

Charles de Secondat, Baron de Montesquieu, provides a curious footnote to this issue in his famous *The Spirit of Laws*.

> Admirable in this respect were the institutions of the principal republics of Greece. The rich employed their money in festivals, musical choruses, chariots, horse-races, and chargeable offices. Wealth was, therefore, as burdensome there as poverty.[9]

ON THE PHYSIOLOGY OF AESTHETICS

The great French intellectual, Blaise Pascal, was one of a number of early philosophers who assumed, by deduction alone, the bicameral nature of mental processes. We describe this today, of course, as the left and right hemispheres of the brain (which are also the official medical terms) and we understand that in general the left hemisphere stores mathematics, language and concepts, while the right hemisphere stores spatial information, music and the emotions. Pascal used the labels 'mathematical' and 'intuitive,' but since he lacked information on our separate hemispheres and their differing nature, his deductions on this subject turn to two kinds of men. It is this subject with which he begins his most famous work, *Pensées*, with the heading, 'The difference between the mathematical and the intuitive mind.'

> In the one the principles are palpable, but removed from ordinary use; so that for want of habit it is difficult to turn one's mind in that direction …
> But in the intuitive mind the principles are found in common use, and are before the eyes of everybody. One has only to look, and no effort is necessary; it is only a question of good eyesight, but it must be good, for the principles are so subtle and so numerous …
> All mathematicians would then be intuitive if they had clear sight, for they do not reason incorrectly from principles known to them; and intuitive minds would be mathematical if they could turn their eyes to the principles of mathematics to which they are unused.
> The reason, therefore, that some intuitive minds are not mathematical is that they cannot at all turn their attention to the principles of mathematics. But the reason that mathematicians are not intuitive is that they do not see what is before them, and that, accustomed to the exact and plain principles of mathematics, and not reasoning till they have well inspected and arranged their principles, they are lost in matters of intuition where the principles do not allow of such arrangement …

---

8 François Fenelon, *Fénelon's Letter to the French Academy* (1716), trans. Barbara Warnick (New York: University Press of America, 1984), 109. François de Salignac de La Mothe-Fénelon (1651–1715) was a courtier, bishop of Cambrai and royal tutor to a grandson of the Louis XIV, the duke of Burgundy.

9 Charles de Secondat, Baron de Montesquieu (1689–1755), *The Spirit of Laws* (1748), trans. Thomas Nugent in *Great Books*, XXXVIII (Chicago: Encyclopedia Britannica, 1952), 45.

> Thus it is rare that mathematicians are intuitive, and that men of intuition are mathematicians, because mathematicians wish to treat matters of intuition mathematically, and make themselves ridiculous, wishing to begin with definitions and then with axioms, which is not the way to proceed in this kind of reasoning …
>
> Intuitive minds, on the contrary, being thus accustomed to judge at a single glance, are so astonished when they are presented with propositions of which they understand nothing, and the way to which is through definitions and axioms so sterile, and which they are not accustomed to see thus in detail, that they are repelled and disheartened.[10]

Thus far, Pascal's deduction of the bicameral nature of brain function is quite impressive. However, as he continues, his deductions do not correspond with what we know through modern clinical research. He finds, for example, two kinds of intellect which we would associate with the left hemisphere, although he associates only one of these with his 'mathematical' side.

> There are then two kinds of intellect: the one able to penetrate acutely and deeply into the conclusions of given premises, and this is the precise intellect; the other able to comprehend a great number of premises without confusing them, and this is the mathematical intellect.[11]

He also concludes, without explanation, that whereas mathematics belong to intellect, judgment and perception are associated with the intuition.[12] He also adds that both understanding and feeling are molded and corrupted by intercourse with society.[13]

The great majority of Pascal's literary works represent the expression of an intensely religious person. Thus we understand that, in the end, the intelligence he has been speaking of above is a spiritual entity, and not mere matter. In a brief reference to the soul, Pascal writes,

> It is impossible that our rational part should be other than spiritual; and if any one maintain that we are simply corporeal, this would far more exclude us from the knowledge of things, there being nothing so inconceivable as to say that matter knows itself. It is impossible to imagine how it should know itself.[14]

It is likewise as a fervent Christian, that Pascal, who in general paints a very depressing portrait of mankind, treats with great suspicion any mental faculty other than Reason. In the following, it is Imagination to which he attributes a negative role.

---

10 Blaise Pascal, *Pensées* (New York: Modern Library, 1941), I, i. Pascal (1623–1662), a brilliant prodigy and largely self-taught, wrote a treatise on the cessation of sounds at age eleven and a paper on Conic Sections at age sixteen. He invented the first mechanical calculator and the barometer, but was foremost a philosopher and writer on theology.

11 Ibid., I, ii.

12 Ibid., I, iv.

13 Ibid., I, vi.

14 Ibid., II, lxxii.

> This arrogant power [Imagination], the enemy of reason, who likes to rule and dominate it, has established in man a second nature to show how all-powerful she is. She makes men happy and sad, healthy and sick, rich and poor; she compels reason to believe, doubt, and deny; she blunts the senses, or quickens them; she has her fools and sages; and nothing vexes us more than to see that she fills her devotees with a satisfaction far more full and entire than does reason. Those who have a lively imagination are a great deal more pleased with themselves than the wise can reasonably be.[15]

The nearest Pascal comes to suggesting that he has deduced that the individual man has two sides to himself is his acknowledgment of their competition.

> There is internal war in man between reason and the passions.
>   If he had only reason without passions …
>   If he had only passions without reason …
>   But having both, he cannot be without strife, being unable to be at peace with the one without being at war with the other. Thus he is always divided against, and opposed to himself.[16]

In the end, Pascal rejects Reason nearly as strongly as intuition. His was in an environment in which discoveries in science, especially in Copernican-Galilean astronomy, and the general harbingers of the Enlightenment were dealing tremendous blows to Christianity. Since the greater part of his book is a defense of Christianity, he cannot completely endorse Reason, which was spreading so much doubt. He rested on Faith, as did so many early Christian philosophers.

> The heart has its reason, which reason does not know. We feel it in a thousand things …
>   It is the heart which experiences God, and not the reason. This, the, is faith: God felt by the heart, not by the reason.[17]

Some philosophers in Catholic France held fast to the old Church dogma that only Reason must control the actions of man. Montesquieu, for example, observes,

> Law in general is human reason, inasmuch as it governs all the inhabitants of the earth: the political and civil laws of each nation ought to be only the particular cases in which human reason is applied.[18]

But as we all know, and as François de la Rochefoucauld charmingly points out, Reason is capable of error.

---

15 Ibid., II, lxxxii.
16 Ibid., VI, ccccxii.
17 Ibid., III, 277.
18 Montesquieu, *The Spirit of Laws*, 3.

Intellectual blemishes, like facial ones, grow more prominent with age.[19]

More to the point, La Rochefoucauld recognized in repeated maxims that there is more to us than Reason.

The steadfastness of the wise is only the art of locking their agitation inside them.[20]

......

The mind is always the dupe of the heart.[21]

......

We all speak well of our hearts, we none of us dare speak well of our minds.[22]

......

Not all those who know their minds know their hearts as well.[23]

La Bruyère acknowledged the same bicameral nature of man when he exclaimed, 'What a discrepancy between the mind and the heart.'[24] He also found this distinction in individual artists.

The plays of Corneille occupy one's mind; those of Racine stir one's heart.[25]

Charles de Saint-Évremond, in a poem contained in a letter to the Duke of Buckingham (1678), suggests rather than be torn between the two it is better to let each have its place.

Sometimes let Reason, with a sovereign sway,
Control all your desires:
Sometimes let Reason to your heart give way,
And fan your warmest fires.[26]

---

19 François de la Rochefoucauld, *The Maxims of La Rochefoucauld*, trans. Louis Kronenberger (New York: Random House, 1959), Nr. 112. François de la Rochefoucauld (1613–1680) joined the army at an early age and spent most of his life in public service. The *Maxims*, his most famous work, was published anonymously in 1665. The duke of Saint-Simon, in his memoirs [*The Memoirs of the Duke of Saint-Simon*, trans. Bayle St. John (London: George Allen, 1926), II, 260], mentions that to his surprise, 'nay, our shame,' he found Rochefoucauld playing chess one day with his servant!

20 Ibid., Nr. 20.

21 Ibid., Nr. 102.

22 Ibid., Nr. 98.

23 Ibid., Nr. 103.

24 La Bruyère, *Characters*, 202.

25 Ibid., 38.

26 Quoted in Charles de Saint-Évremond, *The Letters of Saint-Évremond*, ed. John Hayward (Freeport, NY: Books for Libraries Press, 1971), 205.

And similarly, in another poem,

> To be loved by those you love
> In and out of season,
> Is a sign your feelings move
> In Harmony with Reason.[27]

Regarding this competition between the right and left hemispheres of the brain, one finds an occasional insight which corresponds remarkably well with modern research. We know now that it is the right hemisphere which supplies the emotional content to the language of the left hemisphere in speech as well as the emotional expressions of the face. Something like this seems to be the intent of La Rochefoucauld when he recognizes,

> Tone of voice, look and manner can prove no less eloquent than choice of words.[28]

More extraordinary is his insight that there are forms of understanding unique to the right hemisphere. He does not understand 'right hemisphere,' of course, but his use of 'emotion' here must be taken as a synonym.

> Nature would seem to have hidden deep within us talents and abilities we know nothing about; only strong emotion is able to bring them to light, and to give us at times insights beyond the reach of ordered thought.[29]

Another French musician, Michel de Saint-Lambert, in his *Les Principes du Clavecin* of 1702, makes a similar astonishing deduction. This is one which has only recently been confirmed in clinical research, that is that we carry genetically into birth specific information of a musical nature. We are, in fact, born musicians and Saint-Lambert's insight is quite remarkable. After briefly mentioning some of the abilities needed in performance, he says,

> Though this at first sight may appear a large order, it is nevertheless sure that this extreme accuracy in intonation and rhythm is a gift given to almost all men, like sight and speech. There are very few who do not sing and dance naturally; if it is not with the delicacy and correctness that Art has sought, it is at least with the correctness which Art dictates and which Art itself has derived from Nature. It is already a great asset for those who want to learn music or to play some instrument that they know they have discernment of the ear by nature, that is, the first and most important of these aptitudes.[30]

---

27 Saint-Évremond, Letter to Ninon de Lanclos, 1700, quoted in *The Letters of Saint-Évremond*, 351.
28 *The Maxims of La Rochefoucauld*, Nr. 249.
29 Ibid., Nr. 404.
30 Michel de Saint-Lambert, *Les Principes du Clavecin* (1702), quoted in MacClintock, *Readings in the History of Music in Performance*, 212.

On the Senses

The most interesting seventeenth-century discussion of the role of the senses, which touches on music and aesthetics, is by Nicolas Malebranche, an old-fashioned Church Philosopher still talking about the soul.[31] It is curious, however, that Malebranche, in his *The Search after Truth* (1674), the principal work in which he discusses the senses in their basic relationship to the mind and the soul, he never mentions hearing nor even the topic of music. He begins with his moral conclusion.

> A man who judges all things by his senses, who follows the impulses of his passion in all things, who perceives only what he senses and loves only what flatters him, is in the most wretched state of mind possible. In this state he is infinitely removed from the truth and from his good. But when a man judges things only according to the mind's pure ideas, when he carefully avoids the noisy confusion of creatures, and, when entering into himself, he listens to his sovereign Master with his senses and passions silent, it is impossible for him to fall into error.[32]

Malebranche, like medieval philosophers, places much of what actually belongs to the mind in the 'soul.' Sensations, which Spinoza had called 'confused thoughts,' Malebranche calls 'modifications' of the mind. Again, it is significant that throughout the basic discussion of the senses relative to intellectual understanding, Malebranche only speaks of four of them, omitting the sense of hearing.

> The soul's perceptions of ideas are of two kinds. The first, which are called pure perceptions, are, as it were, accidental to the soul: they do not make an impression on it and do not sensibly modify it. The second, which are called sensible, make a more or less vivid impression on it. Such are pleasure and pain, light and color, tastes, odors, and so on. For it will be seen that sensations are nothing but modes of mind [*manieres d'être de l'esprit*], and it is for this reason that I call all of them *modifications* of the mind.[33]

The capacity for the soul to receive things, he calls 'understanding.' Whenever Malebranche begins to describe in specific physical terms the nature of the perception of the senses, because his philosophy is based on the soul, he is required to lapse into what today can only be regarded as 'weird science.' For example,

---

[31] Nicolas Malebranche, *The Search after Truth*, quoted in *Malebranche, Philosophical Selections*, trans. Thomas Lennon and Paul Olscamp (Indianapolis: Hacket Publishing Company, 1992), 3ff. Malebranche (1638–1715) was born to a well-placed family, his father having been a secretary to Louis XIII and his uncle the viceroy of Canada. In a time of growing skepticism associated with the Enlightenment, Malebranche may be viewed as one of the last of the medieval metaphysicians. He declares,

> I am surprised that Christian philosophers, who ought to prefer the mind of God to the mind of man, Moses to Aristotle, and Saint Augustine to some worthless commentator on a pagan philosopher, should regard the soul more as the *form* of the body than as being made in the image and for the image of God.

[32] Ibid., 6.

[33] Ibid., 8ff.

> Because when we sense pain, or anything else, we ordinarily perceive it through the mediation of the sense organs, men ordinarily say that the senses do the perceiving, without knowing distinctly what they mean by the word sense. They think there is some faculty distinct from the soul that enables it or the body to sense, for they believe that the sense organs really take part in our perceptions. They imagine that the body so aids the mind in sensing that if the mind were separated from the body, it could never sense anything. But they believe all these things only through prejudice, and because in our present state we never sense anything without the use of the sense organs.[34]

As he continues it all becomes more weird. Not being able to say where exactly the soul is, he makes it synonymous with the entire body. Consequently, the eyes are called *its* eyes, the soul's eyes, etc.

> The soul perceives by the senses only sensible and gross objects, either when, being present, they make an impression on the external organs of its body and this impression is communicated to the brain or, when in their absence, the flow of animal spirits make a similar impression in the brain. In this way the soul sees plains and rocks before its eyes, knows the hardness of iron, the point of a sword, and similar things; and these sorts of perceptions are called *feelings* [*sentimens*] or *sensations* [*sensations*].[35]

Again, taking the old church position, he warns of the dangers of these perceptions.

> But our inclinations and passions also act very strongly on us; they dazzle our mind with false lights, cover it, and fill it with shadows. Our inclinations and passions involve us in an infinite number of errors when we follow this false and deceptive light they produce in us.

Malebranche continues his weird science when he discusses the nature of pain, although unwittingly the first part of his thought here is quite correct—the pain is not in the finger.

> I feel pain, for example, when a thorn pricks my finger; but the hole it makes is not the pain. The hole is in the finger—it is clearly conceived—and the pain is in the soul, for the soul senses it keenly and is disagreeably modified by it.[36]

When he summarizes his thoughts in this treatise, he returns to the old church position that the senses cannot be trusted because they provide false information. Again, the sense of hearing is missing.

> Pleasure, pain, taste, heat, color, all our sensations and all our passions, are modifications of our soul. But be that as it may, do we clearly know them? Can we compare heat with taste or smell with color? Do we know the relation between red and green, or even between two shades of

---

34 Ibid., 9ff.
35 Ibid., 19.
36 Ibid., 20.

green? Such is not the case with [geometrical] figures, which we can compare with each other; we know their relations exactly, we know precisely that the square of the diagonal of a square is double that square. What relation is there between these intelligible figures, which are very clear ideas, and our soul's modifications, which are but confused sensations?[37]

In another treatise, Malebranche finally discusses hearing, and music, as one of the senses. In doing so, he falls back to the Church-Scholastic position that music cannot be judged by the ear. It can only be judged as conceptual knowledge; we can hear music, but it has no real meaning except through left brain translation. Thus, in 'Elucidation XI,' he concludes, 'Musicians know nothing.'

> It is true that I can discover exact relations between sounds, that the octave, for example, is two to one, the fifth three to two, the fourth four to three. But I cannot know these relations through the sensation I have of them. If I know that the octave is two to one, it is because I have learned through experience that a given string sounds the octave when, having been plucked at full length, it is then plucked after having been divided into two equal parts. It is because I know that there are twice as many vibrations in an equal amount of time, or something like this. It is because the disturbances in the air, the vibrations of the string, and the string itself are things that can be compared through clear ideas, and because we know distinctly the relations that can obtain between the string and its parts as well as between the rates of different vibrations. But the sounds cannot be compared in themselves, or insofar as they are sensible qualities and modifications of the soul. We cannot know their relations in this way. And although musicians distinguish different consonances very well, this is not because they distinguish their relations through clear ideas. For them, the ear alone judges the difference in sounds; their reason knows nothing. But the ear cannot be said to judge through a clear idea or otherwise than through sensation. Even musicians, then, have no clear idea of sounds taken as sensations or modifications of the soul. Consequently, neither the soul nor its modifications is known through a clear idea, but only through consciousness or inner sensation.[38]

In his *Dialogues on Metaphysics*, Malebranche also follows the old Church insistence that among the senses the eye is the most important. Here also, in turning to the physics of sound as related to the senses, Malebranche shares with many earlier philosophers considerable confusion regarding how sound is actually produced. It seems curious to us that they could often conclude that the sounds were created in the air, rather than by the instrument itself. He also contends that the sounds are heard in the soul, and not in the air. While it is true that pain is sensed in the brain, and not in the finger, this line of thought is not true with respect to music. We understand music in the brain, but it does nevertheless exist in the air.

---

37 Ibid., 73.
38 Malebranche, *Elucidations of the Search after Truth*, trans. Thomas Lennon, in Ibid., 89.

THEODORE. Come, then, let me have the monochord and attend to what I shall do and what I shall say to you. Plucking or drawing this string toward me, I move it from the state in which the binding holds it; and, when I let go, you see—without my having to prove it to you—that it moves for some time this way and that and thus it makes a great number of vibrations and as a consequence many other small commotions which are imperceptible to our senses. For, a straight line being shorter than a curve, a string cannot vibrate, or become alternately straight and curved, unless the parts which compose it lengthen and contract very quickly. Now I ask you, is a body in motion not capable of moving one that it encounters? This string can therefore move the air which surrounds it (and even the subtle matter filling its pores), and this in turn moves something else, and so on to your ear and mine.

ARISTES. That is true. But what I hear is a sound, a sound spread out in the air, a quality which is quite different from vibrations of a string or commotions of air in motion.

THEODORE. Slowly, Aristes. Do not consult your senses, and do not judge on their testimony. It is true that sound is entirely different from air that is moved. But it is precisely for this reason that you have no ground for saying that sound is spread out in the air. For note this: touching this string, I simply make it move, and a string which is moved simply agitates the air that surrounds it.

ARISTES. 'A string which is moved simply agitates the air that surrounds it!' Why, do you not hear it produce a sound in the air?

THEODORE. Clearly I hear what you hear. But, when I want to be apprised of some truth, I do not consult my ears—yet you consult yours, notwithstanding all the good resolutions you made. Enter into yourself then, and consult the clear ideas which Reason contains. Can you conceive that air—or small bodies of whatever shape you please which are agitated in some way or other—is capable of containing the sound which you hear and that a string can produce this sound? Once again, do not consult your ears; and, just to be safe, imagine you are deaf. Consider attentively the clear idea of extension: it is the archetype of bodies; it represents their nature and properties. Is it not evident that the only possible properties of extension are relations of distance? Think seriously about this.

......

ARISTES. I understand clearly that sound is not spread out in the air and that a string cannot produce it. The reasons you gave me appear to be convincing. Since all modalities of bodies consist only in relations of distance, it follows that neither sound nor the power of producing it is contained in the idea of matter. That is enough for me. Still, here is another proof which occurs to me and which is convincing. During a fever I had some time ago, I heard the incessant howling of an animal which was certainly not howling as it was dead. I think also in sleep it happens to you as it does to me that I hear a concert, or at any rate the sound of a trumpet or a drum, even when everything is in total silence. While sick then I heard cries and howls. Even today I remember their giving me a great deal of anxiety. Now these disagreeable sounds were not in the air, although I heard them there as plainly as the sound this instrument makes. Thus, though we hear sounds as if spread out in the air, it does not follow that they are. They are actually only in the soul, for they are just sensations which affect it, modalities which belong to it. I could press the matter even further. Everything you told me up to now leads me to think that there is nothing in objects of our senses similar to the sensations we have of them. These objects correspond [*ont rapport avec*] to their ideas, but it seems to me they have no affinity with our sensations. Bodies are merely extension capable of motion and various shape. This is evident when we consult the idea which represents them.

THEODORE. Bodies, you say, have no resemblance to the sensations we have; and, to know their properties, we must consult not the senses but the clear idea of extension which represents their nature. Keep this important truth well in mind.

ARISTES. It is evident, and I shall never forget it.

THEODORE. Never! Well then, please tell me what an octave is and what is a fifth, or rather instruct me as to what must be done to hear these consonances.

ARISTES. That is very easy. Touch the whole string, and then put your finger there and touch one or the other part of the string, and you will hear an octave.

THEODORE. Why my finger there and not here?

ARISTES. That is because what you would get is a fifth and not an octave. Look, look at that. There, all the notes are marked … You laugh.

THEODORE. I am now very knowledgeable, Aristes. I can make you hear any note I wish. But, if we had broken our instrument, all our knowledge would be in bits.

ARISTES. Not at all. I would make another. It is only a string on a board. Anyone can do that.

THEODORE. Yes. But that is not enough. The consonances must be marked exactly on the board. How would you divide it then to mark where we should put our fingers to hear an octave, a fifth, or other consonances?

ARISTES. I would strike the whole string and, sliding my finger along it, I would locate the sound I wished to mark. For I know music well enough to tune instruments.

THEODORE. Your method is hardly exact since it is only by trial that you find what you are looking for. If you became deaf, or rather if the small nerve which tenses your eardrum and tunes it to your instrument were to loosen, what would become of your knowledge? …

ARISTES. Ah, Theodore! I had already forgotten what I just told you I would never forget … This is because I naturally listen more to my senses than to my Reason. I am so accustomed to consulting my ears that I was not in fact thinking of what you asked me.[39]

The dialogue now turns to the principle of using the eye to mark the proportions of the string in order to establish the desired sounds. The final question raised is why, when one string is struck, a similar string on another instrument will begin to vibrate as well. Malebranche offers the following explanation.

ARISTES. I see the reason for this clearly. Here are two strings with the same sound. Here is yours, and here is mine. When I release my string, it pushes the air towards you, and the air which is pushed moves your string a little bit. Mine again makes in a very short time a number of similar vibrations, each of which moves the air and pushes your string as the first jolt did. This is what makes it vibrate. For several small jolts rightly given will produce a sensible movement. But, when these small jolts come intermittently, they interfere with one another. Thus, when two strings are dissonant—i.e., when they cannot vibrate in equal or multiple times or at any rate in times that are commensurable because they are unequally

---

39   Malebranche, *Dialogues on Metaphysics*, trans. Willis Doney, in Ibid., 173ff.

tensed or are of unequal and incommensurable length or thickness—they cannot move one another. For, if the first moves and pushes the air and second string towards you at the time the second is returning towards me, then it will diminish the motion instead of augmenting it. The vibrations of the strings must then be made in equal or multiple times if there is to be a transfer of motion great enough to be sensible; and their motion will be the more sensible the more the consonance they produce approaches unison. That is why in an octave they move more than in a fifth, and in a fifth more than in a fourth: the two strings begin their vibrations more often at the same instant. Are you happy with this reason?

THEODORE. Quite, Aristes. You have followed the principle of clear ideas. I understand quite well that strings having the same sound move each other, not by 'sympathy' of their sound since sound cannot be the cause of motion, but by agreement in their vibrations that move and shake the air in which they are strung. So long as you reason about the properties of bodies on the basis of ideas of shapes and motions, I shall be happy with you. You have such a good mind that it is difficult for you to engage in bad reasoning while you follow a principle that is clear. In fact, our falling into error so very often derives from the falsity or obscurity of our ideas rather than from weakness of our minds. Geometers make mistakes rarely and Physicists almost always.

ON EDUCATION

The comments by the French philosophers on education are important to a study of the aesthetics of music, not only for their mention of music itself, but for their discussion of the emotions. La Bruyère acknowledges the presumption of the ancient Greek philosophers that education can alter man for the better. He is not sure this is true, but he awards the idea the benefit of doubt.

> Even if it were true, as some people assert, that education cannot give a man a different heart or a different temperament, that it alters nothing basic in him and touches only the surface, I should still maintain that it does him some good.[40]

François Fénelon wrote a number of treatises devoted to the education of children of the aristocracy which include discussion of both emotions and music. First, however, of special interest is his focus on the education of girls, a topic rarely given consideration, for, as he says, most people thought it was enough that they be able to 'look after their households and obey their husbands without asking why.'[41] Fénelon himself believed that women have weaker minds and bodies than men and were therefore not suited for participating in politics, the military, law, philosophy or theology. On the other hand, he reflects, 'nature has given

---

40 La Bruyère, *Characters*, 236.
41 François Fénelon, *Fénelon on Education*, trans. H. Barnard (Cambridge: University Press, 1966), 1. His most extensive treatise was his 'Traité de l'Éducation des Filles.'

them as a recompense industry, neatness and economy, so as to keep them quietly occupied in their homes.'⁴² Having said that, he continues with a general review of the qualities of the female as seen from his perspective.

> When this softness and indolence are joined to ignorance there results a dangerous inclination towards amusements and entertainments. This indeed it is which excites an indiscreet and insatiable curiosity. Those who are well-educated and occupied in serious pursuits have as a rule only a moderate curiosity …
>
> On the other hand, girls who are badly educated and indolent have an imagination which is always straying. Lacking solid nourishment their curiosity turns eagerly towards vain and dangerous objects. Those who have intelligence often develop into *précieuses* and read every book which can feed their vanity. They develop a passion for novels, for plays, for fanciful tales of adventure with a romantic love interest. They give way to empty ideas and grow accustomed to the high-flown language of the heroes of fiction. By so doing they even spoil themselves for ordinary life, for all these fine, but airy, sentiments, these noble passions, these adventures which the fiction writer invents in order to please, have no relation to the motives which hold sway in real life and which decide actual events, nor to the disappointments which one meets in whatever one takes in hand. An unhappy girl, full of the romance and wonder which have fascinated her in these books, is astonished to find in the world no real people who are like these heroes. She longs to live like these imaginary princesses who in novels are always charming, always worshiped, always independent. How she will hate to descend from this romance to the sordid details of housekeeping!
>
> Some girls push their curiosity still further and take upon themselves to express opinions on religious matters, although they are incapable of doing so. But those who have insufficient intellectual aptitude for these curiosities, still have others proportionate to their powers. They are eager to know what is said—a story, a rumor, an intrigue. They like to receive letters and to read those which others receive. They want to be told everything and to tell everything. They are vain and vanity makes them talkative. They are frivolous and their frivolity prevents the reflection which would often help them to keep silence.⁴³

Some characteristics of the female appear to have been a matter of high personal concern with Fénelon, for he mentions them continuously. First on this list is 'craftiness,' although he never defines this. It bothered him that they talk too much and take too long to get to the point. Another 'chief fault' is vanity, of which he cautions, 'there are only a few years difference between one woman who is beautiful and another who is not.'

> Without noticing it they arrive at a certain age when their beauty fades and when they are still charmed with themselves, although the world, far from being so, is disgusted with them.⁴⁴

---

42 Ibid., 2.
43 Ibid., 5ff.
44 Ibid., 71.

Fénelon also considers it a mark against the female that they are more inclined than men toward the emotions.

> Tears cost them nothing; their passions are quick and their knowledge limited. The result is that they neglect nothing in order to succeed, and methods which would not be approved by better regulated persons seem good to them. They rarely use their reason to examine whether something is desirable, yet they spare no pains in order to obtain it.[45]

Turning to the education of children in general, Fénelon mentions the importance of the child's diet and health and allowing the organs to grow strong, but he cautions avoiding 'anything which may excite the passions.' Fénelon is also in possession of some 'weird science' with respect to the child's brain.

> Their brain substance is soft and hardens gradually; as for their mind, it knows nothing and finds everything new. The result of this softness of the brain is that everything is easily impressed on it and the surprise of novelty makes children quickly moved to admiration and extremely curious. It is true also that this moistness and softness of the brain, together with a great heat, give rise to facile and continual movement. This is the cause of that constant activity of children, for they cannot concentrate their attention on any object nor keep their body still in any one place.[46]

We also see here a mistaken view still held by many in the present century, that the infant is born a 'blank slate' which the process of education fills. Because, therefore, children's brains are without any impressions, Fénelon places great emphasis on the character of the people who are allowed access to the children. They learn easily by example, thus,

> They should be shown how often one is despised—or worthy of being so, how often one is miserable when one gives way to one's passions and does not cultivate one's reason.[47]

Music in education is first mentioned by Fénelon as a natural tool to meet the child's natural inclination toward pleasure.

> The ancients understood this matter far better. It was through the pleasures of poetry and music that the chief branches of knowledge, the maxims of virtue and of civilization, were introduced among the Hebrews, the Egyptians and the Greeks. Uneducated people can scarcely believe that, so far removed is it from our own customs.[48]

In meeting the child's need for pleasure, however, one must choose games with great care. Needless to say, 'girls must not associate with boys, or even older girls whose conduct is not well-regulated and dependable.'

---

45 Ibid., 66.
46 Ibid., 9ff.
47 Ibid., 13.
48 Ibid., 21.

> Games which make the child too wild or excited, or which involve bodily actions which are immodest for a girl, as well as frequent visits and conversations which may inspire a taste for paying calls, must be avoided. If one has not already been spoilt by amusement on a large scale and has not conceived some eager passions, one easily finds happiness; its true sources are good health and innocence. But those who have had the misfortune to become accustomed to violent pleasures lose the taste for moderate ones and are always wearying themselves in a restless search for happiness.[49]

With regard to the education of older children, Fénelon warns that there is no need for girls to study other languages, unless they are destined to marry a foreign prince. Otherwise, knowing another language only opens up the possibility of 'reading dangerous books.' In general, the choice of reading for girls must avoid the 'over-exciting' and anything which has a love interest.

It is this concern which leads him to a more detailed discussion of music and the arts in education.

> With music and painting the same precautions are necessary. All the arts imply the same spirit and the same taste. As for music we know that the ancients thought that there was nothing more dangerous to a well-governed state than the introduction of an effeminate type of music. It enervates men and renders them soft and given to pleasure. Languishing and passionate airs are so alluring only because the soul surrenders itself to the charm of the senses and becomes intoxicated with it. For this reason the magistrates at Sparta used to break all instruments whose music was too attractive, and this was one of their most important duties. For this reason Plato also severely rejected all those enervating modes which came from Asia. For an even stronger reason Christians, who ought never to seek pleasure merely for pleasure's sake, should abominate these poisonous amusements.
>
> Poetry and music, if we exclude whatever does not conduce to their true aim, can be very usefully employed to excite in the mind lively and lofty sentiments leading to virtue. How many poetical works there are in Scripture, which apparently used to be sung by the Hebrews! Songs were the first repository, earlier than writing itself, which preserved even more definitely the tradition of things divine among men. We have seen how among heathen people music had power to raise the soul above base thoughts. The Church has thought that the best way to comfort her children is by singing the praises of God. We cannot therefore reject these arts which the Spirit of God Himself has consecrated. Music and poetry, if they be Christian, would be the greatest of all aids to induce disgust with profane pleasures; but owing to the wrong attitude towards these arts which is fashionable in our present society, a taste for them is not without danger. So we should lose no time in showing a young lady, who is susceptible to the influence of music, how much charm there can be in it even if one confines oneself to sacred compositions. If she can sing and appreciate the beauties of music do not hope to keep her forever ignorant of them. Prohibition will only increase her enthusiasm for them. It is much better to give an orderly course to this torrent than to try to stop it.[50]

---

49 Ibid., 25ff.

50 Ibid., 87ff.

A final comment on the education of the young prince, we find interesting. It reflects a thought which took hold in the sixteenth century, that a noble never does anything which requires effort.

> The princes are never made to learn anything by heart, unless they want to, because that takes too much time.[51]

Montesquieu reflects on the differences in society between the ancients and the moderns and concludes that modern society makes the ancient form of education impossible.

> Most of the ancients lived under governments that had virtue for their principle; and when this was in full vigor they performed actions unusual in our times, and at which our narrow minds are astonished.
>
> Another advantage their education possessed over ours was that it never could be effaced by contrary impressions. Epaminondas, the last year of his life, said, heard, beheld, and performed the very same things as at the age in which he received the first principles of his education.
>
> In our days we receive three different or contrary educations, namely, of our parents, of our masters, and of the world. What we learn in the latter effaces all the ideas of the former. This, in some measure, arises from the contrast we experience between our religious and world engagements, a thing unknown to the ancients.[52]

The principal goal which he assigns contemporary education is to provide man with the necessary taste and grace to compliment the best of society.

> A courtly air consists in quitting a real for a borrowed greatness. The latter pleases the courtier more than the former. It inspires him with a certain disdainful modesty, which shows itself externally, but whose pride insensibly diminishes in proportion to its distance from the source of this greatness.
>
> At court we find a delicacy of taste in everything—a delicacy arising from the constant use of the superfluities of life, from the variety, and especially the satiety, of pleasures, from the multiplicity and even confusion of fancies, which, if they are but agreeable, are sure of being well received.
>
> These are the things which properly fall within the province of education, in order to form what we call a man of honor, a man possessed of all the qualities and virtues requisite in [a monarchy].[53]

---

51 Ibid., 115.
52 Montesquieu, *The Spirit of Laws*, 15.
53 Ibid., 14.

ON THE PSYCHOLOGY OF AESTHETICS

One of the most important differences between the twin hemispheres of the brain is that information absorbed by the left hemisphere is always someone else's information, whereas information absorbed in the right hemisphere is primarily experiential in character and personal in nature. It is in this context that it is interesting to find Pascal suggesting that when a writer [or speaker or performer] deals with the emotions, it will be perceived as the listener's own and not that of the author.

> When a natural discourse paints a passion or an effect, one feels within oneself the truth of what one reads, which was there before, although one did not know it. Hence one is inclined to love him who makes us feel it, for he has not shown us his own riches, but ours.[54]

Pascal, in his desire to defend Christianity, returns to the medieval dogma of the Church in his comments on Pleasure. Not only is the general frame of reference negative, but we even find the old attack on the morals of the theater.

> Pleasure, the coin for which we will do whatever is wanted.[55]
>
> ......
>
> When our passions lead us to do something, we forget our duty.[56]
>
> ......
>
> All great amusements are dangerous to the Christian life; but among all those which the world has invented there is none more to be feared than the theater. It is a representation of the passions so natural and so delicate that it excites them and gives birth to them in our hearts....[57]

Pursuits of pleasure and amusement can only be explained as man's attempt to temporarily forget his miserable condition.

> However full of sadness a man may be, he is happy for the time, if you can prevail upon him to enter into some amusement; and however happy a man may be, he will soon be discontented and wretched, if he be not diverted and occupied by some passion or pursuit which prevents weariness from overcoming him. Without amusement there is no joy; with amusement there is no sadness. And this also constitutes the happiness of persons in high position, that they have a number of people to amuse them, and have the power to keep themselves in this state.[58]

---

54 Pascal, *Pensées*, I, xiv.
55 Ibid., I, xxiv.
56 Ibid., II, civ.
57 Ibid., I, xi.
58 Ibid., II, cxxxix.

But even with this justification, Pascal found a problem relative to Christian ethics.

> It is not disgraceful for man to yield to pain, and it is disgraceful to yield to pleasure. This is not because pain comes to us from without, and we ourselves seek pleasure … It is because pain does not tempt and attract us. It is we ourselves who choose it voluntarily, and will it to prevail over us. So that we are masters of the situation; and in this man yields to himself. But in pleasure it is man who yields to pleasure. Now only mastery and sovereignty bring glory, and only slavery brings shame.[59]

Again, it was the medieval Church position that Pleasure is basically bad for the influence it has on man. Pascal seems inclined to extend this to an almost physical definition.

> Our senses perceive no extreme. Too much sound deafens us; too much light dazzles us; too great distance or proximity hinders our view. Too great length and too great brevity of discourse tend to obscurity; too much truth is paralyzing … Too much pleasure disagrees with us. Too many concords are annoying in music.[60]

After Pascal, the French philosophers reflect more of humanism than the Church in writing of the emotions. La Rochefoucauld, although he was wrong in observing that 'The passions are nothing more than varying temperatures of the blood,'[61] was undoubtedly correct when he suggested, 'Each of the passions is a color in the spectrum of self-love.'[62] A number of his other maxims reflect the new focus on man, begun by the humanists and later dignified by the name 'Enlightenment.' A few examples:

> The passions are the only orators who always persuade. They are like some magically infallible law of nature, and the simplest man, endowed with passion, persuades better than the most eloquent man who lacks it.[63]
>
> ……
>
> In the human heart there is an endless procreation of passions: as soon as one is dethroned, another almost always comes to power.[64]
>
> ……
>
> However carefully we disguise our passions to look like piety and honor, the mask proves of no avail.[65]

---

59 Ibid., II, clx.

60 Ibid., II, lxxii.

61 *The Maxims of La Rochefoucauld*, Nr. 564.

62 Ibid., Nr. 531.

63 Ibid., Nr. 8.

64 Ibid., Nr. 10.

65 Ibid., Nr. 12.

It seems appropriate to quote here La Bruyère's similar metaphor,

> All our passions are deceitful: they wear a mask, as far as possible, in front of other people, and they hoodwink themselves.[66]

La Rochefoucauld adds two maxims on the emotion most frequently discussed in all early literature, Love.

> It is difficult to define love: in the soul, it is a thirst for mastery; in the mind, a harmony of thought; in the body, nothing but a delicately hidden desire to possess, after many mysteries, whatsoever one loves.[67]
>
> ......
>
> Judged by most of its reactions, love is closer to hatred than to friendship.[68]

Perhaps it was this emotion Montesquieu was thinking of when he admits that animals lack man's important advantages, but,

> most of them are more attentive than we to self-preservation, and do not make so bad a use of their passions.[69]

Finally, we find interesting a treatise on eloquence by Fénelon, because of the obvious correspondence between the orator as a performer before an audience and the performer of music. Oratory also corresponds with music in that much of the meaning is identified through the emotions.

> Eloquence consists not only in proof but also in the ability to arouse the passions. In order to arouse the passions, it is necessary to portray them. Hence, I believe that all eloquence can be reduced to proving, to portraying, and to striking. Every brilliant thought which does not drive towards one of these three things is only a conceit.[70]

And again,

> The manner of saying things makes visible the manner in which one feels them, and it is this which strikes the listeners the more. In such passages as these, not only are sentences completely unnecessary, but one must neglect their order and their interconnections. Otherwise their passion is no longer like real passion; and nothing is so shocking as passion expressed with pomp and in measured periods.[71]

---

66 La Bruyère, *Characters*, 79.

67 *The Maxims of La Rochefoucauld*, Nr. 68.

68 Ibid., Nr. 72.

69 Montesquieu, *The Spirit of Laws*, 2.

70 François Fénelon, *Fénelon's Dialogues on Eloquence*, trans. Wilbur Howell (Princeton: Princeton University Press, 1951), 92.

71 Ibid., 97.

Later, Fénelon discusses physical movement as an expression of emotion.

> A. For what purpose does the action of the body serve? Does it not serve to express the sentiments and the passions which occupy the soul?
> B. I believe that.
> A. The movement of the body is then a painting of the thoughts of the soul.
> B. Yes.
> A. And that painting ought to be a genuine likeness. It is necessary that everything in it represent vividly and naturally the sentiments of him who is speaking and the nature of the things he speaks of. I mean that he must not, of course, go to the point where his representation becomes trivial and ludicrous.[72]

Fénelon introduces the analogy of music when he contends that an effective orator must have a vocal range with much variety.

> It is a kind of music: all its beauty consists in the variety of its tones as they rise or fall according to the things which they have to express.[73]

If this is not the case, if his voice is not naturally melodious, or is badly managed, it fails to please.

> It does not make any striking impression upon the mind such as it would if it had all the inflections which express feeling. His tones are beautiful bells which should be clear, full, sweet, and pleasant; but, after all, bells which carry no meaning, which have no variety, and as a consequence no harmony and no eloquence.

Fénelon also provides some specific details regarding the relationship of orator and listener, a relationship, again, which also corresponds with the performer of music. The orator, he says, must convince the listener that he is speaking directly to him. The style must be natural, familiar, serious and modest. The passions must be expressed with gesture and not by voice alone. Most important, however,

> It is necessary to feel passion in order to paint it well. Art, however great it be, does not speak as does actual passion. Hence, you will always be a very imperfect orator if you are not affected by the feelings which you wish to portray and to inspire in others.[74]

---

72   Ibid., 99.
73   Ibid., 102ff.
74   Ibid., 104ff.

In considering ornamentation in speech, Fénelon again uses the analogy of music to explain its role.

> B. You would strictly banish all frivolous ornaments from discourse. But tell me by concrete examples how to distinguish them from those which are serious and natural.
> A. Do you like flourishes in music? Don't you prefer animated notes which objectify realities and expressing feelings?
> B. Yes indeed. Flourishes serve only to please the ear; they mean nothing; they arouse no feeling. Formerly our music was full of them; and therefore it was very confused and weak. Then musicians began to discover ancient music. It is a kind of passionate declamation; it acts powerfully upon the soul.
> A. I knew that music, to which you are very sensitive, would serve me in making you understand what concerns eloquence. There must then be a kind of eloquence even in music; and we must eliminate flourishes from eloquence even in music; and we must eliminate flourishes from eloquence as from music. Do you not understand now what I call verbal flourishes—appointed conceits which always return like a refrain, appointed murmurings of languid and uniform periods? There you have false eloquence, and it resembles bad music.[75]

ON THE PHILOSOPHY OF AESTHETICS

A measure of the progress in the general aesthetics of art since the early Renaissance, when it was little more than a pleasant decoration, can be seen in La Bruyère's discussion of the nature of artists and their contribution to society.

> There are certain artists and men of talent whose minds are so vast as the art or science which they profess; they pay back with interest, through their inventive genius, what they owe to that art or science and to its principles; they break away from the art the more to ennoble it, and neglect the rules if these do not lead to greatness or sublimity; they walk alone and unaccompanied, but they soar very high and venture far afield, ever confident and strengthened by the success of the advantages sometimes to be gained from a disregard of the rules. Men of a more sober, timid, moderate cast of mind cannot reach the same heights as these, do not admire them, and indeed cannot understand them, still less seek to imitate them; they stay quietly within their own sphere, and reach a certain point which represents the limit of their capacity and understanding; they go no further, because they see nothing beyond it; they can at best only be first among the second-rate, and attain excellence in mediocrity.[76]

---

75 Ibid., 114ff.
76 La Bruyère, *Characters*, 40.

Thus, he concludes,

> A man who excels in his art and has brought it to its highest pitch of perfection rises, as it were, above that art and becomes equal to all that is noblest and most lofty.[77]

Finally, he suggests that the observer understands these things, if the art work is successful, in the communication of feeling.

> When a book exalts your mind and inspires it with lofty and courageous feelings, seek no other rule to judge it by: it is good, and made by the hand of a master.[78]

Another comment relative to the artist and his work which is worthy of mention, is by Fénelon.

> Art discredits and betrays itself when it makes its methods known.[79]

On Beauty

As mentioned above, the idealistic rules of art bred by the Academy were giving way during the seventeenth century to individual perspective. Pascal makes only one reference to beauty in art which has the old academic ring to it.

> Since everything is cause and effect ... I hold it equally impossible to know the parts without knowing the whole, and to know the whole without knowing the parts in detail.[80]

References to beauty in art in seventeenth-century France are more likely to be associated with nature in some way. In Pascal this seems almost genetic in character.

> There is a certain standard of grace and beauty which consists in a certain relation between our nature, such as it is, weak or strong, and the thing which pleases us.
>   Whatever is formed according to this standard pleases us, be it house, song, discourse, verse, prose, woman, birds, rivers, trees, rooms, dress, etc. Whatever is not made according to this standard displeases those who have good taste.
>   And as there is a perfect relation between a song and a house which are made after a good model, because they are like this good model, though each after its kind.[81]

---

77 Ibid., 48.
78 Ibid., 31.
79 *Fénelon's Letter to the French Academy* (1716), 69.
80 Pascal, *Pensées*, II, lxxii.
81 Ibid., I, xxxiiff.

Having given this definition, Pascal qualifies it with respect to poetry.

> As we speak of poetical beauty, so ought we to speak of mathematical beauty and medical beauty. But we do not do so; and the reason is that we know well what is the object of mathematics, and it consists in proofs, and what is the object of medicine, and that it consists in healing. But we do not know in what grace consists, which is the object of poetry. We do not know the natural model which we ought to imitate.

Pascal displays some hesitation with regard to the individual's ability to judge art. He believed the question is further complicated by the fact that the observer is never the same person, always growing and changing and thus incapable of seeing the art object the same way twice.[82] On the other hand he must have assumed a much greater ability in the artist himself to not only judge, but to know his audience, for he wrote, 'We either carry our audience with us, or irritate them.'[83]

Following Pascal, La Bruyère also mentions beauty in association with the observer.

> The pleasure of criticizing deprives us of the pleasure of being keenly touched by great beauties.[84]
>
> ......
>
> Beautiful things lose some of their beauty when out of place; propriety gives them perfection, and reason lays down the rules of propriety. Thus we do not want to hear a jig in chapel.[85]

Another seventeenth-century philosopher, La Rochefoucauld, only recognizes Beauty in more abstract qualities.

> Truth is the body and breath of perfection and beauty. Nothing, whatever its nature, can be beautiful or perfect that is not all it ought to be or has not all it ought to have.[86]
>
> ......
>
> Intention and performance must be all of one pattern to achieve the fullest effect.[87]

Nicolas Boileau-Despréaux (1636–1711), known today as simply Boileau, is considered to have been an important critic who helped to identify and establish good taste in seventeenth-century French literature. One of his important contributions was the first modern translation of the third century treatise, 'On the Sublime,' by Cassius Longinus, a work which found immediate popularity in Paris and remains a 'Classic' of early literature. As part of

---

82 Ibid., II, cxiv, cxxiii
83 Ibid., I, lvii.
84 La Bruyère, *Characters*, 28.
85 Ibid., 269.
86 *The Maxims of La Rochefoucauld*, Nr. 626.
87 Ibid., Nr. 161.

this publication, Boileau offered his own definition of the Sublime in literature, a definition which seems to us might well be applied to music literature as well.

> The Sublime is a certain power in literature that is able to raise and ravish the soul, and whose source is either greatness of thought and nobility of feeling, or magnificence of phrasing, or a harmonious, intense, and spirited turn of expression.[88]

In another essay, 'Truth and Beauty,' Boileau also makes some comments on beauty, which reflect the renewed interest in Nature exhibited by many of the French writers of this period.

> Only the true is beautiful; only the true is lovable. It ought to prevail everywhere, even in fiction …
> The false is always savorless, tedious, and feeble; but nature is true, and we sense it right away. In all things it is she alone we admire and love.[89]

Among the late Baroque philosophers, Fénelon also associates Truth with Beauty, principles which, it follows, must also have universality.

> As for myself, I wish to know whether things are true before I find them beautiful.[90]
> ……
> Beauty loses none of its value and is more estimable when it is common to all mankind.[91]

Fénelon also recognized one of the most significant definitions of high art, that Beauty in a higher sense is not found in the external qualities.

> The beautiful which is only beautiful, that is, brilliant, is only half beautiful; it must express the passions in order to inspire them. It must captivate the heart to turn it toward the true end of a poem.[92]

The *Essay on Beauty* (1741) by Yves-Marie Andrè (1675–1764) defines Beauty as having four manifestations: *le beau visible, le beau moral, le beau spirituel* and *le beau musical*.[93] The *le beau visible* refers to the light and color of Nature, the use and selection of which is essential to artistic creation. *Le beau moral* includes both personal characteristics such as blood, feeling, and family, as well as the broader civic associations of government and law. *Le*

---

[88] Nicolas Boileau, 'Reflections on Longinus,' quoted in *Selected Criticism*, trans. Ernest Dilworth (New York: Bobbs-Merrill, 1965), 70. Boileau was educated in law, but turned to literature. He became Royal Historiographer at age thirty-eight and seven years later was elected to the Academy.

[89] Boileau, 'Truth and Beauty,' in Ibid., 76ff.

[90] *Fénelon's Dialogues on Eloquence*, 60.

[91] *Fénelon's Letter to the French Academy* (1716), 78.

[92] Ibid., 84. The famous conductor, Celebadache, once told a *Los Angeles Times* interviewer that 'Anyone who thinks music is beautiful, does not understand music. Beauty is only the bait.'

[93] These definitions are discussed in more detail in Robert Finch, *Individualism in French Poetry (1686–1760)* (Toronto: University of Toronto Press, 1966), 90ff.

beau spirituel includes the domain of thought, imagination and again feeling. Finally, *le beau musical* includes the nature of the body as a musical instrument (the voice) and the distinctions made by the ear, in particular those which correspond with the natural overtone series.

Charles Batteux (1713–1780) also addressed the nature of Beauty in his *Les Beaux-Arts réduits à un même principe* (1746). He finds the object of Art to be an absolute, unattainable Beauty, which is perceived through feelings which words cannot express. To attempt to achieve this, Art must have variety, yet unity, originality and if possible an educational value.[94]

On Art versus Nature

Curiously, Pascal did not share the interest of his later contemporaries in this, one of the oldest topics of discussion in aesthetics. Indeed, his few comments seem to emphasize the separation, more than the relationship, between Art and Nature.

> Nature has made all her truths independent of one another. Our art makes one dependent on the other. But this is not natural.[95]
>
> ......
>
> Nature diversifies and imitates; art imitates and diversifies.[96]

Like Pascal, La Rochefoucauld seems to see little value in art attempting to adhere to Nature.

> The only good copies are those that reveal what is silly in the bad originals.[97]
>
> ......
>
> Imitation is always a mistake: the counterfeit displeases for the same reasons that what proves natural, charms.[98]

By the early eighteenth century a significant change had taken place and now Art and Nature were closely linked, as we can see in a comment by Fénelon.

> Sometimes simplicity and exactitude, sometimes sublimity and vehemence, will be in order. A painter who never represents anything but palaces of resplendent architecture will never achieve anything of truth, and will weary us before long. One must follow nature in her changes. After having painted a proud city, one often finds it proper to depict a desert and the huts of shepherds.[99]

---

94 Ibid., 97.
95 Pascal, *Pensées*, I, xxi.
96 Ibid., II, cxx.
97 *The Maxims of La Rochefoucauld*, Nr. 132.
98 Ibid.,
99 *Fénelon's Dialogues on Eloquence*, 119.

The first French writer to address this topic at length was Jean-Baptiste Du Bos, who made the chief criteria of art its approximation to nature. It is in his writings that we begin to find the inclusion of music in the discussion.

> Music has not simply been content to imitate in melody man's inarticulate language, and those natural sounds that he instinctively uses. It has even sought to imitate the many sounds that make a particular impression on him when he hears them in nature. Music uses only instruments to imitate such sounds in which speech has no part. Such imitations are commonly called symphonies. They even now have many different functions in our operas, and they are extremely effective.
>
> In the first place, although this music is purely instrumental, it consistently achieves a truthful imitation of nature …
>
> The imitative truth of a symphony lies in its resemblance to the sound that it seeks to imitate. A symphony that is composed in imitation of a tempest has a truthfulness about it when its melodies, harmonies and rhythms conjure up sounds that are reminiscent of roaring winds and the thunder of waves dashing against each other or breaking against the rocks.[100]

The French philosopher who discussed the relationship of art and nature most thoroughly was Charles Batteux. He was influential in narrowing the concept of the imitation of nature to one of selectivity, imitating the best of nature. It is in this selectivity that art takes on an ethical quality. Our only question regarding Batteux's views is that he makes the fundamental mistake of including music among the other arts, whereas we regard music as quite different because it is never an imitation but rather the 'real thing.'

Batteux, in his classic *Les beaux-arts réduits à un même principe*, begins his discussion of art and nature by describing his discovery of Aristotle's *Poetics*, in which he found certain principles which he believed to be valid with regard to all the arts. Foremost among these was Aristotle's emphasis on imitation, from which Batteux forms his basic perspective of aesthetics, that everything is judged by the degree to which an art imitates nature. This, he finds, is even the basis of the definition of taste.

> The rules of taste derive solely from the principle of imitation. For it follows that if the arts imitate beautiful nature, a taste for beautiful nature must essentially be good taste in the arts.[101]

He also developed the categories of art which are still found in modern criticism, in particular the separation of the fine arts and the utilitarian arts. In his study, Batteux proposed 'The nature of genius, analyzed to establish the character of the arts which it creates,' then divided the arts at large into three broad categories. The mechanical arts serve the needs of

---

100 Jean-Baptiste Du Bos (1670–1742), *Réflexions critiques sur la poësie et sur la peinture* [Paris, 1719], quoted in Peter le Huray and James Day, *Music and Aesthetics in the Eighteenth and Early-Nineteenth Centuries* (Cambridge: Cambridge University Press, 1981), 19ff. Du Bos served in the Foreign Affairs department of the government and later served as secretary of the Académie française.

101 Charles Batteux (1713–1780), *Les beaux-arts réduits à un même principe* [Paris,1746], quoted in Peter le Huray and James Day, *Music and Aesthetics in the Eighteenth and Early-Nineteenth Centuries* (Cambridge: Cambridge University Press, 1981), 42.

man, another category is those arts which have the objective of pleasure, which is the fine arts. The third category has the objective of both pleasure and utility, as for example rhetoric and architecture.[102]

Limiting himself to the second of these categories, he turns to the origin of the fine arts. In his view, earlier man, 'finding the pleasures of simple nature too monotonous,' sought to create 'a new order of ideas and feelings, one that would revive his spirits and enliven his taste.' Because of the limitations of his faculties, his only resource was nature itself. Therefore, Batteux concludes,

> first, that genius—the father of the arts—must imitate nature. Secondly, that genius may not imitate nature just as she is. Thirdly, that taste, for which the arts are made and by which they are judged, finds satisfaction when the artistic choice and imitation of nature has been well managed.[103]

Regarding the quality of imitation available to the artist, Batteux first stipulates that the human mind can only imitate nature in a 'very imperfect manner.' Second, genius which seeks to please 'must not and cannot exceed the bounds of nature itself,' thus 'the men of genius who explore the most only uncover that which already existed.' He also observes that music and dance, in particular, can easily be misused, as in the instance of supplying elements of interest to another form. But this is not imitation,

> If they are to fulfill their proper role, they must get back to imitation, and they should be the artificial portrait of the human passions.[104]

From this he derives his basic definition of taste, 'Nature is the sole object of taste; there can then be only one good taste, which is that of nature.' How, then, does one account for the differences among cultures, as for example the difference between French and Italian taste in music? The best answer Batteux can give is that the different views reflect only perspective, not the object (Nature) itself. He compares this to the artist viewing a model from different perspectives.[105]

Batteux returns to his basic contentions that music must have meaning, otherwise, he says, the tones are nothing more than the empty gestures of the orator or the frivolous ornaments of the writer. And it must imitate nature.

> There is not a musical sound that does not have its model in nature, and which may not at least be the beginning of expression, just as is a letter or a syllable in speech.[106]

---

102 Ibid., 44ff.
103 Ibid., 45.
104 Ibid., 46.
105 Ibid., 47.
106 Ibid., 49ff.

He continues the idea of music imitating nature by discussing the musical representation of storms, streams or a gentle breeze, concluding that 'in nature a simple cry of joy has its own harmony and consonance.'

On Poetry

Perhaps the most influential treatise on aesthetics written during the French Baroque was the *L'Art Poétique* (1674) by Nicolas Boileau. With this publication, Boileau is credited with achieving an important influence on the education of the French public regarding the essentials of good poetry, at a time, in general, when France was producing more critics than writers.[107] Boileau begins his treatise on the art of poetry by suggesting that great poets are born, not made. He concludes that one should not attempt to write poetry unless at one's birth the stars shone with a 'poetic influence.' Those not so blessed, he suggests, should find other kinds of material to write.

Turning to poetry, Boileau begins with some general advice. First, he cautions that whether you compose 'pleasant or sublime' poetry, it must abide by Reason's laws.

> Love reason then; and let whate'er you write
> Borrow from her its beauty, force, and light.[108]

Second, he observes that many poets feel they must choose extravagant subjects, rather than those which are 'plain and natural.'

> [Abandon this idea] and let Italians be
> Vain authors of false glittering poetry.
> All ought to aim at sense …[109]

Third, some poets error by going into too much detail, twenty pages to describe a house, he says.

In the first Canto of his work Boileau addresses mainly style, beginning by recommending avoidance of anything low in character. Most important, he advises variety.

> In writing vary your discourse and phrase;
> A frozen style, that neither ebbs nor flows,
> Instead of pleasing, makes us gape and doze.
> Those tedious authors are esteemed by none,
> Who tire us, humming the same heavy tone.

---

[107] Boileau, *The Art of Poetry*, quoted in Albert Cook, *The Art of Poetry* (Boston: Ginn, 1892), xlvi. The English translation is by Dryden, based on an earlier effort made in 1680 by William Soame.

[108] Ibid., 161.

[109] Ibid.

> Happy who in his verse can gently steer
> From grave to light, from pleasant to severe! …
>
> In all you write be neither low nor vile;
> The meanest theme may have a proper style.[110]

The choice of language and meter must please the ear, but one must be careful not to become so 'pleased with sound' as to depart from Reason. The language must be smooth and lofty, with no 'bombast, noise or affectation.' To do this requires time.

> Take time for thinking; never work in haste;
> And value not yourself for writing fast;
> A rapid poem, with such fury writ,
> Shows want of judgment, not wit.[111]

Then, reconsider 'a hundred times … polish, repolish … and sometimes add, but oftener take away.' Be your own most severe critic, he advises, but also find 'faithful friends' to give their opinion.

In the second Canto, Boileau discusses the nature of a number of specific forms. Pastoral poetry, inspired by similar works by the ancient Greek lyric poets, Boileau found often erred in either picturing characters too elegant for rural settings or too 'low and vile' to be suitable for poetry.

Interestingly enough, Boileau's principal observation regarding the Elegy is that the successful poet must first understand love.

> The Elegy, that loves a mournful style,
> With unbound hair weeps at a funeral pile;
> It paints the lover's torments and delights,
> A mistress flatters, threatens, and invites;
> But well these raptures if you'll makes us see,
> You must know love as well as poetry.[112]

The short Sonnet he found one of the most difficult challenges, with 'set rules for the just measure and the time.'

> A faultless sonnet, finished thus, would be
> Worth tedious volumes of loose poetry.[113]

---

110 Ibid., 163.
111 Ibid., 168.
112 Ibid., 175.
113 Ibid., 178.

The Madrigal 'may softer passions move, and breathe the tender ecstasies of love.' Boileau seemed to have little enthusiasm for the Epigram, but he observed it had a wide audience and that the Italians excelled in it. He objected in general to any form of immodest or obscene language, even in satire. 'Even a song,' he says, 'must have art and sense.'

Canto Three is devoted primarily to Tragedy, which was still composed in poetry. He begins with a nice definition: the purpose of tragedy is to delight us in tears.[114] This is no place, according to Boileau, for heavy, learned discourse, if your goal is to 'move the passions.' 'Confound my ears,' he says, 'but don't instruct my mind.'

Tragedy should observe the three unities of action, time and place, and not imitate the style of the Spanish, which give the observer a character's entire life in one day. He then extends this point to verisimilitude in general.

> Write not what cannot be with ease conceived;
> Some truths may be too strong to be believed.[115]

Similarly, the language and dress of characters should reflect time, local and climate. Boileau had no sympathy for modern revisions which show 'an antique hero like a modern ass.'

Sufficient variety, he finds, can be found by other methods, especially by language.

> Wise nature by variety does please;
> Clothe differing passions in differing dress:
> Bold anger in rough haughty words appears;
> Sorrow is humble and dissolves in tears …
> In sorrow you must softer methods keep,
> And, to excite our tears, yourself must weep.[116]

Boileau offers several guidelines for the choice of plot. First, in his view, no biblical stories are appropriate, for fear invention might weaken belief.

> The Gospel offers nothing to our thoughts
> But penitence, or punishment for faults;
> And mingling falsehoods with those mysteries,
> Would make our sacred truths appear like lies.[117]

In general the poet must avoid too much variety, which Boileau finds makes it dull, but, on the other hand, he recognizes the necessity for rich description to make 'narration lively.' To learn to do this requires time and experience.

---

114 Ibid., 185.
115 Ibid., 187.
116 Ibid., 193.
117 Ibid., 196.

> There must be care, and time, and skill, and pains,
> Not the first heat of inexperienced brains.[118]

For aid in his description, Boileau advises the young poet to study nature, as well as the persons of both town and court.

In the final Canto, Boileau addresses a number of ethical concerns regarding the art of poetry. First he contends that in art, unlike science or the trades, there is no second place, no 'mean betwixt the best and worst,' because no reader is indifferent. If the young poet cannot bear this burden, Boileau advises he be a mason, 'tis a useful art.'[119]

Next, the poet should have an educational goal, to place virtue before the viewer.

> Let all your thoughts to virtue be confined,
> Still offering nobler figures to our mind.
> I like not those loose writers, who employ
> Their guilty muse good manners to destroy,
> Who with false colors still deceive our eyes,
> And show us vice dressed in a fair disguise …
> A virtuous author, in his charming art,
> To please the sense needs not corrupt the heart;
> His heat will never cause a guilty fire;
> To follow virtue then be your desire.[120]

To this end, Boileau does not permit obscene expression, base jealousies or malicious motives. Above all, profit must not be the purpose of poetry.

> Write for immortal fame, nor ever choose
> Gold for the object of a generous muse.
> I know a noble wit may, without crime,
> Receive a lawful tribute for his time
> Yet I abhor those writers who despise
> Their honor, and alone their profits prize,
> Who their Apollo basely will degrade,
> And of a noble science make a trade.[121]

This leads him, in closing, to offer a rather extraordinary view of history.[122] Men began as beasts, feeding on herbs and drinking from rivers. They knew no law, 'their brutal force, on lust and rapine bent.' Only Reason changed these savages and led them from caves to

---

118 Ibid., 202.
119 Ibid., 210.
120 Ibid., 214ff.
121 Ibid., 216.
122 Ibid.

cities. It was poetry which made the accomplishments of Reason possible, beginning with the mythical poets, Orpheus, Amphion and Apollo, followed by Homer and Hesiod. Poetry did this by first charming the ear, and then engaging the heart. But as man became civilized, Boileau found that 'base flattery' and greed corrupted this ancient and noble art.

> Desire of gain dazzling the poets' eyes,
> Their works were filled with fulsome flatteries;
> Thus needy wits a vile revenue made,
> And verse became a mercenary trade.

'Debase not,' he pleas, 'with so mean a vice thy art.'[123]

Boileau had given so many rules for poetry that Fénelon became concerned that language itself had become the point.

> We are tempted to believe that [the French poet] have as much need to consider the arrangement of a syllable as they do the greatest feelings, the most vivid descriptions, and the boldest touches.[124]

Fénelon also wanted to remind his readers that poetry was still a performance medium, not a medium for the eyes.

> The painter and the poet have so close a connection: the one paints for the eyes, the other for the ears. Both the one and the other assume the duty of carrying objects over into the imagination of men. I have given you an example drawn from a poet, in order to make you better understand the matter; for portraiture is still more lively and stronger among the poets than among the orators. Poetry differs from simple eloquence only in this: that she paints with ecstasy and with bolder strokes …
>
> If one does not have this genius to portray, never can one impress things upon the soul of the listener—all is dry, flat, boring.[125]

Jean-Baptiste Du Bos (1670–1742), in his *Réflexions Critiques sur la Poésie et sur la Peinture* (1719) states that the purpose of poetry is not necessarily to provide instruction, but to give pleasure. This is done by stirring the heart of the listener and affecting his feelings.[126] The criterion for judging poetry is therefore whether it does this, and not whether it follows the 'rules.' Just as the listener must assume the innate ability of the poet, so the poet must assume the innate ability of the listener to judge correctly.

---

123 Ibid., 218.

124 *Fénelon's Letter to the French Academy* (1716), 74.

125 *Fénelon's Dialogues on Eloquence*, 93.

126 Ibid., 83ff.

The entire process takes place without the intervention of reason, which operates only afterwards to account for the decision made.[127]

Whether because of the earlier Baïf Academy, with its studies of ancient Greek poetry and music, or the two thousand years of continuous tradition of sung poetry, several of the important French poets of the seventeenth century valued their close associations with music. In the poetry of J. R. de Segrais (1624–1701) one finds references to a number of musical instruments and reference to music as having a special status among the liberal arts.[128] The poetry of Bernard Le Bovier de Fontenelle (1657–1757) also contains many references to music, including a young woman's study of the theorbo and another's passion for opera.[129] More interesting is his admission that he found it necessary to alter his poetry to make it fit the music, as in his *Endymion*.

Finch also offers here an interesting abstract of Fontenelle's view of the origin and earlier development of poetry and music.

> Song probably started as an imitation of bird-song and had no sooner been given a degree of form than, naturally, words were added, to which the rhythmic pattern of the music dictated the form of verse. Then came the early separation of poetry from music. Discriminating ears discovered that by dropping the music another sort of patterned music became enjoyable for its own sake. From then on, poetry, so to speak, gradually annexed musical formalism ... Finally there took place the curious reunion of the two arts with its reversal of their original relations. Nothing prevented independently composed verse from being set to music, since the music which had inspired its form still lingered in its lines ...
>
> Thus, once poetry had annexed as much of music's virtue as possible, music's function was regarded as being simply to heighten the effectiveness of a musical quality henceforth peculiar to poetry itself.

Another poet who was closely associated with music was A. Houdar, known as La Motte, who in fact wrote hymns, cantatas, and eight operas. His first successful opera, *L'Europe galante* (1697), has been called the first French opera to depart from the style of Lully by discarding the ancient heroic format.[130] One poet who began his career writing lyrics for opera was Jean-Baptiste Rousseau (1671–1741). His efforts were not considered successful and henceforth his references to opera were unflattering.[131]

---

127 Finch, *Individualism in French Poetry*, 88.

128 Ibid., 21.

129 Ibid., 47ff. In one of the most famous statements of the late Baroque, Fontenelle, accidentally walking into a young lady's dressing room when he was above ninety years of age, sighed, 'Oh, if I were only eighty!'

130 Ibid., 56ff.

131 Ibid., 101.

The poet Guillaume Amfrye, abbé de Chaulieu (1631–1720) was a personal companion of Lully, sometimes improvising verses to Lully's music at a dinner party in the latter's home.[132] Chaulieu made a point of hearing local music when he traveled and several times refers to his own poetry as his 'lyre.' He also altered his verses when they were to be set with music and in his *Ode contre l'Esprit* made the interesting observation that poetry, in aiming at eloquence, had lost the art of singing.

The poet, Jean-Baptiste Gresset (1709–1777), went so far as to admit that music was superior to poetry as a means of intimate communication.[133] For him it was through love of music that the poet learned to handle such aspects of poetry as genius, taste and its spiritual quality. He believed the goal in poetry of portraying the emotions [*l'art de peindre les sentiments*] was the same as in music. Poetry, he found, also shared with music the ability to also offer enjoyment and to rejoice the heart. With music, poetry and painting he found the same fundamental substance, Truth.

Finally, a few observations on the audience. La Bruyère, already in the seventeenth century, had become exhausted with critics.

> There is no work, however perfect, which would not vanish completely under censorious criticism, if its author chose to believe all the fault-finders who each cut out the passage they like least.[134]

Even in the case of the public, he held in some suspicion regarding their ability to judge.

> Many people go so far as to feel the merit of a manuscript which is read to them, who cannot speak openly in its favor until they have seen what success it will have on society once printed, or what treatment it will get from connoisseurs: they do not venture to express their opinion, and they want to be supported by the crowd and swept along by the multitude. Then they say that they were the first to appreciate the work, and that the public shares their point of view.[135]

By the early years of the eighteenth century, however, the developing importance of communicating feeling to the observer had changed this perspective, as we can see in Fénelon.

> One can only succeed with the consent of those for whom one writes. A writer should never take two steps at a time and should stop to see if he is followed by the multitude.[136]

---

132 Ibid., 68ff.
133 Ibid., 143ff.
134 La Bruyère, *Characters*, 30.
135 Ibid., 28.
136 *Fénelon's Letter to the French Academy* (1716), 75.

5 FRENCH PHILOSOPHERS, II

ON THE AESTHETICS OF MUSIC

During the seventeenth century and the first half of the eighteenth century in France, we believe it is safe to say that most musicians and philosophers thought of music with respect to its relationship with the communication of emotions. This, being a dramatic evolution from the old mathematics-based concepts of music of earlier Scholastic philosophies, is, after all, the very hallmark of the Baroque in music. Nevertheless, since the French philosophers of this period were much engaged in creating aesthetic definitions for the other arts, there were some philosophers who attempted to discover aesthetics principles in music. The central aim of this activity seems to have been to determine the 'rules' by which music could be judged. For example, Jean-Baptiste Du Bos, writing in 1719, attempts to equate music with other arts.

> The basic principles that govern music are thus similar to those that govern poetry and painting. Like poetry and painting, music is an imitation. Music cannot be good unless it conforms to the general rules that apply to the other arts on such matters as choice of subject and exactness of representation.[1]

On the other hand, Yves Marie André, in his *L'Essai sur le beau* (1741), presents an extended defense of why music is a higher art than painting. He primarily points to both the fact that music is heard live, while a painting is frozen in time, and that sounds are more expressive than colors.[2] André also makes some observations on the aesthetic qualities of the conceptual aspects of music. Consonance becomes distasteful with too frequent repetition. Dissonance he describes as both a kind of 'harmonic spice' but also the agent for communicating certain specific emotions, including wild anger, troublous dissension, the horrors of battle and tempestuous storms.[3] André also attempts to explain the nature of unity in music, an

---

[1] Du Bos (1670–1742), *Réflexions critiques sur la poësie et sur la peinture*, quoted in le Huray and Day, *Music and Aesthetics in the Eighteenth and Early-Nineteenth Centuries*, 21. Du Bos served in the Foreign Affairs department of the government and later served as secretary of the Académie française. Du Bos is wrong here, for unlike the other arts music is not an imitation.

[2] Yves Marie André (1675–1764), *L'Essai sur le beau* [1741], quoted in Peter le Huray and James Day, *Music and Aesthetics in the Eighteenth and Early-Nineteenth Centuries* (Cambridge: Cambridge University Press, 1981), 34ff. André was a professor of mathematics at Caen. The present Essay followed three earlier ones on the topics of artistic and moral beauty.

[3] Ibid., 32.

aesthetic principle so valued in the other arts. In music he finds this expressed most clearly in the rules of harmony.

Five years later Charles Batteux attempts to define in more concrete terms the requirements which expressive music and dance must have to be successful. These might be summarized as follows:

1. Every expression must conform to the thing that it expresses, as a dress is tailored for the body.
2. The fundamental character of the subject will determine the expression.
3. Clarity is of prime importance.
4. Each mood must be exactly right. It is the same with feelings as with color.
5. The expression must be lively, and frequently fine and delicate. Everyone is to some extent familiar with the passions. If we only paint the passions halfheartedly, we are no better than the historian or the person who slavishly imitates.
6. The expression must be straightforward and simple; everything that smacks of effort is painful and tiring.
7. The expression must be fresh, especially in music. Here he quotes, without source, a Latin expression, 'We are led to melody by natural instinct.'[4]

Modern clinical research demonstrates that Batteux was quite accurate in the last statement. Not only man, but lower animals appear to be born with some melodic patterns in place.

Finally, Batteux adds that even though music is highly controlled, by conventions of writing time, melody and harmony, these structures do not 'alter or destroy the natural meaning of sounds.' Measure and movement, he finds, are what give life to a composition.

On Beauty in Music

André is the only one of these French philosophers who attempts a detailed analysis of Beauty specifically in music. His purpose appears to have been to attempt to counter the influence of the humanists, with their emphasis on the emotions, by returning to the old focus on Reason. He begins by reflecting on the great reputation of music among the ancient Greeks, but observes that the opinion of some moderns is much more reserved.

> I am aware that some philosophers do not have such an exalted respect for music. Some even hold opinions that are quite to the contrary, claiming that feeling is the sole judge of harmony and that the pleasure of the ear is the only beauty that music affords. They argue moreover, that this pleasure is far too dependent on opinion, prejudice, convention and acquired habit to be the object of firm rules. And, they ask, is not the proof of this obvious enough? Are there any two nations whose musical tastes are the same? Europeans and Orientals, French, Italians, Germans,

---

4 Batteux, *Les beaux-arts réduits à un même principe*, quoted in le Huray and Day, *Music and Aesthetics in the Eighteenth and Early-Nineteenth Centuries*, 50ff.

Spaniards and Englishmen, Turks and Tartars even, has not each race its own particular music which it unquestioningly values above all others? Since each nation is evidently charmed and satisfied by its own music, what more is to be said? Nothing indeed, so far as those peoples are concerned who only conduct their lives and their thoughts in a haphazard way. But for thinking people—for men—something more is needed, namely that in all pleasures reason must at least be on an equal footing with the senses.[5]

André proposes to 'place reason on an equal footing with the senses' by proposing that beauty in music exists on three levels, which he lists as,

1. There is an essential musical beauty that is absolute, wholly independent of human institutions and even divine.
2. There is a natural beauty which comes from the Creator and is not connected to human taste or opinion.
3. There is an artificial musical beauty that is to some degree arbitrary but which none the less is dependent on the eternal laws of harmony.[6]

To attempt to explain the first of these, André imagines a conversation with a person who has just left a concert, while still filled with the impressions of the music. André asks the listener what exactly pleased him in the concert. In the end all the listener can put into words is that he listened to the ordering of the sounds, the propriety of the progressions, the regularity of the flow of time, the tempo, the balance of the ensemble, etc. We would regard this answer as a 'left-brained' one, for the listener only mentions conceptual aspects of the performance. But for André it was apparently not conceptual enough, for he proposes there must be,

a purer pleasure than the sweetness of the actual sounds, and a beauty that does not have its roots in the senses, a particular beauty that charms the mind and which the mind alone perceives and judges.[7]

What this purer pleasure is, in André's view, is a connection between the music and some innate form of rational understanding within the listener.

In other words, sir, during the time that this large ensemble of sonorous instruments was impressing your ear with pleasurable sounds, you experienced deep down within you a master of music who beat time, if I may put it thus, to show how right the music was, and who revealed its principles by means of a light that was superior to that of the senses. These principles are grounded in order, in the structural beauty of the piece, in harmonic numbers, in the rule of proportion and harmonious progression, and in the idea of propriety, a sacred law that allots each part its position, its conclusion and the right path by which to reach its end. Thus while all

---

5   Ibid., 28.
6   Ibid.
7   Ibid., 29ff.

those who took part in the concert were reading their individual parts, you were also reading yours, written in eternal and ineffaceable notes from the great book of reason which is open to all receptive minds.

By the second form of beauty, that which comes from the Creator, André means natural things, beginning with the physics of music, in particular the overtone series. But also he has in mind the body of the listener, which has a kind of receptive harmony: the nerves stretched over bones like strings of an instrument, arteries which beat time and especially the physical components of the ear, throat and mouth. Thus he finds a natural sympathy between the vibrations of music and the body, although he cannot explain how it works. Further, he regards this relationship as the key to understanding emotions in music.

> There is a natural sympathy between certain sounds and the emotions of the soul. There is no question here of explaining how this comes about; all that we need to know is this indubitable fact. There are sounds which have a secret understanding with the heart, and this we cannot deny. Lively sounds inspire courage, languishing sounds appease, laughing sounds cheer, mournful sounds sadden, majestic sounds uplift the soul, harsh sounds irritate, gentle sounds soften.[8]

The third kind of beauty in music, André finds, is that which belongs to the human contribution, including the conventions of art and taste in composition and performance.

On Taste in Music

An early French dictionary of music by Sebastien de Brossard, while it is not addressed to Taste as such, is interesting in its documentation of the wide variety of styles which were generally recognized as early as 1703. His final sentence also implies an aesthetic ranking of these styles.

> Style means, in general, the particular manner or fashion of expressing ideas, of writing, or of doing some other thing. In music, it signifies the manner in which every individual composes, plays or teaches, and all this is very diversified according to the genius of the authors, the country and the nation: as well as according to the materials, the places, the times, the subjects, the expressions, etc. Thus one is wont to say the style of Carissimi, of Lully, of Lambert, etc.; the style of the Italians, of the French, of the Spaniards, etc. The style of gay and joyful music is very different from the style of grave and serious music … therefore we have different epithets in order to distinguish among all these different characters, such as ancient and modern style, Italian, French, and German style, ecclesiastic, dramatic, and chamber style, etc … The Italians

---

8 Ibid., 31.

have expressions for all that we have mentioned, and we shall explain them in the order of their importance.⁹

The most important publication which attempted to define taste in music was by Jean Laurent le Cerf de La Viéville (1647–1710), a French aristocrat who was a strong supporter of Lully and who published a response to Raguenet's *Parallèle des Italiens et des Français* in 1704, called *Comparaison de la musique italienne et de la musique française*. The second part of this publication is an interesting discussion on 'Good Taste in Music,' set in the form of an imaginary discussion between two anonymous noble ladies and the author, whom is called a Chevalier. First, the 'Countess du B' asks if the Chevalier will teach her 'how to distinguish perfectly the beauties of music.' The answer is, unwittingly, a reference to the left and right hemispheres of the brain, for he weighs the merits of judging by feeling versus 'rules.' One might also see this as a perfect representation of the process of modern competitions in musical performance.

> There are two great ways of knowing good and bad things: by our inward feeling and by the rules. We know the good and the bad only by these means. What we see and what we hear pleases us or displeases us. If one listens only to the inward feeling, one will say, 'It seems to me that that is good, or that it is not.' On the other hand, the masters, the skilled, following the observations they have made, have established precepts in every craft. These comprised whatever had seemed to them to be the best and the surest. The established precepts are the rules, and if one consults them regarding what one sees and what one hears, one will say that this is good or is not good, according to such and such a rule, or for such and such a reason. These masters were men; were they incapable of being deceived? The authority of the rules is considerable, but after all it is not a law. Inward feeling is still less sure, because each should distrust his own, should distrust that it is what it should be. Who will dare flatter himself that he has a fortunate nature, endowed with sure and clear ideas of the good, the beautiful, the true? We have all brought into the world the foundation of these ideas, more or less clear and certain, but since our birth we have received, and this it is sad and painful to correct, a thousand false impressions, a thousand dangerous prejudices, which have weakened and stifled within us the voice of uncorrupted nature.
>
> I think that in this uncertainty and confusion the remedy is to lend to the inward feeling the support of the rules, that our policy should be correct and strengthen the one by the other, and that it is this union of the rules and the feeling which forms good taste. To listen attentively to the inward feeling, to disentangle it, and then to purify it by the application of the rules; there is the art of judging with certainty, and therefore I am persuaded that good taste is the most natural feeling, corrected or confirmed by the best rules.¹⁰

---

9 Sebastien de Brossard (1654–1730), *Dictionnaire de Musique* [Paris, 1703], quoted in Paul Henry Lang, 'Musical Thought of the Baroque: The Doctrine of Temperaments and Affections,' in William Hays, ed., *Twentieth-Century Views of Music History* (New York: Scribner's, 1972), 197.

10 Le Cerf de la Viéville, 'Traité du bon goût en musique,' in Oliver Strunk, *Source Readings in Music History* (New York: Norton, 1950), 491ff.

The Countess now begs the Chevalier to please teach her the rules for judging music.

> There are little rules and great rules, madame, and we have touched upon both sorts in our conversation. The little rules are those of composition, on which twenty treatises have been written, of which I do not cite a single one, because I am waiting for somebody to write a twenty-first one that will be good.[11]

The Chevalier gives, as an example of a 'little' rule, the formula that low or high notes should accompany low or lofty concepts. As for the great rules,

> A piece of music should be natural, expressive, harmonious. In the first place, natural, or rather, simple, for simplicity is the first part, the first sign of the natural, which is almost equally an ingredient in these three qualities. In the second place, expressive. In the third place, harmonious, melodious, pleasing—take your choice. These are the three great, the three important rules which one must apply to the airs that the inward feeling has approved, and it is they which in the last resort decide.[12]

As an afterthought the Chevalier adds another rule, 'always to abhor excess. Let us make it a habit and a merit to have contempt, distaste, and aversion without quarter for all that contains anything superfluous.'

The Countess, still not satisfied, wants a simple rule to test whether her judgments were correct. She says, for example,

> Am I not justified in saying that my heart, my ear, and all the rules agree in persuading me that 'Bois épais' is a charming air. And it is by Lully, a new pledge of the correctness of my taste. This other air does not flatter my ear, nor does it touch me; it has neither sweetness nor expression. And it is by Charpentier. Yes, I am judging it rightly; it is bad. Would that be bad reasoning, Chevalier?[13]

The Chevalier cautions the Countess on the dangers of judging on the basis of the composer's name or reputation and, finally, offers her a practical means of judging music.

> You will need to carry in your head two airs representing the two qualities, one good and one bad; that is, good and bad by almost unanimous consent, and two symphonies, one good and one bad, and you must have all their beauties and all their faults at the tip of your fingers. You must have the knowledge of the least of the beauties and faults of these two airs and these two symphonies ever at command and thoroughly familiar, and compare with these models the airs and symphonies you hear.
>
> These latter you will esteem in proportion to their resemblance to the others, and the idea of this resemblance alone, accordingly as it strikes you more or less forcibly, will cause you to say,

---

11 Ibid., 492.

12 Ibid., 493.

13 Ibid., 495.

with greater or less force, 'I like that air; that symphony does not please me.' I am convinced that the ablest connoisseur should not neglect to combine with the judgments based on reasoning these judgments by comparison, from which will be derived an additional clearness, will adapted to confirm our feelings.[14]

The Countess says that if she understands correctly, the more perfectly an air complies with the rules the better it is, and the further it departs from them the worse.' In his response, the Chevalier touches on the important aesthetic principle of universality. To put it in the form of a question, can one trust the judgment of the masses?

There are precepts with regard to this matter. First, infringements of the little rules are as nothing in comparison with violations of the great ones. Listen to a lesson of Holy Week which begins with a sixth, but go out when one begins with a roulade. In the second place, the pleasures of the heart being, by the principles we have established, superior to those of the ear, an air which offends against the laws that are directed toward touching the heart offends more than one which disregards merely those which aim to satisfy the ear. Let us forgive two similar cadences which are too near to each other, or a poor thorough bass, but let us never forgive a melody which is cold and forced …

In the third place, the most beautiful thing is that which is equally admired by the people and by the learned or by all the connoisseurs. Then, after this, I should admire more that which is generally admired by all the people. Finally, that which is admired by all the learned. The learned are the masters of music, the musicians by profession, stubborn about rules. The people is the multitude, the great mass, which has not risen to special knowledge and has only its natural feeling as its guide and as the warrant for its judgments. The connoisseurs are those who are neither altogether of the people nor altogether learned, half the one and half the other, a shade less learned than of the people, that is to say, crediting the rules a shade less than natural feeling …

As to the half-learned, they are in music what they are in any art, in anything whatever, the most contemptible and the most insupportable of all men.[15]

The other noble lady present, the 'Marquis des E,' contributes an interesting observation on universality, as measured by the response of the public, and the recommendation of a system for using that judgment.

That characterization of the people, the connoisseurs, and the learned makes me realize that we must listen to the reasoning of the learned, defer to the feeling of the connoisseurs, and study how the people are moved by theatrical representations can infinitely clarify and facilitate our judgments and help us to make them true. At the first three representations of an opera, let us concern ourselves only with ourselves; it will keep us sufficiently occupied … But at the fourth and later performances let us apply ourselves to studying in what manner and how greatly the people are touched. The value and the degree of value of pieces will certainly be revealed by the impression which they make on the heart of the people and by the vivacity of that impression.

---

14 Ibid., 495ff.
15 Ibid., 496ff.

> When Armida works herself up to stab Rinaldo in the last scene of the second act, I have twenty times seen everybody seized by terror, holding his breath, motionless, all the soul in the ears and eyes, until the air of the violin which ends the scene gave leave to breathe, than at that point breathing again with a murmur of delight and admiration. I had no need to reason. That unanimous response of the people told me with certainty that the scene was of overpowering beauty.[16]

When the noble lady suggests that perhaps one should form one's taste after that of the highest nobles, the Chevalier makes a comment which clearly reflects the beginning of the Enlightenment and the coming Revolution.

> In the matter of taste, mademoiselle, great nobles are only men like ourselves, whose name proves little. Each has his voice and the voices are equal, or at least it is not their quality which will determine their weight.[17]

Another issue which arises in this discussion is whether good taste demands that one give praise where praise is due the performer. The Chevalier adds,

> That is not enough; the degree of praise must correspond to the degree of value of the work. To praise more or less than this is bad taste, and I am persuaded that here is the reef on which the greatest number of people are wrecked. He who can praise with reason and in due proportion will be of a perfect connoisseur.[18]

On the Perception of Music

It is surprising that so few early philosophers concerned themselves with the nature of the perception of music, for it is here that music is so different from the other arts. By this we mean that while the other arts are only a representation of something, music is real, a direct communication between composer and listener. Batteux, the only one of these French writers to discuss perception at all, does not refer to this distinction, but he does touch on a very valid and important point: we do not understand music, as listeners, in anything remotely near the conceptual aspects of it we study in school.

> If I were to say that I could derive no pleasure from a lecture that I did not understand, my confession would in no way seem strange. But if I ventured to say the same of a piece of music, people would ask whether I considered myself enough of a connoisseur to appreciate the merits of so carefully constructed and fine a composition. I would dare to reply yes, for it is a matter of feeling [and not conceptual knowledge]. I do not [while listening to music] pretend in any way

---

16 Ibid., 499.
17 Ibid., 505.
18 Ibid., 504.

> to calculate the sounds, their interrelationships or their connection with the ear. I am speaking here neither of oscillations, string vibrations, nor mathematical proportions. I leave such speculations to learned theorists; these are akin to the grammar and dialectic of a lecture which I can appreciate without going into such details. Music speaks to me in tones: this language is natural to me. If I do not understand it, art has corrupted nature rather than perfected her.[19]

This is perfectly correct, but as he continues, returning to the error of including music and painting in the same category, he seems to lose touch with the importance of what he has just written.

> A musical composition must be judged in the same way as a picture. In the picture I find shapes and colors that I can comprehend; it charms and touches me. What would we think of a painter who was content to throw on the canvas bold shapes and masses of the liveliest color without reference to any known object? The same argument can be applied to music. There is no disparity here, and if there were it would strengthen my argument. The ear is said to be much finer than the eye.[20] I am therefore much more capable of judging a musical composition than a painting.

Curiously, he inserts a footnote here which is entirely inaccurate and is a primary contradiction to his point about listening to feeling in music and not conceptual detail. In the footnote he says a simple song has meaning, but is addressed to the common man, whereas multi-part harmonized music requires 'some kind of musical erudition' to understand its meaning. This is wrong, of course, as abundant evidence all over the earth daily proves people can appreciate music while knowing nothing about it.

Finally, we find some particularly curious observations by Montesquieu on the perception of music under the influence of climate. Under the title, 'Of the Difference of Men in different climates,' he contends,

> Cold air constringes the extremities of the external fibres of the body; this increases their elasticity, and favors the return of the blood from the extreme parts of the heart. It contracts those very fibres; consequently it increases also their force. On the contrary, warm air relaxes and lengthens the extremes of the fibres; of course it diminishes their force and elasticity.
>
> People are therefore more vigorous in cold climates. Here the action of the heart and the reaction of the extremities of the fibres are better performed, the temperature of the humors is greater, the blood moves more freely towards the heart, and reciprocally the heart has more power.

As an example of the influence of climate on music, he observes,

> As climates are distinguished by degrees of latitude, we might distinguish them also in some measure by those of sensibility. I have been at the opera in England and in Italy, where I have seen the same pieces and the same performers: and yet the same music produces such different

---

19 Batteux, *Les beaux-arts*, 48ff.

20 All ancient and medieval philosophers argued just the reverse.

effects on the two nations: one is so cold and phlegmatic, and the other so lively and enraptured, that it seems almost inconceivable.[21]

ON THE PURPOSES OF MUSIC

During the early eighteenth century, in part as a reflection of the Enlightenment, one rarely finds the older purpose for music as being associated with God. But that is what came to mind for André Maugars, in his report of his visit to Rome in 1639, when he recalled a famous Italian singer, Leonora Baroni.

> When she passes from one note to another, she sometimes makes you feel the divisions between the enharmonic and the chromatic modes with such skill and artistry that there is no one who is not greatly pleased by this beautiful and difficult method of singing. She does not need to ask the help of a theorbo player or a violinist, without one of which her singing would be imperfect, for she herself plays these instruments perfectly. Finally, I had the good fortune to hear her sing several times, more than thirty different songs, with second and third verses, which she had composed herself. I must tell you that she did me the special favor of singing with her mother and her sister, her mother playing the lyre, her sister the harp, and she the theorbo. This concert, composed of three beautiful voices and three different instruments, so affected my senses and so ravished my spirit that I forgot my mortal condition and thought I was among the angels enjoying the delights of the blessed. So to address you as a Christian, the purpose of music is, by touching our hearts, to raise them to God, because it is a sample in this world of the eternal joy, and its purpose is not by lascivious gestures to lead us to vice, toward which we are only too much inclined by nature.[22]

On the Communication of Feeling

The more common purpose of music given by these French writers was relative to the communication of feeling, a topic which is a hallmark of the Baroque itself. We see this already very early in the seventeenth century. David de Flurance Rivault, chief tutor to the young Louis XIII, wrote a treatise, 'L'art d'embellir' (1702), which touches briefly on music and includes his belief in the power of music to affect man. He speaks of a certain kind of music which has a tranquilizing effect, and later,

---

21 Charles de Secondat, Baron de Montesquieu, *The Spirit of Laws* (1748), 102ff. He also concludes that the English have a 'disrelish of everything' and an 'impatience of temper' which makes concentration difficult.

22 André Maugars, 'Response faite à un curieux sur le Sentiment de la Musique d'Italie, Ecrite à Rome le premier Octobre 1639,' quoted in MacClintock, *Readings in the History of Music in Performance*, 122ff.

> A well-measured voice can rejoice an afflicted person ... The voice can sometimes bring forth contentment and love; sometimes it can carry away the minds of the hearers to rage and fury: and then again quieten these fumes and calm impassioned souls.[23]

In another place in this same treatise, Rivault provides the memorable phrase, 'The way to grow beautiful is to grow wise, for the wisdom of the soul is a cosmetic for the face.'[24]

Raguenet gives enthusiastic praise for the expression of emotions in Italian music.

> As the Italians are much more brisk than the French, so are they more sensible of the passions and consequently express them more lively in all their productions. If a storm or rage is to be described in a symphony, their notes give us so natural an idea of it that our souls can hardly receive a stronger impression from the reality than they do from the description; everything is so brisk and piercing, so impetuous and affecting, that the imagination, the senses, the soul, and the body itself are all betrayed into a general transport; it is impossible not to be borne down with the rapidity of these movements. A symphony of furies shakes the soul; it undermines and overthrows it in spite of all its care; the artist himself, whilst he is performing it, is seized with an unavoidable agony; he tortures his violin; he racks his body; he is no longer master of himself, but is agitated like one possessed with an irresistible motion.
>
> If, on the other side, the symphony is to express a calm and tranquility, which requires a quite different style, they however execute it with an equal success. Here the notes descend so low that the soul is swallowed with them in the profound abyss. Every string of the bow is of an infinite length, lingering on a dying sound which decays gradually until at last it absolutely expires. Their symphonies of sleep insensibly steal the soul from the body and so suspend its faculties and operations that, being bound up, as it were, in the harmony that entirely possesses and enchants it, it is as dead to everything else as if all its powers were captivated by a real sleep ...
>
> But there is one thing beyond all this which neither the French nor any other nation besides the Italians in the world ever attempted; for they will sometimes unite in a most surprising manner the tender with the sprightly, as may be instanced in that celebrated air, 'Mai non si vidde ancor più bella fedeltà,' which is the softest and most tender of any in the world, and yet its accompaniment is as lively and piercing as ever was composed. These different characters are they able to unite so artfully that, far from destroying a contrary by its contrary, they make the one serve to embellish the other.[25]

Philosophically speaking, the most impressive French writer, among the group we have been examining here, is Jean-Baptiste Du Bos. His thinking was very perceptive and everything he writes on the subject of the expression of emotions in music stands up very well today. Du Bos, an avid opera fan, viewed everything from the aesthetic perspective of Nature. He finds music the most effective of all the arts in speaking directly to the feelings of the observer. It follows, therefore, that he places vocal music above instrumental music, since the

---

23 'L'art d'embellir,' quoted in Yates, *The French Academies of the Sixteenth Century*, 280, fn. 5.
24 Ibid., 279.
25 François Raguenet, 'Parallèle des Italiens et des Français,' (1702), quoted in Strunk, *Source Readings*, 478ff.

latter lacks the verbal precision to exactly determine the emotion being expressed. He did, however, admit the contribution of the orchestral accompaniment in strengthening emotions.

> Do we not perceive that these symphonies enflame us, calm us, soften us, and in short, operate upon us, as effectually almost as Corneille's or Racine's verses.[26]

It is a particularly accurate and important point he makes when he reminds his readers that spoken words are mere symbols of emotion, but carry no actual emotional content in themselves. Sung words, on the other hand, carry the direct emotional meaning of the music. His placing this in the context of Nature is also interesting, for all philologists today consider sung utterances reflecting emotions to precede speech in early man by a considerable period of time. Thus this primitive, emotional communication might well be thought of as 'the work of nature herself.'

> Just as the painter imitates the forms and colors of nature so the musician imitates the tones of the voice—its accents, sighs and inflections. He imitates in short all the sounds that nature herself uses to express the feelings and passions. All these sounds, as we have already shown, have a wonderful power to move us because they are the signs of the passions that are the work of nature herself, from whence they have derived their energy. Spoken words, on the other hand are only arbitrary symbols of the passions. The spoken word only derives its meaning and value from man-made conventions and it has only limited geographical currency.[27]

He adds that the additional 'energy' which words have when sung is what led to the recitative style and hence opera.[28]

Another very important aesthetic point which Du Bos makes is his clarification that the importance of music is not in its external, conceptual features.

> Just as some people are more attracted to the color of pictures than to the expression of passions, so others are only sensible to the pleasures of melody or even to the richness of harmony, and pay not the slightest attention to whether the melody is an effective imitation, or care whether it is consonant with the words to which it is set. Such people do not require the composer to match his melodic lines to the feelings that the words suggest, but are content that his melodies should be pleasing, and even singular. As far as they are concerned it is enough that the occasional word in a recitative shall be treated expressively. There are far too many musicians who are of this mind, and who act as though music were incapable of anything more …
>
> Musical compositions that fail to move us can unequivocally be equated with pictures that have no merit other than their coloring, or with poems that are no more than well-constructed verses. In poetry and painting, technical excellence must serve to express the insights of genius, and to reveal those imaginative beauties that constitute the imitation of nature. In the same

---

26　Jean-Baptiste Du Bos, *Réflexions*, 18.

27　Ibid.,18.

28　Ibid.,19.

way, harmonic richness and variety, ornamentation and melodic originality must be used solely to create and embellish the musical imitation of the language of nature and the passions. The science of composition is, so to speak, the servant which the genius of the musician must keep under his thumb, just as the poet of genius must control his talent for writing verse … Genius is essential to expression, whereas even without genius, it is still possible to compose scholarly music and to produce excellent rhymes.[29]

In Part III of his '*Les beaux-arts réduits à un même principe*,' Batteux presents a brilliant discussion of man's forms of communication. He begins with the definition, 'Men have three means of expressing their ideas and their feelings: speech, the tone of the voice, and gesture.'[30] In defining how these three differ, he begins with two extraordinary deductions, which have since been confirmed in clinical research: that emotions are genetic and that they speak directly 'without detour' through Reason, which is to say, the left hemisphere of the brain.

> Speech expresses passion only by means of the ideas to which the feelings are tied, and as though by reflection. Tone and gesture reach the heart directly and without any detour. In a word, speech is a language of institution, which men have formed for communicating their ideas more distinctly: gestures and tones are like the dictionary of plain nature; they contain a language that we all know upon being born and of which we make use to announce everything that is related to our needs and to the conservation of our being: also they are vivid, short, energetic. What better basis for the arts whose object is to move the soul, than a language all of whose expressions are rather those of humanity itself than those of men![31]

Batteux next proposes that there are three levels of sophistication to these forms of communication. The most elemental level, of speech, tone and gesture, express simple nature, 'the naive portrait of our thoughts and feelings.' The second level is when 'nature is polished by the help of art, to add embellishment to utility.' In the third level, 'one has in view only pleasure,' which is to say, Art.

> From which I conclude first: That the principal object of music and of dance should be the imitation of feeling or of passions: instead of which that of poetry is principally the imitation of actions. But as passions and actions are almost always united in nature, and as they should also be together in the arts, there will be this difference of poetry from music and dance: that in poetry the passions will be employed as means or motives that prepare the action and produce it; and in music and dance the actions will be only a sort of canvas destined to carry, sustain, conduct, and connect the different passions that the artist wishes to express.

From our perspective he has defined correctly here the very essence of music: to express feelings. He elaborates on these distinctions, making the important point that poetry is

---

29 Ibid., 21ff.
30 Batteux, *Les beaux-arts*, 260.
31 Ibid., 260ff.

still 'the language of the mind' whereas music is [a language] of feelings and passions. We would say today, poetry is tied by language to the left hemisphere of the brain, as language, while the experience of music belongs to the province of the right hemisphere, which also contains the emotions.

> Actions and passions are nearly always united and mixed together in everything men do. They are produced and announced reciprocally. They should therefore nearly always be together in the arts. When artists present an action, it should be animated by some passion; similarly when they present passions, they should be sustained by an action. That does not need to be verified by examples. But as the arts, considering the means they employ to express, may be appropriate to express one part of nature rather than another, it follows that the part that should dominate in them is that which is related most to this means of expression.
>
> Thus poetry having chosen speech, which is most particularly the language of the mind, and music and dance having taken for themselves, the one the tones of the voice, and the other the movements of the body, and these two sorts of expressions being dedicated above all to feeling, true poets have had to attach themselves above all to actions and to discourse, and true musicians to feelings and to passions.[32]

Regarding opera, therefore, he says it is the communication of feelings, not the plot, we are interested in. Furthermore, any complex ideas depending on language, such as metaphors, plays on words, etc., 'resists music so strongly.' In contrast, he says, 'that which is an expression of feeling seems to be disposed to it of itself. Tones are half-formed in words; it demands only a little art to draw them out.'

> It is with dance as with music. Declamation necessarily languishes when the soul is not moved, and when there is a question only of instructing: because then all the movements of the body signifying almost nothing, they give no pleasure to those who see them. A gesture is beautiful only when it portrays grief, tenderness, pride; the soul, in a word: if we are dealing with a logical argument, it is ridiculous of itself, because it is useless to the thing one is saying: one reasons in cold blood: and if in quiet reasoning there is a small gesture and a certain natural tone that accompany it, this is to make visible that the soul of the one who is reasoning desires that the truth he is teaching persuade the heart while he is trying to convince the mind of it. Thus it is always feeling which produces that expression.[33]

Batteux does make one fundamental mistake, one often made, by including music in the same category with the other arts. Music is fundamentally different from the other arts in its capacity as a live expressive art form, in which the communication from composer to listener is direct. Arts such as painting and sculpture are representative arts and Batteux is thoroughly incorrect in the way he associates music with them.

---

32 Ibid., 262.

33 Ibid., 263. One could not hope to form a more perfect definition of the art of conducting than is found here.

> There is no need to repeat here that melodic lines and dance movements are only imitations, artificial structures of tones and poetic gestures that are merely realistic. The passions are here as imaginary as are actions in poetry. They are equally and wholly the creation of genius and taste: nothing about them is true, everything is artificial. And if it sometimes happens that the musician or dancer is involved in the actual passion that he is expressing this is entirely accidental and it has nothing to do with the purpose of the art; it is like a painting which ought to be on canvas, but which is found to be on a living skin. Art is only created to deceive.[34]

Batteux concludes this particular discussion with another curious juxtaposition of thought. He begins with a marvelous testimonial to the fact that the importance of music, the feelings, cannot be communicated in words. Here he appears to have been one of a number of early philosophers who seemed to understand, through either intuition or deduction, that the feelings and music of the right hemisphere of the brain are entirely separate from the words and language of the left hemisphere. But, precisely because he was not privileged to the findings of modern brain research—that this is exactly how the two hemispheres are organized and that, while separate, each is valid, and because he mistakenly associated music with painting and sculpture, he unfortunately failed to understand the true significance of his own first two paragraphs.

> It is true, you may say, that a melodic line can express certain passions: love, for instance, or joy, or sadness. But for every passion that can be identified there are a thousand others that cannot be put into words.
> That is indeed so, but does it follow that these are pointless? It is enough that they are felt; they do not have to be named. The heart has its own understanding that is independent of words. When it is touched it has understood everything. Moreover, just as there are great things that words cannot reach, so there are subtle things that words cannot capture, above all things that concern the feelings.
> We may conclude then that although music may be the most exactly calculated art in respect of its tones, and the most geometrically structured in respect of its consonances, even with these qualities it may well have no significance whatever. The analogy might be with a prism, which produces the finest colors but no picture, or with a color keyboard the colors and color sequences of which might amuse the eye, but which would certainly weary the mind.[35]

Finally, he makes another deduction, which is confirmed by modern clinical research, that it is the specific choice of notes for the melody which allow music 'to take on the character of the various passions.'[36] It is in this respect that he finds justification for dissonance in music.

> Not only does dissonance add salt and seasoning, but it serves in a particular way to characterize the musical expression. Nothing is so irregular as the course of the passions of love, anger and

---

34 Ibid., 48.

35 Ibid., 50

36 Ibid., 53.

discord. The voice becomes shrill and then suddenly it takes on an explosive quality, in order to express them. Should art not soften such natural asperities, the truthfulness of the expression will compensate for its roughness. It is the composer's task to use dissonance with care, restraint and intelligence.

ON THE ROLE OF MUSIC IN SOCIETY

During the early years of the eighteenth century there are some interesting discussions on the proper role music should play in society. First, however, it might be interesting to read some descriptions of how La Bruyère found music in society during the immediately previous period.

> At a sermon, at a concert, or in a picture gallery, you may hear precisely contrary opinions uttered to right and to left of you, about precisely the same thing. This inclines me to think that in any sort of work one may venture to include what is good and what is bad; some will like the good things and some the bad.[37]
>
> ......
>
> A man who knows five or six technical terms and nothing more can profess to be a connoisseur in music, in painting, in architecture or in good food; he thinks he gets more pleasure than others do from hearing, seeing and eating; he takes in his fellows, and he is taken in himself.[38]

Even at court, he found little sophistication.

> It is a long-established custom at Court to give pensions and grant favors to a musician, a dancing-master, a comedian, a flute-player, a flatterer, a time-server; they have their accepted merits, their unquestioned and recognized talents, which amuse the great and allow them to relax from their greatness; everyone knows that Favier is a fine dancer and that Lorenzani composes fine motets.[39]

Although the noble should have more taste, La Bruyère found only contentment with the status quo.

> Princes, without being instructed in the rules of art, have a natural sense of comparison: they are born and brought up amidst the finest things, and as it were in the very center of these; and

---

37 La Bruyère, *Characters*, 220ff. Jean de La Bruyère (1645–1696) was born to a bourgeois family, studied law and in 1673 became Treasurer-General of Finance in Caen.

38 Ibid., 146.

39 Ibid., 263.

they compare with these whatever they read and see or hear. Anything that is too much unlike Lully, Racine and Le Brun stands condemned.[40]

One comment, however, seems to reflect the concerns of the coming generation as La Bruyère seems to understand that music should have a higher purpose.

> Men of noble nature seem moved by entertainments, plays and music to a closer and deeper sympathy with the distress of their kindred or friends.[41]

As the discussion of the role of music in society began to attract more serious philosophic interest, we find the discussion once again centered in the practice of ancient Greece, as we can see in Fénlon's letter to the Academy in 1716.

> I turn to the pagans themselves for a judgment on this question. Plato permits no music with the effeminate tones of the Lydians in his Republic. Further, the Lacedaemonians excluded from theirs all complicated instruments which could soften the heart. Music intended only to soothe the ear is merely an amusement for weak and lazy people and is unworthy of a well-regulated republic. Music is good only insofar as it agrees with the sense of the words and as the words themselves inspire virtuous sentiments. Painting, sculpture, and other fine arts should have the same end. Eloquence should also be a part of a design wherein pleasure exists only to counterbalance evil passions and to make virtue attractive …
>
> Poetry is more serious and useful than common people believe. Since the origin of mankind, religion has consecrated poetry to its own use. Before men had a revealed text, the sacred songs they knew by heart preserved the memory of creation and the tradition of God's miracles.[42]

In his *Dialogues on Eloquence*, Fénelon discusses the role of music in ancient and contemporary societies at some length. Here it seems clear that he regards some form of education to be an important necessity for the arts.

> A. You would wish citizens to dislike idleness and to be occupied with very serious matters and to strive always towards the public good?
> B. Yes indeed.
>
> ……
>
> A. You would not permit any of the sciences or any of the arts which serve only for pleasure, for amusement, and for curiosity? What would become of those which belonged neither to the tasks of domestic life nor to the duties of public life?
> B. I would banish them from my republic …
> A. But what would you do with musicians? Would you not agree with those ancient Greeks who never separated the useful from the pleasant? The Greeks, who developed music and poetry,

---

40 Ibid., 160.
41 Ibid., 199.
42 *Fénelon's Letter to the French Academy* (1716), 66ff.

united as one, to so high a perfection, intended that these should serve to ennoble the heart and to inspire great passions. It was by music and poetry that they prepared themselves for battle; they took musicians and musical instruments to war. In line with this came also the trumpets and drums to stir them to an enthusiasm and a sort of madness which they called divine. It was by music and the cadence of verse that they softened ferocious tribes. It was by this harmony that they instilled wisdom along with pleasure into the depths of their children's hearts. They made them sing Homer's verse in order to inspire them in an agreeable way with a contempt for death, for riches, and for the pleasures which weaken the soul; and to stir them to the love of glory, liberty, and native land. Even their dances had a serious aim in their way, and it is certain that they did not dance solely for pleasure. We see by the example of David that oriental peoples regarded dancing as a serious art, analogous to music and poetry. A thousand precepts were mingled in their fables and poems; thus the gravest and most austere philosophy showed itself only with a laughing face. This appeared again in the priest's mysterious dances, which the pagans mingled with their ceremonies for the festivals of the gods. All the arts which consist in melodious sounds, or in movements of the body, or in the use of language—in a word, music, dancing, eloquence, poetry—were devised only to express the passions and to inspire them in the very act of expressing them. By such means as these, mankind wished to impress great thoughts upon the human soul and to bring to men lively and striking pictures of the beauty of virtue and the ugliness of evil. Thus all these arts appeared to be for pleasure, but were in reality among the ancients a part of their deepest striving for morality and religion. Even the chase was an apprenticeship for war. Pleasures the most attractive contained some virtuous lesson. From that source there came to Greece so many heroic virtues, admired by all ages. This first system of education was changed, it is true, and it had indeed its own extreme defects. Its essential defect was that it was founded upon a false and dangerous religion.

C. You just said that this first system of education was changed. Please do not forget to explain that to us.

A. Yes, it was changed. Virtue gives true refinement. But soon, if you do not guard against it, refinement degenerates little by little. The Asiatic Greeks were the first to be corrupted; the Ionians became effeminate; all that coast of Asia became a playhouse of luxury ... All Greece was infected with it. Pleasure, which ought only to be the means to inculcate wisdom, usurped the place of wisdom herself. The philosophers protested. Socrates arose and demonstrated to his misled fellow citizens that the pleasure which they made their goal ought only to be the highway to virtue. Plato, his disciple, ... excludes from his republic every note of music, every appeal of tragedy, every recital of poems, and even the passages of Homer, that did not go to inspire the love of good laws. There you have the judgment which Socrates and Plato pronounce upon the poets and musicians. Are you not of their opinions?

B. I share their sentiments exactly. Man should not tolerate anything that is useless. Since he can find pleasure in serious things, he does not have to seek it elsewhere. If anything can assist the cause of virtue, the identification of virtue with pleasure can do so. On the contrary, when you separate them, you strongly invite men to abandon virtue. Besides, everything that pleases without instructing merely beguiles and softens.[43]

---

43 *Fénelon's Dialogues on Eloquence*, 67ff.

Later he observes that he would also ban tragedy, if it does not have the purpose of instruction while giving pleasure.

Montesquieu, under a heading 'Explanation of a Paradox of the Ancients in respect to Manners,' discusses some of these same issues, although he betrays some fundamental misconceptions about ancient musical practice.

> That judicious writer, Polybius, informs us that music was necessary to soften the manners of the Arcadians, who lived in a cold, gloomy country; that the inhabitants of Cynete, who slighted music, were the cruelest of all the Greeks, and that no other town was so immersed in luxury and debauchery. Plato is not afraid to affirm that there is no possibility of making a change in music without altering the frame of government. Aristotle, who seems to have written his *Politics* only in order to contradict Plato, agrees with him, not withstanding, in regard to the power and influence of music over the manners of the people. This was also the opinion of Theophrastus, of Plutarch, and of all the ancients—an opinion grounded on mature reflection; being one of the principles of their politics. Thus it was they enacted laws, and thus they required that cities should be governed.
>
> This I fancy must be explained in the following manner. It is observable that in the cities of Greece, especially those whose principal object was war, all lucrative arts and professions were considered unworthy of a freeman. 'Most arts,' say Xenophon [*Memorabilia*, V], 'corrupt and enervate the bodies of those that exercise them; they oblige them to sit in the shade, or near the fire. They can find no leisure, either for their friends or for the republic.' It was only by the corruption of some democracies that artisans became freemen. This we learn from Aristotle, who maintains that a well-regulated republic will never give them the right and freedom of the city …
>
> Thus in the Greek republics the magistrates were extremely embarrassed. They would not have the citizens apply themselves to trade, to agriculture, or to the arts, and yet they would not have them idle. They found, therefore, employment for them in gymnastics and military exercises; and none else were allowed by their institution. Hence the Greeks must be considered as a society of wrestlers and boxers. Now, these exercises having a natural tendency to render people hardy and fierce, there was a necessity for tempering them with others that might soften their manners. For this purpose, music, which influences the mind by means of the corporeal organs, was extremely proper. It is a kind of medium between manly exercises, which harden the body, and speculative sciences, which are apt to render us unsociable and sour. It cannot be said that music inspired virtue, for this would be inconceivable: but it prevented the effects of a savage institution, and enabled the soul to have such a share in the education as it could never have had without the assistance of harmony.
>
> Let us suppose among ourselves a society of men so passionately fond of hunting as to make it their sole employment; they would doubtless contract thereby a kind of rusticity and fierceness. But if they happen to imbibe a taste for music, we should quickly perceive a sensible difference in their customs and manners. In short, the exercises used by the Greeks could raise but one kind of passions, viz., fierceness, indignation, and cruelty. But music excites all these; and is likewise able to inspire the soul with a sense of pity, lenity, tenderness, and love. Our moral writers, who declaim so vehemently against the stage, sufficiently demonstrate the power of music over the mind.

If the society above mentioned were to have no other music than that of drums, and the sound of the trumpet, would it not be more difficult to accomplish this end than by the more melting tones of softer harmony? The ancients were therefore in the right when, under particular circumstances, they preferred one mode to another in regard to manners.

But some will ask, why should music be preferable to any other entertainment? It is because of all sensible pleasures there is none that less corrupts the soul.[44]

ON FRENCH VERSUS ITALIAN MUSIC

The enormous popularity of Italian opera which had begun to sweep the continent during the seventeenth century was largely responsible for a debate which engaged many French philosophers on the relative virtues of French and Italian music. We find it particularly interesting that several writers found a disadvantage in French music in the fact that the French composers were too academic in their approach, too bound to the ancient rules of composition. One of these writers was André Maugars, a violist and secretary attached to Cardinal Richelieu, who was sent to Rome in 1639 on a diplomatic mission. Reporting back that 'I have listened carefully to the most celebrated concerts in Rome,' he goes on to compare several aspects of French and Italian music. Among these is the subject of the French composers' dedication to their 'stubbornness in following the rules.'

> In the first place, I find that the Italian composers of church music have more artistry, more knowledge, and more variety than ours; but also that they have more freedom. And for me, since I could not disapprove of this freedom, when it is used discreetly and with skill, which insensibly deceives our feelings, so I cannot approve of the stubbornness of our composers who keep themselves religiously limited in pedantic categories and who feel that they would commit solecisms against the rules of the art if they wrote two successive fifths or if they departed even a little bit from their modes. No doubt it is in these very agreeable departures that the secret of the art consists—since music has figures of speech just like rhetoric, which all tend to charm the listener and deceive him insensibly. To tell the truth, it is not so necessary to amuse ourselves by observing the rules so rigorously that it makes us lose track of a fugue or the beauty of a song, in view of the fact these rules have been invented only to keep young schoolboys under control and prevent them from emancipating themselves before they have reached years of discretion. That is why a judicious man, with full knowledge of the science, is not condemned, by absolute fiat, to stay eternally in this narrow prison and can always soar according as his caprice carries him into some fine experiment, wherever the power of the words and the beauty of the parts shall lead him. This is what the Italians practice to perfection, and as they are much more refined than we in musical matters, they sneer at our musical regularity, and thus they write their Motets with more art, more knowledge, more variety, and more skill than we do ours …

---

44 Montesquieu, *The Spirit of Laws*, 17ff.

As for our composers, if they were willing to emancipate themselves a little more from their pedantic rules and take a few journeys to observe foreign music, my feeling is that they would succeed much better than they are doing now. It is not because I am not aware that we have many who are very capable in France, and among others that illustrious Intendant of the King's music [Antoine Boësset], who can play such lovely chords in his charming motets, in his ravishing songs, and in his manner of singing. All the Italian music will never be powerful enough to make me lose the esteem that I have for his merit and his virtue.

In general, we sin in omission and the Italians in commission. It seems to me that it would be easy for a smart man to write compositions that would have their variety without their extravagances.[45]

A similarly strong complaint against his contemporaries' absorption with the rules was made by François Raguenet, in his famous *Parallèle des Italiens et des Français*, of 1702.

It is not to be wondered that the Italians think our music dull and stupefying, that according to their taste it appears flat and insipid, if we consider the nature of the French melodies compared to those of the Italian. The French, in their melodies, aim at the soft, the easy, the flowing and coherent; the whole melody is of the same key, or, if sometimes they venture to vary it, they do it with so many preparations, they so qualify it, that still the melody seems to be as natural and consistent as if they had attempted no change at all; there is nothing bold and adventurous in it; it is all equal and of one piece. But the Italians pass boldly and in an instant from B-natural to B-flat to B-natural; they venture the boldest cadences and the most irregular dissonance; and their airs are so out of the way that they resemble the compositions of no other nation in the world.

The French would think themselves undone if they offended in the least against the rules; they flatter, tickle, and court the ear and are still doubtful of success, though everything be done with an exact regularity. The more hardy Italian changes the tone and the mode without any awe or hesitation; he makes double or treble improvisations in cadences of seven or eight bars together upon tones we should think incapable of the least division. He will make a swelling of so prodigious a length that they who are unacquainted with it can't choose but be offended at first to see him so adventurous, but before he has done it they will think they can't sufficiently admire him. He will have passages of such an extent as will perfectly confound his listeners at first, and upon such irregular tones as shall instill a terror as well as surprise into the audience, who will immediately conclude that the whole concert is degenerating into a dreadful dissonance; and betraying them by that means into a concern for the music, which seems to be upon the brink of ruin, he immediately reconciles them by such regular cadences that everyone is surprised to see harmony rising again, in a manner, out of discord itself and owing its greatest beauties to those irregularities which seemed to threaten it with destruction. The Italians venture at everything that is harsh and out of the way, but then they do it like people that have a right to venture and are sure of success. Under a notion of being the greatest and most absolute masters of music in the world, like despotic sovereigns they dispense with its rules in hardy but fortunate sallies; they exert themselves above the art, but, like masters of that art whose laws they follow or transgress

---

45 Maugars, 'Response faite a un curieux,' 117ff, 124ff.

at pleasure, they insult the niceness of the ear which others court; they master and conquer it with charms which owe their irresistible force to the boldness of the adventurous composer.[46]

In the writings of Jacques Bonnet-Bourdelot we have a perspective of the French–Italian debate at its height in Paris in 1715.

> You know then, as I do, Monsieur, that there are presently two parties formed on the subject of music; one, the rabid admirers of Italian music, sustained by a small sect of *demi-savants* in this art; nevertheless they are persons of fairly high standing who royally decide and proscribe absolutely French music as being stale and tasteless or entirely insipid. The other party, faithful to the taste of the country and better grounded in the art of music, are unable to suffer without indignation that the good taste of French music is scorned in Paris, and they treat Italian music as bizarre and capricious and as a rebel against the rules of the art.[47]

Bonnet-Bourdelot himself admits that everything about Italian music in general is learned and refined and that the French owe to the Italians the greater part of the practice of ornamentation. On the other hand, he questions Italian taste.

> If we cede to them science and invention, should they not cede to us with the same impartiality the good natural taste we possess, and the tender and noble execution in which we excel: above all, the harmony of our instruments? The enrichments we have added from our own store, should they not be accepted? … Can one not say without offending the partisans of Italian music that their too frequent and misplaced ornaments stifle expression, that they do not sufficiently distinguish their works, being in that like to Gothic architecture, which, too heavily adorned with ornaments, is obscured by them, so that one can no longer distinguish the body of the work?

Ten years later, Le Cerf de la Viéville also made a general criticism of Italian music.

> The Italians find no music good, if it is not difficult, they can scarcely bring themselves to look at it when there are only quarter- and eighth-notes.[48]

For Charles de Brosses, writing in 1739, this entire debate was based mostly on mutual ignorance, that is, the lack of sufficient first-hand experience by either the French or Italians in hearing each other's music.

> It is only up to me to challenge you as an incompetent judge, as every Frenchman would be who tries to pass judgment on Italian music without having heard it in its native country. The

---

46 Raguenet, 'Parallèle des Italiens et des Français,' 477ff.

47 Jacques Bonnet-Bourdelot, *Histoire de la musique et de ses effets depuis son origine, et les progr'es successifs de cet art jusqu'à présent* (Paris, 1715), quoted in MacClintock, *Readings*, 241. Bonnet-Bourdelot (d. 1724) was a nephew of Pierre Bourdelot, an historian who died before finishing his history of music. Jacques' brother, Pierre, took up the project, but he also died before finishing. Jacques took their work, to which he added his own observations, and finished the project.

48 Le Cerf de La Viéville, *Histoire de la Musique* (Amsterdam, 1725), I, 307.

French cannot know better the effect that *Artaxerxes* can produce on the stage than the Italians can feel the effects of *Armide*. I have heard the second and last act of this French opera sung in Rome, at the house of Cardinal Ottoboni; it was the best possible choice of Lully's music; the Italians yawned and we shrugged our shoulders.

Nothing could be more ridiculous; then too, we felt that no voice is capable of singing well any other music than that of its own country. Italian music which we sing in France should not appear more ridiculous than ours does in Rome; be careful not to pass any judgment on it, and certainly, to judge it, almost as much as to sing it, you must know the language perfectly and penetrate the feeling of the words.[49]

As a practical example, De Brosses offers the following anecdote.

The other day in the Paglianini Bookstore I found a treatise on [French and Italian music] written by a Frenchman named Bonnet ... As soon as he comes to Italian music, nothing could be more absurd than everything he says; there is not a shadow of truth nor any appearance of common sense; he cannot endure it; he reveals in a moment that he has never been in Italy, that he does not know a word of the language, and what is worse, that he has never heard real Italian songs ...

The [Italian] musician Menicuccio, having found this book on my table, began to read a few pages, and was astonished at this height of unreason. I took the occasion to remonstrate with him that he was himself unjust in his antipathy for our French music, which he scarcely knows better in spite of the short stay he has made in France; for the Italians are more unjust toward us than the greatest partisans of French music can be toward Italian music.[50]

On French versus Italian Singers

For Raguenet, in 1702, the essential advantage the Italian singers had was a very extrovert and passionate style, which he attributed to their greater experience in singing more complicated music.

The Italians are more bold and hardy in their melodies than the French; they carry their point farther, both in their tender songs and those that are more sprightly as well as in their other compositions; nay, they often unite styles which the French think incompatible. The French, in those compositions that consist of many parts, seldom regard more than that which is principal, whereas the Italians usually study to make all the parts equally shining and beautiful. In short, the invention of the one is inexhaustible, but the genius of the other is narrow and constrained ...[51]

......

---

49 Charles de Brosses, *Lettres familières écrites en Italie en 1739 et 1740* (Paris, 1885), quoted in MacClintock, *Readings*, 268. De Brosses (1707–1777), a magistrate and president of the Parliament of Dijon, was a highly educated man in the fields of art, literature, music and the study of antiquities.

50 Ibid., 269.

51 François Raguenet, 'Parallèle des Italiens et des Français,' (1702), quoted in Strunk, *Source Readings*, 476ff.

Sometimes we meet with a swelling to which the first notes of the thorough bass jar so harshly as the ear is highly offended with it, but the bass, continuing to play on, returns at last to the swelling with such beautiful intervals that we quickly discover the composer's design, in the choice of those discords, was to give the hearer a more true and perfect relish of the ravishing notes that on a sudden restore the whole harmony.

Let a Frenchman be set to sing one of these dissonances, and he will lack courage enough to support it with that resolution wherewith it must be sustained to make it succeed; his ear, being accustomed to the most soft and natural intervals, is startled at such an irregularity; he trembles and is in a sweat whilst he attempts to sing it. Whereas the Italians, who are inured from their youth to these dissonances, sing the most irregular notes with the same assurance they would the most beautiful and perform everything with a confidence that secures them of success.

Music is become exceedingly common in Italy; the Italians sing from their cradles, they sing at all times and places, a natural uniform song is too vulgar for their ears. Such melodies are to them like things tasteless and decayed.[52]

Jean Laurent le Cerf de La Viéville, in his treatise on *Good Taste in Music* (1704), touches on the comparison of French and Italian styles in the context of a discussion on the aesthetic characteristics of a good singer.

A perfect voice should be sonorous, of wide range, sweet, exact [*nette*], lively, flexible. These six qualities, which nature combines only once in a century, are ordinarily present in half measure. A voice of wide range and of a beautiful tone, a touching tone, is a great, a beautiful voice, and the sweeter it is, in addition, a thing rarer in great voices than in others, the more beautiful I believe it to be. A lively and flexible voice is a pretty voice, a pleasing voice, and the more exact it is, in addition, the frequent drawbacks of pretty voices, and the more I shall esteem it …

I reduce the merit of a singer to three things: accuracy, expression, neatness [*propreté*] …

Expression on the part of a singer consists in entering, in a spirited and appropriate manner, into the feeling of the verses he sings, to inform them with passion is the term, as one who understand them and is the first to feel them. On the whole the recitative and the smaller melodies should be sung lightly, the great melodies more consciously, bringing out the full force of each note. It is noticeable that the fault of beginners is to sing too fast, that of the good provincial singers to go a little too slowly. Neatness [*propreté*] is that great mass of little observations, unknown to the Italians but so well known to our own masters, and which by their combined effect afford great pleasure, I assure you. To open the mouth, to produce the tones in the right way, to prepare, ornament, and finish a cadence gracefully, etc.[53]

Robert Donnington also quotes Le Cerf de La Viéville as having written,

The Italian singers pronounce badly … because … they close all their teeth and do not open the mouth enough: except in the florid passages, where they hold it open for a quarter of an hour at

---

52   Ibid., 478.
53   Le Cerf de la Viéville, *Histoire*, 501ff.

a time, without moving the tongue, or the lips … it is only in France that they take the trouble to not open the mouth as they should in singing.[54]

The greatest distinction between French and Italian vocal traditions was, of course, the wide use of castrati by the Italians. De Brosses, visiting Italy in 1739, offers some interesting information on these singers.

> The operation is performed about the age of seven or eight years of age; the child must ask for it himself; the police have imposed this condition to render tolerance for it a little less intolerable. They usually become large and fat like capons, with thighs, buttocks, arms, breast, and neck round and plump like women. When one meets them in a crowd one is astonished when they speak to hear such a tiny child's voice from these colossi …
>
> One must grow accustomed to these castrato voices to enjoy them. Their timbre is as clear and piercing as that of choir boys, and much stronger. It seems to me that they sing an octave above the natural women's voice. Their voices always have a dry and thin quality, far distant from the young and velvety quality of women's voices; but they are brilliant, light, full of *éclat*, very strong, and with a wide range.[55]

Later, he adds,

> The Italians admire the improvised cadences that occur in the finale of every solo melody. For me, they do not please me at all; in addition to being very frequent they always say the same thing. I want to laugh when I see a fat eunuch blow himself up like a balloon, to show the range of his voice for a quarter of an hour without taking a breath in twenty elaborate passages, one after the other.[56]

Regarding the comparison of normal French and Italian voices, De Brosses writes,

> Do not talk to the Italians of the admirable tones of our French music, spun out, sustained tones gradually increased or diminished on the same degree; they would not be capable of understanding you any more than they could provide such sounds. The Italians nevertheless distinguish two kinds of voices: one they call *voce di testa*, which is quite light and suited to the charming little turns they can give to the musical ornaments; the other the chest voice, *voce di petto*, which has sounds more open, more natural, and fuller. In a word, the voices of Italy are agreeable, flexible, seductive to the last degree, but, if all them were put into the beaker, one would not get from all their voices joined together any voice comparable to or approaching that of Catherine Lemaure.

In another place, De Brosses criticizes the Italian tradition for producing singers limited to the theater.

---

54 Quoted in Donnington, *The Interpretation of Early Music*, 525.
55 Brosses, *Lettres*, 275ff.
56 Ibid., 281.

> If you ask a singer to sing a drawing room song, she will not sing without going to the piano to accompany herself, playing the bass with her left hand and the melody, not the chords, with her right hand … So in spite of the small esteem they have for our songs, they praise our gay vaudevilles, our duets and *chansonettes de table*; that is all they like of our music.

Finally, after praising the vocal compositions of Pergolesi, Bernasconi, Scarlatti, Jomelli and Vinci, he adds this interesting note.

> Handel has a great reputation in England; his works are not much known in Italy, and, from what I have seen of his vocal music, I would think him to be inferior to all those whom I have named to you.[57]

On French versus Italian Instrumental Music

During André Maugar's visit to Rome in 1639 he was particularly surprised by an abundance of fine harpists, an instrument rarely reported in literature of this period. He also found the organ performances lacking by French standards, which he attributed to their fewer registers. He then makes a brief summary of national styles of instrumental music.

> We play the lute well and the Italians the archlute. We play the organ agreeably and the Italians learnedly. We play the spinet admirably, and the English play the viol perfectly. I admit that I owe them something and that I have imitated them in their tunings, but not in other things; our French birth and training give us this advantage over all the other nations in that they will never be able to equal us in fine movements, in agreeable diminutions, and particularly in the natural melodies of Courantes and Ballets.[58]

Quite a different impression was given by Raguenet in 1702, after his visit to Italy. In a report which demonstrates his rather detailed knowledge of the instruments in use in both countries, he seemed almost shocked by the aggressive and emotional style of the Italian instrumentalists.

> As to the instruments, our masters touch the violin much finer and with a greater nicety than they do in Italy. Every stroke of their bow sounds harsh, if broken, and disagreeable, if continued….[59]
>
> ……
>
> [The Italian] violins are mounted with strings much larger than ours; their bows are longer, and they can make their instruments sound as loud again as we do ours. The first time I heard our orchestra in the Opéra after my return from Italy, my ears had been so used to the loudness

---

57 Ibid., 285.
58 Maugars, 'Response,' 120, 125.
59 Raguenet, 'Parallèle,' 475.

of the Italian violins that I thought ours had all been bridled ... Their bass-viols are as large again as the French, and all ours put together don't sound so loud in our operas as two or three of those basses do in Italy. This is certainly an instrument much wanted in France; it is the basis on which the Italians in a manner build the whole consort; it is a sure foundation, equally firm as it is deep and low; it has a full mellow sound, filling the air with an agreeable harmony in a sphere of activity extending itself to the utmost bounds of the most spacious places.[60]

......

Moreover, besides all the instruments that are common to us as well as the Italians, we have the oboes, which, by their sounds, equally mellow and piercing, have infinitely the advantage of the violins in all brisk, lively airs, and the flutes, which so many of our great artists have taught to groan after so moving a manner in our moanful melodies, and sigh so amorously in those that are tender.[61]

On the other hand, Raguenet was much more impressed with the actual scoring heard in the Italian ensembles.

As for the accompaniments of the violin [in France], they are, for the most part, nothing but single strokes of the bow, heard by intervals, without any uniform coherent music, serving only to express, from time to time, a few accords. Whereas in Italy, the first and second upper part, the thorough bass, and all the other parts that concur to the composition of the fullest pieces, are equally finished. The parts for the violins are usually as beautiful as the melody itself. So that after we have been entertained with something very charming in the air, we are insensibly captivated by the parts that accompany it, which are equally engaging and make us quit the subject to listen to them. Everything is so exactly beautiful that it is difficult to find out the principal part ... It is too much for one soul to taste the several beauties of so many parts. She must multiply herself before she can relish and digest three or four delights at once which are all beautiful alike; it is transport, enchantment, and ecstasy of pleasure; her faculties are upon so great a stretch, she is forced to ease herself by exclamations; she waits impatiently for the end of the air that she may have a breathing space ...

To conclude, the Italians are inexhaustible in their productions of such pieces as are composed of several parts, in which on the other side the French are extremely limited. In France, the composer thinks he has done his business if he can diversify the subject; as for the accompaniments you find nothing like it in them; without any variety or surprise. The French composers steal from one another or copy from their own works so that all their compositions are much alike.[62]

Raguenet at this point pays tribute to Lully as one who has surpassed all musicians and admits, somewhat in embarrassment, that Lully is an Italian. As for the native French musicians, Raguenet paints a rather dismal portrait of their social recognition.

---

60 Ibid., 486.
61 Ibid., 475.
62 Ibid., 480ff.

> I have seen Corelli, Pasquini, and Gaetani play all together in the same opera at Rome, and they are allowed to be the greatest masters in the world on the violin, the harpsichord, and theorbo or archlute, and as such they are generally paid 300 or 400 pistoles apiece for a month, or six weeks at the most. This is the commonest pay in Italy, and this encouragement is one reason why they have more masters there than we have with us. We despise them in France as people of a mean profession; in Italy they are esteemed as men of note and distinction. There they raise very considerable fortunes, whereas with us they get but a bare livelihood. From hence it is that ten times more people apply themselves to music in Italy than France. Nothing is more common in Italy than performers, singers and music.[63]

Le Cerf de la Viéville, writing in 1705, had the same impression as Raguenet regarding the vigorous Italian ensemble sound. This is mentioned in his treatise on 'Good Taste in Music,' where we also find a brief discussion on the aesthetic characteristics of good instrumental music.

> Of the three qualities to which I reduce the merit of a player, exactness is the principal one, especially for the players of instruments which are played directly by the fingers, without a bow ... Without exactness, what is a piece for the lute or the harpsichord? A noise, a jangling of harmonies in which one understands nothing. I would sooner listen to a hurdy-gurdy. After this precious exactness comes delicacy. It is in instruments what neatness [*propreté*] is in singing ...
>   In truth, [the] Italians carry too far a certain desire to elicit sound from their instruments. My intelligence, my heart, my ears tell me, all at once, that they produce a sound excessively shrill and violent. I am always afraid that the first stroke of the bow will make the violin fly into splinters, they use so much pressure.[64]

The most enlightening comments on Italian instrumental music are found in the record of Charles de Brosses' travel to Italy in 1739. In general, he found a much higher level of orchestral discipline in Italy.

> These people have notions of precision much different from ours and they say much worse things about our playing than about our music.[65]

His most interesting description of Italian instrumental music is of church concerti and he provides many interesting details of their style. His account is another acknowledgment of the superior concepts of orchestration in Italy.

> In a sacred concert performed on Christmas Eve in the Papal chamber of Monte Cavallo, I judged that there were about two hundred instruments; I expected a prodigious noise. In the performance the effect did not seem to me any greater than if there had been only fifty; from this I conjecture that a certain number of violins suffices to give to the air all the sound it is

---

63 Ibid., 487.
64 Le Cerf de la Viéville, *Histoire*, 502ff.
65 Brosses, *Lettres*, 279ff.

capable of enduring, and that a thousand additional ones would not make it louder. As the entire orchestra plays accompaniments, it must take care not to drown out the voices. While the parts of the *ripieno* play harmonic chords, the first violin almost everywhere plays the same melody as the voice; this unison sustains and accompanies it very well. I do not know why we do not play the same way. They have a method of accompanying that we do not understand, which it would be easy for us to introduce into our playing and which greatly increases the power of their music; it is the art of augmenting or diminishing the sound, which I might call the art of shadings or of *chiaroscuro*. This is applied either gradually by degrees, or all at once. In addition to loud and soft, they use also a *mezzo piano* and a *mezzo forte*. These are reflections, half-tints, which give incredible pleasure to the sound color …

They understand how to vary the sound by the variety of the instruments they use, violins, horns, trumpets, oboes, flutes, harps, viols d'amore, archlutes, mandolins, etc. We do not have sufficient diversity in our instruments, which contributes to the monotony of which our music is accused. Their ritornellos are ravishing, and the chorus that follows them is so prettily turned out, so flattering and so surprising, that beside them our French melodies are only sing-song; it is madness to want to compare them.

In summary, De Brosses gives the impression that the Italian music was generally more sophisticated.

I have heard it said a thousand times in France that Italian instrumental music is better than ours, but that we excel in vocal music. It seems to me to be just the contrary and that the Italians think just as I do. For instrumental, they have concerts, with large choirs, or mixed concerts of choirs and solo violins much better than anything we can do in this genre …

Not long ago I took a rather good [French] violinist to a concert at Cardinal Bichi's house, and I had him play the sixth sonata in C minor from Leclair's third book, to see if those people would have the nerve not to find it beautiful; they were not so stupid, but they did not care much for the performer, who really did not play badly. I do not know, but I find French playing dull and insipid compared with theirs; it is not that our hands are not as good on the fingerboard of the violin, we lack the bow hand; they have a thousand delicate turns, a thousand sallies, in a word, an articulation that we are not able to acquire.[66]

ON PERFORMANCE PRACTICE

Maugars, in his report of his visit to Rome in 1639, gives a vivid account of the importance and expectation of improvisation. First he observes that the Italians prefer instrumental music to vocal because 'a single man can produce more beautiful inventions than four voices together, and that it has a charm and freedom which the vocal music does not have.' Then

---

66 Ibid., 282. De Brosses adds a note here that the Italians admit French excel in dancing and that when they give a ball they use French or German minuets, rather than their own music.

he reports having played for a private audience on his viol, after which he was challenged to return and improvise [during a Mass!]—the Italians not believing a Frenchman could do this.

> After the esteem of these good people, it was not yet enough to win absolutely that of the professionals, who are a little too refined and much too reluctant to applaud foreigners. I was informed that they admitted that I played very well alone and that they had never heard anyone play so many parts on the viol, but they had doubts, since I was French, that I was capable of treating and diversifying a subject impromptu. You know, Sir, that that is where I succeed best. Since these words were told to me on the eve of St. Louis's day in the French church, where I was listening to the fine music that was being played, it made me resolve the next morning, emboldened by the holy name of Louis, by national honor, and by the presence of twenty-three Cardinals who were present at the Mass, to mount a pulpit, where having been greeted with applause, they gave me fifteen or twenty notes on a small organ after the third *Kyrie eleison*, which I played with so many variations that they were eminently satisfied, and asked me on behalf of the Cardinals to play once more after the *Agnus Dei*. I counted myself lucky to render this small service to such an eminent company. They sent me another subject, gayer than the first one, which I diversified with so many inventions, with different movements and different speeds, that they were astonished, and came immediately to compliment me, but I retired to my room to rest.[67]

After mention that he also performed for the pope, Maugars continued with some remarks of a more aesthetic nature on improvisation.

> The friendship which you have for me, persuades me, Monsieur, that you will not accuse me of too much vanity in this digression, which I have made only to inform you that it is necessary for a Frenchman who wants to acquire a reputation in Rome to be very well versed in his subject, the more so because they do not think that we are capable of treating a subject impromptu. And certainly no man who plays an instrument deserves to be thought excellent unless he knows how to improvise, and especially on the viol, which being a different instrument because of the small number of strings and the difficulty that exists in fingering all the parts, its true talent is to play around the given subject and to produce fine inventions and agreeable diminutions. But two essential and natural qualities are necessary for this result: to have a lively and strong imagination and quickness of the hand to execute one's ideas promptly; that is why people cold and slow by nature will never succeed well.

In view of some modern theories that Italian music in the Baroque was played without improvisation, Bonnet-Bourdelot's criticism of the excessive improvisation is quite revealing.

> In general one hears in Italian music only a *Basso continuo* always ornamented, which is often a kind of *batterie*, with chords and arpeggios, which casts dust in the eyes of those who are not connoisseurs, and which, reduced to its simplest form, is equivalent to ours. The B. C. are only good to show off the swiftness of hand of those who accompany, either the clavecin or the viol. Also, to outdo these basses already too much ornamented, they vary them again, and the one who

---

67 Maugars, 'Response,' 123ff.

ornaments the most wins. Thus one no longer hears the subject, which appears all too naked in the midst of this great brilliance and remains buried under a jolting of very fast and sparkling sounds, which, passing too lightly, cannot make any harmony against the subject … The voice should dominate and attract the chief attention, but the contrary happens here: one hears only the B. C., which bubbles so loudly that the voice is smothered. There is also a disadvantage in having the basses in batteries and ornamenting *ad lib.*, for it is difficult for a clavecin, a viol, and a theorbo to be able to play together accurately in the same style of ornamentation, no more than can many string instruments or winds; one takes one passage, another the next, which causes an extraordinary cacophony, such that a composer no longer recognizes his work, which appears disfigured; and in the midst of it all, one contents one's self with admiring the rapidity of the hand that is executing the passage! However, there you have the style of execution of the Italian music that is so much extolled.

But this is not the case with Sieur de Lully, great disciple of the beautiful and the true, who would have banished from his orchestra a violin who had spoiled his harmony by some diminution, or a cat's cry badly placed, in imitation of those rigid Grecian inspectors of public spectacles. Can one not compel himself to play music the way it is written? Is it the Italian style to make false harmonies at every turn? …

If this [ornamentation] is suitable to Italian and Latin words, why does one wish to subject the French language to it? Does an Italian control his affairs like a Frenchman? Their tastes, their dress, their customs, their manners, their pleasures, are they not all different? Why does one not wish them to be so in their vocal music as well, and in the playing of instruments? Does an Italian sing like a Frenchman? Why does one want the Frenchman to sing like the Italian? Each nation has different customs; why wish to dress French music in disguise and make her extravagant, she whose language is so wise and so unaffected and cannot bear the least violence, being an enemy of the frequent repetitions and the long fermatas that one tolerates in Italian, or Latin [church], music which do not suit ours at all?

Here one can compare French music to a beautiful woman whose simple natural beauty, without art, draws to her the hearts of all who see her, who has only to appear to please, without fearing defeat by the affected airs of an extravagant coquette who seeks to draw people to her side at any price.[68]

ON OPERA

As the popularity of Italian opera began to spread throughout Europe during the seventeenth century, it prompted increasing debate in France. Not only did the form itself challenge the most basic theater traditions in France, but it was a popular medium, supported commercially, whereas theater in France was a private entertainment for the aristocracy. Issues such as these, not to mention the inherent musical characteristics, fueled a wide variety of views.

---

68 Bonnet-Bourdelot, *Histoire de la musique*, quoted in MacClintock, *Readings*, 243ff.

An early report on opera in Rome, by André Maugars, written before there was much influence felt in France itself, is full of admiration.

> There are a large number of castrati for the Dessus and the Haute-Contre, very beautiful and natural Tenors, and very few deep Basses. They are very certain of their technique and sing the most difficult music at sight. In addition, they are almost all actors by nature, and it is for this reason that they succeed so perfectly in their musical comedies. I have seen them play three or four this last winter, but I must admit that in truth they are incomparable and inimitable in music for the stage, not only for their singing but also for the expression of the words, the postures, and the gestures of the characters they play naturally and very well.
>
> As for their manner of singing, it is much more animated than ours; they have certain inflections of the voice that we do not possess. It is true that they perform their passages with more roughness, but today they are beginning to correct that.[69]

By the end of the seventeenth century, after considerable Italian influence had come to affect the French opera, one observer, La Bruyère, found little to praise.

> The Opera is obviously the first draft of a fine spectacle; it suggests the idea of one.
>
> I don't know how it is that the Opera, with such perfect music and a truly regal expense, sometimes succeeds in boring me.
>
> There are parts of the Opera that leave one wishing for more; one finds oneself occasionally longing for the end of the whole performance: this is for lack of theatrical effects, of action and of interesting matter.
>
> An Opera nowadays is not poetry, but merely verse; it is not a spectacle, since machines vanished under the efficient administration of [Lully] and his tribe: it is a concert, or voices accompanied by instruments. It is an error of judgment and of taste to say, as some do, that machines are merely a childish amusement, fit only for the Marionnettes' Theater; machines enhance and embellish the imaginary action, and maintain the spectators in that delightful illusion which is the chief pleasure the theater offers, by shedding further magic over it. We need no aerial flights, no chariots, no transformation scenes, for the two *Bérénices* or for *Pénélope*: we need them for operas, and the characteristic of that kind of entertainment is to keep one's mind and eyes and ears beyond the same spell.
>
> They did it all, these busy people, they provided the stage sets, the machines, the ballets, the verse, the music, the whole entertainment, even the hall in which it was performed—including the roof and the four walls from their foundation upwards. Who can doubt but that the stag-hunt on the water, the enchanted hunting-party at the Table and the marvelous banquet in the Labyrinth were also their idea? I gather this from their activity and the self-satisfied way in which they congratulate themselves on the success of everything. If I am mistaken, if indeed they contributed nothing towards that splendid and elegant fête which went on for so long and which was planned and paid for by a single man, I wonder at two things: the calm and self-

---

69 Maugars, 'Response,' 122.

possession of the man who set everything in motion, and the fuss and self-importation of those who did nothing at all.[70]

Charles de Saint-Évremond (1613–1703), a distinguished and (rare for France) highly educated noble, expected too much from opera—he expected to have his mind stimulated. By 'mind' he meant, in modern language, the left brain, that is, the rational, conceptual mind. But music does not do this, it never has and never will. Music stimulates the person who is found in the right brain. Therefore, while others were debating French versus Italian opera, Saint-Évremond rejected them both for the lack of depth as entertainment vehicles.

> I shall begin by being very frank and telling you that I do not admire very much the *Comédies en Musique* as we see them at present. I admit that their magnificence pleases me, that the machines are really surprising, that the music is touching in places, that the *tout ensemble* seems marvelous; but you must admit that these marvels soon become tiresome because where the mind comes so little into play the senses necessarily languish after the first pleasure that surprise affords us ... The mind, which has given itself over in vain to outside impressions, turns to revery or is annoyed by its own weakness; finally the weakness is so great that one thinks only of leaving ...
>
> The fatigue which I ordinarily feel at the opera comes from the fact that I have never seen one which did not appear to me as despicable in the conduct of the plot and its verse. Well, it is in vain that the ear is pleased and the eyes charmed if the mind is not satisfied. My spirit agreeing with my intelligence more than with my senses secretly resists the impressions it might receive, or at least it fails to give its glad consent, without which the most voluptuous objects can give me no great pleasure. A piece of stupidity loaded with music, dance, machines and decorations is a magnificent piece of stupidity.[71]

Being by nature, as he explained, incapable of appreciating opera, he could not even understand why everything was sung!

> There is something else in the opera so unnatural that my imagination is hurt by it. That is, having the whole play sung from beginning to end as if the characters presented had ridiculously been adapted to express in music both the commonest and most important events in their lives. Can you imagine a master calling his valet or giving him a task to do by singing; that a friend sing a confidence to a friend; that one should deliberate in a council by singing; that one express his orders in song, or kill men in combat melodiously with sword strokes or spear thrusts?

He admits he does not want to ban all music from the theater, just to leave conversation to speakers and not singers. He does concede some emotions are better sung than spoken.

---

70 La Bruyère, *Characters*, 34ff.

71 Charles de Saint-Évremond, 'Lettre sur les Opera,' quoted in MacClintock, *Readings*, 251ff. Charles de Marguetel de Saint-Denis, seigneur de Saint-Évremond (1613–1703) wrote this material ca. 1680, although it was not published until 1739, long after his death.

> Tender and tragic passions are expressed naturally by a kind of singing; the expression of a beginning love, the irresolution of a soul torn in different directions—these are matters for stanzas, and stanzas are suited to singing.

Nevertheless, in an extraordinary summary of what this kind of opera was, Saint-Évremond writes,

> Opera is a bizarre work of verse and music where the Poet and the Musician, each hampered by the other, take a lot of trouble to create a bad work.

We might add that at the end of his letter he reveals what his real concern is.

> What annoys me the most about this infatuation with opera is that it is about to ruin tragedy, which has been the finest thing we possess, and the one most capable of forming the mind.[72]

He also provides a general outline of what he thinks an opera *should* be. Basically, his appreciation for music extended only so far as incidental music, a fine piece of spoken drama, to which one might add a prologue, intermedi and an epilogue of music—as long as it is in the spirit of the play. Thus, for him, both the mind and the senses would be satisfied.

Having observed 'the little esteem the Italians have for our opera, and the great disgust we have for the Italian ones,' Saint-Évremond treats the reader to a little tour of national characteristics in opera.[73]

> As to the manner of singing, what we call the execution in France, I think with no partiality that no nation can rival ours. The Spanish have admirable throats; but with their graces [*fredons*] and their roulades they seem in their singing to be thinking of rivaling the nightingale in the facility of their throats. The expressiveness of the Italians is false or at least exaggerated, because they do not know exactly the nature and degree of the passions. It is bursting out laughing rather than singing when they express some joyous feeling. If they try to sigh one can hear sobs that are formed violently in the throat, not the sighs with which a loving heart gives vent to its passion in secret. Of a sad reflection they make the most powerful exclamations; tears of absence become funeral weeping; sad things become lugubrious in their mouths; they utter cries of pain instead of laments; and sometimes they express the languor due to passion as a weakness of nature. Perhaps there is some change now in their way of singing and they have profited by their contact with us to acquire a clear-cut, polished execution, just as we have profited from them to acquire the beauties of a greater and bolder composition.
>
> I have seen comedies in England where there was much music. But to speak discreetly, I have never been able to grow accustomed to English singing. I came too late to acquire a taste so differently from any other. There is no nation which shows more courage in the men, and more beauty in the women, more wit in both sexes. But you cannot have everything. Where so many good qualities are common it is no great loss that good taste is so rare …

---

72 Ibid., 256.
73 Ibid., 253ff.

There is no one slower in understanding the sense of the words and entering into the spirit of the composer than the French; there are few who understand quantity less, and who have so much trouble with the pronunciation; but when long study has enabled them to really understand what they are singing, nothing approaches their pleasantness. The same is true for instruments and especially in concerts, where nothing is sure or correct until after an infinity of rehearsals are finished. The Italians, very learned in music, bring their knowledge to our ears with no sweetness whatsoever; the French are not content to rid knowledge of its first roughness, which smacks of the hard work of composing; they find in the secrets of performing something to charm the soul, a *je ne sais quoi* very touching, which they can bring to our very hearts.

Raguenet, in 1702, provides an extensive comparison between French and Italian opera. He begins with those areas in which he finds French opera superior, beginning with the play itself, the quality of the libretto. He also finds much aesthetic virtue in the more balanced vocal forces, particularly the strong bass singers. It is true the Italian operas featured the highest voice, usually a young lady in distress. Raguenet, who took his own life in 1722, would not live long enough to see it was an idiom which would lead to the emotionally expressive music of the Classical Period.

Our operas are written much better than the Italian; they are regular, coherent designs; and, though repeated without the music, they are as entertaining as any of our other pieces that are purely dramatic. Nothing can be more natural and lively than their dialogues; the gods are made to speak with a dignity suitable to their character, kings with all the majesty their rank requires, and the nymphs and shepherds with a softness and innocent mirth peculiar to the plains. Love, jealousy, anger, and the rest of the passions are touched with the greatest art and nicety, and there are few of our tragedies or comedies that appear more beautiful than [the librettist] Quinault's operas.

On the other hand, the Italian operas are poor, incoherent rhapsodies without any connection or design; all their pieces, properly speaking, are patched up with thin, insipid scraps; their scenes consist of some trivial dialogues or soliloquy, at the end of which they foist in one of their best airs, which concludes the scene …

Besides, our operas have a further advantage over the Italian in respect of the voice, and that is the bass, which is so frequent among us and so rarely to be met with in Italy. For every man that has an ear will witness with me that nothing can be more charming than a good bass; the simple sound of these basses, which sometimes seems to sink into a profound abyss, has something wonderfully charming in it. The air receives a stronger concussion from these deep voices than it does from those that are higher and is consequently filled with a more agreeable and extensive harmony. When the persons of gods or kings, a Jupiter, Neptune, Priam, or Agamemnon, are brought on the stage, our actors, with their deep voices, give them an air of majesty, quite different from that of the feigned bases among the Italians, which have neither depth nor strength. Besides, the interfering of the basses with the upper parts forms an agreeable contrast and makes us perceive the beauties of the one from the opposition they meet with from the other, a pleasure to which the Italians are perfect strangers, the voices of their singers, who are for the most part castrati, being perfectly like those of their women.[74]

When it came to the music, however, Raguenet could not help but admire many aspects of Italian singing.

> There is no weak part in any of the Italian operas, where no sense is preferable to the rest of its peculiar beauties; all the songs are of an equal force and are sure to be crowned with applause, whereas in our operas there are I know not how many languishing scenes and insipid melodies with which nobody can be pleased or diverted.
>
> It must be confessed that our recitative is much better than that of the Italians, which is too close and simple; it is the same throughout and cannot properly be called singing. Their recitative is little better than downright speaking, without any inflection or modulation of the voice, and yet there is this to be admired in it—the parts that accompany this psalmody are incomparable, for they have such an extraordinary genius for composition that they know how to adapt charming concords, even to a voice that does little more than speak, a thing to be met with in no other part of the world whatsoever …
>
> I observed in the beginning of this parallel how much we had the advantage over the Italians in our basses, so common with us and so rare to be found in Italy; but how small is this in comparison to the benefit their operas receive from their castrati, who abound without number among them, whereas there is not one to be found in all France. Our women's voices are indeed as soft and agreeable as are those of their castrati, but then they are far from being either so strong or lively. No man or woman in the world can boast of a voice like theirs; they are clear, they are moving, and affect the soul itself …
>
> Add to this that these soft—these charming voices acquire new charms by being in the mouth of a lover; what can be more affecting than the expressions of their sufferings in such tender passionate notes; in this the Italian lovers have a very great advantage over ours, whose hoarse masculine voices ill agree with the fine soft things they are to say to their mistresses. Besides, the Italian voices being equally strong as they are soft, we hear all they sing very distinctly, whereas half of it is lost upon our stage unless we sit close to the stage or have the spirit of divination. Our upper parts are usually performed by girls that have neither lungs nor wind, whereas the same parts in Italy are always performed by men whose firm piercing voices are to be heard clearly in the largest theaters without losing a syllable, sit where you will.
>
> But the greatest advantage the Italians receive from these castrati is that their voices hold good for thirty or forty years together, whereas our women begin to lose the beauty of theirs at ten or twelve years end.[75]
>
> ……
>
> In all our operas we have either some insignificant actor that sings out of tune or time, or some ignorant actress that sings false and is excused, either because she is not as yet thoroughly acquainted with the stage or else she has no voice, and then she is borne with because she has some other way of pleasing the town and withal makes a handsome figure. This never happens

---

74 Raguenet, 'Parallèle,' 474ff.

75 Ibid., 482ff.

in Italy, where there is not a voice but what may very well be liked; they have neither man or woman but what perform their parts so perfectly well that they are sure to charm an audience by their agreeable manner of singing though their voices are not extraordinary, for music is nowhere so well understood as in Italy.[76]

On the other hand, the philosopher, Bonnet-Bourdelot, was one who found almost nothing to praise in Italian opera.

> One can say that Italian music resembles an amiable coquette, although somewhat painted, full of vivacity, always rushing about seeking to sparkle everywhere without reason, and not knowing why; like a scatter brain who shows her passions in everything she does; when it is a question of tender affection she makes it dance the gavotte or gigue. Would not one say that serious matters become comical in her hands, and that she is more suited to *ariettes* and *chansonettes* than to deal with noble subjects? In that, is she not like to those comedians who having talent only for the comic, succeed very badly, turning tragedy to ridicule when they wish to have a hand in it? One must admit that the majesty of French music treats heroic subjects with greater nobility and is more appropriate to the cothurnus and the theater; whereas in Italian music all the passions appear alike: joy, anger, sorrow, happy love, the lover who fears or hopes—all seem to be painted with the same features and the same character; it is a continual gigue, always sparkling or leaping.[77]

He was particularly suspicious of anything involving technique, for its tendency to detract from the sentiment of the words in the opera.

> We have difficulty to accustom ourselves to the strange intervals in the recitatives of their songs, which sometimes exceed an octave, in which even the most skillful find difficulty with just intonation. Above all, the long *tenutos* make the listener impatient because they are misplaced; these holds, which we also use and which are rarely suitable except on words of repose, they make indifferently on all the words that end with vowels. I do not say there may not be a great deal of art in having a violin and a bass frolic below one of these long fermatas, but what has liberty to do with this sound that lasts a quarter of an hour? Where is the taste and expression in all of that? It very often happens that Italian music expresses something quite different from the words. I hear a Prelude that is fast and furious: I then think that some lover, repelled by the coldness of his lady, is going to give way to spite and abuse Love; not at all: it is a tender lover who praises the price of his constancy, who calls Hope to his aid, or who makes a declaration of love to his mistress.

Bonnet-Bourdelot makes a curious and revealing observation on French opera in an apparent reference to the famous French salons.

---

76 Ibid., 484.
77 Bonnet-Bourdelot, *Histoire*, 242ff.

> There are, however, women who decide the merit and destiny of works in the spectacles, and whom we must seek to please, above all in that art which seems to be made for them.[78]

Another unusually interesting passage regarding opera involves a quotation from St. Augustine which we do not find in the extant works of that Church father.

> But to arrive at perfection in such a fine spectacle, it is necessary to have persons of talent who understand perfectly the principles on which St. Augustine placed the perfection of harmony, arranged in nine degrees: the first in the mind, the second in good judgment, the third in the imagination, the fourth in the emotions, the fifth in the word, the sixth in the melody, the seventh in the sound, the eighth in desire, and the ninth in the composition.
>
> These principles embody also the perfection of the nine Muses, whom the Ancients considered divinities. Thus, to compose a perfect opera it takes at least a poet, a musician, a mathematician, a ballet master, a painter—all of whom excel in their art—and a superintendent of great perception to oversee the construction and execution of the work. Also a great prince, or a republic as powerful as that of Venice, should pay the expenses *à discretion*, for it is necessary that everything be suitable to such a great subject, which is ordinarily drawn from a fable or history or is allegorical.[79]

The reference to 'a great prince' refers to the fact that opera in France at this time was sponsored by the nobility, whereas in Italy it was a private, commercial concern. Bonnet-Bourdelot returns to the French tradition when he observes,

> One must admit that all these representations are at least as indebted for their perfections to the magnificence and generosity of sovereigns who have paid for them as to those who composed them; otherwise music would still be limited to the chant of the church, and bounded by private concerts, as may be seen in states where spectacles are not yet enjoyed.[80]

In summary, he finds,

> One can say also without ostentation that the French operas outdo those of Italy by the size and beauty of the choruses, by the *agréments* of the recitative, as well as by the authority of execution by the instruments of the orchestra, whose symphony is inimitable, as well as by the magnificence of the ballet *entrées* and the *danses élevées, danses bases,* or *danses figurés* ... executed by dancers who know the art of characterizing the passions through movements of the dance with grace and a nobility worthy of admiration that is not found in Italy.[81]

Charles de Brosses gives us a lengthy and very interesting account of Italian opera at the end of the Baroque. He begins his discussion of French and Italian opera by acknowledging

---

78 Ibid., 249ff.
79 Ibid., 249.
80 Ibid.
81 Ibid.

that Italy has larger and more beautiful opera houses than France, mentioning in particular one in Rome built by a French gentleman in the service of Queen Christina. He makes the curious observation that in Italy the audience never sits on the stage. This is done only in France, where 'a thousand people go to the comedy more for the spectators than for the spectacle.'[82] His following remarks reflect the fact that Italian opera was much more public than that in France.

> The parterre is filled with benches, like a church, where people sit. It is no less noisy for that reason; it is a clam shell of cabals in favor of the artists, of applause when the favorite of one faction is singing … in a word, a racket so disturbing, so indecent, that the first row of loges becomes uninhabitable. It is turned over to the disreputable women because it is too close to the parterre …
>
> Respectable people rent the second, third, and even, if the hall is crowded, the fourth row of loges; the highest ones are for the common people …
>
> [The loges being rented by the season], I come there as I would to my own house. You use your lorgnette to see who of your acquaintance is there, and you visit each other if you want to. The taste that those people have for spectacles and music is shown more by their presence than by the attention they pay. When the first performances are over, when the silence is rather modest, even on the parterre, it is not good manners to listen except in the interesting passages …
>
> I took it into my head to play chess one time when I was almost alone in the La Valle theater with Rochement, at the charming *Dangerous Liberty* … which amuses me more than their great tragedies. Chess is wonderfully suited to fill in the emptiness of those long recitations, and the music to interrupt one's too great attention to chess.

Opera being a public, commercial enterprise in Italy, De Brosses explains that one who wishes to produce an opera must rent a theater, contract singers, instrumentalists, workmen and decorators, and 'often winds up going bankrupt.'

In one interesting observation, De Brosses comments on the Italian tendency for several composers to use the same libretto.

> A lyric poem once set to music is common property; composer musicians are not rare; whenever one of them wants to work he seizes upon a poem already published, already set to music by several others; for this he makes new music to the same words. They especially take the operas of Metastasio; there are scarcely any of them that the famous masters have not worked on by turns. This method is useful and easy; one should use the same method in France, where operas often fail through the fault of the poet, it being impossible to compose good music to bad words.[83]

Tartini, according to De Brosses, complained of instrumental composers in Italy attempting to write for the voice, instead of remaining with their field of expertise.

---

82 Brosses, *Lettres*, 271ff.

83 Ibid., 273. De Brosses adds here that he had several times encouraged Rameau to compose operas in a different style than Lully and reports Rameau answering that he was afraid of being accused of vanity and of trying to surpass the old masters.

I have been begged to write for the theaters of Venice, and I have never been willing, knowing full well that a throat is not the fingerboard of a violin. Vivaldi, who tried to compose in both genres, was always hissed in one, while he succeeded in the other.[84]

Turning now to comparing the style of opera in France and Italy, De Brosses points out that the French prefer strange and fanciful plots, sacrificing Truth and realism in order to bring together,

> a great number of diverse amusements and the perpetual amusement of the senses. For that we have done well to choose fables, enchantments, magic, which leans toward the marvelous, machines, the intrusion of divinities, varieties of festivals, dances and spectacles.[85]

The Italians, on the other hand, seem to regard opera as a means of adding music to make tragedy more effective than if it were simply recited.

> This idea would be good if it were correct; but it has only a first appearance of truth. Indeed, in the violent movements of the soul, song, which is a kind of exaggerated voice, becomes quite natural, and it is very true that a strongly passionate sentiment will move the hearers more strongly when it is joined to music than it does with simple declamation; but except for these great movements, song becomes ridiculous in a tragedy.

This leads De Brosses to make a personal objection to the handling of the emotions in French opera and finally to state his preference for tragedy over opera, for the reason of mind above the senses.

> Another and greater fault of our best musical tragedies is that, at the moment when the action has moved you the most, you are diverted from your emotion because your eyes are occupied by a dance and your ears by a song, each of which forms an amusement of another kind and lets the sentiment grow cold, which the action must reheat when it returns to the stage. The opera, because it tries to present too many pleasures at one time, decreases the enjoyment: also, with many agreeable moments, there are moments of boredom, which the good French [spoken] tragedies do not have, where the interest produces its effect without diversion; it grows by degrees, and from act to act finds the heart stirred by the preceding act.
>
> The partisans of opera will say that one does not go to the opera for the subject, but for the accessories of the music, the spectacle, and the dance; that is true: it is also what makes me prefer comedy and tragedy, because the pleasures of the mind are more lively than those of the eyes or ears.[86]

---

84 Ibid., 277.

85 Ibid., 283. De Brosses mentions with regret that Pergolesi had just died at age twenty-three [actually, twenty-six]. Had he lived, says De Brosses, he might have become as famous as his teacher, Vinci, whom he says was regarded as the Lully of Italy.

86 Raguenet, 'Parallèle,' 484.

In general, however, De Brosses had genuine appreciation for the music of Italian opera.

> The Italians like to have all kinds of songs, which create the many different pictures of which music is capable. They have some very noisy ones, full of music and harmony, for brilliant voices; others have agreeable singing with delicate turns of phrase for fine and flexible voices; others are passionate, tender, touching, true in their expression of feelings, which are of a nature suitable for theatrical expression and for enhancing the play of the actor … This music is so beautiful, so astonishing, it paints objects with such art and such truth, that one is quite willing to pardon still greater faults, like that of making a character stay on the stage to sing a very long aria at a time when danger urges him to flee.

De Brosses found recitative in general boring, claiming one day he asked an Englishman if he found the French recitative 'as flat and ridiculous' as that of the Italians. 'Just as ridiculous,' said the Englishman, 'I assure you that both are equally boring and insupportable in the highest degree.'

He was particularly pleased with the new form which we recognize as opera buffa.

> These little farces have only two or three comic characters; the music is simple, gay, natural, comic in its expression, lively, and laughable in the highest degree … Add to that the air of truth with which it is presented by the musicians and the actors, and the strange precision of the execution. These *bouffons* weep, laugh loudly, work hard, do all kinds of pantomime, without missing the tempo by an eighth of a second. I admit that these kinds of plays, when they are like the *Maître de Music* by Scarlatti, the *Serva padrona*, *Livietta e Tracollo* by my charming Pergolesi, give me more pleasure than any of the others. The intellectuals who esteem only their serious plays laugh at me for my infatuation for these farces. But I stick to my opinion that the less serious the music is, the better Italian music succeeds.[87]

By 1746, the element of the drama is all but swept aside. Although Batteux offers an almost Wagnerian plea for the unity of the arts, he confesses that in opera 'if music is to be preeminent, it alone has the right to display all its wares. The stage is hers to command. Poetry and dance take the second and third places.'

EDUCATIONAL MUSIC

In his discussion of French and Italian music, Raguenet makes a brief reference to the musical education of children in 1702.

> [It is no wonder the Italians excel in music] when we consider that they learn music as we do to read; they have schools among them where their children are taught to sing as soon as our learn their A B C's; they are sent thither whilst they are very young and continue there for nine

---

87 Brosses, *Lettres*, 286ff.

or ten years, so that by the time our children are able to read true and without hesitation, theirs have been taught to sing with the same judgment and facility. To sing at sight with them is no more than to read so with us. The Italians study music once for all and attain it to the greatest perfection; the French learn it by halves, and so making themselves never masters of it, they are bound always to be scholars.[88]

FUNCTIONAL MUSIC

We find little discussion of Church music among the French literary philosophers of the seventeenth century, most of them would have no doubt agreed with the tactful comment by La Bruyère,

> Not every sort of music is fit to praise God with, or to be heard in His sanctuary.[89]

Charles de Brosses concludes his discussion of French and Italian music with a brief, but interesting, reference to Italian church music.

> I might add a couple of words on church music; we hear it often, for every time there is a service in a church there is music, and there are so many churches here, each of which has so many feasts! They perform not only motets but also concertos, sometimes with two choirs, which answer each other from two lofts, from one side of the church to the other.
> There was a superb instance of this sort of music at the Gesù on New Year's Day, but still inferior than that at Saint Cecilia, where a Spaniard gave a motet of his own composition, the most beautiful I have heard in Italy. The choirs of their motets are admirable, but the chants are lacking in the nobility and gravity suitable to their subjects. I would praise their knowledge and their harmony but not their taste. Our motets by Lalande are more beautiful and better constructed than theirs. The music in Latin does not have the same popularity as that in the vulgar tongue; little of it is performed outside the church. I would have trouble in telling you which are the most celebrated composers. As to the old Carissimi … for heaven's sake, do not speak of him in Italy for fear of being looked upon as a sugarloaf hat; those who succeeded him have gone out of fashion a long while ago. For a long time in Venice they praised the psalms in the vulgar tongue of a certain Benedetto Marcello; they are in three or four voices with basso continuo, without an orchestra. Those that I have heard appeared learned to me, but sad and devoid of a singing quality.[90]

Finally, Jean-Baptiste Du Bos, in his essay on poetry and painting of 1719, makes a few comments about military music. He refers to the fact that this kind of music has long been

---

88 Raguenet, 'Parallèle,' 484.
89 La Bruyère, *Characters*, 303.
90 Brosses, *Lettres*, 286ff.

demonstrated in practice and that civilized people have often made use of these instruments in their religious rites. Military music has long inspired the soldiers, 'and even on occasion to damp that courage down.' He finds military music still in use, but not so respected as in the past.

> Perhaps we would have studied the art of playing military instruments with the care that the Ancients did, were it not for the fact that the din of firearms prevents the instruments from being clearly heard. Although we have given little thought to the perfection of military instruments, although we have seriously neglected the art of playing them—one that was so highly valued by the Ancients—and although we now regard the people who play such instruments as of the lowest rank, the basic principles of the art are still alive in our camps.[91]

ENTERTAINMENT MUSIC

The few references we find to Entertainment Music among the important French philosophers suggest an unsurprising sense of contempt. La Bruyère, for example, observes,

> It is an old and well-tried policy of States to let their people be lulled amid festivities and entertainments, luxury, pomp and pleasure, vanity and indolence; to let them satisfy themselves with emptiness and relish frivolity; by means of which indulgence, what great strides are made towards despotism![92]

La Rochefoucauld, even though speaking of music in analogy, suggests that popular music then, as now, was short lived.

> Some people are like a popular song, taken up only for a time.[93]

---

91 Du Bos, *Réflexions*, 20.

92 La Bruyère, *Characters*, 166.

93 Rochefoucauld, *Maxims*, Nr. 211. François de la Rochefoucauld (1613–1680) joined the army at an early age and spent most of his life in public service. The *Maxims*, his most famous work, was published anonymously in 1665.

6   DESCARTES

RENÉ DESCARTES (1596–1650), after losing his mother at an early age, received from his father a financial inheritance which allowed him to spend his life in contemplation, free from the necessity of employment. His education was in Jesuit schools, centered primarily in mathematics, a background which inspired him to attempt to apply the same step-by-step process to philosophy. In the course of so doing, he felt the necessity to rid himself of possible error in all prior learning by starting over, educating himself from the beginning. In setting out on this course, he wanted to find some universal beginning point which could not be questioned and thus he formulated the most single famous sentence in philosophy, *Cogito ergo sum* [I think, therefore I am]. This concept of starting with the individual, conscious self was in itself a revolution. Even though the humanists of the Renaissance had helped rediscover the individual, in the Catholic countries such as France there was still preserved in the universities a Scholastic tradition a thousand years old which emphasized God before self.

From the perspective of self, Descartes concentrates on knowing. How do we know anything? How do we know anything is real? It is fun to follow him around in circles: since we sense things while dreaming that are evidently not real, how do we know what the senses perceive when we are awake are real and how do we distinguish between states of sleep and being awake? But in the end, since his arguments are mixed together with so much weird science, for the modern reader he becomes a bore. Particularly so since the real object of his thinking was in trying to prove there is a God.[1] He retreads a thousand years of Church dialog and ends up where they did: if you wish to believe God is real, you must believe it on Faith, not on the basis of the evidence of the senses or of indisputable conclusions of the intellect.

Cartesian philosophy began to be taught in universities in the Low Countries while Descartes was still living in that area. Some professors were very critical of his work and in these cases Descartes responded as a person rather than a philosopher. One of these squabbles caught our attention because Descartes mentions one of the most remarkable women of

---

1   In a Letter to Marin Mersene, April 15, 1630, quoted in *Descartes Philosophical Letters*, trans. Anthony Kenny (Oxford: Clarendon Press, 1970), 10ff. Marin Mersenne (1588–1648) was a Friar Minim and extensive writer, to whom we have devoted a separate chapter. Descartes makes it clear here how sincere this perspective was.

> I think that all those to whom God has given the use of this reason have an obligation to employ it principally in the endeavor to know Him and to know themselves. That is the task with which I began my studies; and I can say I would not have been able to discover the foundations of Physics if I had not looked for them along that road.

the Baroque.² Descartes is complaining here about Voetius, a professor of theology at the University of Utrecht.

> This Voetius has also spoilt Mlle de Schuurman: she had excellent gifts for poetry, painting and other gentle arts, but these last five or six years he has taken her over completely so that she cares for nothing but theological controversies, and all decent people shun her.³

ON THE PHYSIOLOGY OF AESTHETICS

At the very beginning of his 'Rules for the Direction of the Mind,' Descartes points out that the arts differ from other intellectual pursuits in several significant ways. First, no one man can excel in them all and to excel in even one requires concentration on one. Further, the hand trained for harp playing, cannot be used for other pursuits, such as agriculture. All this is by way of introducing his observation that it was the arts which convinced the other intellectual disciplines that one must be a specialist in only one subject, devoting his entire life to that alone. Descartes, on the other hand, thought everyone should study all known knowledge, in all fields, at least once in their lives. Further, he believed that since all sciences were so closely interconnected, it made more sense to study them all rather than to isolate one.

An increasing number of philosophers were arriving, through deduction or intuition, at the understanding that man has a bicameral brain. While their labels would differ (modern medicine made the official names 'left' and 'right'), it was becoming increasing clear that there was more than one way of knowing. Descartes, in presenting his labels, quickly makes them unequal: only the left brain can be trusted.

> There are two ways of arriving at a knowledge of things—through experience and through deduction ... We must note that while our experiences of things are often deceptive, the deduction or pure inference of one thing from another can never be performed wrongly by an intellect which is in the least degree rational.⁴

But of the left brain world, Descartes found only two subjects so pure and simple that 'nothing of experience can render them uncertain.' It followed that it was the step-by-step teaching

---

2   Maria Schuurman (1607–1678) was so talented she was known as the 'Minerva of Holland.' She was a talented artist and sculptor, but also active in mathematics and philosophy. During her lifetime she was particularly known for her ability in languages, reading eleven and speaking seven. One of her contemporaries paid her the generous compliment, 'If all the languages of the earth should cease to exist, she herself would give them birth anew.'

3   Letter to Mersenne, November 11, 1640, quoted in Descartes, *Philosophical Letters*, 81.

4   'Rules for the Direction of the Mind,' (1628), Rule Two. Unless otherwise indicated the translations are taken from *The Philosophical Writings of Descartes*, trans. John Cottingham, Robert Stoothoff and Dugald Murdoch (Cambridge: Cambridge University Press, 1985). In Rule Twelve, Descartes extends this to say the man has four basic faculties, 'understanding, imagination, sense and memory,' of which only the first is capable of understanding truth, and the role of the other three is one of support.

principle of these two, arithmetic and geometry, that he attempted to turn into a method for the study of all subjects.

By 1641, in a letter to Henricus Regius, a professor of medicine at Utrecht and one of the philosopher's supporters, Descartes reveals the degree to which his perspective had become exclusively left-brained.

> There is only one soul in man, the rational soul; for no actions can be reckoned human unless they depend on reason.[5]

By the time he published his 'Principles of Philosophy,' in 1646, Descartes had become even more focused on the left hemisphere of the brain. Now he says, 'We possess only two modes of thinking: the perception of the intellect and the operation of the will.' Everything else, experience, sensory perception, imagination, desire, etc., 'can be brought under these two headings.'[6]

There are some charming views of Descartes' belief in Reason in his correspondence at this time with Princess Elizabeth of Bohemia. In 1645, the princess was suffering from 'a slow fever and a dry cough.' Descartes wrote her that the commonest cause of slow fever was sadness and its cure was the mastery of *reason* over the passions.[7] But when Elizabeth challenged Descartes, pointing out that she found it necessary to make decisions on the basis of her experience, and not on Reason, Descartes quickly retreated.

> I do not doubt that your Highness' maxim is the best of all, namely that it is better to guide oneself by experience in these matter than by reason. It is rarely that we have to do with people who are as perfectly reasonable as men ought to be, so that one cannot judge what they will do simply by considering what they ought to do; and often the soundest advice is not the most successful.[8]

It is particularly interesting that Descartes assumed that some left brain knowledge was genetically in place at birth. In a letter to Mersenne in 1630, Descartes writes, 'There is no single [law] that we cannot understand if our mind turns to consider it. They are all *inborn in our minds*.'[9] This is also stated in his 'Rules for the Direction of the Mind.'

> I am convinced that certain primary seeds of truth naturally implanted in human mind …[10]

But did Descartes mean the brain by 'mind?' Physiologically, he leaves some doubt. In a letter to the Jansenist theologian, Antoine Arnauld, Descartes clearly suggests that the mind

---

5   Letter to Regius, May, 1641, quoted in Descartes, *Philosophical Letters*, 102.
6   'Principles of Philosophy' (1644), I, 32.
7   Descartes, *Philosophical Letters*, 161.
8   Letter to Elizabeth, May, 1646, quoted in Ibid., 195. Elizabeth (1618–1680) was a princess Palatine of Bohemia.
9   Letter to Mersene, April 15, 1630, quoted in Ibid., 11.
10 'Rules for the Direction of the Mind,' IV.

is something other than the brain. He writes, 'The mind, which is incorporeal.'[11] Another suggestion that the thought of the mind as something other than the brain can be seen in his curious contention that the infant has no mind.

> Infants are in a different case from animals: I should not judge that infants had minds unless I saw that they were of the same nature as adults.[12]

On the Senses

Early in his career, Descartes seemed confused about the seat of the senses. In a letter of 1637 to Mersenne he includes the senses as part of the soul.

> You argue that if the nature of man is simply to think, then he has no will. I do not see that this follows; because willing, understanding, imagining, sensing and so on are just different ways of thinking, and all belong to the soul.[13]

On the other hand, in a letter of the same year to another correspondent, discussing one of his critics, he identifies the senses with the brain.

> He expresses surprise that I recognize no sensation save that which takes place in the brain.[14]

By 1641, in his 'Meditations on First Philosophy,' Descartes appears to have begun to distrust the senses.

> During the past few days I have accustomed myself to leading my mind away from the senses; and I have taken careful note of the fact that there is very little about corporeal things that is truly perceived, whereas much more is known about the human mind, and still more about God.[15]

Today we attribute the understanding of a spatial object, such as a triangle, to the special properties of the right hemisphere of the brain. Descartes denies the senses are necessary to understanding spatial objects, observing,

---

11 Letter to Arnauld, July 29, 1648, quoted in Descartes, *Philosophical Letters*, 235.
12 Letter to More, April 15, 1649, quoted in Ibid., 251. Henry More was bursar of Christ's College, Cambridge.
13 Letter to Mersene, February 27, 1637, quoted in Ibid., 32.
14 Letter to Plempius, October 3, 1637, quoted in Ibid., 37ff. Plempius (1601–1661) was a professor of medicine at the University of Louvain.
15 'Meditations on First Philosophy' (1641), IV.

For I can think up countless other shapes which there can be no suspicion of my ever having encountered through the senses, and yet I can demonstrate various properties of these shapes, just as I can with the triangle.[16]

In his sixth meditation, of his 'Meditations on First Philosophy,' he reviews at length his reasoning by which he reaches the conclusion that neither internal nor external information of a sensory nature can be trusted and indeed were often mistaken.[17] This was, of course, the view propagated for a thousand years by the Church. Descartes goes further, however, by adding that he distrusts what might be learned from Nature for the same reason, because it comes from the senses. Later in this work, he observes that the great gift we have from Nature is Reason.

> The first request I make of my readers is that they should realize how feeble are the reasons that have led them to trust their senses up till now, and how uncertain are all the judgments that they have built up on the basis of the senses. I ask them to reflect long and often on this point, till they eventually acquire the habit of no longer placing too much trust in the senses ...
> In this way they will be exercising the intellectual vision which nature gave them, in the pure form which it attains when freed from the senses; for sensory appearances generally interfere with it and darken it to a very great extent.[18]

In this publication, Descartes simply concludes that we must accept the fact that we are created with the potential for error.

> It is quite clear from all this that, notwithstanding the immense goodness of God, the nature of man is a combination of mind and body is such that it is bound to mislead him from time to time.[19]

By three years later, in his 'Principles of Philosophy,' Descartes has arrived at the extraordinary conclusion that no information from the actual senses reaches the brain.

> By means of our senses we apprehend nothing in external objects beyond their shapes, sizes and motions ... We actually experience the various sensations as they are produced in the soul, and we do not find that anything reaches the brain from the external sense organs.[20]

As we have noted, the basic role which Descartes assigns the senses reflects a long-held Church position. We are reminded here that he was once contemplating a treatise on

---

16 Ibid., V.
17 One of his principal examples, involving pain, is that of the so-called 'phantom limb,' where a patient continues to feel pain in a limb no longer existent. Descartes also mentions the 'phantom limb' in the letter mentioned above to Plempius of October, 1637.
18 'Second Set of Replies,' to 'Meditations on First Philosophy.'
19 'Meditations on First Philosophy,' VI.
20 'Principles of Philosophy,' IV, 198.

astronomy, but was frightened into silence by the Inquisitions's trial of Galileo. Thus, we cannot help but wonder if he privately considered the value of the informaton obtained by the senses in a higher perspective than the Church would have approved, for in an *unpublished* manuscript notebook found after his death we find,

> Man has knowledge of natural things only through their resemblance to the things which come under the senses. Indeed, our estimate of how much truth a person has achieved in his philosophizing will increase the more he has been able to propose some similarity between what he is investigating and the things known by the senses.

ON THE PSYCHOLOGY OF AESTHETICS

For a confirmed left-brained thinker like Descartes, who was most at home in mathematics and geometry, it is perhaps to be expected that he felt somewhat uncomfortable in subjects which we identify today with psychology. Not being subject to Reason, as he understood it, Descartes found in a concept such as Pleasure something of a 'confused' nature. As he observed in a letter to Princess Elizabeth in 1645,

> Pleasures are of two kinds: those that belong to the mind itself, and those that belong to the whole human being, that is to say to the mind as joined to the body. These last present themselves in a confused manner to the imagination and often appear much greater than they are, especially before we possess them; and this is the source of all the evils and all the errors of life.[21]

Descartes had the same sense of discomfort in discussing the emotions, although it was a subject upon which he wrote a great deal. He begins his discussion of the 'passions' by noting that no other knowledge among the ancient philosophers is so deficient. He attributes this to the fact that since we all feel the passions within, there is no need to look outside for observation. Also he says the emotions of the soul might be called 'perceptions,' for they are 'only evident knowledge' … and confused and obscure.

> For experience shows that those who are the most strongly agitated by their passions are not those who know them best, and that the passions are to be numbered among the perceptions which the close alliance between the soul and the body renders confused and obscure.[22]

He declares that every passion is also an action, observing 'we should recognize that what is a passion in the soul is usually an action in the body.'[23] Regarding the various actions of the body, Descartes never tired of comparing the body to a machine. In a memorable con-

---

21 Letter to Elizabeth, September 1, 1645, quoted in Descartes, *Philosophical Letters*, 169.
22 'The Passions of the Soul' (1649), xxxviiiff.
23 Ibid., ii.

versation with the extraordinarily bright Queen Christina of Sweden, he was expounding on the body as a mechanism and she responded, 'That's strange, I never noticed my watch ever having baby watches!' On another occasion, more related to the topic of the emotions, Descartes uses the organ as a metaphor for the basic body mechanism which results in the perception of the emotions.

> You can think of our machine's heart and arteries, which push the animal spirits into the cavities of its brain, as being like the bellows of an organ, which push air into the wind-chests; and you can think of external objects, which stimulate certain nerves and cause spirits contained in the cavities to pass into some of the pores, as being like the fingers of the organist, which press certain keys and cause the air to pass from the wind-chests into certain pipes. Now the harmony of an organ does not depend on the externally visible arrangement of the pipes or on the shape of the wind-chests or other parts. The functions we are concerned with here does not depend at all on the external shape of the visible parts which anatomists distinguish in the substance of the brain, or on the shape of the brain's cavities, but solely on three factors: the spirits which come from the heart, the pores of the brain through which they pass, and the way in which the spirits are distributed in these pores.[24]

The 'animal spirits' referred to here, Descartes defines as,

> The parts of the blood which penetrate as far as the brain serve not only to nourish and sustain its substance, but also and primarily to produce in it a certain very fine wind, or rather a very lively and pure flame, which is called the *animal spirits*.[25]

For a time, Descartes seems to have struggled with the question of where the emotions are actually located. We get a hint of this, perhaps, in a letter to Henricus Regius.

> To say of the passions that their seat is in the brain is very paradoxical … For although the spirits which move the muscles comes from the brain, the seat of the passions must be taken to be part of the body which is most affected by them, which is undoubtedly the heart. So I would say: 'The principal seat of the passions in so far as they are corporeal, is the heart, since that is principally affected by them; but in so far as they affect also the mind, their seat is in the brain, since only the brain can directly act upon the mind.'[26]

By 1644, however, he had worked out a much detailed explanation for the physiology of the emotions. Unfortunately, from here on, as the reader will discover, his thinking included much 'weird science.' In his 'Principles of Philosophy,' Descartes explains that emotional awareness comes through small nerves, scattered throughout the body.

---

24 'Treatise on Man,' 166.
25 Ibid., 129.
26 Letter to Regius, May, 1641, quoted in Descartes, *Philosophical Letters*, 103.

> The nerves which go to the stomach, esophagus, throat, and other internal parts whose function is to keep our natural wants supplied, produce one kind of internal sensation, which is called 'natural appetite.' The nerves which go to the heart and the surrounding area, despite their very small size, produce another kind of internal sensation which comprises all the disturbances or passions and emotions of the mind such as joy, sorrow, love, hate and so on. For example, when the blood has the right consistency so that it expands in the heart more readily than usual, it relaxes the nerves scattered around the openings, and sets up a movement which leads to a subsequent movement in the brain producing a natural feeling of joy in the mind; and other causes produce the same sort of movement in these tiny nerves, thereby giving the same feeling of joy. Thus, if we imagine ourselves enjoying some good, the act of imagination does not itself contain the feeling of joy, but it causes the animal spirits to travel from the brain to the muscles in which these nerves are embedded. This causes the openings of the heart to expand, and this in turn produces the movement in the tiny nerves of the heart which must result in the feeling of joy ... Or again, if the blood is too thick and flows sluggishly into the ventricles of the heart and does not expand enough inside it, it produces a different movement in the same small nerves around the heart; when this movement is transmitted to the brain it produces a feeling of sadness in the mind, although the mind itself may perhaps not know of any reason why it should be sad. And there are several other causes capable of producing the same feeling. Other movements in these tiny nerves produce different emotions such as love, hatred, fear, anger and so on; I am here thinking of these simply as emotions or passions of the soul, that is, as confused thoughts, which the mind does not derive from itself alone but experiences as a result of something happening to the body with which it is closely conjoined. These emotions are quite different in kind from the distinct thoughts which we have concerning what is to be embraced or desired or shunned.[27]

By the time Descartes had finished his treatise on 'The Passions of the Soul,' in 1649, he had obviously made some first-hand observations of human brains, although this had been only possible by looking at dead brains in corpses. He noticed the folds in the cerebellum and concluded that in a live brain there were spaces where these folds are. It was the 'animal spirits,' a fine part of the blood, sent from the brain, traveling into these cavities and entering 'pores' in the brain's surface which carried emotions to the soul. The soul itself produces actions [everything we do by will] and some passions, although the soul also receives other passions.[28]

> Thus, when we see the light of a torch and hear the sound of a bell, the sound and the light are two different actions which, simply by producing two different movements in some of our nerves, and through them in our brain, give to the soul two different sensations. And we refer these sensations to the subjects we suppose to be their causes in such a way that we think that we see the torch itself and hear the bell, and not that we have sensory perception merely of movements coming from these objects.[29]

---

27 'Principles of Philosophy,' IV, 316ff.
28 'The Passions of the Soul,' xvii.
29 Ibid., xxiii.

To this he adds an additional type of passions.

> The imaginings which depend solely on the fortuitous movement of the animal spirits may be passions just as truly as the perceptions which depend on the nerves ... Everything the soul perceives by means of the nerves may also be represented to it through the fortuitous course of the spirits. The sole difference is that the impressions which come into the brain through the nerves are normally more lively and more definite than those produced by the spirits.[30]

The real centerpiece of all this weird science is the pineal gland, a small gland in the brain, to which Descartes assigned nearly everything for which he could not otherwise discover a physical location. To be fair to Descartes, we must note that the medical profession, after two thousand years of research, still has no idea what function this gland performs. But, on the other hand, research has proven that several of the functions which Descartes attributes to this gland are incorrect. In various treatises he says this gland is the seat of the imagination and the common sense,[31] the passions as well as the seat of the soul.[32] With regard to the latter, this gland being the seat of the soul, Descartes gives a very precise description of his theory in a letter of 1640 to Lazare Meysonnier, a professor, doctor and astrologer at Lyons. One can see here that Descartes was evidently bothered by the question, that since we have two eyes, two ears, etc., how *two* senses could feed information to the brain which would result in *one* understanding?

> I will answer the question you asked me about the function of the little gland called [pineal]. My view is that this gland is the principal seat of the soul, and the place in which all our thoughts are formed. The reason I believe this is that I cannot find any part of the brain, except for this, which is not double. Since we see only one thing with two eyes, and hear only one voice with two ears, and altogether have only one thought at a time, it must necessarily be the case that the impressions which enter by the two eyes or by the two ears, and so on, unite with each other in some part of the body before being considered by the soul. Now it is impossible to find any such place, in the whole head, except this gland; moreover it is situated in the most suitable possible place for this purpose, in the middle of all the concavities; and it is supported and surrounded by the little branches of the carotid arteries which bring the spirits into the brain.[33]

In the 'Passions of the Soul,' Descartes words this differently. Here the pineal gland is not the soul itself, but it is the agent which acts on the soul.

---

30 *Ibid.*, xxvi.

31 'Treatise on Man,' 129 and 'Meditations on First Philosophy,' VI.

32 'Principles of Philosophy,' IV, 316ff.

33 Letter to Meyssonnier, January 29, 1640, quoted in Descartes, *Philosophical Letters*, 69ff. He discusses this again at some length in a letter to Mersenne of December 24, 1640.

> We can easily understand that these images or other impressions are unified in this [pineal] gland by means of the spirits which fill the cavities of the brain. They cannot exist united in this way in any other place in the body except as a result of their being united in this gland ...
>
> Thus, for example, if we see some animal approaching us, the light reflected from its body forms two images, one in each of our eyes; and these images form two others, by means of the optic nerves, on the internal surface of the brain facing its cavities. Then, by means of the animal spirits that fill these cavities, the images radiate toward the little [pineal] gland which the spirits surround: the movement forming each point of one of the images tends towards the same point on the gland as the movement forming the corresponding point of the other image, which represents the same part of the animal. In this way, the two images in the brain form only one image on the gland, which acts directly upon the soul and makes it see the shape of the animal.[34]

We must also observe at this point that in his private letters, Descartes sometimes refers to the soul as not being a gland, but an incorporeal concept. Thus, in a letter to the French philosopher, Jean de Silhon, on the existence of God and the human soul, Descartes observes,

> Man, that is his soul, is a being or substance which is *not at all corporeal*, whose nature is solely to think, and that this is the first thing one can know with certainty.[35]

Similarly, in a letter to Mersenne,

> In the case of the soul the matter is even clearer. As I have shown, the soul is nothing but a thing which thinks ... It is true that a thing of such a nature cannot be imagined, that is, *cannot be represented by a corporeal image*.[36]

Aside from this discrepancy, correspondence with Descartes reveals that his theories of the function of the pineal gland aroused many questions, particularly among the medical profession. Mersenne writes of some objections he had heard in 1640 and wonders why the medical profession had not discovered the role of this gland. Descartes answers,

> I would not find it strange that the gland should be found decayed when the bodies of lethargic persons are dissected, because it decays very rapidly in all other cases too. Three years ago at Leyden, when I wanted to see it in a woman who was being autopsied, I found it impossible to recognize it, even though I looked very thoroughly, and knew well where it should be, being accustomed to find it without any difficulty in freshly killed animals. An old professor who was performing the autopsy, named Valcher, admitted to me that he had never been able to see it in any human body. I think this is because they usually spend some days looking at the intestines and other parts before opening the head.[37]

---

34 'The Passions of the Soul,' xxxiiff.
35 Letter to Silhon, May, 1637, quoted in Descartes, *Philosophical Letters*, 34.
36 Letter to Mersene, July, 1641, quoted in Ibid., 106.
37 Letter to Mersenne, April 1, 1640, quoted in Ibid., 72

Mersenne writes again in July 1640, enclosing a letter he had received from a doctor questioning Descartes' theories about the pineal gland. Descartes answers Mersenne that he sees no argument to refute and adds two more properties for the pineal gland. First, he suggests it may be responsible for people who 'become troubled in their minds without any known cause.'

> Moreover, all the alterations which take place in the mind, when a man sleeps after drinking, for instance, can be attributed to some alterations taking place in this gland.[38]

Descartes finds yet another role for the pineal gland in the explanation of memory. Memory occurs, according to Descartes, when the will to remember,

> makes the gland lean first to one side and then to another, thus driving the animal spirits towards different regions of the brain until they come upon the one containing traces left by the object we want to remember.[39]

Finally, Descartes attributes to the pineal gland the occurrence that the same images can result in different passions in different people. The reason for this, he says, is that not all brains are constituted in the same way.

> Thus the very same movement of the gland which in some excites fear, in others causes the spirits to enter the pores of the brain which direct them partly into nerves which serve to move the hands in self-defense.[40]

With that brief introduction to Descartes' weird science regarding the physiology of emotions, we move to his definition of psychological aspects of the emotions. After presenting the definition of human passions as 'something which moves the soul to want the things for which they prepare the body,'[41] Descartes concludes there are only six principal ['primitive'] passions: wonder, love, hatred, desire, joy and sadness. All others are contained in these, or composed of them.[42]

Wonder, is a 'sudden surprise of the soul' which causes it to devote unusual attention to objects that 'seem to it unusual and extraordinary.' Since this passion is concerned primarily with knowledge, it is not accompanied by changes in the heart or blood. A stronger form of Wonder, astonishment, has an added element of surprise which 'causes the spirits in the cavities of the brain to make their way to the place where the impression of the object of wonder is located.' Descartes observes,

---

38 Letter to Mersenne, July 30,1640, quoted in Ibid., 75.
39 'The Passions of the Soul,' xlii.
40 Ibid., xxxixff.
41 Ibid., xl, li.
42 Ibid., lxixff.

Although it is only the dull and stupid who are not naturally disposed to wonder, this does not mean that those with the best minds are always the most inclined to it.

Excessive Wonder may become a habit, he notes, when we fail to correct it.
Regarding Love and Hatred,[43]

> Love is an emotion of the soul caused by a movement of the [animal] spirits, which impels the soul to join itself willingly to objects that appear to be agreeable to it. And hatred is an emotion caused by the spirits, which impels the soul to want to be separated from objects which are presented to it as harmful.

Descartes distinguishes between benevolent love (a wish for the well-being of the object) and concupiscent love (to desire the object) and notes that there is an abundance of passions which are also associated with love: the desire of the ambitious for glory, the miser for money, the drunkard for wine, etc. He also associates affection, friendship and devotion with whether we esteem the object as less, equal or more than ourselves.

Desire is a passion in which an agitation of the soul caused by the animal spirits disposes the soul to wish, in the future, for something agreeable.[44] Descartes finds there is no opposite for Desire, but that there are many kinds: curiosity for knowledge, desire for glory, desire for vengeance, etc.

Joy and Sadness,[45] he defines as follows,

> Joy is a pleasant emotion which the soul has when it enjoys a good,[46] which impression in the brain represent to it as its own ... Sadness is an unpleasant listlessness which affects the soul when it suffers discomfort from an evil or deficiency which impressions in the brain represent to it as its own.

Next Descartes explains the physical manifestation associated with these basic passions,[47] excepting Wonder which is located only in the brain. In the case of Love,

> the pulse has a regular beat, but is much fuller and stronger than normal; we feel a gentle heat in the chest; and the digestion of food takes place very quickly in the stomach. In this way this passion is conducive to good health.

---

43 Ibid., lxxixff.
44 Ibid., lxxxviff.
45 Ibid., xciff.
46 In a letter to Princess Elizabeth, November, 1646, quoted in John Blom, *Descartes* (New York: New York University Press, 1978),197, Descartes observes,
>   I also even dare to believe that interior joy has some secret force to render fortune more favorable.
47 'The Passions of the Soul,' xcviff.

In Hatred,

> the pulse is irregular, weaker and often quicker; we feel chills mingled with a sort of sharp, piercing heat in the chest; and the stomach ceases to perform its function, being inclined to regurgitate and reject the food we have eaten, or at any rate to spoil it and turn it into bad humors.

In Joy,

> the pulse is regular and faster than normal, but not so strong or full as in the case of love; we feel a pleasant heat not only in the chest but also spreading into all the external parts of the body along with the blood which is seen to flow copiously to these parts; and yet we sometimes lose our appetite because our digestion is less active than usual.

In Sadness,

> the pulse is weak and slow, and we feel as if our heart had tight bonds around it, and were frozen by icicles which transmit their cold to the rest of the body. But sometimes we still have a good appetite and feel our stomach continuing to do its duty, provided there is no hatred mixed with the sadness.

Desire,

> agitates the heart more violently than any other passion, and supplies more spirits to the brain. Passing from there into the muscles, these spirits render all the senses more acute, and all the parts of the body more mobile.

Descartes now elaborates on the physical manifestations associated with the passions.[48] We will cite, as an example, only those associated with Love.

> These observations, and many others that would take too long to report, have led me to conclude that when the understanding thinks of some object of love, this thought forms an impression in the brain which directs the animal spirits through the nerves of the sixth pair to the muscles surrounding the intestines and stomach, where they act in such a way that the alimentary juices (which are changing into new blood) flow rapidly to the heart without stopping in the liver. Driven there with greater force than the blood from other parts of the body, these juices enter the heart in greater abundance and produce a stronger heat there because they are coarser than the blood which has already been rarefied many times as it passes again and again through the heart. As a result the spirits sent by the heart to the brain have parts which are coarser and more agitated than usual; and as they strengthen the impression formed by the first thought of the loved object, these spirits compel the soul to dwell upon this thought. This is what the passion of love consists in.

---

48 Ibid., ciiff.

Like many early philosophers, Descartes incorrectly believed that it was the eyes which communicate emotions. We know today, through extensive research, that it is only the facial expressions which express emotions and in greater part in the left side of the face (corresponding to the right hemisphere of the brain). Further, the basic facial expressions as they correspond to basic emotions are, like the emotions themselves, universal and in place genetically before birth. But, in case the reader is curious, here are the observations by Descartes.

> There is no passion which some particular expression of the eyes does not reveal. For some passions this is quite obvious: even the most stupid servants can tell from their master's eye whether he is angry with them. But although it is easy to perceive such expressions of the eyes and to know what they signify, it is not easy to describe them. For each consists of many changes in the movement and shape of the eye, and these are so special and slight that we cannot perceive each of them separately, though we can easily observe the result of their conjunction. Almost the same can be said of the facial expressions which also accompany passions. For although more extensive than those of the eyes, they are still hard to discern. They differ so little that some people make almost the same face when they weep as others do when they laugh ... [Also] the soul is able to change facial expressions, as well as expressions of the eyes, by vividly feigning a passion which is contrary to one it wishes to conceal. Thus we may use such expressions to hide our passions as well as to reveal them.[49]

He does mention, in passing, the reading of expressions on the face, when discussing the nature of words as symbols.

> Words, as you well know, bear no resemblance to the things they signify, and yet they make us think of these things, frequently without our paying attention to the sound of the words or to their syllables. Thus it may happen that we hear an utterance whose meaning we understand perfectly well, but afterwards we cannot say in what language it was spoken. Now if words, which signify nothing except by human convention, suffice to make us think of things to which they bear no resemblance, then why could nature not also have established some sign which would make us have the sensation of light, even if the sign contained nothing in itself which is similar to this sensation? Is it not thus that nature has established laughter and tears, to make us read joy and sadness on the faces of men?[50]

Finally, in a letter to Pierre Chanut, French ambassador to Sweden, Descartes acknowledges the genetic nature of the emotions, but contends that the prenatal fetus has only four 'passions': joy, love, sadness and hatred. It was the unconscious retention of the confused prenatal emotions which complicated our judgments of the passions in later life, Descartes suggested.

> Those four passions, I think, were the first we felt, and the only ones we felt before our birth. I think they were then only sensations or very confused thoughts, because the soul was so attached

---
49 Ibid., 412ff.
50 'The World or Treatise on Light,' 4.

to matter that it could not do anything except receive impressions from the body ... Before birth love was caused only by suitable nourishment, which entered in abundance into the liver, heart, and lungs and produced an increase of heat: this is the reason why similar heat still always accompanies love, even though it comes from other very different causes ... The other bodily conditions which at the beginning of our life occurred with these four passions still accompany them. It is because of these confused sensations of our childhood, which continue connected to the rational thoughts by which we love what we judge worthy of love, that the nature of love is difficult for us to understand.[51]

ON THE PHILOSOPHY OF AESTHETICS

Except for music, Descartes mentions topics related to aesthetics in the arts only in passing. For example, a passage in a letter to Henry More suggests that Descartes supported the concept that art should imitate Nature.

It seems reasonable, since art copies nature, and men can make various automata which move without thought, that nature should produce its own automata, much more splendid than artificial one. These natural automata are the animals.[52]

The only comment Descartes made in reference to the theater suggests that our rational-minded philosopher was a bit uncomfortable with strong emotions.

I agree that the sadness of tragedies would not please as it does if we feared that it might become so excessive as to make us uncomfortable.[53]

Descartes refers to poetry several times. On one occasion he calls upon his rational analytical powers to describe the creative urge for Princess Elizabeth.

The inclination of your Highness to compose verse during her illness made me remember Socrates, who, as Plato tells us, had a similar desire while he was in prison. And I believe this humor issues from a strong agitation of the animal spirits that would be able utterly to upset the imagination of those who do not possess a well settled brain, but can only make a little warmer those more stolid, and dispose them to poetry. And I consider this transport a mark of a mind stronger and more elevated than the common.[54]

---

51 Letter to Chanut, February 1, 1647, quoted in Descartes, *Philosophical Letters*, 210ff.
52 Letter to More, February 5, 1649, quoted in Ibid., 244.
53 Letter to Elizabeth, November 3, 1645, quoted in Ibid., 184ff.
54 Letter to Elizabeth, February 22, 1649, quoted in Blom, *Descartes*, 238ff.

A comment in his 'Discourse on the Method' has quite a different character.

> Those with the most pleasing conceits and the ability to express them with the most embellishment and sweetness would still be the best poets, even if they knew nothing of the theory of poetry.[55]

As in other cases, perhaps Descartes' most private observations are found in an unpublished notebook found after his death.

> It may seem surprising to find weighty judgments in the writings of the poets rather than the philosophers. The reason is that the poets were driven to write by enthusiasm and the force of imagination. We have within us the sparks of knowledge, as in a flint: philosophers extract them through reason, but poets force them out through the sharp blows of the imagination, so that they shine more brightly.[56]

Finally, reflecting his extensive reading, Descartes mentions in a letter to Pierre Chanut the centuries old theme by poets, that the pain of love outweighs the pleasure.

> Love gives pleasure; and though the poets often complain of it in their verses, I think that men would naturally give up loving if they did not find it more sweet than bitter.[57]

ON THE AESTHETICS OF MUSIC

The 'Compendium of Music,' Descartes' earliest treatise, appears to have been written during lulls while he was serving in the army of Prince Maurice of Nassau in 1617. In spite of this early demonstration of his interest in music, he would never mention it again in his treatises, except in passing or when in need of a metaphor. It is particularly odd that he never mentions music in his treatise on the passions, for this subject was closely associated with music in all similar European treatises.

Of course, we must assume that Descartes had discovered in the subsequent years of writing that music was a subject which did not lend itself easily to the kind of rational thought process which he had advocated. In addition, there is a passage in the 'Discourse on the Method' which refers to the long Scholastic tradition in the universities, where the 'speculative' had long been taught, but only recently the 'practical.' Although this passage is not addressed specifically to music, since these terms, 'speculative music' and 'practical music' were so long associated with music by the academic world, we think it might therefore be another reason why Descartes wrote so little on music after the first treatise. Perhaps he

---

55 'Discourse on the Method' (1637), I, 7.
56 From a manuscript notebook found after the death of Descartes.
57 Letter to Chanut, February 1, 1647, quoted in Descartes, *Philosophical Letters*, 216.

concluded that it was practical music which went to the heart of the essence of music, and not the old 'speculative music' approach of the universities. At the same time, he may have felt he lacked the experience to discuss 'practical music.'

> It seemed to me that much more truth could be found in the reasonings which a man makes concerning matters that concern him than in those which some scholar makes in his study about speculative matters. For the consequences of the [practical study] will soon punish the man if he judges wrongly, whereas the [speculative study] has no practical consequences and no importance for the scholar except that perhaps the further they are from common sense the more pride he will take in them, since he will have had to use so much more skill and ingenuity in trying to render them plausible.[58]

On the Purpose of Music

Descartes' definition of music is also its purpose, to communicate emotions to the soul of the listener.

> The basis of music is sound; its aim is to please and to arouse various emotions in us. Melodies can be at the same time sad and enjoyable; nor is this so unique, for in the same way writers of elegies and tragedies please us most the more sorrow they awaken in us …
> The human voice seems most pleasing to us because it is most directly attuned to our souls.[59]

In his treatise, 'The Passions of the Soul,' Descartes contends that every passion of the soul is usually accompanied by an action in the body.[60] In the 'Compendium of Music' he appears to have this in mind when he offers some observations on the physical manifestations of musicians while performing.

> Few are aware how in music with diminution [*musica valde diminuta*], employing many voices, this time division is brought to the listener's attention without the use of a beat [*battuta*]; this, I say, is accomplished in vocal music by stronger breathing and on instruments by stronger pressure, so that at the beginning of each measure the sound is produced more distinctly; singers and instrumentalists observe this instinctively, especially in connection with tunes to which we are accustomed to dance and sway. Here we accompany each beat of the music by a corresponding motion of our body; we are quite naturally impelled to do this by the music. For it is undoubtedly true that sound strikes all bodies on all sides, as one can observe in the case of bells and thunder … Since this is so, and since, as we have said, the sound is emitted more strongly and clearly at

---

58 'Discourse on the Method' (1637), I, 9ff.

59 Descartes, *Compendium of Music*, trans. Walter Robert (Rome: American Institute of Musicology, 1961), 11. As has been our practice in earlier volumes, we are interested only in discussion which touches on aesthetics in music, and not in theoretical discussions.

60 'The Passions of the Soul,' ii.

the beginning of each measure, we must conclude that it has greater impact on our spirits, and that we are thus roused to motion. It follows that even animals can dance to rhythm if they are taught and trained, for it takes only a physical stimulus to achieve this reaction.[61]

Descartes adds a few more observations on the relationship of tempo and the communication of emotions. Slower tempi, he suggests, 'arouses in us quieter feelings such as languor, sadness, fear and pride.' Faster tempi arouses 'faster emotions, such as joy.'[62]

The most intriguing comment by Descartes is that he would like to 'discuss the various powers which the consonances possess of evoking emotions,' but that the topic exceeds the scope of his treatise. We may have been disappointed if he wrote more on this subject, however, for when he addresses this topic in a letter to Mersenne he seems to abandon any meaningful hope to establish aesthetic principles.

> It is one thing to say that a consonance is sweeter than another, another to say it is more pleasing. Everyone knows that honey is sweeter than olives, yet many would prefer to eat olives, not honey. Thus, everyone knows that the fifth is sweeter than the fourth, the fourth sweeter than the major third, this in turn sweeter than the minor third. Yet there are places in which the minor third is more pleasing than the fifth, others, indeed, where a dissonance is more pleasing than a consonance.[63]

On the Perception of Music

Descartes, with his predilection to systematic thought, devotes the greater part of his treatise to the perception of music. He begins with a series of propositions, called 'Preliminaries,'[64] for which he provides the reader little further discussion.

1. All senses are capable of experiencing pleasure.
2. For this pleasure a proportional relation of some kind between the object and the sense itself must be present. For example, the noise of guns or thunder is not fit for music, because it injures the ears …
3. The object must be such that it does not fall on the sense in too complicated or confused a fashion …
4. An object is perceived more easily by the senses when the difference of the parts is smaller.
5. We may say that the parts of a whole object are less different when there is greater proportion between them.

---

61 Descartes, *Compendium of Music*, 14ff.
62 Ibid., 15.
63 Quoted in Bianconi, *Music in the Seventeenth Century*, 56.
64 Descartes, *Compendium of Music*, 11ff.

6. This proportion must be arithmetic, not geometric, the reason being that in the former there is less to perceive, as all differences are the same throughout.

In the last three of these, Descartes appears to have been thinking primarily of time, for later he contends,

> Time in sound must consist of equal parts, for these are perceived most easily according to point 4 above, or it must consist of parts which are in a proportion of 1:2 or 1:3; this progression cannot be extended, for only these relations can be easily distinguished by the ear, according to points 5 and 6. If time values were of greater inequality, the ear would not be able to recognize their differences without great effort, as experience shows; for should I, for example, place five even notes against one, it would be almost impossible to sing.[65]

7. The most pleasing sense-objects are neither those which are most easy to perceive nor those which are most difficult; but those which are not so easy as to fail to satisfy the natural desire of the senses to operate on their objects nor yet so difficult as to tire the senses.
8. Finally, it must be observed that variety is in all things most pleasing.

In a letter to Mersenne in 1630, Descartes makes a lengthy discussion of aesthetics, concluding that neither 'beauty' nor 'pleasure' can be given meaningful definitions in music since everything is a matter of individual preference.

> You ask whether one can discover the essence of beauty. This is the same as your earlier question, why one sound is more pleasant than another, except that the word 'beauty' seems to have a special relation to the sense of sight. But in general 'beautiful' and 'pleasant' signify simply a relation between our judgment and an object; and because the judgments of men differ so much from each other neither beauty nor pleasantness can be said to have any definite measure. I cannot give any better explanation than the one I have long ago in my treatise on music; I will quote it word for word, since I have the book before me.
>
> [Here he quotes Nr. 7, above]
>
> To explain what I meant by difficult or easy perception I instanced the divisions of a flower bed. If there are only one or two types of shape arranged in the same pattern, they will be taken in more easily than if there are ten or twelve arranged in different ways. But this does not mean that one design can be called absolutely more beautiful than another; to some men's fancy one with three shapes will be the most beautiful, to others it will be one with four or five and so on. But whatever will please most men could be called the most beautiful without qualification; but what this is cannot be determined.
>
> Secondly, what makes one man want to dance may make another want to cry. This is because it evokes ideas in our memory: for instance those who have in the past enjoyed dancing to a certain tune feel a fresh wish to dance when they hear a similar one; on the other hand, if a man never heard a galliard without some affliction befalling him, he would certainly grow sad when

---

65 Ibid., 13.

he heard it again. This is so certain that I reckon that if you whipped a dog five or six times to the sound of a violin, he would begin to howl and run away as soon as he heard that music again.[66]

Descartes makes only a few additional observations on the perception of music. He discusses the aesthetic nature of various intervals, the most interesting observation being that the fifth 'sounds neither as sharp to the ear as the major third or as languid as the octave; it is the most pleasing of all consonances.'[67]

His comment regarding the bass voice, 'it must strike the ear more forcibly in order to be heard distinctly,' is interesting as an early recognition of what we call the 'pyramid principle,' a means of solving through performance the tendency of the brain to boost the perception of upper partials.[68]

Finally, in another instance of weird science, Descartes mistakenly believed some form of memory in the musical performer resided in the actual fingers, hands and arms. This first appears in a letter of January 1640 to Lazare Meysonnier.

> I think also that some of the impressions which serve the memory can be in various other parts of the body: for instance the skill of a lute player is not only in his head, but also partly in the muscles of his hands and so on.[69]

Descartes mentions this again in a letter to Mersenne in March of the same year with more detail.

> I think that it is the other parts of the brain, especially the interior parts, which most serve memory. I think that all the nerves and muscles can serve it, too, so that a lute player, for instance, has a part of his memory in his hands: for the ease of bending and disposing his fingers in various ways, which he as acquired by practice, helps him to remember the passages which need these dispositions when they are played.[70]

In a letter to Mersenne in August of this same year, Descartes speculates that the memory of childhood events is attributed to the fact that 'we have done the same things again and renewed the impression by remembering the events from time to time.' Our left-brained philosopher would have been very surprised to know that modern clinical research suggests that memories of childhood are invariably associated with the emotions.

---

66 Letter to Mersene, March 18, 1630, quoted in Descartes, *Philosophical Letters*, 7ff.

67 Descartes, *Compendium of Music*, 23.

68 Ibid., 48.

69 Letter to Meyssonnier, January 29, 1640, quoted in Descartes, *Philosophical Letters*, 70.

70 Letter to Mersenne, April 1, 1640, quoted in Ibid., 71.

7 FRENCH DRAMA

IN CATHOLIC FRANCE the influence of the Church had managed to suppress the dramatic arts until it was officially encouraged by cardinal Richelieu. Although strong Church objections would continue throughout the seventeenth century, the remarkable talents of Corneille, Molière and Racine made it popular with aristocratic society and thus establishing forever the theater in France.

The vigorous intellectual atmosphere in Paris, which resulted in so much discussion of opera and philosophy, also produced much commentary on the role of this new movement in dramatic poetry. While much of this discussion focused on the relationship of modern French theater to the writings of the ancient Greeks, in particular Aristotle, there are many comments which we believe might reflect on the aesthetic climate in general. Therefore, we begin by briefly reviewing the chronological development of the aesthetic principles of the French theater during the Baroque.

An early commentary is François Ogier's *Préface au Lecteur*, attached to Jean de Schélandre's play, *Tyr et Sidon* (1628), which comments on the purpose of drama.

> Poetry, and especially that which is written for the theater, is composed only for pleasure and amusement, and this pleasure can arise only from the variety of the events which are represented on the stage.[1]

He argues that imitating the ancients is of limited value, due to the different times and customs of France of his day. These differences should be reflected in the theater, but in a subject such as philosophy the central object in all countries should be the search for basic values and Truth.

> I confine myself here to poetry alone, and say that the too intense eagerness of wishing to imitate the ancients has caused our best poets to fail to attain either the reputation or the excellence of the ancients. They did not consider that the taste of nations is different, as well in matters pertaining to the mind as in those of the body, and that, just as the Moors, and without going so far, the Spaniards, imagine and prefer a type of beauty quite different from that which we prize in France, and just as they desire their sweethearts to have a different figure, and features other than those that we desire to see in ours, to such a degree that there are some men who

---

1   Quoted in Barrett Clark, *European Theories of the Drama* (New York: Crown Publishers, 1959), 119. Ogier (d. 1670) was a native of Paris, entered the church at an early age and became '*prédicateur du roi*.' It is known that he was present at Münster in 1648 for the signing of the Treaty of Westphalia.

will form an idea of their beauty from the same features that we should consider homely, just so, it must not be doubted that the minds of nations have preferences quite different from one another, and altogether dissimilar feelings for the beauty of intellectual things, such as poetry; but philosophy, nevertheless, has no part in this matter: for it expects, to be sure, that the minds of all men, under whatever sky they may be born, shall agree in one and the same opinion concerning the things necessary for the sovereign good, and it strives as far as possible to unite them in the search after truth, because there can be but one truth; but as for matters that are merely amusing and unimportant, such as this of which we are speaking, it allows our opinions to take whatever direction they please, and does not extend its jurisdiction over this matter.[2]

Ogier also discussed the new dramatic form called *Tragi-comédie*, which he says was introduced by the Italians. Whereas the ancient Greek drama theorists carefully separated the comic and the tragic, Ogier finds this a meaningful form, reflecting the true nature of man's life.

To say that it is improper to show in a single play the same persons speaking now of serious, important, and tragic matters, and immediately after of commonplace, vain, and humorous things, is to be unacquainted with the nature of human life, whose days and hours are very often interrupted by laughter and by tears, by joy and by sorrow, according as they are filled with happiness or troubled by misfortune. Some one of the gods endeavored formerly to mingle joy with sorrow in order to make of them a single compound; he was unable to accomplish this, but then he joined them behind one another. That is why they ordinarily follow so closely after one another, and nature herself has shown us that there is scarcely any difference between them, since artists note that the movements of muscles and nerves that give an expression of laughter to the countenance, are the same that serve to make us weep and assume the expression of sorrow by which we manifest extreme grief.[3]

In 1637 Jean Chapelain published a treatise called, *Les Sentimens de l'Académie françoise sur la Tragi-comédie du Cid*. This paper reflects an intellectual debate which followed the enormous success of Corneille's *Le Cid*, first produced in 1636. A number of jealous 'arbiters of taste' in Paris attacked the work for treating an unacceptable subject and for violating the rules of drama. After several counterattacks, including one by Corneille himself, the question was taken up by the Academy and the eventual report was written primarily by Champelain. In this report Chapelain discusses the purpose of drama, and the nature of 'Pleasure.'

Nature and Truth have put a certain value to things, which cannot be altered by that which chance or opinion set up; to attempt to judge them by what they seem, and not what they are, is to condemn oneself at the outset. It is true enough that the great Masters are not themselves in very close agreement on this point. Some, too much inclined, it seems, toward pleasure, hold that delight is the true purpose of dramatic poetry; others, more sparing of men's time and holding it too dear to be given over to amusements which yield only pleasure and no profit,

---

2 Ibid., 121.
3 Ibid., 122.

maintain that its real end is to instruct. Though each expresses himself in such different terms, it will on closer examination be seen that both are in agreement; and if we judge them with what favor we should, we shall see that those who claim pleasure as the sole end are too reasonable to exclude anything that is not conformable to reason. We must believe—if we would do them justice—that by pleasure they mean the pleasure which is not the enemy but the instrument of virtue, and which purges men, insensibly and without disgust, of their vicious practices, and which is useful because it is good, and which can never leave regret in the mind for having surprised it, nor in the soul for having corrupted it. And so they only seem to disagree with the others, for it is true that if the pleasure they demand be not profit itself, it is at least the source whence of necessity it flows; and that wherever there is pleasure there is profit, and that both are produced from the same sources.[4]

As this discussion continues, Chapelain includes music as an illustration for his contention that it is not enough to please, but a work of Art must also observe the rules 'of the experts'—an obvious reference to the Academy itself.

Hence, they are at one, and we agree with them both, and we can all of us together say that a play is good when it produces a feeling of reasonable content. But, as in music and painting, we should not consider every concert and every picture good if it please the people but fail in the observance of the rules of their respective arts, and if the experts, who are the sole judges, did not by their approval confirm that of the multitude. Hence we must not say with the crowd that a poem is good merely because it pleases, unless the learned and the expert are also pleased. Indeed, it is impossible that there can be pleasure contrary to Reason, unless it be to a depraved taste—as, for instance, a liking for the bitter and the acid.

In a posthumous work, *Sommaire d'une Poétique dramatique*, Chapelain defines Tragedy as the noblest form of drama, in which the playwright imitates the actions of the great, while comedy treats actions of people of middle or low condition and has a happy ending. Tragi-comedy, which he mentions is very popular in France, he finds closer to Tragedy. The Pastoral he considers a type of Tragi-comedy, dealing with shepherds, but in an elevated manner with higher sentiments. In his summary, he adds the element of the emotions.

In plays, poets depict, besides action, the various manners, customs and passions of human beings.[5]

The relationship of modern theater with that of the ancients was also addressed in François Hédelin's *La Pratique du théâtre* (1657).[6] The rules of theater established by the ancients had

---

4   Ibid., 125ff. Chapelain (1595–1674) was reared by his parents to have a literary career, of which his most important production was an epic poem, *La Pucelle*. Chapelain frequented the salon at the Hôtel de Rambouillet, where he became friends with Malherbe, Corneille and Richelieu.

5   Ibid., 127.

6   François Hédelin (1604–1676), was also known as Abbé d'Aubignac, after an estate he was given for his services as tutor to the nephew of Cardinal Richelieu. His treatise on dramatic theory is remembered today for its emphasis that plays should be performed, not read.

their significance, he believed, in the fact that they were based on Reason. To the objection that the ancients sometimes violated their own rules, he answered,

> Reason, being alike all the world over, does equally require everybody's submission to it, and if our modern authors cannot without offense be dispensed from the rules of the stage, no more could the Ancients; and where they have failed I do not pretend to excuse them …
>
> I must not omit, for the glory of the Ancients, that if they have sometimes violated the art of dramatic poems, they have done it for some more powerful and inducing reason than all the interest of the play could amount to.[7]

To those who pointed out that the productions of ancient Greek and Roman plays were not always successful in modern Paris, Hédelin replied that this was due only to poor translations and to subjects, such as ancient history, which held little interest for modern Frenchmen.

Hédelin devotes considerable attention to the nature of the subject of a play, although prefacing his remarks by observing that 'there is no story so rich but that an ill poet may spoil its beauty.' First, to be successful, a play must not offend the moral standards of the age in which it is presented. It was for this very reason, he points out, that the *Théodore* of Corneille did not receive the appreciation it deserved.

> It is in itself a most ingenious play, the plot being well carried and full of variety, where all the hints of the true story are made use of to advantage, the changes and turns very judicious and the passions and verse worthy of the name of so great a man. But because the whole business turns upon the prostitution of Theodora to the public stews, it would never please.[8]

To be popular with the public, he contends that the subject of a play must be founded on one of three things; noble passions, an intricate and pleasing plot or upon some extraordinary spectacle. Of these we are particularly interested in his discussion of the 'passions' in drama, an element by which, he says, 'the spectators are ravished and their soul continually moved with some new impression.' First, he warns of the danger of emotional excess.

> Violent passions too often repeated do, as it were, numb the soul and its sympathy … It is for this reason that some of our poets who had contrived in every act a memorable incident and a moving passion did not find that the success answered their expectation.

At this time Jean de La Bruyère, in his famous book, *Characters*, also makes an interesting observation on the emotions of the plays and their relationship to the observers.

> Why is it that we laugh so freely at the theater and yet are ashamed to weep there? Is it less natural to be moved by what is pitiful than to be amused by what is ridiculous? Are we deterred by the fear of distorting our features? Such distortion is greater in excessive laughter than in the

---

7 Clark, *European Theories*, 129ff.
8 Quoted in Ibid., 131.

bitterest grief, and we avert our faces to laugh as well as to weep in the presence of the great and of all those whom we respect ... The extreme violence we do to our feelings by restraining our tears, and the false laughter with which we try to conceal them, clearly proves that the natural effect of great tragedy should be to make us all weep quite openly, with one accord, in other another's presence, with no further concern than to wipe our eyes; moreover, after having agreed to indulge in tears, we might discover that we generally run less risk of weeping in the theater than of dying of boredom there.[9]

We have mentioned, in the Introduction, that, in contrast to the other arts, it is the uniqueness of music that it is not a representation of feeling, but a direct communication of feeling between composer and listener. Hédelin indirectly refers to this in his discussion of the representation of the emotions on the stage.

The subjects full of passions last longer and affect us more, because the soul which received the impression of them does not keep them so long nor so strongly as our memory does the events of things; nay, it often happens that they please us more a second seeing, because that the first time we are employed about the event and disposition of the play and by consequent do less enter into the sentiments of the actors; but having once no need of applying our thoughts to the story, we busy them about the things that are said, and so receive more impressions of grief or fear.[10]

It is often asked, Hédelin writes, whether a subject must be a true story. No, he says,

The stage does not present things as they have been, but as they ought to be, for the poet must in the subject he takes reform everything that is not accommodated to the rules of his art, as a painter does when he works upon an imperfect model.[11]

With regard to the purpose of drama, Hédelin assigns a strong goal to education. By the poet adding to the action 'diverse pithy and bold truths,'

It is principally that the stage ought to be instructive to the public by the knowledge of things represented.[12]

Cardinal Richelieu, at the time he was in power, encouraged the arts and considered himself an authority on the theater. In 1635 he invited five young poets to compose one act each for Richelieu's *La Comédie des Tuileries*. Pierre Corneille, one of those chosen to be honored, refused. With the great success of *Le Cid* (1636), Corneille became the target of much jealousy and criticism. Richelieu took the opportunity to send the play to the French Academy, which had been founded the previous year, to have them examine its literary merits, that is,

---

9   La Bruyère, *Characters*, 35ff. Jean de La Bruyère (1645–1696) was born to a bourgeois family, studied law and in 1673 became Treasurer-General of Finance in Caen.

10 Clark, *European Theories*, 133.

11 Ibid., 132.

12 Ibid., 135.

to determine if it breaks the 'rules.' Behind this, however, was Richelieu's anger that the play glorified Spain to an extent, at a time when France was not friendly to Spain, politically. In 1640, Corneille dedicated his *Horatius* to Richelieu, no doubt in an effort to regain his favor. One can sense in these lines by the greatest French poet of the seventeenth century, the real power of Richelieu's influence on all aspects of Parisian life.

> You have facilitated our knowledge of [the theater], since we need no other study to attain this than to fix our eyes on Your Eminence when you honor with your presence and your attention the recital of our poems. It is there, reading your face what pleases and displeases you, that we learn with certainty what is good and what is bad, and derive unfailing rules of what should be followed and what avoided; it is there that I have often learnt in two hours what my books could not have taught me in ten years.[13]

In 1648, in a published commentary on *Le Cid*, Corneille makes his first extended public defense of his most famous play.[14] He mentions that many of those who have supported him in this debate have pointed out that the rules of Aristotle were intended for his own time and not for modern France. He continues, however, by mentioning some of the most important principles of Aristotle.

> That great man has treated the art of poetry with such skill and judgment that the precepts he has left us on this subject are for all times and all peoples; and very far from trifling with details of the proprieties and the concords, which can be different according as these two circumstances are different, he goes straight to the heart's reactions whose nature does not change. He has shown what emotions tragedy should stir in the hearts of its spectators; he has sought the necessary conditions both in the characters portrayed and the events introduced to effect these emotions; for this purpose he has left us the means which would have produced their effect everywhere since the creation of the world and which will still be capable of producing it, as long as there are theaters and actors …
>
> And indeed I should be the first to condemn *Le Cid* if it sinned against those great and sovereign maxims that we owe this philosopher; but, very far from agreeing that this is so, I dare say that this happy composition has only had such an outstanding success because it entwines the two master conditions that this great master demands of tragedies of the highest order, and which are so seldom found together in a single work … The first condition is that he who suffers and is persecuted should not be altogether bad nor altogether good, but a man good rather than bad, who by some characteristic of human weakness, not criminal, falls into a misfortune he does not deserve; the second is that the persecution and the peril should not come from an enemy, not from somebody indifferent to him, but from someone who would love the sufferer and should be loved by him.

To some degree, Pierre Corneille never recovered his composure from the debate over his play. Years later, 1660, he wrote a treatise called *Discourse on the Uses and Elements of*

---

13   Quoted in Samuel Solomon, *Pierre Corneille, Seven Plays* (New York: Random House, 1969), 104.

14   The 'Examen,' which is part of this publication, explains in detail why he 'broke the rules,' such as 'the unities.'

Dramatic Poetry as the final of many efforts to explain his understanding of aesthetics in the theater. He gives the principal purpose of tragedy as being pleasure, although he adds, 'it is impossible to please according to the rules without at the same time supplying a moral purpose.'[15] Corneille finds four kinds of plays which provide this moral purpose.

> The first sort of play is that which contains maxims and moral instructions, scattered throughout. These should be sparingly used and only on the rarest occasions inserted in general discourses, and then in small doses, especially when they are put into the mouth of an impassioned character …
>
> The second use of dramatic poetry is in the simple description of the vices and virtues, which never misses its effect if well conceived, and if the marks of it are so clear that one cannot confuse the two nor take vice for virtue …

He quotes Aristotle as saying, 'The success of virtue against misfortunes and perils excites us to embrace it, and the fatal success of crime and injustice is capable of enlarging the nature of it, through the fear of the misfortune.' It is in this that the third use of the theater consists, just as the fourth consists in the purgation of the passions through the means of pity and fear.

Corneille defines the subject of tragedy as 'an illustrious, extraordinary, serious subject,' while the subject of comedy is 'a common, playful subject.'

> Both have this in common, that the action must be complete and finished, that is, in the event which finishes it the spectator must be so clearly informed of the feelings of all who have had a part in it that he leaves with his mind quiet and doubting of nothing.

Corneille makes several interesting comments about the role of the emotions in tragedy.

> There is this difference between the dramatic poet and the orator, that the latter can exhibit his art and make it extraordinary with full freedom, and the other must hide with care, because it is never he who speaks, and those whom he has speak are not orators.

But, he does not mean by this that the emotions are less important in the theater.

> I do not mean to say that when an actor speaks he cannot inform the listener about many things, but he must do so through the passion which moves him, and not through a simple narration … The poet especially must remember that when an actor is alone in the theater it is taken for granted that he is thinking to himself, and speaks but to let the listener know what he thinks. Therefore it would be an unforgivable error if another actor should by this means learn his secret. One excuses that in a passion which is so violent that it is forced to burst out, even though one has no one to listen to.

---

15 Clark, *European Theories*, 140ff. Pierre Corneille (1606–1684) received a Jesuit education in the classics and received a law degree in 1624, a field in which he worked for a time in government. His *Le Cid* has been called the beginning of modern French tragedy.

Finally, there are a few interesting remarks on drama theory to be found in the prefaces of Corneille's plays. In a preface to *Le Cid*, published some years later, in a discussion of the importance of the stage action, he observes that 'what is open to the eye is much more moving than what one only learns through the ear.'[16] He elaborates on this relationship between the spectator and the stage in his 'Examen' attached to the publication of *Cinna*.

> The spectator loves to be absorbed in the action on the stage before him and not to be obliged, in order to understand what he sees, to think about what he has previously seen, and to cast back his memory on the first acts while the last are before his eyes. This is the inconvenience of complicated plays ... It is not found in plays with simple plots; but as the former doubtless need more wit to conceive them and more art to follow them through, the latter, not having the same weight from the side of the plot, require more force in the verse, the arguments and feelings to sustain them.[17]

In his preface, 'To the Reader,' of his *Nicomedes*, Corneille adds two additional thoughts on drama theory. First he observes that 'love and passion should be the soul of tragedy,' although this play stresses only the nobility of soul.[18] He also remarks that while this play had success in production, he is somewhat concerned whether it will enjoy equal reputation when read in the printed form.[19] Several French writers at this time remind us that drama, like music, has both a written form and a performance form.

That 'love and passion should be the soul of tragedy,' seems quite different from the central features as given by Aristotle, which Corneille quotes above and appears to endorse. The question is made more confusing by a statement in his 'Discourse on Tragedy,' where Corneille notes that in *Le Cid* 'duty of birth and care of honor' are given precedence over Love, of which he adds, 'I never let it take the first place.' Then, in the 'Examen' he wrote for *Polyeucte*, he attributes the power of this play in large part to the element of Love.

> Its style is not as powerful nor as majestic as that of *Cinna* and *Pompey*, but it has something more moving, and the tenderness of human love in it mingles so pleasingly with the fortitude of the divine, that its performance has delighted at the same time both the devout and the fashionable.[20]

One philosopher who was doubtful of the value of following official rules in writing plays, even those of the ancients, was Saint-Évremond. In his *De la Tragédie ancienne et moderne* (1672), he begins by using the example of Hédelin himself.

---

16 Quoted in Solomon, *Pierre Corneille*, 18.

17 Ibid., 197ff.

18 Quoted in Pierre Corneille, *Polyeuctus, The Liar, Nicomedes,* trans. John Cairncross, (Middlesex: Penguin Books, 1980), 236.

19 Ibid., 237.

20 Quoted in Solomon, *Pierre Corneille*, 280.

> There were never so many rules to write a good tragedy by, and yet so few good ones are now made that the players are obliged to revive and act all the old ones. I remember that the Abbé d'Aubignac wrote one according to the laws he had so imperiously prescribed for the stage. This piece had no success, notwithstanding which he boasted in all companies that he was the first French writer that had exactly followed the precepts of Aristotle; whereupon the prince of Condé said wittily: 'I am obliged to Monsieur d'Aubignac for having so exactly followed Aristotle's rules, but I will never forgive Aristotle for leading Monsieur d'Aubignac to write so bad a tragedy.'
>
> It must be acknowledged that Aristotle's *Art of Poetry* is an excellent piece of work; but, however, there is nothing so perfect in it as to be the standing rules of all nations and all ages. Descartes and Gassendi have found out truths that were unknown to Aristotle. Corneille has discovered beauties for the stage of which Aristotle was ignorant; and our philosophers have observed errors in his *Physics*.[21]

Saint-Évremond suggests that the theater should not involve itself with sacred subjects, which only have the result that both the play and religious beliefs suffer. He did suggest that the Old Testament stories would be much more successful in Paris than stories centering on the ancient Greek religious rites, although he notes that the clergy would be the first to complain.

> I am apt to believe that the priests would not fail to exclaim against the profanation of these sacred histories, with which they fill their conversations, their books, and their sermons.[22]

It is particularly interesting that Saint-Évremond represents a rare example of a philosopher who questioned the famous Aristotelian concept of catharsis.

> Among a thousand persons that are present at the theater, perhaps there may be six philosophers that are capable of recovering their former tranquility by the assistance of these prudent and useful meditations; but the multitude will scarce make any such judicious reflections, and we may be almost assured that what we see constantly represented in the theater, will not fail, at long run, to produce in us a habit of these unhappy motions.
>
> Our theatrical representations are not subject to the same circumstances as those of the Ancients were, since our fear never goes so far as to raise the superstitious terror, which produced such ill effects upon valor. Our fear, generally speaking, is nothing else but an agreeable uneasiness, which consists in the suspension of our minds; it is a dear concern which our soul has for those objects that draw its affection to them.[23]

On the other hand, when he offers his own version of catharsis it is not so far removed from the ideas of Aristotle.

---

21 Clark, *European Theories*, 164. Charles de Marguetel de Saint-Denis, sieur de Saint-Évremond (1610–1703) was trained in law, but spent much of his career in the military. A letter critical of the Treaty of the Pyrenees forced him to leave France and live his remaining years in London.

22 Ibid., 165.

23 Ibid., 166.

> We ought, in tragedy, before all things whatever, to look after a greatness of soul well expressed, which excites in us a tender admiration. By this sort of admiration our minds are sensibly ravished, our courage elevated, and our souls deeply affected.[24]

Among his observations on contemporary theater, perhaps the most interesting and enlightening comments which reflect on the manners of his time are those in which he considers the verisimilitude of the passion, Love.

> We are obliged to mingle somewhat of love in the new tragedy, the better to remove those black ideas which the ancient tragedy caused in us by superstition and terror. And in truth there is no passion that more excites us to everything that is noble and generous than a virtuous love …
>
> Love has a certain heat which supplies the defect of courage in those that want it most. But to confess the truth, our authors have made as ill an use of this noble passion as the Ancients did of their pity and fear …
>
> We have an affected tenderness where we ought to place the noblest sentiments. We bestow a softness on what ought to be most moving; and sometimes when we mean plainly to express the graces of nature, we fall into a vicious and mean simplicity.
>
> We imagine we make kings and emperors perfect lovers, but in tragedy we make ridiculous princes of them; and by the complaints and sighs which we bestow upon them where they ought neither to complain nor sigh, we represent them weak, both as lovers and as princes.
>
> Our great heroes in the theater generally make love like shepherds; and thus the innocence of a sort of rural passion supplies with them the place of glory and valor.
>
> If an actress has the art to weep and bemoan herself after a moving lively manner, we give her our tears, at certain places which demand gravity; and because she pleases best when she seems to be affected, she shall put on grief all along, indifferently …
>
> I am in good hopes we shall one day find out the true use of this passion, which is now become too common. That which ought to sweeten cruel or calamitous accidents, that which ought to affect our very souls, to animate our courage and raise our spirits, will not certainly be always made the subject of a little affected tenderness or of a weak simplicity.[25]

In contrast to this we should note a letter from Corneille to Saint-Évremond of 1668, in which the playwright observes,

> I have hitherto been of the opinion, that Love was a passion attended with too much weakness to be predominant in an heroic play: I would have it to be the ornament, but not the substance; and that great souls should not be affected by it, any farther than it is consistent with nobler impressions.[26]

---

24 Ibid., 167.
25 Ibid., 166ff.
26 Quoted in Saint-Évremond, *The Letters*, 73.

Finally, at the beginning of the eighteenth century, we find some interesting observations on the theater by François Fénelon, beginning with his rather unusual definition of the principal forms.

> First, tragedy must be separated from comedy. The former portrays great events which excite violent passions; the latter is limited to portraying the morals of men in a deprived state.[27]

Second, he introduces the traditional philosophical subject of 'Art versus Nature,' a topic which had become much discussed at this time in France.

> Tragedy must not corrupt the imitation of true nature. While it is possible to depict nature favorably and on a large scale, still every man must always speak in a very human way.[28]

Having read a summary of the theater from the perspective of the drama theorists, now we turn to the philosophy expressed in the plays themselves.

ON THE PHYSIOLOGY OF AESTHETICS

The comedies of Molière[29] had as their paramount purpose the reflection of contemporary society as he saw it. It is no surprise, therefore, to find a satirical reference to the Church's ancient position that man must always be governed by Reason. In *The Learned Ladies* [I, i] Armande says to her sister,

> Instead of being a bound slave to the dictates of a man, unite yourself, sister, in marriage with philosophy, which raises us above the whole human race and gives supreme sovereignty to the Reason, subjugating to its laws the animal instincts whose gross appetites lower us to the level of the beasts.

And in Molière's *Don Garcia of Navarre* (II, v), Don Garcia, thinking of love, says to himself,

> Beware ... lest the bewildering thoughts of your mind tend to make you believe too easily the testimony of your senses. Consult your reason; take it alone for guide.

In Molière's *The Compulsory Marriage* (scene iv), the philosopher Pancrace makes the significant point that unlike other representations (such as painting, presumably), words are direct representatives of Rational thought.

---

27 *Fénelon's Letter to the French Academy*, 84. François de Salignac de La Mothe-Fénelon (1651–1715) was a courtier, bishop of Cambrai and royal tutor to a grandson of the Louis XIV, the duke of Burgundy.

28 Ibid., 88.

29 Molière was the stage name for Jean Baptiste Poquelin (1622–1673). His early years in the theater were unsuccessful and his father had to rescue him from a debtor's prison. Eventually his work attracted the attention of the king, and the critic, Boileau, and he remained successful until his death.

On the other hand, as everyone knows letting Reason rule is not always so easy. Sometimes there is a choice between following Reason and following the emotions, or, as we know in terms of modern brain research, a competition between the left and right hemispheres of the brain. Racine[30] acknowledges this struggle in the dedication to Henrietta of England of his *Andromache*, when he mentions that she cried at the first reading of the play. Then he adds,

> But, Madam, it is not only with your heart that you judge the worth of a work, it is with an intelligence that no false brilliance may deceive.

In Marivaux's *The Game of Love and Chance* (Act Three),[31] Sylvia *wants* a struggle between Reason and the emotions.

> Because it costs him so much to overcome himself, he will be all the more precious to me. He thinks that by marrying he will grieve his father, betray his birth and jeopardize his fortune. These are great obstacles—and I want the satisfaction of triumphing over them … I want him to struggle. I want to see a fight between passion and Reason.

Finally, we might also mention one place where Molière refers to an observation made by all the early poets since the time of the ancient Greeks, that pleasurable emotions are soon followed by their contraries. In *The Blunderer* (IV, v), Anselme advises Léandre,

> Let me tell you again that those ardent longings, those youthful transports, may give us a few pleasant moments, but that this bliss is of short duration, and, as our gratified passion cools, long unhappy days follow.

ON THE PHILOSOPHY OF AESTHETICS

One important question of aesthetics in the arts which we find reference to in these plays, is whether Art should imitate Nature. In a humorous moment in Molière's *The Sicilian, or Love makes a Painter* (scene xi), as an artist is painting a portrait of a lady, the question arises whether the artist should imitate Nature or improve upon it.

> ADRASTUS. There's nobody but would esteem it a great glory to put his hand to such a work. I have no great skill; but the original here, will of itself supply the inability, and be a means of doing something fine.
> ISIDORA. The original is but indifferent, but the painter's skill will cover its defects.

---

30 Jean Racine (1639–1699, born La Ferté-Milon), reared by his grandmother, was educated by Jansenist schools in Paris and philosophy at the Collège d'Harcourt. His family urged him to prepare to be a priest, but by 1664 he was writing plays. By 1677 he had concluded that theater was an immoral influence and he turned his efforts to history.

31 Pierre de Marivaux (1688–1763), born Pierre Carlet, was a minor playwright and novelist.

ADRASTUS. The painter can perceive none; and all he desires is ability to represent the charms to the eyes of the world as great as he sees them.
ISIDORA. If your pencil flatters as much as your tongue, you will draw my picture with but little resemblance.
ADRASTUS. Heaven, who formed the original, has made it impossible to flatter it.

This question was one of considerable importance to Molière, in fact one which might affect his personal security. Since his purpose was the satire of contemporary manners, obviously there was risk if he imitated Nature so perfectly that the person being satirized recognized himself. Thus Molière several times takes an opportunity to remind the viewers that his purpose is not to literally copy Nature, but only to create stereotypes. In his *The Impromptu of Versailles* (scene iv), Brécourt presents Molière's philosophy after two characters argue whether the character they saw in a play was intended to be them.

I say, it is neither one nor the other. You are both of you fools, to think of applying these characters to yourselves; it is just what I heard Molière complain about the other day. Speaking to some people who accused him as you have done, he said that nothing annoyed him so much as being charged with taking off a specific person in the characters he makes; his object is to paint manners without wishing to interfere with individuals: all the characters he portrays are imaginary persons, simply phantasms, which he clothes according to his fancy to amuse the audience. He would be very sorry had he ever indicated anyone in particular. If anything were capable of making him give up the writing of comedies, it would be the resemblances which people constantly think they find, and out of which his enemies maliciously seek to make capital, that they may do him a bad turn with regard to certain persons whom he had never had in mind … Since it is the business of comedy to represent generally all the defects of men, and specifically the men of our own age, it is impossible for Molière to draw any character which cannot be met with in the world; if he is to be accused of having had in mind all the persons in whom one can see the defects which he describes, he will assuredly not write any more comedies.

A character in his play named Molière, adds,

Do you think he has exhausted, in his comedies, everything that is ridiculous in human nature? And, without going away from the Court, are there not still a score of characters he has not touched upon? For example, are there not those who profess the greatest friendship imaginable, and who, when one's back is turned, amuse themselves by tearing each other to pieces? Are there not crawling sycophants, insipid flatterers, who never season with a little salt the adulation they give, all of whose blandishments have a faint sweetness which makes one's heart sick to hear it? Are there not cowardly worshipers of success, faithless idolaters of fortune, who burn incense before you in prosperity, and revile you in adversity? Are there not those who are always discontented with the Court, useless followers, troublesome parasites, men, I say, who render importunities in place of services, and who seek to be rewarded for having besieged the Prince for ten years or more?

And again, in his Preface to *The Affected Ladies*, Molière observes,

> I should have liked to have shown that throughout it keeps within the bounds of fair and honest satire; that the most excellent things are liable to be caricatured by wretched asses who deserve to be whipped; and that these ridiculous imitations of what is most perfect have been at all times the subject of comedy. And for the same reasons that the true scholar and the truly brave have never as yet thought fit to be offended at the doctor or the swaggerer in a comedy,—no more than the judges, princes, or kings to see Trivelin or any other upon the stage ridiculously mimic the judge, prince or king—in the same manner the true *Précieuses* would be wrong to be vexed when I satirize those absurd people who wretchedly imitate them.

The reference to the *Précieuses* is a reference to the salon held at the Hôtel de Rambouillet. In Scene X, Molière refers to the performance of songs at such salons.

One member of society who Molière no doubt enjoyed portraying in satire was the courtier. These instances are valuable as reflections of seventeenth-century court manners. In his *The Impromptu of Versailles* (scene i), the character Molière, 'an absurd marquis,'[32] instructs one of the actors who is to play a courtier,

> You must assume a calm manner, a natural tone of voice and gesticulate as little as possible.

In another place, Molière has a courtier express himself in the kind of logic one might find in Church argument.

Sganarelle, in *Don Juan* (V, ii), observes,

> Good precepts are better than fair words, fair words are found at court, at court are courtiers, courtiers follow the fashion, fashion comes from fancy, fancy is an attribute of the soul, the soul is that which gives us life.

In Molière's *The Impromptu of Versailles* (scene i), he similarly gives us a view of the manners of the poet. The character Molière says to another character, who is to portray a playwright,

> You play a poet's part, and you ought to be fully taken up with your impersonation; indicate the pedantic air he preserves throughout his intercourse with the fashionable world, his sententious tone of voice, and precise pronunciation of every syllable.

---

32 In Molière's *The Impromptu of Versailles* (scene i), the character Molière remarks,

> A marquis now days is the funny man of a play; just as in all the old comedies there was always a clownish valet to make the audience laugh, so in all our plays now, there must always be a ridiculous marquis to amuse the company.

On the Purpose of Drama

In this repertoire of plays three distinct purposes of stage plays are given. One purpose is to provide pleasure, as we see in a passage which begins with an observation on the quality of contemporary theater and its rapid movement toward an emphasis of entertainment. In Molière's *The School for Wives Criticized* (scene vi), the playwright, Lysidas, observes,

> One must admit that this sort of comedy is not really a comedy: there is a great difference between all these trifles and the excellence of serious plays. Nevertheless everybody accepts them nowadays: people do not run after anything else, and there is a lamentable emptiness where great works are acted, whilst the silly pieces have all Paris to listen to them. I confess that my heart bleeds many a time: it is a disgrace to the nation.

This gives rise to a general discussion of the aesthetic purpose of theater.

> URANIE. It is very strange that you poets always condemn those pieces every one runs after and speak nothing but good of those which no one goes to see. You exhibit an unconquerable aversion towards the one and an inconceivable affection for the other ...
>
> DORANTE. I should much like to know whether the grand rule of all rules is not the art to please: if a play put on the stage does not attain that end it has not followed a good course. Can the whole public be in error in these matters, and may not each one be a judge of what pleases him therein?
>
> URANIE. I have noticed one thing in these gentlemen: those who talk most of these canons and now more about them than others, produce the comedies which no one thinks good.
>
> DORANTE. And that shows, Madam, how little attention we need pay to their tiresome objections. For, in fact, if the plays which are according to rule do not please, and those which please are not according to rule, it must of necessity, be that the rules are badly made. So let us mock at the sophistry wit which they would shackle the public taste, and only judge of the play by the effect it has upon ourselves. Let us give ourselves up in all good faith to whatever stirs our hearts deeply, without searching for reasons to prevent our enjoying.
>
> URANIE. When I see a comedy I regard only whether it interests me, and if I am greatly delighted, I never ask if I am wrong, or if the rules of Aristotle forbid me to laugh ... I marvel at the hair-splitting refinements of certain folk upon things which we know by instinct.

We get a somewhat different perspective on this question in Molière's *The Impromptu of Versailles* (scene v), when the character, Mlle. Molière, speaks of aesthetics of drama with the playwright, Du Croisy.

> MILLE. MOLIÈRE. Why does he write wretched plays that all Paris goes to see, in which he depicts people so accurately, that everyone recognizes himself? Why does he not write comedies like those of Monsieur Lysidas? No one would be against him then, and all the authors would speak well of them ...

> Du Croisy. That is so: I have the advantage of not having enemies, and all my works have the approbation of the learned.
>
> Mille. Molière. You are quite right in being satisfied with yourself. That is worth more than all the applause of the public, and all the money which the plays of Molière may bring. What matters it to you whether people come to your comedies, provided they are approved by your peers?

And finally, in *The Countess of Escarbagnas* [I, iv], Molière gives us a character who wants only a pleasure to be shared with his friends. Here a comedy is about to be given in a private palace and the Countess announces that she has given the footman instructions not to let anyone in so there will not be a 'crush.'

> The Viscount. If that be so, Madam, I have to tell you that I must cancel the performance, I do not take any pleasure in it when there is not a large company.

Another purpose of stage plays was to express the emotions. Racine, in his Preface, says of a tragic moment in *Berenice*,

> I make bold to say that it renews pretty effectively in the audience's hearts the emotion the rest of the play had succeeded in arousing.

He suggests that some had criticized his play supposing that it did not follow the 'rules,' even though they admitted it did not bore them and in fact moved them in places. What else can they ask for, wonders Racine?

> Let them place on our shoulders the burden of interpreting the difficulties of the *Poetics* of Aristotle; let them keep for themselves the pleasure of weeping and being touched; and let them allow me to say to them what a musician once said to Philip, King of Macedon, who asserted that a song was not according to the rules:
> 'God forbid, my lord, that you ever be so unfortunate as to know these things better than I!'

We might also mention that in the preface to *The Theban Brothers*, Racine observes that 'Love, which as a rule plays so great a part in tragedies, has a very minor role in this one.'

The third purpose of stage plays was education, to enlighten the viewers. We find Racine, in the Preface to his final play, *Phaedra*, a disillusioned playwright who has concluded that the ideal purpose of drama is to improve man. Speaking of this play, he says,

> The passions are displayed only to show all the disorder of which they are the cause; and vice is everywhere depicted in colors which make the deformity recognized and hated. That is properly the end which every man who works for the public should propose to himself; and it is that which the first tragic poets kept in sight above everything. Their theater was a school where virtue was not less well taught than in the schools of the philosophers.

Molière, of course, in his comedies achieves this through exposing the manners of society to the observer. In a lengthy preface to the publication of his *Tartuffe* ('the Hypocrite'), Molière admits it is 'a Comedy which has made a great disturbance.' In his earlier works, which satirized ladies and doctors, his characterizations were taken in good humor. But, he says, 'Hypocrites won't take a jest.'

The chief attack on *Tartuffe*, the author reports, was a religious one, that it 'offends Piety.' Molière adds that at the present time plays in general are under attack by some Fathers of the Church and he also admits that 'there have been times wherein Comedy has been corrupted.'

> And what is there in the world but what is daily corrupted? There is nothing so innocent but what man may make criminal; no Art so wholesome, whose intentions they are not capable to overthrow; nothing so good in itself, but what they can turn to an ill use.

Medicine, for example, also makes possible poison and philosophy 'has often been publicly employed to maintain Impiety.' But, Molière argues, this play 'does not at all tend to ridicule the things that ought to be revered.' On the contrary,

> If the business of the Drama is to correct the vices of mankind, I don't see for what reason any vice should be privileged. This vice is of a much more dangerous consequence than all the others; and we have found that the stage has a good hand at correction. The finest strokes of a serious Morality are sometimes less effectual than those of satire; and nothing reprehends most men better than the description of their faults. It is a great blow to the vicious, to expose them to the laughter of all the world. People can endure to be reproved, but not to be ridiculed. They would willingly be knaves, but not fools.

On the Public

Molière, it would seem, considered the acceptance by the public as the final judgment as the to value of his comedies. As he observes in the Preface of his *The Impertinents*,

> I refer myself to the sentence of the Multitude, and I think it as hard to oppose a work which the Public approves, as it is to defend one which it condemns.

In another place, Molière suggests that the reaction by the public actually changed his own evaluation of one play. In the Preface of his *The Affected Ladies*, after observing that one of his plays has been published without his knowledge, he concludes,

> Not that I intend here to play the bashful author and depreciate my own comedy out of delicacy. I should inconsistently offend all Paris if I accused it of having applauded a senseless thing; for as the public is the supreme judge of all these kinds of works, it would be impertinence in me

to question its judgment; and had I entertained the worst opinion in the world of my comedy before it was acted, I am now bound to believe it to be worth something, since so many people have agreed to speak in its favor.

In one play we are perhaps justified to discover a hint that Molière had a perfectly normal enjoyment of a favorable acceptance of his work. In his *The School for Wives Criticized* (scene vi), the playwright, Lysidas, reveals his enjoyment of praise.

> LYSIDAS. I am rather late, Madam, but I had to read my play at the house of the marchioness of whom I spoke to you; and the praises bestowed upon it kept me an hour longer than I expected.
> ÉLISE. Praise has magic power to detain an author.

Marivaux took the same position regarding the value of the public's judgment as did Molière. In his *Money Makes the World Go Round*, he concludes with a *Divertissement*[33] which asks,

> The audience, we admit, knows best.
> Have we, we wonder, passed the test?

Racine, in contrast, saw much irony in the value of the public's evaluation of a play. In the Preface to *The Litigants*, his only comedy, he observes,

> Most people care not a fig for the intention or the diligence of authors. My trifle was immediately scrutinized as closely as a tragedy. Even those who had laughed the loudest trembled lest they had not laughed according not the rules, and took it ill that I had not thought more earnestly of the proper way to make them laugh. Others fancied that it was correct for them to be bored, and that the affairs of the Law Courts could not possibly furnish fit matter for the amusement of the nobility. The play was soon after performed at Versailles. There the highest in the land did not hesitate to laugh; and those who had imagined it to be disreputable to laugh in Paris, were perhaps compelled to laugh at Versailles to save their reputations.

Racine is also the most outspoken on the subject of the professional critic. In the Preface to his *Alexander the Great*, he complains,

> I should have achieved nothing had I paid heed to the subtleties of certain critics who would subject public taste to the distempers of a sick mind, who go to the theater with the set object of not enjoying themselves, and who fancy they can prove to the whole audience, by shaking their heads and by affected leers, that they are deeply versed in the *Poetics* of Aristotle.

---

33 Marivaux's *The False Servant* also concludes with a *Divertissement* which includes singing and dance.

ON THE AESTHETICS OF MUSIC

In the comedies of Molière there are two instances in which he provides a humorous record of the music making of amateurs. The *The Affected Ladies* (scene x), presents a nice satire of upper class dilettantes who compose music although they know nothing about it. The Marquis of Mascarille is discussing poetry, as a refinement of the upper class, with two ladies. He first reads his poem, a madrigal, and then announces he has also composed music for it.

> MASCARILLE. I must sing you the tune I made to it.
> CATHOS. Ah! you have learnt music?
> MASCARILLE. Not a bit of it!
> CATHOS. Then how can you have set it to music?
> MASCARILLE. People of my position know everything without ever having learnt.
> MADELON. Of course it is so, my dear.
> MASCARILLE. Just listen, and see if the tune is to your taste [he warms up his voice]. The brutality of the season has greatly injured the delicacy of my voice; but it is of no consequence; permit me, without ceremony: *(he sings)*
> > Oh! oh! I was not taking care.
> > While thinking not of harm, I watch my fair.
> > Your lurking eye my heart doth steal away.
> > Stop thief! Stop thief! Stop thief! I say.
>
> CATHOS. What soul-subduing music! One would willingly die while listening.
> MADELON. What soft languor creeps over one's heart!
> MASCARILLE. Do you not find the thought clearly expressed in the song? *Stop thief, stop thief.* And then as if one suddenly cried out *stop, stop, stop, stop,* stop thief. Then all at once, like a person out of breath—*Stop thief!*
> MADELON. It shows a knowledge of perfect beauty, every part is inimitable, both the words and the melody enchant me.
> CATHOS. I never yet met with anything worthy of being compared to it.
> MASCARILLE. All I do comes naturally to me. I do it without study.
> MADELON. Nature has treated you like a fond mother, you are her spoiled child.

In Molière's *Le Bourgeois Gentilhomme* we are given an extended view of the household music in the home of a socially aspiring businessman, named Mr. Jourdain. Although the treatment is satire, there is also much here that reflects on views of music in general. Act One begins with a music master, a dancing master, three singers, two violinists and four dancers on stage. The music master mentions that he has had his student compose a song while they all are waiting on the gentleman to wake up. The initial dialogue is concerned with describing what it is like for artists who work in such an environment.

> MUSIC MASTER. We have found the very man we both wanted. He brings us in a comfortable little income, with his notions of gentility and gallantry which he has taken into his head; and it would be well for your dancing and my music if everybody were like him.

DANCING MASTER. No; not altogether. I wish, for his sake, that he would appreciate better than he does the things we give him.

MUSIC MASTER. He certainly understands them but little; but he pays well, and that is nowadays what our arts require above all things.

DANCING MASTER. I must confess, for my part, that I rather hunger after glory. Applause finds a very ready answer in my heart, and I think it mortifying enough that in the fine arts we should have to exhibit ourselves before fools, and submit our compositions to the vulgar taste of an ass. No! say what you will, there is a real pleasure in working for people who are able to appreciate the refinements of an art; who know how to yield a kind recognition to the beauties of a work, and who, by felicitous approbations, reward you for your labor …

MUSIC MASTER. I grant it; and I relish them as much as you do. There is certainly nothing more refreshing than the applause you speak of; still we cannot live on this flattering acknowledgment of our talent. Undiluted praise does not give competence to a man; we must have something more solid to fall back on, and the best praise is the praise of the pocket. Our man, it is true, is a man of very limited capacity, who speaks at random upon all things, and only gives applause in the wrong place; but his money makes up for the errors of his judgment. He keeps his discernment in his purse, and his praises are golden. This ignorant, commonplace citizen is, as you see, better to us than that clever nobleman who introduced us here.

DANCING MASTER. There is some truth in what you say; still I think that you set a little too much value on money, and that it is in itself something so base that he who respects himself should never make a display of his love for it.

MUSIC MAN. Yet you receive readily enough the money our man gives you.

The businessman, Mr. Jourdain finally appears and, after soliciting compliments on the new dressing gown he has had made, he asks to see what 'little drollery' the music and dancing masters have prepared.

MUSIC MASTER. I should like, first of all, for you to hear a song which [my student] has just composed for the serenade you asked of me. He is one of my pupils, who has an admirable talent for this kind of thing.

MR. JOURDAIN. Yes; but you should not have had it done by a pupil; you were not too good for the business yourself.

MUSIC MASTER. You must not be deceived, Sir, by the name of pupil. These kinds of pupils know sometimes as much as the greatest masters; and the Air is as beautiful as possible. Only just listen to it.

MR. JOURDAIN. *(to his servants)* Hand me my dressing gown, so that I may hear better …

THE PUPIL *(sings)*
*All night and day I languish on; the sick man none can save
Since those bright eyes have laid him low, to your stern laws a slave …*

MR. JOURDAIN. This song seems to me rather dismal; it sends one to sleep; could you not enliven it a bit here and there?

MUSIC MASTER. We must, Sir, suit the music to the words.

This performance has reminded the businessman of a song which he now sings. At its conclusion, he asks 'Now, isn't it pretty?'

> Music Master. The prettiest thing in the world.
> Dancing Master. And you sing it very well.
> Mr. Jourdain. Do I? I have never learned music.
> Music Master. You ought to learn it, Sir, as you do dancing. These are two arts which are closely bound together.
> Dancing Master. And which open the human mind to the beauty of things.
> Mr. Jourdain. Do people of rank learn music also?
> Music Master. Yes, Sir.

Upon hearing this, the businessman decides to study music. On second thought, he remembers he has also engaged a fencing teacher and a professor of philosophy and therefore fears he may not have time. The music and dancing masters, in response, begin to speak of the purposes and virtues of their arts.

> Music Master. Philosophy is something, no doubt; but music, Sir, music …
> Dancing Master. Music and dancing, Sir; in music and dancing we have all that we need.
> Music Master. There is nothing so useful in a state as music … Without music no kingdom can exist … All the disorders, all the wars that happen in the world, are caused by nothing but the lack of music …
> Mr. Jourdain. How is that [possible]?
> Music Master. Does not war arise from a lack of concord between them?
> Mr. Jourdain. True.
> Music Master. And if all men learned music, would not this be the means of keeping them in better harmony, and of seeing universal peace reign in the world?

Mr. Jourdain accepts this idea and now the music master proposes that the businessman see the musical composition which the student has composed. A female and two male singers, dressed as shepherds, now prepare to sing the music, which the music master promises will 'represent the different passions which can be expressed by music.' Jourdain asks why such Intermezzi always involve shepherds. The interesting answer is one which was occasionally given as an objection to opera itself, that 'normal' people do not discuss their affairs in singing.

> When we make people speak to music, we must, for the sake of probability, adopt the pastoral. Singing has always been affected by shepherds, and it is not very likely that our princes or citizens would sing their passions in dialogue.

During Act Two this dialogue between the music and dancing masters and the businessman continues, now focusing on music of a concert nature as the Music Master recommends that Mr. Jourdain establish his own salon.

MUSIC MASTER. But, Sir, this is not enough; a gentleman magnificent in all his ideas like you, and who has taste for doing things handsomely, should have a concert at his house every Wednesday or Thursday.
MR. JOURDAIN. But why should I? Do people of quality have concerts?
MUSIC MASTER. Yes, Sir.
MR. JOURDAIN. Oh! very well! Then I too must have some. It'll be fine?
MUSIC MASTER. Very. You must have three voices: a treble, a counter-tenor, and a bass; which must be accompanied by a bass-voil, a theorbo lute, and a harpsichord for the thorough-basses, with two violins to play the harmony.[34]

Mr. Jourdain requests that singers for the dinner table not be forgotten.

A fencing master comes on the scene and a brief argument ensues over the relative value of each of their arts. Now a professor of philosophy is introduced and speaks with disdain for the arguments at hand.

Is there anything more base and more shameful than the passion which changes a man into a savage beast, and ought not reason to govern all our actions?

Shortly the philosopher equates music and dancing with 'the trades of prize-fighter, street-singer, and mountebank,' which brings insults upon him from the music, dancing and fencing masters.

Another interesting view of music in contemporary seventeenth-century France describes the public, which a character finds is a poor judge of music. In Molière's *The School for Wives Criticized* (scene v), the Chevalier Dorante comments on both the lower and upper class audience members at the theater, including a specific reference to musical concerts.

Speaking generally, I would place considerable confidence in the approval of the pit, for, among those who frequent it, there are several who are capable of criticizing a play by the accepted canons, and the remainder form their opinion in the right way, which is to see things as they are, without blind prejudice, or affected compliance, or ridiculous refinement …

It angers me to see these people make themselves ridiculous, in spite of their rank; they are so conceited that they are continually talking boldly of everything, no matter how ignorant they may be. They shout applause at the worst passages of a play, and never cheer those that are good; and, when they see a picture, or hear a concert, blame and praise just in the same wrong-headed way.

---

34 In III, iii, Jourdain's wife complains there was a 'regular din of violins and singers, that are a positive nuisance to all the neighborhood.'

On the Purposes of Music

The purpose of music most commonly given in early literature is to soothe the listener. Molière, exaggerating for the purpose of humor, carries this idea almost to the point of music therapy. In *Love the Best Physician* (III, vii), Clitander announces,

> I've brought several singers, musicians and dancers, to celebrate the feast and make merry. Call them in. These are people I brought with me, and which I use daily, to pacify by their harmony and dancing the disturbances of the mind.

In the *Monsieur de Pourceaugnac* (I, viii) two doctors recommend a series of draconian treatments for de Pourceaugnac, including bleeding (from a vein in the head) and that he should be 'purged, de-obstructed, and evacuated by suitable purgatives.' But first, one doctor recommends, before anything else,

> I think he ought to be cheered by pleasant conversation, songs, and instruments of music.

Indeed, in Scene Ten, a stage direction calls for two 'Italian Musicians dressed as grotesque doctors,'[35] who sing to cheer up de Pourceaugnac.

> *Do not let yourself be killed*
> *By melancholic grief.*
> *Our harmonious song's for you,*
> *We have to make you laugh.*
> *We are only here to cure.*

Another purpose of music given in this repertoire is for the purpose of romance, for which, judging by one comment, music had become almost obligatory. In the Intermezzo given between the second and third acts during the first performance of Molière's *The Princess of Elis*, Moron observes,

> Most women now are taken by the ear; they make everybody learn music: and nobody succeeds with them, but by the Sonnets and Verses they sing to them. I must learn to sing that I may do like others.

A contrary opinion is found in Marivaux's *Double Infidelity* (Act Two), where Sylvia wonders why men go to all the trouble to court a girl who is not interested. She laments, 'All this waste of concerts and plays.'

There is a particularly clever scene which deals with the use of music for romance in Molière's *The Hypochondriac* (II, v). In addition, Molière takes the opportunity here to include some common contemporary complaints, including the reputed bad influence of the theater,

---

35 In II, xi, the stage direction calls for 'Two singing lawyers.'

poets who object to having to alter their verses to fit music and the frequency of pastoral scenes. This scene begins as Argan wants Cléante to prepare his daughter, Angélique, to sing before his guests. Cléante, who is secretly Angélique's lover, arranges for the two of them to improvise lyrics to the music of a previously composed chamber opera. The scene begins,

> Argan. *(to Cléante)* Monsieur, just get my daughter to sing before the visitors.
> Cléante. I was awaiting your commands, Monsieur. I thought we might entertain the company by singing with Mademoiselle a scene from a small opera that has recently been written. See, here is your part.
> Angélique. I?
> Cléante. Please do not make any objection, but allow me to explain to you the scene we have to sing. I have no voice for singing; but it will suffice here if I can make myself understood. You will be so kind as to make allowances for me, since I have to superintend the singing of the young lady.
> Argan. Are the lines good?
> Cléante. The opera is, strictly speaking, impromptu, and you will only hear rhythmical prose sung, or some sort of irregular verse, such as passion and necessity might suggest to two persons, who sing these things spontaneously, and speak on the spur of the moment.
> Argan. Very good. We will listen.

As Angélique begins to sing her part as a shepherdess, the father remarks, 'I did not think my daughter was clever enough to sing like this, at first sight, without making any mistakes.' As the singing continues, and becomes rather heated in passion between the two lovers, the father becomes suspicious.

> Argan. No, no; we have heard enough. Your opera sets a very bad example. The shepherd Tireis is an impertinent fellow, and the shepherdess Philis an impudent minx, to talk like this in the presence of her father. Show me the score. Come, come where are the words you have sung? There is nothing but music here.
> Cléante. Are you not aware, Monsieur, that a method has recently been invented whereby the words and the notes are expressed by the same signs?

The most fundamental purpose of music is, of course, to communicate feelings. Again, Molière exaggerates this idea, reminding us of the German absorption with the 'Doctrine of the affections' at this time. In *The Sicilian* (Scene ii) a discussion of a potential serenade leads to an interesting discussion of tonality relative to feeling.

> Adrastus. Are the musicians here?
> Haly. Yes.
> Adrastus. Bid them come hither. I'll have them sing here 'till break of day, to see if their music will draw this charming creature to some window.
> Haly. Here they are. What shall they sing?
> Adrastus. What they think fit.

HALY. It shall be a *Trio* then, which they sung to me the other day.
ADRASTUS. No, no; I don't like that.
HALY. Ah. Sir, 'tis a charming B sharp.
ADRASTUS. What the Devil do you mean with your B sharp?
HALY. Sir, I stand up for B sharp: You know I understand Music. B sharp charms me. No key is so harmonious as B sharp. Pray hear this *Trio*.
ADRASTUS. No, I'll have something that's tender and soft, something that may put me into a gentle musing.
HALY. I see you're for B flat; but there's a way to satisfy both of us. They shall sing you a certain scene of a little comedy which I have heard them rehearse. It is of two love-sick shepherds, full of languor, who upon B flat, come separately to make their complaints in a wood, afterwards they discover to each other the cruelty of their mistress; and, thereupon, comes a jovial shepherd, with an admirable B sharp, who rallies their weakness.
ADRASTUS. Well, let's hear it.

Scene Three now begins with the lyrics for a song by three musicians, '*If, with the sad recital of my woes …*'

There is one instance of the use of music for prophesy, found in fact in one of the few Racine plays which mentions music. *Athaliah*, not only has a singing chorus, but the appearance of unidentified 'music' on stage to enhance the religious atmosphere. Referring to this scene in the Preface, Racine reflects on the use of music for prophesy in the Old Testament.

> This scene, which is a kind of episode, brings in music very naturally, by the custom which several prophets had of entering into their holy trances to the sound of instruments: witness that troop of prophets who came before Saul with the harps and lyres which were borne before them.

MUSIC IN THE STAGE DIRECTIONS

Perhaps in rebellion to the popularity of opera, the French playwrights in general, unlike the great traditions of Elizabethan theater, include very little music in their plays. The indication of musicians on stage is particularly rare, but certainly one of the more interesting examples is found in Molière's *Monsieur de Pourceaugnac*, which concludes with a stage direction reading 'Several Masques of all kinds, some in the balconies and others in the street, enjoy themselves with diverse songs, dances and other innocent delights.' The subsequent dialogue includes lyrics for a 'Chorus of Singers.' Another intriguing occasion is found in Molière's *The Compulsory Marriage* (Scene vi), where the stage direction calls for 'Gypsies, furnished with tabors,' who enter singing and dancing.

There are two plays in which we find indications of unusually large music ensembles present. The Intermezzo which begins Molière's *The Magnificent Lovers* begins with the stage direction, 'The scene opens with the pleasant sound of a great many instruments.' Similarly,

Molière's *Le Bourgeois Gentilhomme* begins with a stage direction reading 'The overture is played by a consort of many instruments.'

ART MUSIC

Among the occasional references to the performances of songs in these plays, there is one which is unusual because it involves a discussion of the failure of a performance. In Marivaux's one act play, *Money Makes the World Go Round*, Apollo enters with some singers and dancers. After a song, the lyrics for which are given, we find the following dialogue:

> APOLLO. I'm afraid you were not too happy with this, Mr. Grangewell.
> GRANGEWELL. Oh, don't pay any attention to me. I'm deaf to music.
> SPINETTA. I was falling asleep.
> APOLLO. And you, madam, were you disappointed too?
> LYDIA. The music was elegant enough, but the performance seemed a little chilly to me.
> PLUTUS. That's because the singers are hoarse. A little greasing of throats is what's needed.
> APOLLO. Gently! You needn't pay my performers.
> A SINGER. What? The gentleman makes us a present—why should you care? It won't prevent you from paying us. In fact, the sooner the better.

In Corneille's *The Liar* (I, v), Alcippe spreads the word that a serenade played in boats on the water has been given a young lady.

> ALCIPPE. It's said that someone gave a concert for a girl.
> DORANTE. On water?
> ALCIPPE. Yes.
> DORANTE. Water can fire love's flame.
> PHILISTE. Sometimes.
> DORANTE. And this was all last night?
> ALCIPPE. It was …
> DORANTE. The music?
> ALCIPPE. Not at all to be disdained.

Later in this scene, Dorante explains that he organized the serenade, now providing more details.

> I'd hired five boats to make a better show;
> In each of four of them I placed a band
> Whose music would entrance the saddest heart.
> Violins in the first; voices and lutes
> Came next, then flutes, and oboes in the fourth,

From which in turn came waves of harmony
Lulling the ear with sweetness infinite.[36]

There are two places in Molière where the impact of the music on the listener is mentioned. In *The Princess of Elis* (III, ii), Euryalus recalls,

> The sweetness of her voice made itself evident in that perfectly delightful song she deigned to sing, her wonderful tones penetrated to the depths of my soul, and held all my senses so enraptured that they could not recover their self-possession.

And in *The Magnificent Lovers* (I, ii), Timocles remarks 'I have had my love sung by the most touching voices.'

Finally, we should mention that in a performance of *The Magnificent Lovers*, Molière himself, playing the character, Clitidas, sang a song in Act Two, Scene Three.

FUNCTIONAL MUSIC

There are two specific references in this repertoire to the use of music for dance. In Molière's *The Affected Ladies* (scene xiii) musicians are engaged for a dance and they first play for Mascarille, who sings as he dances a solo dance. Then, as he dances with Madelon, he criticizes the musicians.

> MASCARILLE. The liberty of my heart will dance a couranto as well as my feet. Play in time, musicians. Oh! what ignorant fellows! There is no possibility of dancing with them. Devil take you, can't you play in time? Steady, you village scrapers.
> JODELET. (dancing in his turn) Gently, don't play so fast, I have only just recovered from an illness.

Marivaux's *The Test* concludes with Dorian announcing, 'Send for the village fiddlers, and let's end the day with a dance.'

ENTERTAINMENT MUSIC

We find a nice satire on the life of the court musician in Molière's *The Impromptu of Versailles* (scene i). Here a character named Molière is trying to organize a rehearsal for a little play to be given before Louis XIV. He has had so little time he has written no dialogue and expects

---

36 This serenade is referred to again in II, iii.

the actors to improvise it.[37] When one of them asks why he did not request more time of the king, he comments,

> Ah! Mademoiselle, kings like nothing better than prompt obedience: opposition meets with little favor at their hands. Things are only acceptable at the time they are wanted; and to try to delay their entertainment is to take all the charm of it away, so far as they are concerned. They want pleasures which never keep them waiting;[38] so those that are the soonest ready are always the most agreeable to them. We should never consider ourselves when they desire anything of us: our only business is to please them; and when they command anything of us, we ought instantly to be only too glad to take advantage of the urgency of their desires. It is better to do badly what they ask of us, than not to do it soon enough; if one has the shame of unsuccessful work, there is always the renown of having instantly obeyed their commands.

Regarding the the comment above, on obeying the king, we find in Molière's dedication of *Les Facheux* to the king,

> I had a pleasure in obeying you, which was much more useful to me than Apollo and all the Muses.

Another view of private music for the entertainment of nobles is found in Alain-René Lesage's *Turcaret* (II, vi), where Frontin invites a guest to dinner.

> FRONTIN. And to add to the gaiety of the occasion, you will be entertained with music and instruments.
> THE BARONNE. Music, Frontin?
> FRONTIN. Yes, Madame. The proof of it is that I am also to order a hundred bottles of [wine] for the musicians to drink.
> THE BARONNE. A hundred bottles!
> FRONTIN. It's none too much, Madame. There will be eight ensemble players, [and] four Italians from Paris, three sopranos, and two fat tenors.
> M. TURCARET. Upon my word he's right. It will be none too much.

Lyrics for drinking songs are found in Molière's *Le Bourgeois Gentilhomme* (IV, i)[39] and *The Mock-Doctor* (I, vi),

---

37 In fact, in the Preface to *The Impertinents*, Molière tells us he was required by the court to write this play in only fifteen days.

> In the little time that was allowed me it was impossible for me to execute so great a design, and think much upon the choice of my characters, and disposition of my subject.

38 In one of Louis XIV's most famous remarks, made to a servant whose job was to open the door through which the king passed, Louis warned, 'You almost made me wait.'

39 In this comedy (IV, xi) a little musical play is acted out, including a song with Turkish lyrics. The music for this was composed by Lully.

What pleasure's so great, as the bottle can give,
What music so sweet, as thy little gull, gull!

Additional examples of entertainment music in Molière are found in *The Compulsory Marriage* (scene viii), where violins are engaged for the entertainment of the wedding guests, and in *Tartuffe* (II, iii), when Dorine refers to a ball to be held at carnival time when there will be 'a good band [*la grand'bande*] with two musettes and perhaps *Fagotin*[40] and marionnettes.'

---

40 The musette was the specially made small bagpipes which were popular with the court, which counted among its entertainments pretending they were peasants. The meaning of 'Fagotin' is unclear, but may mean small bassoons, as the musettes were sometimes played as small oboes (i.e., with the canter alone). In modern French, 'fagotin' can mean a small monkey dressed in clothes or a clown. Various English translations of this passage give such diverse solutions as 'the learned ape' and 'an animal act.'

8   FRENCH FICTION

THE DEBATE OVER THE QUESTION of the ideals of ancient Greece versus contemporary virtues which permeated all facets of French intellectual society is also mentioned in the works of fiction. Montesquieu, in his *Persian Letters*, which describe an imaginary visit to Paris by a Turk, and his subsequent comments on the manners of society he found there, makes fun of the serious attention given to the ancient philosophers.

> I confess, though, I am rather disgusted with those talented personages; for instead of making themselves useful to their country, they waste their abilities on the most childish trifles. For example, when I arrived in Paris, I found them quite excited over the most trivial question imaginable: it was that of the reputation of a Greek poet, as to the place of whose birth and the time of whose death the world has remained in ignorance for two thousand years. Both parties acknowledge that he was an excellent poet; the dispute turned solely on the degree of his excellence.[1]

When Fénelon discusses this debate, he provides us with an interesting explanation of the continued popularity of literary works set in a pastoral setting, after the model of the ancient lyric poets.

> When poets wish to charm men's imaginations, they lead them far from great cities and cause them to forget the extravagance of their century. They put them back into the golden age and, rather than portraying turbulent courts and great men unhappy in their greatness, they show us shepherds dancing on flowery grass under the shade of a grove in a delightful season ...
>
> Nothing more plainly marks a spoiled nation than our disdainful luxury which rejects the ancients' frugal simplicity. It was depravity such as this which overthrew Rome.[2]

Abbé Prévost, in his *Adventures of A Man of Quality*, writes of the positive influence which the early literature had brought to society. He observes that 'the time was past when people

---

1. Montesquieu, *The Persian Letters* (London: Athenaeum, 1901), 66. Later, in Ibid., 262, he describes a gentleman in Paris who is so enchanted by ancient Rome that he not only collects artifacts, but travels on the old Roman roads, even though it requires him to travel miles out of his way. Charles-Louis de Secondat, Baron de Montesquieu (1689–1755), was born to a family of sufficient wealth that he was able to spend much of his time in study. Although his *L'Esprit des lois* (1748) is better known today, the *Persian Letters* became very popular and inspired Voltaire's *Lettres sur les Anglais*.
2. *Fénelon's Letter to the French Academy*, 109. François de Salignac de La Mothe-Fénelon (1651–1715) was a courtier, bishop of Cambrai and royal tutor to a grandson of the Louis XIV, the duke of Burgundy.

of quality could afford to despise art and letters.'³ In this same work he also gives us a glimpse of the character of the courtier.

> Do you believe, my dear Marquis (continued I, laughing), that you will ever be really fit for this little system of treachery and bad faith? Do you feel yourself disposed to flatter in public and injure in secret, to feign to serve those whom you would ruin? That is what a skillful courtier must constantly put in practice.⁴

It would seem that a certain educational purpose had become associated with fictional literature, especially with respect to preparing youth to take their place among the 'people of quality.' Marivaux, for example, in the Preface of his novel of manners, *La vie de Marianne*, defines the purpose of this type of novel to be one of education.

> The reading of that part of history that relates to human life and manners has been always considered by allowed judges as one of the best methods of instructing and improving the mind. When we see the heart laid open, and the secret springs and movements that actuate it exposed and set in one impartial light with their different good and evil tendencies, we are enabled to form a true estimate of human nature and are taught what ought or ought not to be our own conduct in every similar instance.⁵

These entertaining novels are especially valuable for the education of youth, he maintains, for,

> Those who have been concerned in the important business of education must know that the love of pleasure is the most natural and easy inlet to young minds.

The 'allowed judges,' mentioned by Marivaux, refers first and foremost to the French Academy, which was another source of humor for Montesquieu in his *Persian Letters*.

> I have heard a good deal of talk about a sort of tribunal called the French Academy. There is none in the world less respected; for it is said that no sooner has it issued one of its decrees than the people set about breaking it and establishing laws of their own which the Academy has to observe.⁶

Today the French Academy is primarily concerned with judging which words are to become part of the French language. The frequent examples of foreign words, especially American

---

3   Abbé Pierre Prévost, *Adventures of A Man of Quality*, trans. Mysie Robertson (London: Routledge & Sons, 1930), 66. Prévost (1697–1763), following a failed love affair, entered a Jesuit cloister which he described as,

>   the tomb; that is the name which I give to the venerable order in which I buried myself, and where remained so effectively dead for some time that my relations and friends knew not what had become of me.

4   Ibid., 104.

5   Marivaux, *The Virtuous Orphan*, trans. Mary Collyer (Carbondale: Southern Illinois University Press, 1965), 3ff. Pierre de Marivaux (1688–1763), born Pierre Carlet, was a minor playwright and novelist.

6   Montesquieu, *The Persian Letters*, 138.

expressions, which are used by the public to the utter dismay of the Academy are perfect examples of what Montesquieu had in mind.

We might mention another aspect of French intellectual life which Montesquieu takes a little jab at, the tradition of Scholasticism in the universities. He tells a wonderful story about a man who had been unable to sleep for thirty-five days. Ordinary physicians, at a loss, proposed to give him opium, but a friend took him to a holistic doctor (a man who 'does not practice medicine, but has a multitude of remedies') who gave him a six-volume study of law. After reading a few pages, the man fell asleep.[7]

ON THE PHYSIOLOGY OF AESTHETICS

In Crébillon, fils, in his epistolary novel, *Letters from the Marchioness de M****, makes reference to the topic of man's struggle to balance his rational and emotional parts of himself when he comments, 'The language of the lips does not always imitate the sentiments of the heart.'[8]

Montesquieu, discussing the role of the senses in his *Persian Letters*, takes the old Church position that the senses are confusing and distort truth.

> Must the senses then, divine mollah, be the sole judges of the purity or impurity of things? But, inasmuch as objects do not affect all men in the same manner—for what produces an agreeable sensation in some excites disgust in others—it follows that the testimony of the senses cannot serve as a guide, unless it be asserted that each individual can decide for himself according to his fancy.[9]

It is, of course, a virtue of the Arts, and in particular Music, that man can decide for himself.

ON THE PSYCHOLOGY OF AESTHETICS

The only general discussion of the emotions which seem worthy of quotation is a comment by Marivaux, in his novel *Le Paysan Parvenu* (1735). He discusses Love as a biological urge versus 'sentiment,' which he finds is going out of fashion.

> There are many love affairs in which the heart plays no part—more of them even than of the others—and, in the main, nature depends upon these for achieving her ends, and not on our sentimental delicacies, which are useless to her. Most often it is we ourselves who indulge in tenderness so as to embellish our passions, but it is nature who makes us passionate, and it is

---

7   Ibid., 269.

8   Claude Prosper Jolyot de Crébillon, fils, *Letters from the Marchiness de M*** to the Count de R****, ed. Josephine Grieder (New York: Garland, 1972), 110.

9   Montesquieu, *The Persian Letters*, 35.

from her that we derive the reality that we doll up with the respectabilities for that is my name for sentiments which nowadays we have almost ceased dolling up; it is going out of fashion at the time I am writing this.[10]

ON THE PHILOSOPHY OF AESTHETICS

Fénelon's *Telemachus* portrays some of the principal Arts as still being primarily functional in purpose, much as they were in ancient Greece.

> Painting and sculpture were arts which Mentor did not think fit to be laid aside; but he was against suffering many hands to apply themselves that way. He erected a public school to teach those arts, with masters, who had an excellent taste, to examine the young disciples. Such arts, says he as are not absolutely necessary, ought not to admit of anything that's ordinary or indifferent; and therefore none ought to be allowed to learn them, but lads or a very promising genius, and who are likely to attain to the utmost perfection in them. As for others, who have their capacity turned to arts less noble, they will be very profitably employed about the ordinary occasions of the commonwealth. The only use, said he, that ought to be made of carvers and painters, is to preserve the memory of great men and great actions; and therefore, it is in public buildings and tombs where you ought to preserve the representations of what has been performed in any extraordinary manner for the service of the country.[11]

On the other hand, in this same work Fénelon stresses the role of his emotions in the artist, something we should not expect to be emphasized in functional art.

> Do you think, Telemachus, that a great painter labors from morning until night, that he may dispatch his work the sooner? No; such slavery and subjection would damp the flame of his fancy; he would no longer work from his genius; all must be done irregularly and by sallies, according as his relish moves him, and his spirit stimulates him. Think you that he spends his time in grinding the colors and preparing the pencils? no, that's the business of his servant. His province is that of thought and contrivance; he studies nothing but to strike bold strokes that may give sweetness, a noble air, life and passions to his figures; his head runs upon the sentiments and way of thinking of those heroes he is about to represent; he transports himself into the ages wherein they lived, and re-mounts into all the circumstances that ever attended them:

---

10   Pierre Carlet de Chamblain de Marivaux, *Up From the Country*, trans. Leonard Tancock (New York: Penguin Books, 1980), 206.

11   Fénelon, *The Adventures of Telemachus, Son of Ulysses*, Book XII, (London: Garland Publishing, 1979, facsimile of the 1720 edition), I, 280. It was as tutor for the Duke of Burgundy that Fénelon wrote the most widely read French book of its time, and the following century, the *Continuation of Homer's Odyssey*. However, this book, known today as *The Adventures of Telemachus*, angered Louis XIV in its description of a tyrant. Fénelon and his friends were banished from the court, the printer was arrested and the police attempted to confiscate all copies.

To this kind of enthusiasm he must join a judgment that must restrain and chastise his luxuriant fancy, proportionable in all its parts.[12]

In his *Persian Letters*, Montesquieu describes poets much as they were sometimes described in ancient Greece.

> If I am not becoming too troublesome, would you inform me who is that man in front of us? He is very badly dressed, makes grimaces sometimes, and speaks a language different from that of the others. He has not wit enough to talk, but talks to show that he has. That grotesque specimen of humanity, he answered, is a poet. Such fellows as that say that they are born what they are, which is true—quite as true as that they are born to be almost always the laughing-stock of the human race; so they are the objects of universal contempt. Hunger has brought the person you speak of into this house; he is well received by its master and mistress, for their good nature makes them courteous to everybody.[13]

He treats the dramatic poets somewhat better.

> The next day he led me into another room. This contains the poets, he said, that is to say, the authors whose task it is to fetter common sense and overwhelm reason under the pretense of adorning it …
>
> You are now in the presence of the dramatists, who, in my opinion, are the only real poets and the only true masters of the passions. There are two kinds of them: the comic dramatists, who are the source of such agreeable emotions, and the tragic, who can throw us into the most violent excitement and agitation.[14]

In Alain René Lesage's *Le Diable boiteux*, an entire chapter is given over to a debate between tragic and comic playwrights who are residents in an inn. They are both from France and have come to Madrid to try their luck. The tragic poet, as an illustration of the power of his art, describes an occasion when he read one of his tragedies in the home of a wealthy lady in Paris.

> Well, at the first scene, the hot tears ran down her cheeks; during the reading of my second act, she was obliged to change her handkerchief; her sobs were beyond her control in the third; at the end of the fourth she was nearly in hysterics; and I expected, at the catastrophe, that she would have absolutely died with the hero of my piece.[15]

---

12   Fénelon, *The Adventures of Telemachus, Son of Ulysses*, Book XXII, II, 235ff.
13   Montesquieu, *The Persian Letters*, 86.
14   Ibid., 247ff.
15   Alain René Lesage, *Asmodeus, or The Devil on Two Sticks* (1707) (The Bibliophilist Society, 1932), 219ff. Lesage (1668–1747) was educated by the Jesuits at Vannes and traveled to Paris to study law. After serving as a tax collector, he became disgusted and turned to writing.

Soon the two playwrights are arguing the relative merits of their art. The tragic poet says,

> My pieces are printed as often as they are played. This, now, never occurs with comedies; printing exhibits their feebleness. Comedies being but trifles, the lighter productions of mind ... Softly! my tragic friend; softly! interrupted the comic playwright, you are getting somewhat warm. Speak, I beg of you, of comedy with less irreverence to me. Do you think, now, a comic piece less difficult to write than tragedy! Undeceive yourself! It is far less easy to make good men laugh, than it is to make them weep. Learn that a subject drawn from ordinary life requires talent of as high an order as do the stilted heroes of antiquity.

At the end of the chapter the Devil brings the argument to a close by observing that this question has been debated forever. He concludes that each medium requires a special genius, observing,

> I say that it is not more easy to compose a comic than a tragic piece, for if it were so, we must conclude that a tragic poet would be more capable of writing comedy, than the best comic author; which is not borne out by experience.

Finally, Marivaux, warns the artist of the moral danger in valuing the judgment of the public.

> We are generally more jealous of the vain applause and consideration of the multitude than desirous of the value and esteem of the wise and thinking few and, consequently, not enough solicitous after our own integrity, the only true honor.[16]

ON THE AESTHETICS OF MUSIC

In Fénelon's *Telemachus*, we find the ancient Greek's use of 'harmony' as a metaphor for good government, with the head of state being analogous to the conductor.

> The government of a kingdom demands a certain harmony, like Music, and just proportions, like that of architecture. If you will allow me, I will again make use of the comparison of these arts, and make you conceive what ordinary understandings those men have who govern by the detail. He who in a consort of music sings only some certain parts, although he sings them perfectly well, he is no more than a singer; he alone is the master of music who governs the whole consort, and at once regulates all the parts of it.[17]

In this same book, Fénelon makes the important point that one learns about music from performance, not from books.

---

16   Marivaux, *The Virtuous Orphan*, 66.
17   Fénelon, *The Adventures of Telemachus, Son of Ulysses*, Book XXII, II, 235. He continues with a similar distinction between the mason and the architect.

Who is it that taught you to know good and bad poets? It was frequent reading and reflection with such persons as had a true taste that way. Who is it that procured you that judgment in music? It was the same application of mind in observing musicians.[18]

On the Perception of Music

Cyrano de Bergerac's *Other Worlds* [*L'Autre Monde*] of 1650 is a reflection of society's interest in the possibility of life on the other planets at a time when, even though astronomy had fostered this interest, telescopes were not yet sufficient to reject the possibility that even the Moon might be inhabited. It is indeed to the Moon that the central figure of this novel first travels and a citizen of that body explains both the nature of hearing and provides a curious explanation for how music communicates emotions to the listener.

> The operation of hearing is not more difficult to conceive and for the sake of brevity let us simply consider the case of the notes of a lute touched by the hands of a virtuoso. You will ask me how I can possibly perceive something so far away from me and which I cannot see at all. Does a sponge come out of my ears and soak up this music in order to bring it to me? Or does the musician beget another little musician inside my head with a little lute and instructions to sing the same tunes to me like an echo? No; the miracle is due to the fact that the plucked string strikes the air which is composed of little bodies and drives it into my brain, gently piercing it with these little bodily nothings. If the string is taut the note is high, because it drives the atoms more vigorously and once the organ is thus penetrated it furnishes my imagination with sufficient of them from which to make its picture. If it is not so taut, it happens that when our memory has not yet completed its image, we are obliged to repeat the same sound to it; so that, for example, from the materials furnished by the measures of a saraband, it takes enough to complete the portrait of this saraband.
>
> But this operation is by no means as wonderful as those by which we are moved now to joy, now to anger with the aid of the same organ. This occurs when in the course of their movement the little bodies meet others inside us which are moving in the same manner, or whose own shape makes them susceptible to the same type of vibration. The new arrivals excite their hosts to imitate their motion and in this way when a violent tune encounters the fire of our blood, it makes it take up the same dance and excites it to thrust itself outwards, and that is what we call 'the ardor of courage.' If the sound is sweeter and has only the strength to raise a lesser, more quavering flame, by causing this to travel along the nerves and membranes and through the apertures in our flesh, it excites that tickling sensation which we call 'joy.' The other passions are aroused in the same way, according to the greater or lesser violence with which these little bodies are hurled at us, according to the motion resulting from their contact with other impulses and according to the mobility they find in us.[19]

---

18 Ibid., Book XXIV, II, 270.
19 Cyrano de Bergerac, *Other Worlds*, trans. Geoffrey Strachan (London: Oxford University Press, 1965), 84ff.

One characteristic, with regard to the perception of music, which most interested both the ancient philosophers and those of the Middle Ages, was that music is the only art which you cannot see. It is from this perspective that we find in Fénelon's *Telemachus* King Inachus's description of Music as an 'odor,' as if you can *smell* music, if you cannot see it.

> He holds in his hand a golden harp, and with eternal raptures sings the wonderful works of the gods: from his heart and his mouth an exquisite odor takes its being; the melody of his lyre and the voice were enough to ravish the gods as well as men.[20]

On the Purposes of Music

Only in Fénelon's *Telemachus*, among the fictional works, do we find insights into the purpose of music, and here they are all related to the communication of emotions.

> This said, Termosiris gave me a flute, of such sweetness, that the echoes of the hills, which carried the sound of every side, soon drew each neighboring shepherd round about me. My voice was endued with a Divine harmony: I found myself transported and moved, as by a superior power, to sing the graces which Nature has conferred upon the country. We passed the days and part of the nights in singing together.[21]
>
> ......
>
> The hollow valleys shall ring again with the consorts of shepherds, who along the crystal brooks shall sing to their pipes both of their amorous pains and pleasures.[22]

In one place Fénelon casts this more in the example of the 'ethos' of the ancient Greeks, the ability of music to change the character of the listener.

> Apollo [came to] teach the shepherds what are the charms of harmony; soften their savage hearts, show them the amiableness of virtue, and make them feel how sweet it is to enjoy, in this retirement, the innocent delights that nothing can deprive a shepherd of.[23]

---

20 Fénelon, *The Adventures of Telemachus, Son of Ulysses*, Book XIX, II, 158ff.
21 Ibid., Book II, I, 36.
22 Ibid., Book XII, I, 286.
23 Ibid., Book I, I, 36.

ART MUSIC

Fénelon's *Telemachus* is rich in descriptions of art music set in pastoral scenes, reminiscent of the ancient lyric poets.

> Every day was a festival; nothing was heard but the warbling of the birds, or the soft whispering of the zephyrs, sporting amidst the trembling boughs, or the murmur of a transparent stream descending from some rock, or songs which the Muses inspired into the shepherds who followed Apollo.[24]

And,

> There was at Tyre a young Lydian called Malachon, of marvelous beauty, but voluptuous, effeminate, and swallowed up in pleasure; his own study was how to preserve the delicacy of his complexion, to comb his flaxen locks, which waved upon his shoulders, to perfume himself, to adjust his robe in the nicest manner, to sing amorous songs to the music of his lute.[25]

He paints a rather romantic picture of Egypt, with meadows full of grazing cattle, workers bending under the weight of fruit they are harvesting, and,

> Shepherds that made the Echoes on every side repeat the melodious sound of their warbling flutes and pipes.[26]

In another place, he credits the Egyptians with the invention of 'instruments of music to ravish the soul.'[27]

We might also mention that in this same book, Fénelon writes a line which reminds us of the minstrel schools of the late Middle Ages.

> And now the shepherd comes home again with his flute, and sings to the assembled family such new songs as he learnt in the adjacent hamlets.[28]

Other references to art music are found in Marivaux's *La vie de Marianne*, where there is a brief mention of a specially composed song honoring newlyweds, 'a very fine epithalamium sung to soft music,'[29] and in Cyrano de Bergerac's *Other Worlds*, where a visitor from the Earth visits the Sun and finds there, among other implausible curiosities, people who have turned themselves into birds. These birds and the visitor engage in a musical dialogue,

---

24 Ibid., Book II, I, 35.
25 Ibid., Book III, I, 65
26 Ibid., Book II, I, 22.
27 Ibid., Book VIII, I,184.
28 Ibid. Book XII, I, 284.
29 Marivaux, *The Virtuous Orphan*, 506. An epithalamium is a wedding song.

the description of which suggests that the author himself had heard art songs which were emotionally quite sensitive.

> We serenaded one another by turns with the musical stories of our mutual loves. In my airs I sang that I was not only comforted but that I even rejoiced at my disaster since it had won me the honor of being lamented in such beautiful songs …
>
> I replied in my turn with all the raptures, all the tenderness, and all the subtleties of a passion so moving that two or three times I saw it on the branch ready to die of love. In truth, I mixed so much skill with the sweetness of my voice and surprised its ear with touches so cunning and ways so little frequented by its own species, that I had its fair soul at the mercy of all the passions to which I wished to subject it.[30]

Curiously, opera is not as frequently mentioned in fiction as it is in all other forms of literature. It is no doubt an accurate reflection of the times that in Crébillon, fils' *Letters from the Marchioness de M****, opera is described as a place to meet one's lover.

> If it must be so, my Lord, I permit you to be at the opera, and am infinitely obliged to you for your industry, to be informed what box I shall appear in; and since you so much desire it, I shall take care to have you accommodated with a place: But, as tender as the music may be, all opera nights are not alike; and whatever soft things you may tell me, with relation to Armida and Rinaldo, I shall remember too well that I have been the one, ever to allow you to be the other.[31]

Alain René Lesage, in his *Le Diable Boiteux*, presents two descriptions, remarkable in their detail, of serenades. While the novel is set in Madrid, we may assume his familiarity with serenades was gained in Paris. The first passages gives us much information about the musicians, and their literature of the latest songs sung in a 'sweet' style. First we are told of the arrangements.

> You may assure your cousin that I will in all things follow her advice; and that tomorrow, without fail, in the middle of the night, the street shall resound with one of the most gallant concerts that was ever heard in Madrid. And away went the intendant to secure the assistance of a celebrated musician, to whom he communicated his project, and whom he charged with the care of its execution.[32]

The lady herself is alerted that Don Como, governor of the pages, will 'gratify you with the sound of music and sweet voices, in an evening serenade.'

> The night came, and with it appeared, before the balcony of the lady, two carriages, from which descended the gallant Como and his confidant, accompanied by six musicians, vocal and instrumental, who commended a very decent concert, which lasted for a considerable time.

---

30 Bergerac, *Other Worlds*, 161.
31 Crébillon, fils, *Letters from the Marchiness de M*** to the Count de R****, 259.
32 Lesage, *Asmodeus, or The Devil on Two Sticks*, 99ff.

They performed many of the newest airs, and sang all the songs in vogue whose verses told the power of love in uniting hearts despite the obstacles of fortune, and the inequality of rank; while at every couplet, which the general's daughter perceived to be directed to herself, her merriment knew no bounds.

When the serenade was over, and the performers had departed in the carriages which brought them, the crowd which the music had attracted dispersed, and our lover remained in the street with Domingo alone.

Later we are told that this concert, 'including the carriages and the enormous quantity of wine which its bibulous performers had consumed, cost Don Como upwards of a hundred ducats.'

The second serenade which Lesage describes is unique for its high drama. Here Asmodeus, Zambullo and Don Cleophas are out walking when they hear instruments tuning at the end of the street, preparing for a serenade.

I am a great admirer of this sort of concert, replied Zambullo; let us by all means get near them; there may chance to be some decent voices among the lot ...

The serenade was commenced by the instruments alone, which played some new Italian songs; and then two of the voices sang alternately the following couplets:

List, while the thousand charms I sing,
Which round thee such enchantment fling,
that even Love has plumed his wing
    To seek thy bower.
Thy neck, that shames the mountain snow,
Thy lip, that mocks the peach's glow,
Bit Cupid's self a captive bow
    Beneath thy power ...

The couplets are gallant and delicate, cried the Student. They seem so to you, replied the Devil, because you are a Spaniard: if they were translated into French, for instance, they would not be greatly admired. The readers of that nation would think the expressions too figurative; and would discover an extravagance of imagination in the conceptions, which would be to them absolutely laughable. Every nation has its own standard of taste and genius, and will admit no other: but enough of these couplets, continued he, you will hear music of another kind.

Follow with your eyes those four men who have suddenly appeared in the street. See! they pounce upon the serenaders: the latter raise their instruments to defend their heads, but their frail [instruments] yield to the blows which fall on them, and are shattered into a thousand pieces.

Two cavaliers come to the rescue, one of whom paid for the serenade and is killed by the attackers.[33]

---

33   Ibid., 161ff.

Finally, as we have maintained throughout these volumes, it is the evidence of the contemplative listener which confirms the presence of Art Music. In Fénelon's *Telemachus* we find,

> He played on his flute, and all the other shepherds resorted to the shady elms and limpid streams, to listen to his songs.[34]

In another place he makes this point much more vivid.

> Mentor took up a harp, and played on it in so masterly a manner, that Architoas let his drop from him in very spite: his eyes struck fire; his troubled face turned pale; everybody took notice of his disorder and confusion: but at the same moment Mentor's harp entirely transported the souls of all the bystanders; none of them hardly durst breathe, for fear of breaking in upon the profound silence, and so losing something of the divine music, still fearing least it would be too soon over. Mentor's voice was by no means effeminate, but tuneable, strong, and expressive of every passion he turned it to.[35]

The subjects of his songs included the praises of Jupiter, the wisdom of Minerva, the misfortunes of young Narcissus and of the death of Adonis.

> All that heard him broke into resistless tears, and felt a secret pleasure in weeping. When he gave over singing, the Phoenicians looked at one another with amazement: one said, this is Orpheus, for thus with his harp he used to soften the wild beasts.

One who wished to congratulate the singer was so overcome with emotion he could not speak,

> Arichitoas ... did now begin to bestow on Mentor some commendations, but he blushed at the same time and could not proceed.

FUNCTIONAL MUSIC

Curiously, there is little reference to true functional music in the fictional works, although we find music for dancing in Montesquieu's *Persian Letters*, where he describes a pastoral festival in the kingdom of the Troglodytes,

> They instituted festivals in honor of the gods. Maidens, adorned with flowers, and young men celebrated them with dancing and rustic minstrelsy; then followed banquets ... It was at these gatherings that artless nature spoke.[36]

---

[34] Fénelon, *The Adventures of Telemachus, Son of Ulysses*, Book II, I, 34.

[35] Ibid., Book VIII, I, 179ff.

[36] Montesquieu, *The Persian Letters*, 27. The Troglodytes are mentioned in both Aristotle and Herodotus as bestial tribes living in Africa.

And Brantôme mentions a tradition in villages of the use of the tabor and flute to accompany the young girl to the church on her wedding day.[37]

There is also a brief reference to military in Fénelon's *Telemachus*, which speaks of 'trumpets that filled the air with martial clangors.'[38]

ENTERTAINMENT MUSIC

There are two references to banquet music in Fénelon's *Telemachus*,

> Adoam caused a magnificent repast to be brought in ... the rowers seats were all filled with musicians playing upon the flute: Architoas now and then made them pause, to introduce the sweet harmony of his voice and lyre, fit to be heard at the table of the gods, and to ravish the ears of Apollo himself.[39]
>
> ......
>
> At other times Ulysses appeared to him of a sudden in those feasts where joy shines forth amidst delights, and where you might hear the soft harmony of a voice, with a harp more melodious than the harp of Apollo, or the voice of all the Muses.[40]

Finally, Alain René Lesage, in his *Le Diable boiteux*, briefly refers to a trio sung in a tavern by 'a lusty Flemish captain, a chorister of the French opera, and an officer of the German guard.' They have been drinking since eight in the morning and, for honor of country, each is determined to be the last standing.[41]

---

37 Brantôme, *Lives of Fair and Gallant Ladies*, trans. A.R. Allinson (New York: Liveright, 1933), 367.
38 Fénelon, *The Adventures of Telemachus, Son of Ulysses*, Book X, I, 230.
39 Ibid., Book VIII, I, 177ff.
40 Ibid., Book XVIII, II, 123.
41 Lesage, *Asmodeus*, 25.

9 ON FRENCH MANNERS

OUR PURPOSE IN THIS CHAPTER is to present a sampling of first-hand observations of manners relative to the practice of music, taken from letters and memoirs of the aristocracy. We begin with a comment on the general cultural environment, as expressed in a letter from Charles de Saint-Évremond to the playwright, Corneille, in 1668.

> I believe the influence of ill taste is upon the decline; and that the first piece you shall give the public will show, by the return of their former applause, both the recovery of good sense and the restoration of reason.[1]

The 'ill taste' among the aristocracy, of which Saint-Évremond speaks, is described in much more vivid terms in a letter by the Duchesse d'Orléans.

> All the young people are dreadfully debauched and given to every vice, nor are they above lying and cheating and they think that it would be a disgrace to take pride in being honorable people; all they can do is guzzle, debauch others, and use filthy language, and whoever among them is the most unmannerly is admired and esteemed the most.[2]

In a letter of 1698 she begins to complain that her own son is falling into this pattern of life, observing,

> He has changed so much that one does not recognize either his face or his temperament, and since he leads this life he no longer takes pleasure in anything; his pleasure in music, which used to be a passion, is gone too.[3]

While the Duchesse praises her son's 'pleasure in music,' above, she placed quite a different value on actual musicians. In a letter of 1699, regarding the character of the Monsieur, she

---

1   Saint-Évremond, Letter to d'Hervart, February, 1675, quoted in *The Letters of Saint-Évremond* (Freeport, NY: Books for Libraries Press, 1971), 76. Charles de Marguetel de Saint-Denis, sieur de Saint-Evremond (1610–1703) was trained in law, but spent much of his career in the military. A letter critical of the Treaty of the Pyrenees forced him to leave France and live his remaining years in London.

2   Letter to the Duchess Sophie, May 18, 1685, quoted in Charlotte-Elisabeth Orléans, *A Woman's Life in the Court of the Sun King*, trans. Elborg Forster (Baltimore: Johns Hopkins University Press, 1984), 53. In a letter of 1700 [Ibid., 123], she mentions that the Duke d'Estrées was placed in the Bastille after a wild drinking spree in which several houses were set on fire. Elisabeth Charlotte, Duchesse d'Orléans (1652–1722), born Liselotte von der Pfalz, was a sister-in-law to Louis XIV. After the king's death, her son became Regent.

3   Ibid., 106.

observes that he 'prefers the company of lowly people, of painters and musicians, to that of people of rank.'[4] This attitude reflects an attitude which had become increasingly prominent since the latter part of the sixteenth century, that a gentleman should not engage in music because he should never spend his time on any activity which requires extraordinary effort. We can see this clearly in a letter of 1647 by Saint-Évremond, when he observes,

> Study has something cloudy and melancholy in it, which spoils that natural cheerfulness, and deprives a man of that readiness of wit, and freedom of fancy, which are required for polite conversation.[5]

Fifteen years later, we find the gentleman's viewpoint has not changed.

> I never was much addicted to reading; and if I employ any hours that way, they are the most idle, without design, without order, when I cannot enjoy the conversation of ingenious Gentlemen, and find myself debarred from pleasurable entertainments. Do not therefore expect that I should speak to you profoundly of those things, which I have but cursorily examined, and upon which I have but slight reflections …
>
> Mathematics have, indeed, much more certainty: but when I consider the profound meditation they require, and that they draw us from the actions and pleasures, to employ us entirely in speculation, its demonstrations seem to me to be very dearly bought; and a man must be very fond of Truth to pursue it at that price.[6]

When contemplating a visit to London, Saint-Évremond at least expressed a preference for music over science, as he explains to d'Hervart.

> I cannot understand how I can have made you think that I was going to apply myself to [scientific experimentation], for of all things in the world, it is least to my taste … Should I visit England … I should prefer the duke of Buckingham's violin to his laboratory, however curious it might be.[7]

There was, in this regard, an exception made for aristocratic ladies, music being an acceptable means of spending a life of insignificant employment. No doubt many of them became proficient musicians as we can see in the instance when the Duchesse d'Orléans regrets that a talented young lady, Louise-Adélaïde, is going to become a nun.

> It is a pity for this girl; she has many good traits, is most pleasing in appearance, tall, well-built, with a pretty and pleasant face, a beautiful mouth, and teeth like pearls; she dances well, has a

---

4   Letter to the electress Sophie, July 26, 1699, Ibid., 114.
5   Quoted in Saint-Évremond, *The Letters*, 1.
6   Ibid., 32ff.
7   Ibid., 94ff.

lovely voice and is a fine musician who can sing from sight anything she likes, without grimacing and very prettily.[8]

The Duchesse d'Orléans, who often complains of court manners, finds the nobles superficial even in the emotions they feel for their departed friends. She relates that after the funeral of the Dauphine, the court immediately resumed its cardplaying, 'hunting in the afternoon, music at night.'

If this were a matter of strength of character one might perhaps appreciate it and admire them for it, but that is not the reason, for as long as they see the sad spectacle they cry, but as soon as they leave the room they laugh again and forget all about it.[9]

This attitude is confirmed by the Duke of Saint-Simon who observes that even the death of Louis XIV, after having reigned seventy years, was little regretted and that few persons felt a sense of loss, apart from his personal servants.[10]

ON THE PHYSIOLOGY OF AESTHETICS

We find a very interesting reference to man's struggle between Reason and the emotions, or between his left and right hemispheres of the brain, in a letter of 1671 by Saint-Évremond to the Mareschal de Créqui.

> I can say one thing of myself, as extraordinary as true, that I never felt in myself any conflict between Passion and Reason. My Passion never opposed what I resolved out of duty; and my Reason readily complied with what a sense of pleasure inclined me to. I don't aim at praise on account of this easy agreement; on the contrary, I confess I have often been the more vicious for it. Not out of any perverse disposition to evil, but because the vice was entertained as a pleasure, instead of appearing as a crime.[11]

As an older man, he writes another correspondent,

> How unhappy is my condition! I have lost everything on the side of Reason, and I see nothing for me to pretend to on the side of Passion.[12]

---

8   Letter to the Raugräfin Luise, March 31, 1718, quoted in Charlotte-Elisabeth Orléans, *A Woman's Life*, 212.
9   Letter to the duchess Sophie, June 12, 1690, quoted in Ibid., 69.
10 Saint-Simon, *The Memoirs*, III, 28.
11 Quoted in Saint-Évremond, *The Letters*, 114.
12 Saint-Évremond, Letter to Duchesse Mazarin, 1676, Ibid., 168.

ON THE PHILOSOPHY OF AESTHETICS

In one of the letters by Saint-Évremond we find a rare comment by one of these nobles on a genuine topic of aesthetics, the question whether Art should imitate Nature.

> Nature is various in men; and Art, which is nothing but an imitation of Nature, ought to vary as she does.[13]

In another letter, he comments on the influence on literature caused by the fascination with the ancient writers, an expression of the continuing movement we call humanism.

> The good sense which is often found in our writings is generally borrowed from antiquity, rather than of our own growth. I would have the moderns inspired by the wit of the ancients, but would not have them steal it, and pass it for their own. I allow them to teach us how to think well, but hate to make use of their thoughts …
>
> What have we to do with a new author, who puts forth nothing but old productions; who sets himself out with the fancies of the Greeks, and imposes on the world their knowledge for his own? A vast number of rules, made three thousand years ago, are set up to be the standard of what's written now days; without considering that neither the subjects to be treated, nor the genius to be regulated are the same.[14]

In discussing poetry, Saint-Évremond again touches on the idea that the noble must not exert himself too much.

> Poetry requires a peculiar genius, that agrees not overmuch with good sense. It is sometimes the language of Gods, sometimes of Buffoons; rarely that of a Gentleman …
>
> Not but that there is something noble in making agreeable verses; but we must have a great command of our genius, otherwise the mind is possessed with something foreign, which hinders it from the free management of itself. 'He's a blockhead,' says the Spaniard, 'that can't make two verses, and a fool that makes four.' I believe, if this maxim prevailed over all the world, we should lack a thousand fine works, the reading of which gives us a very delicate pleasure; but this saying respects men of business, rather than professed poets …
>
> Comic poets are of all most proper for the converse of the world: for they make it their business to draw to the life what passes in it, and to express the sentiments and passions of men.[15]

The last sentence refers to the poet who writes comedies for the theater. In another letter, Saint-Évremond makes an interesting observation on the use of the emotions versus Reason in the two important French authors of tragedy.

---

13   Letter to Duchesse Mazarin, 1676, quoted in Ibid., 164.
14   Ibid., 163ff.
15   Letter to Mareschal de Créqui, [1671], quoted in Ibid., 117ff.

Corneille is admired for the expression of an heroic grandeur of soul, for the force of the passions, and sublimity of discourse. Racine's merit consists in sentiments which are more natural, in thoughts that are more clear, and in a diction that is more pure, and more easy. The former ravishes the soul, the latter makes a conquest of the mind. The latter gives no room for the reader to censure, the former does not leave the spectator in a condition to examine.[16]

In the correspondence of the Duchesse d'Orléans, we find numerous references to the opposition by the Church to the theater. To the Electress Sophie she complains,

> We almost had no more plays; the Sorbonne, in order to please the king, wanted to have them forbidden. But I understand that the archbishop of Paris and Père de la Chaise told the king that it was too dangerous to banish honorable entertainments because this would drive the young people even deeper into abominable vices … As long as plays are not completely done away with, I shall always go to see them, however loudly the preachers in their pulpits are made to howl against them. Two weeks ago during a sermon against plays, when the preacher said that the theater stirs the passions, the king turned to me and said, 'He is not preaching against me, since I no longer go to see plays, but against all of you who love them and go to see them.' I said, 'Although I love plays and go to see them, Monsieur d'Agen is not preaching against me, for he speaks only of those who let their passions be aroused by plays, and that is not my case; I only let myself be entertained, and there is nothing wrong with that.' The king did not say another word.[17]

She complains on this subject again in a letter of 1698 to Raugräfin Luise.

> I already wrote to you what I think of parsons and priests who forbid comedies, so I will say nothing more about it, except to add that if these reverend gentlemen were able to see a little further than their noses, they would understand that the common people's money is not wasted on comedies. In the first place, actors are poor devils who make their living from the theater, and furthermore, comedies give pleasure, pleasure gives health, health gives strength, and strength makes people work better; so in fact they should order rather than forbid them.[18]

One of the more striking comments by the Duchesse d'Orléans is about manners in the theater, allowing the public on the stage during the production, something confirmed by other observers.

> I just cannot enjoy it here because the Parisians are so boorish that they stand and sit around on the stage in droves, so that the actors have no room to play; it is most annoying. Yesterday we saw a new tragedy that is not too bad; but the actors were held back by all the people.[19]

---

16 Letter to Duchesse Mazarin, 1676, quoted in Ibid., 298.
17 Letter to the Electress Sophie, December 23, 1694, quoted in Charlotte-Elisabeth Orléans, *A Woman's Life*, 85ff.
18 Letter to the Raugräfin Luise, June 17, 1698, quoted in Ibid., 109.
19 Letter to the Raugräfin Luise, November 23, 1719, quoted in Ibid., 243.

Finally, there is this rather disdainful, aristocratic observation by Saint-Évremond on critics.

> The elevation of the mind leaves some little things for exact critics to lay hold on; and it is a comfort which great wits ought not to grudge those of a moderate size. Let poor wretches, to whom Nature has not been indulgent, put themselves as forward as they can by the labor of so crabbed a study.[20]

ON THE AESTHETICS OF MUSIC

There are a number of references by the aristocratic ladies which suggest they were active performers, listeners, collectors and even composers of songs. Several times in her correspondence, Mme de Sévigné mentions singing in private. For example, in a letter of 1695,

> I have received your two letters from Chaulnes, my dear cousin; we found some verses in them that delighted us; we have sung them with extreme pleasure, and more than one person will tell you so.[21]

In an earlier letter to the Count de Grignan, she apologizes,

> I should likewise have sent you the music you desired, but have not yet been able to procure it.[22]

The Duchesse d'Orléans provides very interesting information about the nature of some of these songs privately sung by the ladies.

> I also have a very big book of songs. It was given to me by the good Grande Mademoiselle [the niece of Louis XIII] before she died, and it amuses me very much. At the late Monsieur's court there were many clever people who made up the funniest songs. There are people in Paris who have ten or twelve big volumes of these old songs and take very good care of them. In France one can find out about every period from songs, because songs are written about everything. They are a much better way to learn about the court than the history books; for these are full of flattery, but in the songs they sing what is really going on.[23]

Even Saint-Évremond, who often claimed he was not particularly fond of formal concerts and opera, nevertheless could quote the lyrics of popular songs in his correspondence, as for example in a letter to the Comte de Lionne in 1668.

---

20 Letter to Duchesse Mazarin, 1676, quoted in Saint-Évremond, *The Letters*, 166.

21 François Sévigné, *Letters of Madame de Sévigné*, ed. Richard Aldington (London: Routledge, 1937), II, 195. In a letter of 1680 [Ibid., II, 76], she uses the figure of speech, 'We are in good tune when we are together.'

22 Ibid., I, 21.

23 Letter to the Electress Sophie, January 24, 1700, quoted in Charlotte-Elisabeth Orléans, *A Woman's Life*, 121.

*Pains of Love are sweeter far
Than all the other pleasures are.*[24]

In a letter to the same the following year, we find,

> Now you are perfectly cured, relish the pleasure of it, and let me make melancholy reflections on the song you have taught me:
>
> > *But oh! when Age benumbs our veins,
> > No longer sprightly Joy remains!*
>
> If there be any songs as agreeable as this in the music of [*Les Plaisirs de l'Isle enchantée*], I desire you to send them to me [arranged with accompaniment].[25]

On the Purposes of Music

As the correspondence and memoirs by these French aristocrats rarely mention general philosophical problems in aesthetics, we are not surprised to find the same is true with regard to music. We should like to mention, however, two comments relative to the purpose of music. First, in a letter to the Earl of St. Albans in 1677, Saint-Évremond writes of the familiar purpose of music to soothe the listener. He recommends, in this case, preparing for approaching death in the manner of Monsieur des Yveteaux of Paris.

> He died at eighty years of age, causing a saraband to be played to him, a little before he expired, that his soul, as he expressed himself, might slide away the easier.[26]

Mme de Sévigné mentions, if indirectly, the purpose of music to communicate feeling in a letter to Mme de Grignan. She recalls that after a performance of Molière's *Tartuffe*, the minuet and gigues played at a ball 'nearly reduced me to tears, for they brought you so fresh to my remembrance.'[27]

Saint-Évremond, in a letter to d'Hervart on the subject of opera, is particularly interesting for its contention that music communicates feelings, but spoken words communicate action.

> I do not deny but that the music may be very beautiful in some places, and the dances marvelous, but that opera, seeing how it is composed, should be perfect in every part, is an impossibil-

---

24 Quoted in Saint-Évremond, *The Letters*, 63.

25 Ibid., 79.

26 Ibid., 189. In Vigneuil-Marville [Bonaventure Argonne], *Mélanges d'Histoire et de Littérature* (Paris, 1725), I, 177, this same Frenchman is described.

> He ended his days in a world of his own, dressed as a shepherd, the birds hopping on to his flute piped to an imaginary flock.

27 Letter of 1671, in Sévigné, *Letters*, I, 68.

ity ... There is nothing so ridiculous as having an action sung, whether it be the deliberation of a Council, the giving of orders in battle, or anything else. Where the Gods are concerned there may be singing: every Nation has worshiped them in song, and chanted their praises. We can sing what we feel and suffer, for grief and affection are naturally expressed by a kind of tender and melancholy song. But our actions require no other expression but the spoken word. Moreover, operas are so contrived that all the spirit of the production is lost in our enjoyment of the music, which is not worth it, however enchanting it may be. For where the mind has too little to do, it is impossible, in the long run, that our senses, which we are most eager to please, should not begin to languish. The best poet is obliged to degrade himself in favor of the musician, since his lines must be arranged, less for the meaning he would have them represent, than for the convenience of the musician and the smoothness of his songs.[28]

To another correspondent, however, he is quick to note that he himself is not moved by the emotions of opera!

> The passionate songs at the opera make no impression upon me of themselves; they have no manner of influence over me.[29]

On Opera

In the correspondence of several persons we are given the information that the opera, like the theater, was under attack by the Church. A letter of 1680 by Mme de Sévigné mentions in passing the censorship of opera.

> The opera (of *Proserpine*) is superior to every other. The Chevalier tells me he has sent you several of the airs, and that he saw a gentleman who said he had sent you the words; I dare say you will like it. There is a scene in it, between Mercury and Ceres, which requires no interpreter to be understood; it must have been approved, since it has been performed; but you will judge for yourself.[30]

The Duchesse d'Orléans, as well, cannot understand why the Church is opposed to opera and plays, as she mentions in a letter to the Electress Sophie in December 1694.

> If the rumors that are flying are true, the boredom here will soon get worse, for they say that all operas and plays are to be done away with and that the Sorbonne has orders to work on this. I am certain that this will be no more to Your Grace's taste than it is to mine, and what seems most peculiar is that they go after such innocent things and forbid them, even though the most dreadful vices are in vogue now, such as murder by poison, assassination, and abominable sod-

---

28 Letter to d'Hervart, February, 1675, quoted in Saint-Évremond, *The Letters*, 161ff.

29 Letter to Duchesse Mazarin, 1676, quoted in Ibid., 168.

30 Sévigné, *Letters*, II, 57ff.

omy; but nobody objects to these and the preachers only preach against the poor plays, which do not hurt anyone and in which one sees vice punished and virtue rewarded.[31]

In a letter of 1701, she mentions that the king no longer attends the opera[32] and in 1709 she reveals,

> My confessor does not forbid me to go to the opera or to the theater, except on the day before confession; he would be pleased if I did not go at all, but since I know what I do there is not sinful I have no scruples whatsoever about it.[33]

There are a few interesting comments relative to the practice of opera performance in the Court at this time. Saint-Simon recalls the celebration of the marriage of the Duke de Burgundy lasted several days and suggests that such festivities often concluded with an opera.

> The king took them into the theater, where Destouches's opera of *Issé* was very well performed. The opera being finished, everybody went his way, and thus these marriage-fêtes were brought to an end.[34]

Regarding this same duke, who became the Regent following the death of Louis XIV, Saint-Simon tells us that he regularly attended the opera at five o'clock and sometimes returned with an 'opera girl' as one of his mistresses.[35] In another place he observes that the opera in question was in the Palais Royal, that it was well-guarded on the days of a performance and that a machine had been built to cover the pit when the opera was used for balls.[36] Of another noble, he mentions that 'Paris loved Monseigneur, perhaps because he often went to the opera.'[37]

One of Saint-Simon's most interesting comments is relative to the vanity of Louis XIV.

> Without voice or musical knowledge, he used to sing, in private, the passages of the opera prologues that were fullest of his praises! He was drowned in vanity; and so deeply, that at his

---

31 Letter to the electress Sophie, December 16, 1694, quoted in Charlotte-Elisabeth Orléans, A Woman's Life, 85.

32 Ibid., 140. In a letter of 1716, however, she mentions the king was fond of music.

33 Ibid., 176.

34 Saint-Simon, *The Memoirs*, I, 109.

35 Ibid., III, 59.

36 Ibid., III, 61. The duke also observes [Ibid., III, 125],

> The Regent, without having the horrible vice or the favorites of Henry III, had even more than that monarch become notorious for his daily debauches, his indecency, and his impiety.

> In another place [Ibid., III, 410], the duke mentions that the Regent had said he would like to die suddenly. After the latter's death, Saint-Simon reflected,

> I shudder to my very marrow, with the horrible suspicion that God, in His anger, granted his desire.

37 Ibid., I, 206.

> public suppers—all the Court present, musicians also—he would hum these self-same praises between his teeth, when the music they were set to was played![38]

ART MUSIC

Among the correspondence and memoirs of the French aristocrats we also find some interesting descriptions of, and information regarding, actual performances which they heard. In a letter of 1676 Mme de Sévigné seems to imply there was rather frequent music at court.

> There is always music, to which [the king] occasionally listens, and which has an admirable effect; in the meantime, he chats with the ladies, who are accustomed to have that honor.[39]

The Duke of Saint-Simon agrees that Louis XIV regularly listened to music in 'Madame de Maintenon's rooms,' and on one occasion describes this as 'a grand concert.'[40]

Among the participants, Saint-Évremond mentions 'Mademoiselle Sivert, who sings Italian songs better than any I have heard in my life'[41] and the Duke of Saint-Simon recalls one noble lady, Madame la Duchesse, who 'had the art of writing witty songs.'[42] Regarding 'witty' songs, the Duchesse d'Orléans mentions in several of her letters popular songs written in satire of the king. In one letter she suggests that these feelings were not deeply felt.

> I know the French; they may be angry at their king, but their anger goes no further than the singing of songs against his Majesty, and for all that, every one of them would rather starve to death than leave their king without money.[43]

Nevertheless, in another letter she mentions,

> I am sending Your Grace a song ... expressing discontent with the king and the prince de Conti, which I could not send through the mail.[44]

We have mentioned in the Introduction that functional music could become art music under circumstances that included a contemplative listener. We have such a case, regarding more serious vocal music, when Mme de Sévigné writes of the funeral service for Chancellor Peter Seguier in 1672.

---

38   Ibid., II, 359.
39   Quoted in Sévigné, *Letters*, I, 238.
40   Saint-Simon, *The Memoirs*, II, 348.
41   Letter to d'Hervart, July, 1669, quoted in Saint-Évremond, *The Letters*, 96.
42   Saint-Simon, *The Memoirs*, I, 83.
43   Letter to the electress Sophie, December 22, 1702, quoted in Charlotte-Elisabeth Orléans, *A Woman's Life*, 149.
44   Ibid., 150.

As for the music, it was fine beyond all description. Lully exerted himself to the utmost and was assisted by all the king's musicians. There was an addition made to that fine *Miserere*, and there was a *Libera* which filled the eyes of the whole assembly with tears. I do not think the music in heaven could exceed it.[45]

Regarding instrumental music at court, Saint-Évremond mentions several harpsichordists in his correspondence, beginning with a performance by Jacques Chambonnières, the great keyboard player employed by Louis XI.

Monsieur de Chambonnière's Corantos, which you sent me, are pretty, but they are not his best; the Sarabande is very agreeable, and in his true manner. I once heard him play a Suite of Corantos in a concert at the Duc de Joyeuse's, with which I was enraptured. I have asked you to send me his *Springtime*, for which Monsieur Servien wrote the words; it begins with a Coranto, continues with a Sarabande, and ends with a Chaconne. I shall be obliged if you can send them all, as well as *Young Zephyrs* and the Suite of Corantos. All this is a burden, but as they are old pieces, they will not be difficult to obtain, and you could certainly have them copied by some scholar who is familiar with Monsieur de Chambonnière's style.[46]

In other places he mentions 'Baillon, who is an excellent performer on the harpsichord,'[47] and an English artist.

It would be agreeable to visit Mrs. Bond. You are certain there of winning a little, and of hearing the harpsichord played better than anyone you can hear in England.[48]

Nevertheless, in a letter of 1671, he comments,

The elegant harmony of concerts, engages me not so much.[49]

The Duchesse d'Orléans, in a letter during one of the coldest winters in recent memory, describes a failed concert.

Last night we had a concert, but it was not very good because half of the musicians could not make their way up the hill in their hackney coach, for all the streets are icy.[50]

---

45 Sévigné, *Letters*, I, 110.
46 Letter to d'Hervart [1669], quoted in Saint-Évremond, *The Letters*, 93ff.
47 Letter to Duchesse Mazarin, 1691, quoted in Ibid., 294.
48 Letter to Mme de la Perrine, ca. 1700–1703, quoted in Ibid., 370.
49 Letter to Mareschal de Créqui, [1671], quoted in Ibid., 115.
50 Letter to the Electress Sophie, February 7, 1709, quoted in Charlotte-Elisabeth Orléans, *A Woman's Life*, 171.

FUNCTIONAL MUSIC

As might be expected for a court environment, this literature contains references to a wide variety of functional music. One of the more curious of these is in a letter of 1680 by Mme de Sévigné which mentions the execution of a noble lady, Catherine Monvoisin, who enjoyed a local reputation in Paris as a provider of poison to needy nobles. Among the latter was Racine, of whom it was rumored that he murdered his mistress, Thérèse du Parc.[51] Mme de Sévigné described 'La Voisin' singing psalms in mockery in her cell in the days before her execution.

There are numerous references to more traditional Church music. Saint-Évremond makes his most fervent comments about music when it is that of the Church, as we can see in a letter to Monsieur Justel in 1681.

> Nor is your austerity less wild in the silencing our music, than in condemning our images. You ought to remember that David recommended nothing so earnestly to the Jews, as the celebrating of the praises of the Almighty with all sorts of instruments. Music in churches exalts the soul, purifies the mind, moves the heart, inspires and raises devotion.[52]

The Duchesse d'Orléans, Elisabeth Charlotte, being German-born, was usually bored when hearing the music of the Church sung in Latin and French. On one occasion when a cough kept her from sleeping for three days,

> I remembered that I always sleep in church as soon as I hear preaching and nuns singing. Therefore I drove to a convent where there was to be a sermon. The nuns had barely begun to sing when I went to sleep, and I slept throughout the three-hour service; that made me feel much better.[53]

She mentions this again a few years later.

> If your Grace were Catholic and had to go to mass, she would find it even more boring, for not only is it always exactly the same, but one never hears anything but the singing of vowels, like 'aaaa eeee oooo iiii'; it is enough to make one burst out of one's skin with sheer impatience.[54]

The Duke of Saint-Simon mentions that the musicians of Louis XIV always sang an anthem when he went to mass.[55]

---

51 To protect Racine, the king had the court records suppressed, hence the details are lost to history.
52 Quoted in Saint-Évremond, *The Letters*, 234.
53 Letter to the Duchess Sophie, March 19, 1693, quoted in Charlotte-Elisabeth Orléans, *A Woman's Life*, 81.
54 Letter to the Electress Sophie, January 15, 1696, quoted in Ibid., 89. In a letter of 1719, she mentions that Louis XIV never used trumpets and timpani in church.
55 Saint-Simon, *The Memoirs*, III, 22.

The Duchesse d'Orléans also writes of the music of the Lutheran church.

> What has become of the hymns that used to be sung in Hanover during Advent? In my day, no Advent passed without the hymn 'Now Comes the Heathens' Savior …' It seems to me that the Lutherans rarely have musical instruments in their churches; in my day we did not have any and everyone sang together, just as Your Grace does in her church. It seems to me that singing alone is much more entertaining than the finest instrumental music. If the angels in heaven can assume human shape and human voices, they must sing beautifully, but I doubt that Our Lord is all that amused by instruments.[56]

In another letter she mentions the Lutheran hymn, 'O Man Repent Your Grievous Sins.'

> I still know the melody and at least six stanzas of this very long hymn. It is really much more agreeable when one can sing along instead of having to listen to some bawling in a language that one does not even understand.[57]

And in yet another letter she mentions the music for New Year's.

> 'In dulci jubilo-ho-ho, sing, Christians, and rejoy-hoy-hoyce, our hearts' deli-hi-hight lies in praesepio-ho-ho, and sparkles like the su-hu-hun, matris in gremio-ho-ho, alpha es et o-ho-ho, alpha es et o.' If Your Grace has not sung this herself today, I am certain at least that the timpani and trumpets have played it for her, since today is New Year's Day for Your Grace.[58]

We have a glimpse of ceremonial music heard by the public, when the Duchesse d'Orléans describes a ceremony to lay a cornerstone.

> Today I rose a good hour later than usual because I had gone to bed an hour late yesterday. I did not return from Paris until ten o'clock at night; I had driven there at half past ten in the morning in order to perform a most tiresome and long-winded ceremony in a monastery called l'Abbeye au Bois, namely, the laying of a cornerstone for a new church. I was quite embarrassed, for I was received to the sound of timpani, trumpets, shawms, pipes, tambors and gun salutes. I had to walk through an alley along the foundation with all that noise ahead of me … You can imagine how this attracted the populace. Before this fine procession I had already heard mass with beautiful music at the monastery. At the place of the foundation stone the priests sang three psalms in Latin and also recited some prayers of which I did not understand a word.[59]

---

56 Letter to the Electress Sophie, December 16, 1699, quoted in Charlotte-Elisabeth Orléans, *A Woman's Life*, 118.

57 Ibid., 158. In a letter to Sophie of May 24, 1705, she mentions an interesting anecdote regarding the death of the Emperor Leopold.

> When the emperor, having received the sacraments, asked the doctors whether they knew of anything else that might help him. When they answered this question with 'No,' he called for all his musicians, sang hymns to their accompaniment, and thus died singing.

58 Letter to the Electress Sophie, March 8, 1699, quoted in Ibid., 111.

59 Letter to the Raugräfin Luise, June 9, 1718, quoted in Ibid., 213ff.

We find descriptions of rather unusual functional music when the Duke of Saint-Simon relates the drums began to march through Paris at five o'clock in the morning when the king requested the Parliament to meet at the Tuileries[60] and an instance in 1717 when 'guards with drums at each end of the street' were used to control traffic.[61]

Regarding music for dance, Mme de Sévigné, referring to the son of one of her noble lady friends mentions, 'he took an hautboy with him, and they danced till midnight.'[62] The Duchesse d'Orléans, on the other hand, complains,

> I spent the first days of carnival being sick and the last days being bored by watching poorly danced minuets.[63]

The Duke of Saint-Simon mentions the capture of military timpani—an important symbol of victory in the field.

> We took all their cannon … a quantity of flags, and some pairs of timpani. The victory was complete.[64]

ENTERTAINMENT MUSIC

Several correspondents refer to the elaborate entertainment music provided at Versailles. A letter of Mme de Sévigné, of 1676, mentions 'they went afterwards in gondolas upon the canal, where there was music.'[65] The Duchesse d'Orléans describes the entertainments given on Monday, Wednesday and Fridays by the king in a new gallery built to connect his apartments with those of the queen. These evenings, called, '*jours d'appartement,*' began with the men and women assembling separately,

> Thereupon everyone goes to the salon of which I spoke, and from there to a large room where there is music for those who want to dance. From there one goes to a room where the king's throne stands. There one finds various kinds of music, concerts and singing. From there one goes into the bedchamber, where three tables for playing cards are set up, one for the king, one for the queen and one for Monsieur. From there one goes to a room that could be called a hall, where more than twenty tables, covered with green velvet cloth with a gold fringe, have been put up for all kinds of games. From there one goes to a large antechamber containing the king's billiard table, and then to another room with four large tables for the collation, all kinds of things

---

60 Saint-Simon, *The Memoirs*, III, 138ff.

61 Ibid., III, 223.

62 Sévigné, *Letters*, II, 138.

63 Letter to the electress Sophie, February 10, 1701, quoted in Charlotte-Elisabeth Orléans, *A Woman's Life*, 129.

64 Saint-Simon, *The Memoirs*, I, 33.

65 Sévigné, *Letters*, I, 239.

like fruit cakes and preserves ... After one is done with the collation, which is taken standing up, one goes back to the room with the many tables; now everyone sits down to a different game, and it is unbelievable how many varieties of games are being played: lansquenet, trictrac, picquet, l'hombre, chess, ... every conceivable game. When the king and the queen come into the room, no one gets up from the game. Those who do not play, like myself and a great many others, just stroll from room to room, now to the music and now to the game room, for one is allowed to go wherever one wishes; this lasts from six until ten, when one goes to supper.[66]

In a letter of 1695, she reveals her own preference, 'if there is *appartement* I listen to the music.'[67]

We also find some description of the musical performances hosted by lesser nobles. A letter of Mme de Sévigné of 1677 describes the music at a party in a garden of the Hôtel de Condé.

There were water-works, bowers, terraces, six hautboys in one corner, six violins in another, the most melodious flutes; a supper which seemed to be prepared by enchantment, an admirable bass-viol, and a resplendent moon, which witnessed all our pleasures.[68]

She also writes of her visit to the Marquis de Termes in 1677.

They brought one of the musicians belonging to the opera with them; he plays better than Lully, and amuses us highly. There is, besides, a little impertinent hump-backed fellow, who is always singing, and who imagines himself an admirable performer; he is a perpetual source of laughter to us.[69]

The Duke of Saint-Simon mentions entertainment music provided for banquets by the king's famous ensemble, the 'twenty-four violins.' He relates that on the annual fête of St. Louis (August 25) the order of the day was that,

The drums and oboes, assembled beneath the king's windows, should play their accustomed music as soon as he awoke, and that the twenty-four violins should play in the ante-chamber during his dinner.[70]

He describes the celebration of the Peace of Utrecht, in April 1713, as including a *Te Deum* sung at Notre Dame, a fireworks display and a great banquet at the Hôtel de Ville for the leading officials of Paris with music performed by the king's 'twenty-four violins.'[71]

---

66 Letter to the electress Wilhemine-Ernestine, December 6, 1682, quoted in Charlotte-Elisabeth Orléans, *A Woman's Life*, 38ff.
67 Ibid., 86.
68 Quoted in Sévigné, *Letters*, I, 262.
69 Ibid., II, 1.
70 Saint-Simon, *The Memoirs*, II, 351.
71 Ibid., II, 248.

We should mention another instance of entertainment music recalled by the Duke of Saint-Simon, although it was probably not appreciated by the guest of honor. He tells of a palace joke by which the Swiss guards with drums were sent in to awaken a lady in the morning 'by their horrid din.'[72]

Finally, Mme de Sévigné gives us a brief glimpse of the local peasant music near her country estate.

> I am vexed that you cannot see the *bourrées* of this country; it is the most surprising sight imaginable; the peasantry dance in as true time as you do, and with such an activity, a sprightliness that, in short, I am quite in raptures with them. I have a little band of music every evening, which costs me a mere trifle.[73]

---

72 Ibid., I, 258.
73 Letter of 1676, quoted in Sévigné, *Letters*, I, 226.

10   VOLTAIRE, AS PHILOSOPHER

François Marie Arouet (1694–1778), known as Voltaire,[1] was the son of a successful attorney and a lively and intelligent woman who hosted a minor salon in Paris. His father advised him, 'Literature is the profession of the man who wishes to be useless to society and a burden to his relatives, and to die of hunger.' The son responded by becoming one of the most prolific writers of the Baroque, supporting his family and dying wealthy. His works include drama, poetry, history, fiction and above all philosophy.

Voltaire arrived in Paris in 1715 as France was in transition from the era of Louis XIV to the regency for the young Louis XV. His brilliant wit, and sharp tongue, soon brought him to the attention of high society and earned him several visits to the Bastille. One comment remembered from this time followed an announcement that the regent, for reasons of the economy, had sold half the horses of the royal stables. Voltaire suggested it might have been better if he dismissed half the asses at court!

During these first years in Paris he also spent much time visiting the famous salons, where the most enlightening intellectual discussions of Paris were enjoyed.[2] While we must presume this was stimulating for the young man, he would later describe these salons as,

> A large number of little groups exists in Paris, each presided by a woman who begins to cultivate her mind as her beauty declines. One or two men of letters are the prime ministers of this little kingdom. If you neglect to enroll yourself among the courtesans, you are regarded as belonging to the enemy, and you are crushed. Notwithstanding your merits you grow old in disgrace and poverty. Places intended for men of letters are not awarded to talent but as the result of intrigue.[3]

Among many of his contemporaries in Catholic France, which had remained unchanged by the Reformation, Voltaire was most infamous for his writings about religion. Although he never failed to state that he believed in God, his attacks focused on a long list of rather vulnerable topics, such as the selling of indulgences, errors and impossibilities in the accounts

---

1   He took the name Voltaire, a name which had been in his mother's family, while in the Bastille.
2   These salons were a mandatory visiting place for important dignitaries visiting Paris, including Americans such as Thomas Jefferson and Ben Franklin.
3   Letter to Le Fèvre (ca. 1740), in Voltaire, *Select Letters of Voltaire*, trans. Theodore Besterman (London: Nelson, 1963), 71ff.

of the Scriptures (such as the Flood[4]) and the general topic of money—the wealth of the Churchmen vowed to poverty then representing about a third of the wealth of France.

Voltaire was particularly hard on all forms of Church-encouraged superstitions and relics, as for example the church of Puy-en-Velay which claimed to possess the foreskin of Jesus.[5] As time went on, he became more outspoken about the Roman Church. In a letter to Catherine, Empresses of Russia, he observed,

> I confess, your Majesty, that I loathe the papal government: I find it ridiculous and abominable: it has brought stupidity and bloodshed to half of Europe for too many centuries.[6]

He was thinking of this when writing under the topic 'Heresy' in his *Philosophical Dictionary*. Heresy, he notes, was,

> A Greek word, signifying 'belief, or elected opinion.' Is it not greatly to the honor of human reason that men should be hated, persecuted, massacred, or burned at the stake, on account of their chosen opinions?[7]

But for all of this, Voltaire was not a theologian. Rather, as he once wrote to Frederick the Great, 'Humanity is the principle of all my thought.'[8] It was also his perspective of humanity at large which inspired many of his comments on government. One example:

> We are every day asked, whether a republican or a kingly government is to be preferred? The dispute always ends in agreeing that the government of men is exceedingly difficult. The Jews had God himself for their master; yet observe the events of their history. They have almost always been trampled upon and enslaved.[9]

Volaire appears to have been intellectually uncomfortable in Paris and indeed lived much of his remaining life elsewhere. His observations of Paris life usually reflect a rather superfi-

---

[4] Voltaire, in his *Philosophical Dictionary*, 'Universal Deluge,' in *The Works of Voltaire* (New York: St. Hubert Guild, 1901), VIII, 75, observed of the Flood,

> I do not comprehend how God created a race of men in order to drown them, and then substituted in their room a race still viler than the first.

The *Philosophical Dictionary* evolved after Voltaire had been asked to contribute a number of articles to the famous *Encyclopédie* of Diderot and d'Alembert. It was published in 1764, although Voltaire repeatedly disavowed it, as for example in a letter to Etinne-Noël Damilaville (September 19, 1764).

[5] *Philosophical Dictionary*, 'Superstition,' in Ibid., XIV,18. He also quotes here a letter purported to have been left by Jesus after he visited a French church in 1771.

[6] Letter to Catherine of Russia (November, 1770), in *Voltaire and Catherine the Great*, trans. A. Lentin (Cambridge: Oriental Research Partners, 1974), 93.

[7] *Philosophical Dictionary*, 'Heresy,' X, 36.

[8] Letter to Frederick the Great (October, 1737), in *The Selected Letters of Voltaire*, trans. Richard Brooks (New York: New York University Press, 1973), 64.

[9] *Philosophical Dictionary*, 'Democracy,' VIII, 83.

cial society, a place 'made for young women and sensual men, the country of madrigals and powder puffs. But elsewhere are to be found reason, talent, etc.'[10] To a correspondent he writes,

> I am leading no life at all. I am being carried, being swept far away in a whirlwind. I come and go; I have supper at one end of town and the following day at the other end. One must fly from the company of three or four intimate friends to the Opera, to the Comédie, to see curiosities the way a foreigner would, to embrace a hundred persons a day, to make and receive a hundred declarations of friendship.[11]

Nothing reveals Voltaire's disgust at this superficial society more clearly than his description of their reaction to the Abbeville Affair, in which an eighteen-year-old young man, charged with blasphemy and mutilating a crucifix, had his hand cut off, his tongue removed and was then burned at the stake.

> People barely speak of these things for a moment and then rush on to the Opéra-Comique.[12]

One of the Parisian institutions which Voltaire frequently demeaned was the famous Academy. A typical example is found in a letter to Le Fèvre.

> After forty years of work you bring yourself to seek by intrigue that which is never given to merit alone: you cabal like all the others to enter the *Académie française* and to deliver in a broken voice, on the day of your reception, a discourse which on the next day will be forgotten forever.
> This *Académie française* is the subject of all literary men's secret hopes, it is a mistress against which they launch songs and epigrams until they have obtained its favors, and which they neglect as soon as they have entered into possession.
> It is not surprising that they wish to enter a body in which merit is always to be found, and by which they hope, though more or less in vain, to be protected. But you will ask me why they all speak so badly of it until they are admitted, and why the public, which has a good deal of respect for the *Académie des sciences*, treats the *Académie française* with so little consideration. It is because the labors of the *Académie française* are seen by all, and the others are veiled. Every Frenchman thinks that he knows his language, and prides himself on having taste, but he does not pride himself on being a physicist. Mathematics will always be a sort of mystery to the nation at large, and consequently something worthy of respect; algebraic equations do not expose themselves to epigrams, nor to songs, nor to envy; but the public judges severely immense collections of mediocre verse, of discourses, of harangues, and of those panegyrics which are sometimes as false as the eloquence with which they are recited.[13]

---

10 Letter to Pierre-Robert Le Cornier de Cideville (February, 1737), in *The Selected Letters*, 63ff.
11 Letter to Mme. de Champbonin (September, 1739), in Ibid., 79.
12 Letter to Jean D'Alembert (July, 1766), in *Ibid.*, 265. It might be added that when the boy was apprehended, he had a copy of Voltaire's *Philosophical Dictionary*—which was added to the fire.
13 Letter to Le Fèvre (ca. 1740), in *Select Letters*, 72. Voltaire makes some of these same points again in his 'The Professon of Letters,' in *The Works of Voltaire*, XXXVII, 73ff.

In an essay on the Royal Society of London, Voltaire dismisses the importance of such institutions in general.

> All the great men have either been formed before the institution of academies, or at least without any assistance from them.[14]

In several places we can see the disappointment of Voltaire that he came too late to participate in the period of Louis XIV. His, in contrast, was a period of decay in both society and the arts. In an essay on 'Courtiers,' he reflects,

> There was a time when the arts were cultivated in France by persons of the first distinction; even the courtiers applied themselves to the Fine Arts, in spite of that dissipation, the taste for trifles, and that passion for intrigue, which are the deities of this country. It appears to me, that at present, learning is not the reigning taste at court.[15]

Similarly, in a letter to the English ambassador to Constantinople, Voltaire observed,

> Everything, in these days, conspires to reduce France to that state of barbarism from which Louis XIV and Cardinal Richelieu had delivered her: that a curse on that policy knows not the value of the fine arts! ... Under the greatest princes the arts have always flourished, and their decay is often succeeded by that of the state itself: history will supply us with ample proofs of it.[16]

Today, when little of his voluminous output attracts much attention, Voltaire is remembered primarily for his associations with others, beginning with his long on again, off again, friendship with that great musician-poet-king, Frederick the Great. Certainly we can sense the excitement he felt in Berlin, as compared to Paris.

> Well, here I am finally in this place, formerly savage, which is today as much embellished by the arts as ennobled by glory. A hundred and fifty thousand victorious soldiers, no attorneys, the opera, the theater, philosophy, poetry, a hero-philosopher and poet, grandeur and grace, granadiers and muses, trumpets and violins, Platonic banquets, society and liberty! Who would believe it.[17]

Voltaire is also remembered together with Rousseau, and others, as being one of the philosophers who prepared the intellectual climate for the French Revolution. Clearly, he would have been surprised to know that Louis XVI would later observe of Rousseau and

---

14 'The Royal Society and Academies,' in *The Works of Voltaire*, XXXIX, 96.
15 'On Courtiers who have Cultivated Learning,' in Ibid., XXXIX, 75.
16 Letter to Mr. Falkener, in Ibid., X IX, 11.
17 Letter to Charles Augustin Feriol (July 24, 1750), in *Select Letters*, 108.

himself, 'Those two men have destroyed France.'¹⁸ But, it is just as evident that he recognized the changes taking place.

> I am informed that an inquisition against literature is being instituted. They noticed Frenchmen were beginning to develop their wings, and they are clipping them. It is not good for a nation to take it into its head to think. This is a dangerous vice that must be left to the English.¹⁹

ON THE PHYSIOLOGY OF AESTHETICS

For all the centuries during which Church and university philosophers had been arguing that man must be ruled by Reason, Voltaire could not help but reflect on how poorly it had been valued.

> When one considers that Newton, Locke, Clarke, and Leibniz would have been persecuted in France, imprisoned at Rome, and burned at Lisbon, what are we to think of human reason?²⁰

He was also cautious that there may be forms of Reason which we do not understand, such as perhaps some form of Reason beyond our awareness.

> There are poets who make verses sleeping; geometricians who measure triangles. All proves to us that there is a power which acts within us without consulting us.²¹

Voltaire observes that the same vowel sounds are used in all languages and from this he develops a very interesting discussion on the development of language as the basis of rational thought.

> Yet all nations …, even the Hottentots and Kaffirs, pronounce the vowels and consonants as we do, because the larynx in them is essentially the same as in us—just as the throat of the rudest boor is made like that of the finest opera-singer, the difference, which makes of one a rough, discordant, insupportable bass, and of the other a voice sweeter than the nightingale's, being imperceptible to the most acute anatomist; or, as the brain of a fool is for all the world like the brain of a great genius.²²

---

18 Quoted in Voltaire, *Life of Voltaire* (Third Edition), 526.
19 Letter to Jean D'Alembert (May 1764), in *The Selected Letters*, 249.
20 'Decartes and Newton,' in *The Works of Voltaire*, XXXVII, 174.
21 *Philosophical Dictionary*, 'Man,' in Ibid., XI, 190.
22 *Philosophical Dictionary*, 'The Alphabet,' in Ibid., V, 9ff.

Voltaire then makes some very astute deductions regarding the origin of language, deductions which are generally believed by modern philologists. He suggess that language began with simple emotional utterances, later clarified by the addition of gesture.

> May we not, without offending anyone, suppose that the alphabet originated in cries and exclamations? Infants of themselves articulate one sound when an object catches their attention, another when they laugh, and a third when they are whipped, which they ought not to be …
>
> From exclamations formed by vowels as natural to children as croaking is to frogs, the transition to a complete alphabet is not so great as may be thought. A mother must always have said to her child the equivalent of come, go, take, leave, hush!, etc. These words represent nothing; they describe nothing; but a gesture makes them intelligible.

He adds that he is astonished when he reflects on the ages it must have taken to go from this to sentences.

He concludes this discussion by observing that as words were invented they soon became charged with subjective inferences, from their association with religion, from magic, from necromancy, etc., thus losing their value as invariable symbols. Thus, he says, 'the alphabet was the origin of all man's knowledge, and of all his errors.'

Under 'Abuse of Words,' in his *Philosophical Dictionary*, Voltaire goes to some lengths to demonstrate that language, and books, 'rarely give us any precise ideas' and are often taken by the listener in an incorrect sense.[23] In this regard, in another place he mentions that he finds it curious that 'the same word (Adoration) that is used in addressing the Supreme Being is also used in addressing a mistress.'

> We not infrequently go from hearing a sermon, in which the preacher has talked of nothing but *adoring* God in spirit and in truth, to the opera, where nothing is to be heard but *the charming object of my adoration*, etc.[24]

Voltaire was also keenly aware that there is more to man than Reason, that there is a feeling side which, in the course of daily actions, may be even more important.

> What will I gain from knowing the path of light and the gravitation of Saturn? These are sterile truths. One feeling is a thousand times more important.[25]

He recognizes this duality in Racine.

> Yes, I consider Racine unquestionably the best of our tragic poets, the only one who has spoken both to the heart and to reason.[26]

---

23 Ibid., 53ff.
24 Ibid., 70.
25 Letter to Pierre-Robert Le Cornier de Cideville (February, 1737), in *The Selected Letters*, 63.
26 Letter to Aleksandr Sumarokov (February, 1769), in Ibid., 283.

and in himself, in a comment following an illness late in life in which he correctly associates music with the feeling side, 'Today I am deprived of both wit and music.'[27]

In attempting to elaborate on the coordination of these two sides of man, Voltaire makes an interesting observation. Among artists, the painter paints with his right hand (left hemisphere), at least in the case of the great majority who are right-handed. This is particularly interesting because in the case of sculptors, all of them hold the chisel in the left hand (right hemisphere), that is to say, plan the progress of the art work using the left hand, with the right hand serving only as a dumb hammer.

> What is most rarely to be met with is the combination of reason with enthusiasm. Reason consists in constantly perceiving things as they really are …
>
> How is reasoning to control enthusiasm? A poet should, in the first instance, make a sketch of his design. Reason then holds the crayon. But when he is desirous of animating his characters, to communicate to them the different and just expressions of the passions, then his imagination kindles, enthusiasm is in full operation and urges him on like a fiery courser in his career. But his course has been previously traced with coolness and judgment.[28]

Voltaire makes some additional references to the positive associations with the right hand, something we have cited in numerous examples throughout history in these volumes. The origin for this is in the fact that it is only the left hemisphere which can speak, and in the further documented fact that the left hemisphere tends to deny the existence of the right hemisphere (left hand). Thus, for example, Voltaire mentions 'the simple and innocent practice yet taught in country places to children—that of kissing their right hands in return for a sugar plum.'[29] He also uses a figure of speech relative to the King of Sweden who 'sometimes ate with King Augustus, whom he had dethroned, and that he always gave him the right hand....'[30] It is also interesting that in one of his essays, Voltaire mentions that the French Academy had actually published a study on the subject of right hand preference, although he sees no potential value in such a study.

> We could have very well dispensed, for instance, with such disquisitions as the origin of the preference due to the right hand over the left.[31]

Lacking the knowledge of modern medical discoveries regarding the location of rational and emotional faculties in separate hemispheres, Voltaire can only recognize these separate faculties without hope for understanding their physical nature.

---

27 Letter to Gabriel Cramer (c. 1772–1773), in Ibid., 295.
28 *Philosophical Dictionary*, 'Enthusiasm,' in *The Works of Voltaire*, VIII, 241ff.
29 *Philosophical Dictionary*, 'Kiss,' in Ibid., XI, 54.
30 Letter to Marshal Schulenburg [September 15, 1740], in Ibid., XXI, 54.
31 'The Royal Society and Academies,' in Ibid., XXXIX, 100. Voltaire mentions this again in his *Philosophical Dictionary*, under 'Society and Academies.'

Man is an acting, feeling, and thinking being; this is all we know of the matter: it is not given to us to know either what renders us feeling or thinking, or what makes us act, or what causes us to be.[32]

On the Senses

Voltaire also reflects several contemporary lines of thought regarding the role of the senses in intelligence, another subject which lacked consensus despite centuries of discussion. In his essay, 'The Ignorant Philosopher,' he states that all knowledge comes by way of the senses, discounting any kind of genetic knowledge. Speaking of the writings of an Englishman, named Cudworth, Voltaire reflects.

> He confirms me in the opinion I always entertained:
> That nothing obtains a place in our understanding but through our senses.
> That there are no innate ideas.[33]

Voltaire also was acquainted with the commentary of Descartes on this subject, which he humorously notes must be correct, being opposed by the English.

> All antiquity maintains that our understanding contains nothing which has not been received by our senses. Descartes, on the contrary, asserts in his 'Romances,' that we have metaphysical ideas before we are acquainted with the nipple of our nurse. A faculty of theology proscribed this dogma, not because it was erroneous, but because it was new. Finally, however, it was adopted, because it had been destroyed by Locke, and an Englishman must necessarily be in the wrong. In fine, after having so often changed opinion, the ancient opinion which declares that the senses are the inlets to the understanding is finally proscribed.[34]

Curiously, Voltaire accepts without question Descartes 'weird science' regarding the pineal gland, a small gland in the brain whose function remains unknown today, but to which Descartes attributed numerous functions without offering the slightest evidence for his theories.

> By some inconceivable mechanism, sensitiveness is diffused throughout my body, and thought in my head alone. If the head be cut off, there will remain a very small chance of its solving a problem in geometry. In the meantime, your pineal gland, your fleshly body, in which abides your soul, exists for a long time without alternation, while your separated head is so full of animal spirits that it frequently exhibits motion after its removal from the trunk. It seems as if at this

---

32 *Philosophical Dictionary*, 'Soul,' in Ibid., XIII, 279.
33 'The Ignorant Philosopher,' in Ibid., XXXV, 257.
34 *Philosophical Dictionary*, 'Sensation,' in Ibid., XIII, 188ff.

moment it possessed the most lively ideas, resembling the head of Orpheus, which still uttered melodious song, and chanted Eurydice, when cast into the waters of the Hebrus.

Voltaire himself seems at a loss to explain the physical relationship of the senses and the rational process, but he clearly recognized this was an essential part of man.

> If life be the faculty of sensation, whence this faculty? In reply to this question, all the learned quote systems, and these systems are destructive of one another. But why the anxiety to ascertain the source of sensation? It is as difficult to conceive the power which binds all things to a common center as to conceive the cause of animal sensation. The direction of the needle towards the pole, the paths of comets, and a thousand other phenomena are equally incomprehensible.
>
> Properties of matter exist, the principle of which will never be known to us; and that of sensation, without which there cannot be life, is among the number.
>
> Is it possible to live without experiencing sensation? No. An infant which dies in a lethargy that has lasted from its birth has existed, but not lived.
>
> Let us imagine an idiot unable to form complex ideas, but who possesses sensation; he certainly lives without thinking, forming simple ideas from his sensations. Thought, therefore, is not necessary to life, since this idiot has lived without thinking.[35]

He also makes a remarkable observation worthy of contemplation.

> Is it not an amusing thing, that our eyes always deceive us, even when we see very well, and that on the contrary our ears do not?[36]

Voltaire also addresses other topics which he finds critical to the larger question of how man functions intellectually. One, which he mentions in his essay, 'The Ignorant Philosopher,' is the importance of knowledge gained by personal experience etc.

> Let us never introduce the Holy Scriptures into our philosophical disputes; these are things too heterogeneous, and they have no relation to it. The point here is to examine what we can know by ourselves, and this is reduced to a very narrow compass. We must give up all pretensions to common sense not to agree that we know nothing in the world but by experience; and certainly, if it is only by experience, and by a succession of groping and long reflection, that we obtain some feeble and slight ideas of body, of space, time, infinity, and God Himself; it would not be worth while for the Author of nature to put these ideas into the brain of every fetus, in order that only a very small number of men should make use of them.[37]

Another topic which Voltaire obviously felt compelled to confront was the nature of the 'soul,' the central subject of Church philosophy. But for all his courageous intellectual brilliance, this was a topic for which Voltaire was at a loss.

---

35 *Philosophical Dictionary*, 'Life,' in Ibid., XI, 136ff.
36 *Philosophical Dictionary*, 'Prejudice,' in Ibid., XII, 290.
37 'The Ignorant Philosopher,' in Ibid., XXXV, 225.

> Reason tells me that God exists, but this same reason also tells me I cannot know what He is …
> Therefore, I observe sadly that nothing ever written about the soul can teach us the slightest
> truth.[38]
>
> ……
>
> How, then, shall we be bold enough to affirm what the soul is? We know certainly that we
> exist, that we feel, that we think. Seek we to advance one step further—we fall into an abyss of
> darkness; and in this abyss, we have still the foolish temerity to dispute whether this soul, of
> which we have not the least idea, is made before us or with us, and whether it is perishable or
> immortal?[39]

In the end, Voltaire concludes the soul cannot be known.

> I acknowledge then my ignorance; I acknowledge that four thousand volumes of metaphysics
> will not teach us what our soul is.[40]

Nevertheless, he does not hesitate to use the word in a colloquial sense, as when he mentions,

> The musical instrument maker places, and shifts forward or backward, the soul of a violin, under
> the bridge, in the interior of the instrument: a sorry bit of wood more or less gives it or takes
> from it a harmonious soul.[41]

On Philosophy

Perhaps it was his sense of failure in being able to explain the soul that helped him acknowledge that there is much that philosophy cannot explain. In his essay, 'The Ignorant Philosopher,' he documents this in a charming observation.

> Aristotle's child being at nurse, attracted into his mouth the nipple which he sucked, forming with
> his tongue, which he drew in, a pneumatic machine, pumping the air, and causing a vacuum:
> while his father, quite ignorant of this, said at random, that 'nature abhors a vacuum …'
> We are all, great as we may be, like these children; we perform admirable things, and there
> is not a single philosopher who knows how they are done.[42]

---

38 Letter to Frederick the Great (October, 1737), in *The Selected Letters*, 65.
39 *Philosophical Dictionary*, 'Soul,' in *The Works of Voltaire*, XIII, 264ff.
40 Ibid., 275.
41 Ibid.
42 'The Ignorant Philosopher,' in Ibid., XXXV, 260ff.

He also seemed concerned that philosophy had become fashionable in Paris.

> Philosophy is merely a fashion in France coming after a number of others and which will give way in turn. But no art, no science ought to be fashionable. They must all go hand in hand and be constantly nurtured. I have no desire to pay tribute to fashion; I want to go from an experiment in physics to an opera or comedy and not ever have my sense of taste dulled by study.[43]

Voltaire's most direct effort at defining philosophy reads,

> Philosopher, 'lover of wisdom,' that is, 'of truth.' All philosophers have possessed this two-fold character; there is not one among those of antiquity who did not give examples of virtue to mankind, and lessons of moral truth …
>
> The philosopher is no enthusiast; he does not set himself up for a prophet; he does not represent himself as inspired by the gods.[44]

In another place, Voltaire adds that it was not the ideas contained in books which rendered philosophers their power over civilization, but rather the ideas expressed in their actions.

> Oh! you say to me, the books of Luther and Calvin have destroyed the Roman Catholic religion in half of Europe? …
>
> You deceive yourself very grossly, when you think that you have been ruined by books. The empire of Russia is two thousand leagues in extent, and there are not six men who are aware of the points disputed by the Greek and Latin Church. If the monk Luther, John Calvin, and the vicar Zwingli had been content with writing, Rome would yet subjugate all the states that it has lost; but these people and their adherents ran from town to town, from house to house, exciting the women, and were maintained by princes …
>
> It was not the Koran which caused Mahomet to succeed: it was Mahomet who caused the success of the Koran …
>
> You fear books, as certain small cantons fear violins. Let us read, and let us dance—these two amusements will never do any harm to the world.[45]

It was Voltaire's conclusion that action-oriented philosophers, such as those he has mentioned above, must pay a price as a result of being too far in front of ordinary men.

> Men of letters who have rendered the most service to the small number of thinking beings scattered over the earth are isolated scholars, true sages shut up in their closets, who have neither publicly disputed in the universities, nor said things by halves in academies; and such have almost all been persecuted. Our miserable race is so created that those who walk in the beaten path always throw stones at those who would show them a new one …

---

43 Letter to Pierre-Robert Le Cornier de Cideville (April, 1735), in *The Selected Letters*, 44.
44 *Philosophical Dictionary*, 'Philosopher,' in *The Works of Voltaire*, XII, 169.
45 *Philosophical Dictionary*, 'Liberty of the Press,' in Ibid., XI, 133ff.

> Compose odes in praise of Lord Superbus Fatus, madrigals for his mistress; dedicate a book of geography to his porter, and you will be well received. Enlighten men, and you will be crushed.[46]

Among those who will be the first to 'crush' him are his fellow believers, the philosophers of the Church.

> The stiff Lutheran, the savage Calvinist, the proud Anglican high churchman, the fanatical Jansenist, the Jesuit always aiming at dominion, even in exile and at the very gallows, the Sorbonnist who deems himself one of the fathers of a council; these, and some imbecile beings under their respective guidance, inveigh incessantly and bitterly against philosophy. They are all different species of the canine race, snarling and howling in their peculiar ways against a beautiful horse that is pasturing in a verdant meadow, and who never enters into contest with them about any of the carrion carcasses upon which they feed, and for which they are perpetually fighting with one another.[47]

ON THE PSYCHOLOGY OF AESTHETICS

Voltaire understood, intuitively, that the common form of emotions are universal, common to all men. In his discussion of this point, however, he confuses what we call emotions today with involuntary physical actions.

> All feeling is instinct. A secret conformity of our organs to their respective objects forms our instinct. It is solely by instinct that we perform numberless involuntary movements, just as it is by instinct that we possess curiosity, that we run after novelty, that menaces terrify us, that contempt irritates us, that an air of submission appeases us, and that tears soften us.[48]

It is interesting that Voltaire defines Love as being more associated with the involuntary processes than with what we think of as emotion today.

> It is the embroidery of imagination on the stuff of nature.[49]

Voltaire's most interesting discussion of the emotions with respect to art is found in his comments under 'Enthusiasm,' which he claims the Greeks understood to mean, 'emotion of the bowels, internal agitation.'[50] This definition differs from that of earlier philosophers, who generally state that the Greeks meant by this word a kind of 'divine madness.' We rec-

---

46 *Philosophical Dictionary*, 'Letters,' in Ibid., XI, 117ff.
47 *Philosophical Dictionary*, 'Philosopher,' in Ibid., XII, 180.
48 *Philosophical Dictionary*, 'Instinct,' in Ibid., X, 241.
49 *Philosophical Dictionary*, 'Love,' in Ibid., XI, 138.
50 *Philosophical Dictionary*, 'Enthusiasm,' in Ibid., VIII, 238ff.

ognize today that the observer has an individual understanding of the universal emotions communicated by art. Voltaire's recognition of this fact is perhaps a bit extreme.

> How many shades are there in our affections! Approbation, sensibility, emotion, distress, impulse, passion, transport, insanity, rage, fury. Such are the stages through which the miserable soul of man is liable to pass.
>
> A geometrician attends at the representation of an affecting tragedy. He merely remarks that it is a judicious, well-written performance. A young man who sits next to him is so interested by the performance that he makes no remark at all; a lady sheds tears over it; another young man is so transported by the exhibition that to his great misfortune he goes home determined to compose a tragedy himself. He has caught the disease of enthusiasm.

Voltaire's discussion of Pleasure and Pain begins with the physical association with the emotions. He observes that other animals than man have the muscle necessary to create a smile, although none do. Similarly, he notes that none cry, 'with the exception of a dog when dissected alive.' 'Man,' he says, 'is the only animal which laughs and weeps.'

> It is not all joy which produces laughter: the greatest enjoyments are serious. The pleasures of love, ambition or avarice, make nobody laugh.[51]

Voltaire wanted to distinguish levels of Pleasure, but he does not become very specific other than as a matter of language.

> Pleasure is more transient than happiness, and happiness than felicity. When a person says—I am happy at this moment, he abuses the word, and only means I am pleased. When pleasure is continuous, he may then call himself happy. When this happiness lasts a little longer, it is a state of felicity.[52]

Voltaire does not discusses types of Pain, but he was intrigued by tears.

> Tears are the silent language of grief. But why? What relation is there between a melancholy idea and this limpid and briny liquid filtered through a little gland into the external corner of the eye which moistens the conjunctiva and little lachrymal points, whence it descends into the nose and mouth by the reservoir called the lachrymal duct, and by its conduits? Why in women and children, whose organs are of a delicate texture, are tears more easily excited by grief than in men, whose formation is firmer?
>
> Has nature intended to excite compassion in us at the sight of these tears, which soften us and lead us to help those who shed them?[53]

---

51 *Philosophical Dictionary*, 'Laughter,' in Ibid., XI, 58ff.
52 *Philosophical Dictionary*, 'Happy,' in Ibid., X, 5.
53 *Philosophical Dictionary*, 'Tears,' in Ibid., XIV, 69ff.

ON THE PHILOSOPHY OF AESTHETICS

On Art and Society

Although his conclusion here seems odd, Voltaire recognized that true art has no function.

> All the arts are pretty much the same. There is a certain point, beyond which all is matter of mere curiosity. These ingenious but useful truths are like the stars, which are placed at such an infinite distance from us that we reap not the least advantage from their beams.[54]

This comment notwithstanding, in other places Voltaire finds important value for society in the arts. For example, as his closing comment in *Ancient and Modern History*, he contends,

> When a nation has an acquaintance with the arts, and its inhabitants are not absolutely enslaved, or carried away by a foreign conqueror, that nation will rise from its ruins, and regain its strength.[55]

The significance of this, in view of the frequent discussion in France regarding the relationship of contemporary art with the principles of the ancient Greek philosophers, may be seen in Voltaire's interesting observation that the sciences of antiquity enjoyed no contemporary relevance.

> Ancient history, ancient astronomy, ancient physics, ancient medicine (up to Hippocrates), ancient geography, ancient metaphysics, all are nothing but ancient absurdities which ought to make us feel the happiness of being born in later times.[56]

One can see why Voltaire, in his discussion of the proper way to write history, viewed the arts as reliable hallmarks of a society.

> Take away the arts and the progress of the mind, and you will find nothing in any age remarkable enough to attract the attention of posterity.
>
> ……
>
> I wish to write a history not of wars, but of society; and to ascertain how men lived in the interior of their families, and what were the arts which they commonly cultivated … My object is the history of the human mind, and not a mere detail of petty facts; nor am I concerned with

---

54 'The Royal Society and Academies,' in Ibid., XXXIX, 101.
55 'Ancient and Modern History,' in Ibid., XXX, 315.
56 *Philosophical Dictionary*, 'Axis,' in Ibid., VI, 181.

the history of great lords …; but I want to know what were the steps by which men passed from barbarism to civilization.[57]

It is the relationship of the arts with society, which appears to have motivated Voltaire to write his article on 'Taste' for his *Philosophical Dictionary*. The heart of this article deals with the nature of 'national taste,' and, of course, it reflects his knowledge and experience in Paris. He begins his discussion on Taste by comparing taste in art with the sense of taste from which the metaphor has its origin.[58]

> The taste, the sense by which we distinguish the flavor of our food, has produced, in all known languages, the metaphor expressed by the word 'taste'—a feeling for beauty and defects in all the arts. It is a quick perception, like that of the tongue and the palate, and in the same manner anticipates consideration. Like the mere sense, it is sensitive and luxuriant in respect to the good, and rejects the bad spontaneously; in a similar way it is often uncertain, divided, and even ignorant whether it ought to be pleased; lastly, and to conclude the resemblance, it sometimes requires to be formed and corrected by habit and experience.

Voltaire now makes a very important point relative to 'taste' in the arts. An art work, he says, must appeal to our feelings, and not to our intellect. Curiously, later he will contend that *good* taste is a matter of learning. For the moment he continues with his original metaphor in his attempt to further define taste in the arts.

> To constitute taste, it is not sufficient to see and to know the beauty of a work. We must feel and be affected by it. Neither will it suffice to feel and be affected in a confused or ignorant manner; it is necessary to distinguish the different shades; nothing ought to escape the promptitude of its discernment; and this is another instance of the resemblance of taste, the sense, to intellectual taste; for an epicure will quickly feel and detect a mixture of two liquors, as the man of taste and connoisseur will, with a single glance, distinguish the mixture of two styles, or a defect by the side of beauty …
>
> As a physical bad taste consists in being pleased only with high seasoning and curious dishes, so a bad taste in the arts is pleased only with studied ornament, and feels not the pure beauty of nature.
>
> A depraved taste in food is gratified with that which disgusts other people: it is a species of disease. A depraved taste in the arts is to be pleased with subjects which disgust accomplished minds, and to prefer the burlesque to the noble, and the finical and the affected to the simple and natural: it is a mental disease.

---

57 Quoted in Will Durant, *The Story of Philosophy* (New York: Simon & Schuster, 1961), 169. In 'The Political Testament of cardinal Alberoni,' *The Works of Voltaire*, XXXVII, 147, Voltaire adds,

> In my opinion, history should not speak of the living: she should imitate the judgments of the Egyptians, who never decided concerning the merit of their countrymen until they were no more. The characters of great men are always viewed in a false light during their lifetime.

58 *Philosophical Dictionary*, 'Taste,' in *The Works of Voltaire*, XIV, 44ff.

Voltaire now turns to a point which he firmly believed in, that good taste in the arts is, in part, a matter of education.[59] Several inconsistencies are present here, the first being that he also recognizes the possibility of Universality in art. That is, art appreciated by everyone, including the uneducated. Second, he states that art *contains* beauty in *itself*. But if beauty is in the object, and not in 'the eye of the beholder,' then the only purpose of education would be to teach the 'rules,' which is in opposition to his initial statement that art appeals to feeling rather than our 'knowing' of its beauty. He also suggests that good taste may not always be a matter of education, but of birth—an aristocracy of taste. Some people, he says, are incapable.

> A taste for the arts is, however, much more a thing of formation than physical taste; for although in the latter we sometimes finish by liking those things to which we had in the first instance a repugnance, nature seldom renders it necessary for men in general to learn what is necessary to them in the way of food, whereas intellectual taste requires time to duly form it. A sensible young man may not, without science, distinguish at once the different parts of a grand choir of music; in a fine picture, his eyes at first sight may not perceive the gradation, the chiaroscuro perspective, agreement of colors, and correctness of design; but by little and little his ears will learn to hear and his eyes to see …
>
> If an entire nation is led, during its early culture of the arts, to admire authors abounding in the defects and errors of the age, it is because these authors possess beauties which are admired by everybody, while at the same time readers are not sufficiently instructed to detect the imperfections …
>
> It is said that there is no disputation on taste, and the observation is correct in respect to physical taste, in which the repugnance felt to certain ailments, and the preference given to others, are not to be disputed, because there is no correction of a defect of the organs. It is not the same with the arts which possess actual beauties, which are discernible by a good taste, and unperceivable as a bad one; which last, however, may frequently be improved. There are also persons with a coldness of soul, as there are defective minds; and in respect to them, it is of little use to dispute concerning predilections, as they possess none.

He now makes one more attempt to define good taste.

> Is there not a good and a bad taste? Without doubt; although men differ in opinions, manners, and customs. The best taste in every species of cultivation is to imitate nature with the highest fidelity, energy, and grace. But is not grace arbitrary? No, since it consists in giving animation and sweetness to the objects represented. Between two men, the one of whom is gross and the other refined, it will readily be allowed that one possesses more grace than the other....

On the subject of National Taste, he first provides an historical hypothesis and then gives a recent illustration from the history of France.

---

59   In another place [*Philosophical Dictionary*, 'Happy,' in X, 7], he observes,

> In matters of art, it is necessary to instruct man; in affairs of morals, he should be left to think for himself.

Taste may become vitiated in a nation, a misfortune which usually follows a period of perfection. Fearing to be called imitators, artists seek new and devious routes, and fly from the pure and beautiful nature of which their predecessors have made so much advantage. If there is merit in these labors, the merit veils their defects, and the public in love with novelty runs after them, and becomes disgusted, which makes way for still minor efforts to please, in which nature is still more abandoned. Taste loses itself amidst this succession of novelties, the last one of which rapidly effaces the other; the public loses its 'whereabout,' and regrets in vain the flight of the age of good taste, which will return no more, although a remnant of it is still preserved by certain correct spirits, at a distance from the crowd …

As an artist forms his taste by degrees, so does a nation. It stagnates for a long time in barbarism; then it elevates itself feebly, until at length a noon appears, after which we witness nothing but a long and melancholy twilight. It has long been agreed, that in spite of the solicitude of Francis I, to produce a taste in France for the fine arts, this taste was not formed until towards the age of Louis XIV, and we already begin to complain of its degeneracy.

Voltaire continues his discussion of National Taste by advancing a contention that climate may affect choice, as does the natural sociability of a nation's people. He also returns to the idea of an aristocracy in taste, pointing to the connoisseur, and eventually concludes that in a large city perhaps only one-half of one percent of the people actually have good taste. Certainly, he says, you won't find it among businessmen, lawyers or members of the government!

In general, a refined and certain taste consists in a quick feeling of beauty amidst defects, and defects amidst beauties. The epicure is he who can discern the adulteration of wines, and feel the predominating flavor in his viands, of which his associates entertain only a confused and general perception.

Are not those deceived who say, that it is a misfortune to possess too refined a taste, and to be too much of a connoisseur; that in consequence we become too much occupied by defects, and insensible to beauties, which are lost by this fastidiousness? Is it not, on the contrary, certain that men of taste alone enjoy true pleasure, who see, hear, and feel, that which escapes persons less sensitively organized, and less mentally disciplined?

The connoisseur in music, in painting, in architecture, in poetry, in medals, etc., experiences sensations of which the vulgar have no comprehension …

It is afflicting to reflect on the prodigious number of men—above all, in cold and damp climates—who possess not the least spark of taste, who care not for the fine arts …

It is necessary to select the capital of a great kingdom to form the abode of taste, and yet even there it is very partially divided among a small number, the populace being wholly excluded. It is unknown to the families of traders, and those who are occupied in making fortunes, who are either engrossed with domestic details, or divided between unintellectual idleness and a game at cards. Every place which contains the courts of law, the offices of revenue, government, and commerce, is closed against the fine arts …

In a town like Paris, peopled with more than six hundred thousand persons, I do not think there are three thousand who cultivate a taste for the fine arts. When a dramatic masterpiece is represented, a circumstance so very rare, people exclaim: 'All Paris is enchanted,' but only three thousand copies, more or less, are printed.

Taste, then, like a philosophy, belongs only to a small number of privileged souls.

In an essay devoted to criticizing the writings of Pascal, Voltaire again seems to suggest that taste in the arts, and specifically music, is a matter feeling and not knowledge.

PASCAL. All our reasoning terminates in yielding to sensation.
VOLTAIRE. Our reasoning must yield to sensation, in matters of taste, not in those of knowledge.

......

PASCAL. Those who judge of work by rule, are with respect to other men, like those who have a watch, in comparison with those that have none …
VOLTAIRE. In works of taste, in music, poetry, and painting, taste serves as a watch, and that man who judges of them only by rule, judges wrong.[60]

We find here again Voltaire's concept of an aristocracy in taste.

PASCAL. The common people have in general a very just taste, an instance of which is in their preferring public sports, hunting, and so forth, before poetry, and the polite arts.
VOLTAIRE. It would seem as if it had been proposed to the people to choose a game at bowls, or to make verses. But this is not the case. Those whose organs are more grossly formed, seek after those pleasures in which sentiment has the least share; while, on the other hand, those of delicate sensations wish for the more refined pleasures, where we must live.

ON THE ARTIST

In a letter to Père Porée, Voltaire contends that the artist learns by experience, and not from books.

No matter how many books are written on the technique of painting by those who know their subject, not one of them will afford as much instruction to the pupil as will the sight of a single head by Raphael.

The principles of all the arts, which depend upon imagination, are simple and easy; they are based upon nature and reason … The composer of *Armide* and *Issé* [Lully], and the worst of composers, worked according to the same musical rules.[61]

---

60 'Remarks on M. Pascal's Thoughts,' in Ibid., XXI, 250, 256.
61 Letter to Père Porée (1730), quoted in Clark, *European Theories* (New York: Crown, 1959), 279.

Voltaire, as Philosopher

He makes the same point in his *Philosophical Dictionary*.

> No one can ever learn in a book to weave stockings, nor to polish diamonds, nor to work tapestry. Arts and trades are learned only by example and practice.[62]

By 'learning by example,' Voltaire means, of course, emulating the masters of art. Emulation, in turn, may have its root in envy.

> I believe Mandeville, the author of the 'Fable of the Bees,' is the first who has endeavored to prove that envy is a good thing, a very useful passion ...
>
> He thinks that without envy the arts would be only moderately cultivated, and that Raphael would never have been a great painter if he had not been jealous of Michelangelo.
>
> Mandeville, perhaps, mistook emulation for envy; perhaps, also, emulation is nothing but envy restricted within the bounds of decency.[63]

In a whimsical mood, he concludes,

> That it is better to excite envy than pity is a good proverb. Let us, then, make men envy us as much as we are able.

To another correspondent, he observes, 'I know that jealousy pursues the arts everywhere.'[64]

Voltaire also finds emulation a factor in the relationship of whole societies and art.

> Emulation in art has changed the face of the continent, from the Pyrenees to the icy sea. There is hardly a prince in Germany who has not made useful and glorious establishments.[65]

In another place, Voltaire points out that emulation has its limits. 'Glory,' he says, 'is the portion of inventors in the fine arts; imitators have only applause.'[66] And again,

> In an art or profession, the man who has far distanced his rivals, or who has the reputation of having done so, is called great in his art, and appears, therefore, to have required merit of only one description in order to obtain this eminence; but the great *man* must combine different species of merit.[67]

With respect to real individual genius in the arts, he clearly understood that such men possessed something beyond learning or emulation.

---

62 *Philosophical Dictionary*, 'Casting,' in *The Works of Voltaire*, VII, 19.
63 *Philosophical Dictionary*, 'Envy,' in Ibid., VIII, 244ff.
64 Letter to Pierre-Robert Le Cornier de Cideville (February, 1737), in *The Selected Letters*, 64.
65 *Philosophical Dictionary*, 'Fine Arts,' in *The Works of Voltaire*, VI, 69.
66 *Philosophical Dictionary*, 'Glory,' in Ibid., IX, 201.
67 *Philosophical Dictionary*, 'Greatness,' in Ibid., IX, 320.

> It must be confessed that in the arts having genius as their basis, everything is the product of instinct.[68]

By 'instinct' here, Voltaire apparently meant that the true genius is born and not made.

> We use the word 'genius' indifferently in speaking of … an artist, or a musician … Now an artist, however perfect he may be in his profession, if he have no invention, if he be not original, is not considered a genius. He is only inspired by the artists his predecessors, even when he surpasses them …
> Poussin, who was a great painter before he had seen any good pictures, had a genius for painting. Lully, who never heard any good musicians in France, had a genius for music …
> Genius, conducted by taste, will never commit a gross fault … Genius, without taste, will often commit enormous errors; and, what is worse, it will not be sensible of them.[69]

In another place, he adds,

> The gift of nature is an imagination inventive in the arts—in the disposition of a picture, in the structure of a poem. It cannot exist without memory, but it uses memory as an instrument with which it produces all its performances.[70]

The primary characteristic of this 'gift of nature,' that the artist is born with, Voltaire finds to be the quality of his imagination.

> Active imagination, which constitutes men poets, confers on them enthusiasm, according to the true meaning of the Greek word, that internal emotion which in reality agitates the mind and transforms the author into the personage whom he introduces as the speaker; for such is the true enthusiasm, which consists in emotion and imagery …
> In general, the imaginations of painters when they are merely ingenious, contribute more to exhibit the learning in the artist than to increase the beauty of the art …
> In all the arts, the most beautiful imagination is always the most natural.[71]

Curiously, later in this same article, he observes,

> We do not create a single idea or image. I defy you to create one …
> We make no images; we only collect and combine them.[72]

---

68 Letter to Denis Diderot (April, 1773), in *The Selected Letters*, 298.
69 *Philosophical Dictionary*, 'Genius,' in *The Works of Voltaire*, IX, 194.
70 *Philosophical Dictionary*, 'Imagination,' in Ibid., X, 162.
71 Ibid., 164ff.
72 Ibid., 168.

On General Aesthetic Principles in Art

Regarding Beauty, Voltaire again returns to the idea that in art definitions must be found in the senses, and in feeling, the 'heart,' and not in Reason.

> The beautiful, which only strikes the senses, the imagination, and what is called the spirit, is then often uncertain; the beauty which strikes the heart is not.[73]

In a commentary on the writings of Pascal, he attempts to illustrate the sensory pleasures of poetry, as opposed to the 'meaning' of the words themselves.

> PASCAL. As we say poetical beauty, we likewise should say geometrical and medicinal beauty, and yet we do not say so; the reason is, we know very well what is the object of geometry, and what is the object of physic; but we do not know what that is, in which the charm of beauty consists, which is the object of feeling. We do not know what this natural model is, which we ought to imitate, and for want of this knowledge, we have invented and adopted certain odd terms, such as golden age, miracle of our fine fatal laurel, beautiful stars, and so forth, and this jargon is called poetical beauty; but were any person to figure to himself a woman, dressed after this model, he would see a handsome young lady covered with looking-glasses, and bound in tinsel chains.
>
> VOLTAIRE. This is very false. We should not say geometrical beauty, nor medicinal beauty, because a theorem and a purge do not affect the senses in an agreeable manner; because we give the name of beauty to those things only that charm the senses, as music, painting, eloquence, poetry, regular architecture, and so forth. The reason given by M. Pascal is equally false with his reflection. He well knows what it is that forms the object of poetry. It consists in painting with strength, clearness, delicacy and harmony. Poetry is harmonious eloquence. M. Pascal must have had little taste, to say that fatal laurel, beautiful star, and such like stuff, are practical beauties; and the editors of his 'Thoughts' must have been little versed in polite literature, otherwise they would not have printed a reflection so unworthy of its illustrious author.[74]

Voltaire mentions this again in his *Philosophical Dictionary*.

> How ridiculous is it in Pascal to say: 'As we say poetical beauty, we should likewise say geometrical beauty, and medicinal beauty ...'
> The pitifulness of this passage is sufficiently obvious. We know that there is nothing beautiful in a medicine, nor in the properties of a triangle; and that we apply the term 'beautiful' only to that which raises admiration in our minds and gives pleasure to our senses.[75]

---

73 *Philosophical Dictionary*, 'The Beautiful,' in Ibid., VI, 228.
74 'Remarks on M. Pascal's Thoughts,' in Ibid., XXI, 256.
75 *Philosophical Dictionary*, 'Aristotle,' in Ibid., VI, 44.

One specific element which Voltaire associates with Beauty, is Grace.

> Grace, in painting and sculpture, consists in softness of outline and harmonious expression; and painting, next to sculpture, has grace in the unison of parts, and of figures which animate one another, and which become agreeable by their attributes and their expression.[76]

Regarding the aesthetic question often discussed by all early philosophers, whether art should imitate nature, we find Voltaire clearly of the opinion that the imitation of nature is a primary necessity. In his essay criticizing the writings of Pascal, he makes this clear.

> PASCAL. How vain an art is that of painting, which attracts our admiration by the resemblance of things, whose originals we do not admire.
> VOLTAIRE. Certainly the merit of a portrait does not consist in the goodness of heart of the person it resembles, but in the likeness it bears to him. We admire Caesar in one sense, and his statue, or his image on canvas, in another.[77]

And again in his *Philosophical Dictionary*,

> Thus, in all languages, the heart burns, courage is kindled, the eyes sparkle; the mind is oppressed, it is divided, it is exhausted; the blood freezes, the head is turned upside down; we are inflated with pride, intoxicated with vengeance. Nature is everywhere painted in these strong images, which have become common …
> Nature alone is spontaneously eloquent. The precepts always follow the art. Tisias was the first who collected the laws of eloquence, of which nature gives the first rules.[78]

We should mention, in this regard, his tribute to Molière in a letter to Aleksandr Sumarokov.

> I have not seen Paris for twenty years. People have informed me that Molière's plays were no longer being performed there. The reason, in my opinion, is that everyone knows them by heart … His only aim was to portray nature, and without a doubt he was the greatest painter of nature.[79]

Voltaire makes one very interesting, and striking, reference to Universality in art.

> We demand why the same man, who has seen with a dry eye the most atrocious events, and even committed crimes with *sangfroid*, will weep at the theater at the representation of similar events and crimes? It is, that he sees them not with the same eyes; he sees them with those of the author and the actor. He is no longer the same man; he was barbarous, he was agitated with furious passions, when he saw an innocent woman killed, when he stained himself with the blood of his friend; he became a man again at the representation of it. His soul was filled with

---

76 *Philosophical Dictionary*, 'Grace,' in Ibid., IX, 306.
77 'Remarks on M. Pascal's Thoughts,' in Ibid., XXI, 260.
78 *Philosophical Dictionary*, 'Eloquence,' in Ibid., VIII, 197ff.
79 Letter to Aleksandr Sumarokov (February, 1769), in *The Selected Letters*, 283.

a stormy tumult; it is now tranquil and void, and nature re-entering it, he sheds virtuous tears. Such is the true merit, the great good of theatrical representation, which can never be effected by the cold declamation of an orator paid to tire an audience for an hour.[80]

Regarding Voltaire's specific comments on aesthetics in individual arts, we have, of course, given his reflections on drama in another chapter. His most interesting comments on painting are etched in satire. He remarks that while other countries do not appreciate French music, painting tends to be more universal for it imitates Nature, which is the same everywhere.

The only true test of a painter's merit is the judgment of foreigners. It is not enough that he has a party, and is praised by scribblers; his works must be in request, and bear a high price.[81]

His strongest remarks on painting are reserved for an attack on the famous Academy of Art in Paris.

Academies are, without doubt, extremely useful to form pupils, especially when the directors aim at the sublime in painting; but if they are men of groveling taste, if their manner is dry and minute, if their figures are ungraceful, their pieces painted like fans; their pupils are the dupes of imagination, or aiming at the applause of a bad master. There is a sort of fatality attending academies. None of the works styled academic, of any kind, have been works of genius. Suppose an artist extremely solicitous lest he should not hit the manner of his fellow academicians, his productions will infallibly be stiff and disgusting. But if a man is free from these prejudices, and aims only at copying nature, it is ten to one that he succeeds. Almost all the eminent painters either flourished before the establishment of the academies, or got the better of the prejudices contracted there.

Some of Voltaire's most interesting comments on poetry are found under the subject of 'Style,' in his *Philosophical Dictionary*. He first points out that the artist is under some influence of the subject itself, the architecture of 'a temple not being the same thing as a common house, nor music of a serious opera that of a comic one.'[82] This reflects the fact that, according to Voltaire, however complicated the question may become, it is always reduced to either 'the simple' or the 'elevated.'

Thinking primarily of poetry, Voltaire finds several general categories of style, beginning with 'the feeble.'

Weakness of the heart is not that of the mind, nor weakness of the soul that of the heart. A feeble soul is without resource in action, and abandons itself to those who govern it. The *heart* which is weak or feeble is easily softened, changes its inclinations with facility … and may subsist with a strong *mind*; for we may think strongly and act weakly.

---

80 *Philosophical Dictionary*, 'Tears,' in *The Works of Voltaire*, XIV, 71.
81 'The Age of Louis XIV,' in Ibid., XXIII, 304.
82 *Philosophical Dictionary*, 'Style,' in Ibid., XIV, 6ff.

The 'Flowery Style,' is an appropriate metaphor, says Voltaire, for flowers are showy without strength.

> This style belongs to productions of mere amusement; to idylls, eclogues and descriptions of seasons or gardens ...
> The flowery style detracts from the interest of tragedy, and weakens ridicule in comedy. It is in its place in French opera, which rather flourishes on the passions than exhibits them.

'Coldness of Style,' Voltaire finds primarily limited to poetry, eloquence, music and painting and not in architecture, geometry, logic and metaphysics, which 'cannot be properly called warm or cold.' This style is often associated with 'a sterility of ideas,' or from 'a deficiency of soul.'

> We may allay a fire which is too intense, but cannot acquire heat if we have none.

Although he does not go into detail, Voltaire suggests that the mixing of styles is difficult. We are not satisfied, he says, by the 'whistle of Rabelais' in the midst of the 'flute of Horace.'

ON THE AESTHETICS OF MUSIC

On the Nature of Music

In a letter to a connoisseur of art, Voltaire reveals that he understood quite correctly the fundamental nature of music, that it communicates 'passions' and not the intellect. It is not, he says, an *idea*.

> It seems to me that sculpture and painting are like music: they do not express ideas. An ingenious song cannot be performed by a musician; and a clever allegory, intended only for the intellect, cannot be expressed either by the sculptor or the painter. I believe that a subtle idea, in order to be represented, must be animated by passion, be characterized in a non-equivocal manner, and above all that the representation of this idea must be as pleasing to the eye as it is to the mind.[83]

That music was an 'idea,' or consisted of concepts, was propagated by the Scholastic tradition of the University of Paris. This long professed dogma of 'speculative music' demanded that music be judged by knowledge of theoretical concepts and not by the ear. Voltaire makes fun of this idea in the course of a fictional debate among the inmates of the hospital *Quinze Vingt*.

---

83 Letter to Anne Claude Philippe de Tubières Grimoard de Pestels de Levis, Comte de Caylus (ca. January, 1739), in *Select Letters*, 59.

> A deaf man reading this short history, acknowledged that these blind people were quite wrong in pretending to judge of colors; but he continued firmly of the opinion that deaf people were the only proper judges of music.[84]

Voltaire also makes a few observations about the development of musical style and traditions. Two of these comments contain interesting references to Rameau.

> The rude beginnings of every art acquire a greater celebrity than the art in perfection; he who first played the fiddle was looked upon as a demigod, while Rameau had only enemies. In fine, men, generally going with the stream, seldom judge for themselves, and purity of taste is almost as rare as talent.[85]

......

> 'Easy' applies not only to a thing easily done, but also to a thing which appears to be so. The pencil of Correggio is easy, the style of Quinault is much more easy than that of Despréaux, and the style of Ovid surpasses in facility that of Persius.
> This facility in painting, music, eloquence, and poetry, consists in a natural and spontaneous felicity, which admits of nothing that implies research, strength, or profundity. Thus the pictures of Paul Veronese have a much more easy and less finished air than those of Michelangelo. The symphonies of Rameau are superior to those of Lully, but appear less easy.[86]

Finally, twice Voltaire mentions music with regard to language. The first is the case of a word whose musical roots are quite forgotten today.

> Enchantment (*incantatio*) comes, say some, from a Chaldee word, which the Greeks translate 'productive song.'[87]

The second instance contrasts the performer and composer.

> The word *able* is applicable to those arts which exercise at once the mind and the hand, as painting and sculpture. We say of a painter or sculptor, *he is an able artist*, because these arts require a long novitiate; whereas a man becomes a poet nearly all at once ...
> A mere player of an instrument is *able*; a composer must be more than able; he must have genius.[88]

---

[84] 'The Ignorant Philosopher,' in *The Works of Voltaire*, XXXV, 293.
[85] *Philosophical Dictionary*, 'Amplification,' in Ibid., V, 153.
[86] *Philosophical Dictionary*, 'Ease,' in Ibid., VIII, 174.
[87] *Philosophical Dictionary*, 'Enchantment,' in Ibid., VIII, 222.
[88] *Philosophical Dictionary*, 'Able,' in Ibid., V, 28. He adds, that to say 'an *able* courtier,' implies blame rather than praise, since it too often means an able flatterer.

On the Perception of Music

In his discussion of the various kinds of Love, Voltaire points to the love of Art, including music, as a kind of love which is without any reference to self. In view of the fact that today we regard music as a fundamental means of expressing feeling, it is certainly incorrect to suggest that the listener receives nothing from his experience.

> If we must pass from the thorns of theology to those of philosophy, which are not so long and are less piercing, it seems clear that an object may be loved by anyone without any reference to self, without any mixture of interested self-love ... We view some masterpiece of art, in painting, sculpture, architecture, poetry, or eloquence; we hear a piece of music that absolutely enchants our ears and souls; we admire it, we love it, without any return of the slightest advantage to ourselves from this attachment; it is a pure and refined feeling; we proceed sometimes so far as to entertain veneration or friendship for the author; and were he present should cordially embrace him.[89]

Voltaire seems to have been unusually interested in the relativity of the perception of music as sound.

> The harmony of a concert, to which you listen with delight, must have on certain classes of minute animals the effect of terrible thunder; and perhaps it kills them.[90]
>
> ......
>
> He who, for the first time in his life, hears the noise of a cannon or the sound of a concert, cannot judge whether the cannon be fired or the concert be performed at the distance of a league or of twenty paces. He has only the experience which accustoms him to judge of the distance between himself and the place whence the noise proceeds. The vibrations, the undulations of the air carry a sound to his ears, or rather to his sensorium, but this noise no more carries to his sensorium the place whence it proceeds than it teaches him the form of the cannon or of the musical instruments.[91]

On the Current Musical Scene

Voltaire was clearly a participant in the discussion at this time of the relative merits of ancient and modern aesthetics in the arts. In his essay, 'Revolutions in the Tragic Art,' he writes of the functional role of music in religion in ancient times.

---

89 *Philosophical Dictionary*, 'Love of God,' in Ibid., XI, 144.
90 *Philosophical Dictionary*, 'Appearance,' in Ibid., VI, 7.
91 *Philosophical Dictionary*, 'Distance,' in Ibid., VIII, 136.

These public diversions were, among the Greeks, connected with their religious ceremonies. It is well known that among the Egyptians, songs, dances and representations made an essential part of the ceremonies reputed sacred. The Jews borrowed these customs from the Egyptians, as every ignorant and barbarous nation endeavors to imitate its learned and polite neighbors; hence those Jewish festivals, those dances of priests before the ark, those trumpets, those hymns, and so many other ceremonies entirely Egyptian.[92]

In another place he speaks of Functional Music in both ancient Greece and modern Paris.

Law was promulgated in Athens nearly as in Paris we sing a song on the Pont-Neuf. The public crier sang an edict, accompanying himself on the lyre.
It is thus that in Paris the rose in bud is cried in one tone; old silver lace to sell in another; only in the streets of Paris the lyre is dispensed with.[93]

The philosophical debate over the artistic rules of the ancient Greeks and the 'moderns' had continued since the sixteenth century. Voltaire was struck by those who were so enamored by the past that they seemed oblivious to the accomplishments of their own era. He singled out the Englishman philosopher, William Temple, as one who 'closed his eyes to the wonders of his contemporaries, and opened them only to admire ancient ignorance.'[94]

'What,' he says, 'has become of the charms of that music which so often enchanted men and beasts, fishes, birds, and serpents, and even changed their nature?' This enemy to his own times believed implicitly in the fable of 'Orpheus,' and, it should seem, had never heard of the fine music of Italy, nor even of that of France, which *do not* charm serpents, it is true, but *do* charm the ears of the connoisseur.

In a review of Renaissance music in France, Voltaire seems generally uninformed of the scope of musical activity during the period of François I, in particular the important art music played by *Les Grands Hautbois*. He also appears to have no knowledge of Machaut and his period.

The arts that do not depend absolutely upon the mind, such as music, painting, sculpture, architecture, etc., made but small progress in France before that period which we distinguish by the name of the age of Louis XIV. Music was as yet in its infancy; all that we knew were some songs, and a few melodies for the violin, the guitar, and the oboe, most of which were composed in Spain. The taste, the skill of a Lully, amazed the world; he was the first who in France introduced bases, stops, and fugues. However easy and simple his compositions may now appear, the execution of them must have cost him some trouble. There are at this time a thousand people who understand music for one who was proficient in the days of Louis XIII, and the art has, by degrees, arrived at perfection.

---
92 'Revolutions in the Tragic Art,' in Ibid., XXXIX, 152.
93 *Philosophical Dictionary*, 'Singing,' in Ibid., XIII, 208.
94 *Philosophical Dictionary*, 'Ancients and Moderns,' in Ibid., V, 159ff.

> What music may have gained in composition it seems to have lost in expression, for the modern refinements of this art are calculated to tickle the ear rather than wake or assuage the passions of the heart.
>
> Few great towns are now without a public concert; whereas then there was not one, even in Paris. The king's orchestra, of twenty-four violins, was all the music of France. The different species of science belonging to music, and its dependent arts, made such progress that, about the end of Louis XIV's reign, the art of notating dances was invented; so that it may now be truly said we dance by book.[95]

He makes several interesting references to the period of Louis XIV, beginning with a reference to the participation of the nobles.

> The word Academy became so celebrated that when Lully, who was a sort of favorite, obtained the establishment of his Opera, in 1692, he had interest enough to get inserted in the patent, *that it was a Royal Academy of Music, in which Ladies and Gentlemen might sing without demeaning themselves.* He did not confer the same honor on the dancers; the public, however, has always continued to go to the Opera, but never to the Academy of Music.[96]

To one of his correspondents, Voltaire writes of the musical awareness of Louis XIV.

> Do not regard Louis XIV merely as a happy man who had no part in the glory of his reign. He alone reformed the taste of his Court in more than one field. He chose Lully as his musician, depriving Lambert of his license because Lambert was mediocre and Lully was excellent. He knew how to distinguish wit from genius. He gave Quinault the subjects of his operas, directed the paintings of Le Brun, sustained Corneille and Racine against their enemies.[97]

In one of his essays he makes another reference to the reputation of Lully.

> There is an immense difference between consecrated ground and profane ... the value of the ground is increased in proportion to that of the man. That in which Molière was interred has acquired reputation. Now as this man was buried in a chapel, he cannot be damned, like Mademoiselle Le Couvreur and Romagnesi, who were buried upon the highway ... I have no doubt of the salvation of Jean Baptiste Lully, fiddler to the king's sister, king's musician, superintendent of the king's music, who played in *Cariselli* and *Pourceaugnac* and was, moreover, a Florentine; he is gone to heaven as surely as I shall go thither myself; that is evident, for he has a fine marble monument at St. Eustache's church: he was not thrown upon a dung-hill: fortune rules the globe.[98]

---

95 'Ancient and Modern History,' in Ibid., XXX, 112ff.

96 *Philosophical Dictionary*, 'Academy,' in Ibid., V, 58ff. Later in this volume, under 'Anecdotes,' Voltaire quotes a book by Durand, *Anecdotes Littéraires* (1752), III, 183, as follows,

> Louis XIV was so much pleased with the opera *Isis* that he ordered a decree to be passed in council by which men of rank were permitted to sing at the opera, and receive a salary for so doing, without demeaning themselves. This decree was registered in the Parliament of Paris.

97 Letter to John Hervey (ca. June, 1740), in *Select Letters*, 66ff.

98 'Dialogue between the Intendant des Menus and the abbé Brizel,' in *The Works of Voltaire*, XXXVII, 244.

Finally, Voltaire's reading seems to have been so extensive that he noticed even some interesting trivia regarding music. The first, actually, we find quite interesting.

> Thus, after Newton discovered the nature of light, Castel, to outdo him, suggests an ocular harpsichord.[99]

This is a reference to the French mathematician, Castel, and his treatise *Optique des Couleurs* (1740), which discussed the correspondence between melody and color. To demonstrate his theories, he apparently constructed an *clavecin oculaire*.

The other passage which caught our eye leaves us disappointed that Voltaire failed to provide more details.

> I know that men have disorders in their brain. We have seen a musician die mad, because his music did not appear good enough.[100]

On Opera

Voltaire comments frequently on opera, in part no doubt, due to the fact that it was generally a much discussed topic in France. We suspect he was not an avid fan of the music itself, for his commentary deals mostly with various aspects of the literary content of opera. Nevertheless, in one essay, he correctly points out that the purpose of opera is not conceptual ideas, but the expression of emotions.

> All those glittering thoughts to which men have given the appellation of wit, ought never to have been admitted into great works, composed for the instruction of the public, or calculated to move the passions. I would not even hesitate to say they ought to be banished from our operas. Music expresses the passions, the sentiments, and the images: but what accents are able to express an epigram? Quinault has formerly been sometimes neglected, yet he was always natural.[101]

While today we think of Europe as having a single musical culture, whereas it's languages, food and customs vary distinctly, it is interesting that Voltaire could remark, 'In no art are national characteristics more marked than in that of music.'[102] In making this statement it is evident he was thinking primarily of opera, although again he concentrates on language.

> French music, especially the vocal, is disliked by all other nations. It cannot be otherwise, because the French prosody or versification differs from that of every other country of Europe.

---

99 Letter to Mdlle Quinault (May, 1776) in *Voltaire in His Letters*, 257.
100 'The Ignorant Philosopher,' in *The Works of Voltaire*, XXXV, 284.
101 'Wit,' in Ibid., XXXVII, 62ff. Quinault was the librettist associated with Lully.
102 'The Age of Louis XIV,' xxxii, in Ibid., XXIII, 300.

> We make the pauses always upon the last syllable, whereas all others make it upon the penult, or antepenult, as the Italians. Our language is the only one that has words terminating in *e* mute, and those *e*'s that are not pronounced in ordinary discourse ... Hence it comes, that most of our airs and recitative are insupportable to those who have not been accustomed to them. The climate denies us that flexibility of voice which it gives the Italians, and it is not custom among us, as at Rome and other Italian courts, to make eunuchs of men, in order to render their voices finer than those of women. All these things, joined to the slowness of our singing, which, by the bye, forms a strange contrast with our native vivacity, will always make the French music disagreeable to any but Frenchmen ...
>
> Jean Baptiste Lully, who was born at Florence in 1633 [sic, 1632], and came to France at the age of fourteen, when he could perform on no instrument but the violin, was the parent of French music. He knew how to suit his art to the genius of the language, which was the only sure way to succeed: but at that time the Italian music had not begun to deviate from that gravity and noble simplicity which we still admire in Lully's recitative.

Voltaire disagrees with the criticism by the great French critic, Boileau, that the lyrics which Quinault furnished Lully were unmusical.

> Those hackneyed thoughts, so wanton yet so tame,
> That Lully strove to warm at music's flame.

Voltaire maintains here that it was in fact Quinault's diction which 'animated the music still more than Lully's art did the words.'

This last comment is given more extended discussion in a long letter of 1767 to Chabanon. Here he seems critical of the actual melodies of Lully and finds his strength in his understanding of the French language. The composer Voltaire praises here was Jean Benjamin de La Borde (1734–1794), a now forgotten composer of more than thirty operas. He was guillotined during the French Revolution.

> I am not too much of an expert in C G C and F C F. I am hard of hearing, a bit deaf. However, I confess to you that there are tunes in *Pandora* that have given me considerable pleasure. In spite of myself, I remember for example:
>
> > *Ah! You have grandeur and glory for yourself.*
>
> Other tunes have made a great impression on me and still leave a confused noise in my eardrum ...
>
> I agree that most of Lully's ariettas are trivial tunes and Venetian barcaroles. Therefore, they are not remembered as being good but as being facile. But if one only has taste, one can fix all of poetic art and all four acts of *Armide* in one's memory. Lully's declamation is so perfect a recitative that I recite it entirely by following his notes and by only softening its intentions. [It has] a very great effect on the audience, and no one remains unmoved. Lully's declamation then is in nature. It is adapted to language; it is the expression of feeling.

> If this admirable recitative no longer produces the same effect today as in the beautiful age of Louis XIV, it is because we no longer have any actors. They are in short supply in every genre, and besides Lully's ariettas have done his recitative harm and people penalize his recitative for the weakness of his symphonies. One must admit that there is considerable arbitrariness in music. All I know is that there are things in M. de La Borde's *Pandora* that have given me extreme pleasure.¹⁰³

In his article on singing, in the *Philosophical Dictionary*, Voltaire, focusing again more on language than singing, suggests that others were critical of Lully.

> It is very probable that the *melopée*, or modulation, regarded by Aristotle in his poetic art as an essential part of tragedy, was an even, simple chant, like that which we call the preface to mass, which in my opinion is the Gregorian chant, and not the Ambrosian, and which is a true *melopée*.
>
> When the Italians revived tragedy in the sixteenth century the recitative was a *melopée* which could not be written; for who could write inflections of the voice which are octaves and sixths of tone? They were learned by heart. This custom was received in France when the French began to form a theater, more than a century after the Italians. The *Sophonisba* of Mairet was sung like that of Trissin, but more grossly; for throats as well as minds were then rather coarser at Paris. All the parts of the actors, but particularly of the actresses, were noted from memory by tradition. Mademoiselle Buaval, an actress of the time of Corneille, Racine, and Molière, recited to me, about sixty years ago or more, the commencement of the part of Emilia in *Cinna*, as it had been played in the first representations by La Beaupré. This modulation resembled the declamation of the present day much less than our modern recitative resembles the manner of reading the newspaper.
>
> I cannot better compare this kind of singing, this modulation, than to the admirable recitative of Lully, criticized by adorers of double crochets, who have no knowledge of the genius of our language, and who are ignorant what help this melody furnishes to an ingenious and sensible actor.¹⁰⁴

And once again, Voltaire incorrectly suggests that it is Quinault, and not Lully, whom history will remember.

> Quinault was much superior in his way to Lully. The former will always be read, whereas the latter, setting aside his recitative, cannot even be sung: yet in his own time [Quinault] was supposed to be indebted to Lully for his reputation: but time judges all things.¹⁰⁵

Interestingly enough, Voltaire himself served as the librettist for several operas by Rameau. The only one of these which he discusses at any length in his correspondence is *Samson* (1733), which was never produced. Rameau later used some of this music in *Zorocastre* in 1749, using a new librettist.

---

103 Letter to Michel-Paul Gui de Chabanon (December, 1767), in *The Selected Letters*, 267ff.
104 *Philosophical Dictionary*, 'Singing,' in *The Works of Voltaire*, XIII, 209ff.
105 'Notes on Some of the Writers who Lived in the Age of Louis XIV,' in Ibid., XXXVIII, 207.

> I committed a great blunder by writing an opera, but the desire to work for a man like M. Rameau carried me away. I thought only of his genius and did not understand that mine is not at all suited for the lyric genre. Therefore I informed him some time ago that I would rather have written an epic poem than fill in someone else's outlines. I certainly do not scorn that sort of work. None of it is despicable, but this is a talent which I believe I lack entirely. Perhaps with tranquility of mind, care, and the advice of my friends, I may succeed in achieving something less unworthy of the talents of our Orpheus. But I predict that the production of this opera will have to be postponed until next winter. It will only be improved and be more sought after by the public. Our great musician, who doubtless has enemies in proportion to his merit, must not feel sorry that his rivals are getting ahead of him. The point is not to be performed soon, but to be successful. It is better to be applauded late than to be hissed early.[106]

Another letter on the same subject, two years later, includes the following.

> I would hope that the indulgence with which this work has just been received might encourage our great composer Rameau to place renewed confidence in me and complete his opera on Samson along the lines I have always had in mind. My work was solely for him, I departed from the ordinary road in the poem only because he does the same in music. I thought it time to open opera to a new career. Since the beauties of Quinault and Lully have become commonplace on the tragic stage, few persons will be bold enough to advise M. Rameau to create music for an opera in which love is absent from the first two acts. But he must have the courage to set himself above prejudice ... Let his self-interest and pride give him courage; let him promise to act entirely in concert with me; let him especially not wear his music out by having it played from house to house; let him adorn the pieces I have written for him with new beauties. I will send him the play when he wishes; M. de Fontenelle will be the examiner. I feel sure that the Prince de Carignan will be its patron and that, in the end, of all the works by this great musician it will unquestionably bring him the greatest honor.[107]

Voltaire also writes extensively on the subject of national styles in opera. His most extensive discussion of this aspect of opera is contained in an essay on ancient and modern tragedy, addressed to an Italian bishop.[108] He begins with the interesting contention that music, specifically opera, has contributed to the decline of Italian tragedy.

> If your nation has not always equaled the ancients in tragedy, it is not to be attributed to your language, which is copious, flexible, and harmonious, adapted to all subjects: but it is in my opinion, extremely probable that the great progress you have made in music has in some measure put a stop to your improvement in tragedy: one perfection has destroyed another ...
> One of your most celebrated authors tells us, that since the golden age in Athens, Tragedy, deserted and forsaken, wanders about from country to country in search of some kind friend that will assist and restore her to her former honors, but has as yet found none; if he means by

---

106 Letter to M. Berger (ca. February, 1734), in *The Selected Letters*, 32.
107 Letter to M. Berger (February, 1736), in Ibid., 52ff.
108 Contained in a letter to cardinal Quirini, bishop of Brescia, quoted in *The Works of Voltaire*, XXXVII, 116ff.

this that no nation among the moderns has theaters where choruses are almost always on stage, singing strophes, antistrophes, and epodes, accompanied with serious dances; that we do not set our actors on stilts, or cover their faces with masks that express joy on one side and grief on the other: if he means that the declamation of your tragedies is not notated and accompanied with instruments, he is certainly in the right, and I don't know whether all this is not rather in our favor; perhaps our manner, by approaching more nearly to nature, is fully as eligible as that of the Greeks, which had much more splendor and magnificence.

But if he only designed to insinuate that this noble art is not in general so much considered since the restoration of letters as it was formerly; that there are nations in Europe who have treated with ingratitude the successors of Sophocles and Euripides; that our theaters are not like those superb edifices which the Athenians were so proud of; and that we do not take the same pains as they did in representations, which have become so necessary in large and opulent cities; we cannot but entirely agree with him.

Where shall we find any public spectacle at present that can give us any idea of the Greek stage? Perhaps in your tragedies, or operas. What say the critics, an Italian opera like the theater of Athens? Yes, the Italian recitative is exactly the *mélopée* of the ancients, a declamation in notes, and accompanied with instruments of music: this *mélopée*, which is tiresome and disagreeable in your bad tragic operas, is admirable in those few which are good. The choruses which you have added in late years approach still nearer to the ancient chorus, as the music in them is different from that of the recitative; in the same manner as the strophe, antistrophe, and epode, among the Greeks were set to music, though they differed from the *mélopée* of the dialogue …

I am sufficiently aware that these tragedies, which are so agreeable from the music and magnificence of the spectacle, have indeed one fault which the Greeks always avoided; a fault which has often turned pieces finely written, and in all other respects extremely regular, into monstrous and unnatural productions; I mean, the fault of bringing into every scene little songs and catches that interrupt the action, merely to show off the quavers of an effeminate voice that exerts itself to the utter destruction of probability and good sense. [Metastasio] has taken several of his tragedies from French writers, and has, by the force of his genius in some measure remedied this absurdity, which has become, as it were, necessary. The words of his songs or sonnets embellish the subject; they are full of pathos and passion …

But what are the greatest beauties when out of their proper place? What would an Athenian audience have said, if Oedipus and Orestes, just in the very minute of discovery, the most interesting part of the drama, had entertained them with quavering out a fine air …? We must therefore, after all, acknowledge that the opera, so bewitching to an Italian ear by its musical attractions, though on the one hand it may be said to have revived, has notwithstanding on the other, in effect, destroyed the true Greek tragedy.

Our French opera deviates still more from the right point: as our *mélopée* differs more than yours from natural declamation, and is withal more languid. It will not allow our scenes their proper length, but requires short dialogues and little sententious remarks, every one of which makes a kind of sonnet.

Let those who are thoroughly acquainted with the state of literature in other nations, and whose knowledge is not confined to the melodies of our own ballets, recollect that admirable scene in 'La Clerienza di Tito,' between Titus and his favorite, who had conspired against him ... Or let them read the soliloquy that follows ...

These two scenes, comparable to the finest which Greece ever produced, if not superior to them; these two scenes, worthy of Corneille when he is no declaimer, or of Racine when he is not flimsy; these two scenes, which are not founded on opera love, but on the noblest sentiments of the human heart, are at least three times as long as the longest scenes in our musical tragedies: but these would not be allowed in our Lyric theater, which is only supported by maxims of gallantry, and ill-painted passions, except the *Armida*, and some fine scenes in *Iphigenia*, works more admired than imitated among us.

Among the many faults of our operas, we have, like you, a number of little detached songs, even in the most tragical parts, and which are more inexcusable than yours, because they have less affinity to the subject; the words are generally submitted entirely to the composers, who not being able to express themselves in the manly and vigorous terms of our language, require soft, vague, and effeminate words, foreign to the action, and adapted as well as they can to little ballads, like those which at Venice are called 'Barcarole.' Where, for instance, is the connection between Theseus, just discovered by his father on the point of being poisoned by him, and this ridiculous speech:

The wisest men often fall in love,
And engage themselves they know not how.

But with all these faults I am still of the opinion, that our good tragic operas, such as *Atys*, *Armida* and *Theseus*, may give us some idea of the Greek theater, because they are sung like the ancient tragedies, and because the chorus, even defective as it now is, consisting of tedious panegyrics on the morality of love, does notwithstanding, in some measure, resemble the Grecian chorus, by continuing on the stage almost throughout the piece ...

Several learned men, who are well acquainted with the works of antiquity, seem to think with me, that they are at once the copy and the destruction of the Athenian stage; a copy of it, as they admit of the *mélopée*, the choruses, machines, and deities, and at the same time the destruction of it; as they have taught our young men to be fonder of sound than sense; to prefer the tickling of their ears to the improvement of their minds; the non-sense of sing-song to sublimity of sentiment; and have besides contributed to the success of many insipid and ill-written performances, which have been supported by a few pleasing songs: and yet, in spite of all these faults, that enchantment which arises from a happy mixture of fine scenes, choruses, dances, symphony, and a variety of decorations, bears all before it, and silences even criticism itself; insomuch that the best comedy or tragedy we have is never seen so often by the same people with half the pleasure that a middling opera is. Beauties which are regular, noble, and severe are seldom much sought after by vulgar minds.

In another place, Voltaire also suggests that the tradition of the long romantic poems, such as those by Ariosto and Tasso, may have also lost favor because of opera.

What has chiefly contributed to their fall is the great perfection the stage has arrived at. In a good tragedy, or a good opera, we meet with a much greater number of sentiments than are to be found in all these enormous volumes: these sentiments are at the same time much better expressed, and there appears a much clearer knowledge of the human heart.[109]

In a discourse addressed to the French people, he acknowledges the debt of French opera to Italy.

> You will allege that you are extremely successful in comic operas: but can you deny that you are indebted to Italy for your comic as well as your serious operas?[110]

But, in a letter to Chabanon, he longs for a new savior of French opera.

> I am willing to believe that Orpheus was a great musician, but if he were to return among us to create an opera, I would advise him to attend the school of Rameau.
> I certainly realize that today the [Parisians] only have their comic opera, but I am persuaded that geniuses like you can bring the age of Louis XIV back to them. You are the one to rekindle the remains of the sacred fire that has not yet been completely extinguished.[111]

Another general observation, in his essay, 'The Ignorant Philosopher,' speaks of the censorship of literature and the changing of taste.

> Most philosophical works are like La Fontaine's 'Tales,' which were at first burned, but were in the end brought upon the stage at the Comic Opera.[112]

Voltaire is at his outspoken best when he surveys the general decline of opera, which he dates from the preferences of the court of Louis XIV. Thinking of Duché, a valet de chambre of Louis XIV, Voltaire notes,

> His opera of *Iphigenia at Tauris* is his best piece. It is written in the sublime taste; and, though it is but an opera, it affords a strong idea of the best things in the Greek tragedies. This taste did not last long, and soon after we were reduced to simple ballets, consisting of detached acts, made solely for the sake of introducing the dances; thus, even the opera began to degenerate, at the same time that almost every other theatrical production was on the decline.[113]

It is apparent that Voltaire had little appreciation for the inevitable dance in opera, as we can see in a sarcastic remark in a letter to Catherine the Great.

---

109 'Notes on Some of the Writers who Lived in the Age of Louis XIV,' in Ibid., XXXVIII, 277.
110 'A Discourse to the Welsh,' in Ibid., XXXVII, 94.
111 Letter to Michel-Paul Gui de Chabanon (September, 1764), in *The Selected Letters*, 253.
112 'The Ignorant Philosopher,' in *The Works of Voltaire*, XXXV, 298.
113 'Notes on Some of the Writers who Lived in the Age of Louis XIV,' in Ibid., XXXVIII, 283.

> For some time now there has been an excellent dancer at the Paris opera. She is said to have very lovely arms. The last comic opera was not very successful, but another is to be put on which will be the wonder of the world.[114]

Returning to Voltaire's views on the decay of opera, we find another somewhat sarcastic comment, which follows a brief summary of the evolutionary climb of mankind.

> Finally, after other ages, things got to the point at which we see them. Here we represent a tragedy in music; there we kill one another on the high seas of another hemisphere, with a thousand pieces of cannon. The opera and a ship of war of the first rank always astonish my imagination. I doubt whether they can be carried much farther in any of the globes with which the heavens are studded.[115]

He seemed particularly disturbed that librettists and composers relied on such things as the ancient myths, rather than legitimate plot, to attract the audience.

> An Asiatic, who should travel to Europe, might well consider us as pagans; our week days bear the names of Mars, Mercury, Jupiter, and Venus; and the nuptials of Cupid and Psyche are painted in the pope's palace; but, particularly, were this Asiatic to attend our opera, he would not hesitate in concluding it to be a festival in honor of the pagan deities.[116]
>
> ......
>
> At the opera, and in more serious productions, the gods are introduced descending in the midst of tempests, clouds, and thunder; that is, God is brought forward in the midst of the vapors of our petty globe. These notions are so suitable to our weak minds that they appear to us grand and sublime.[117]

Some of the most curious remarks on opera by Voltaire are on the subject of manners. In a letter to the English ambassador to Constantinople, he mentions something discussed by other writers, namely that the audience felt free to make their way onto the stage.

> We ought certainly to reflect, that everything in this world depends upon custom and opinion: the court of France have danced on the stage with the actors of the opera, and we thought there was nothing strange in it, but that the fashion of this kind of entertainment should be discontinued.[118]

In a letter of August 1765 to Mme Clairon, Voltaire mentions this again relative to the king himself.

---

114 Letter to Catherine of Russia (August, 1771), in *Voltaire and Catherine the Great*, 113.
115 *Philosophical Dictionary*, 'Man,' in *The Works of Voltaire*, XI, 186.
116 *Philosophical Dictionary*, 'Contradictions,' in Ibid., VII, 264.
117 *Philosophical Dictionary*, 'Heaven of the Ancients,' in Ibid., X, 17.
118 Letter to Mr. Falkener, in Ibid., X IX, 15.

Louis XIV, at the peak of his greatness, danced with dancers from the opera house within view of all Paris when he returned from the celebrated campaign of 1672.[119]

Some of Voltaire's reflections on contemporary manners were clearly intended to be humorous. In an essay, we find a fictional observer is worried that the theater is taking away the audience of the church. An 'Italian' answers,

> The case is not the same at Rome, and in the other states of Europe. When a fine mass has been sung at St. John of Lateran, or St. Peter's church, with grand choruses in four parts, and when twenty castrati have sung a hymn with quavering voices, all is ours; those who composed the congregation go in the evening to drink chocolate at the opera of St. Ambrose, and nobody takes umbrage at this. Churchmen take care not to excommunicate [the famous singers] la Signora Cuzzoni, la Signora Faustina, la Signora Barbarini, and above all Signor Farinelli, knight of Calatrava, and actor of the opera, who is possessed of diamonds as big as my thumb.[120]

In 1732 Voltaire wrote to a friend, Pierre Robert le Cornier de Cideville,

> The opera is a public meeting place where people assemble themselves on certain days, without knowing why.[121]

Finally, it was while attending the opera with the actress Adrienne Le Couvreur that Voltaire uttered one of his most famous remarks. He was approached by an unfriendly Chevalier de Rohan-Chabot who demanded, 'Mr. Voltaire, what *really* is your name?' Voltaire retorted, 'My name begins with me, your's ends with you.'

ART MUSIC

Voltaire rarely discusses specific performances or even circumstances of performance. We find interesting one reference to the long tradition of sung poetry, which now in England had evolved into larger choral forms.

> It is surely of all the employments in a great house, that which is the most useless. The kings of England, who have preserved in their island many of the ancient usages which are lost on the continent, have their official poet. He is obliged once a year to make an ode in praise of St. Cecilia, who played so marvelously on the organ or psalterium that an angel descended from the ninth heaven to listen to her more conveniently—the harmony of the psaltery, in ascending from this place to the land of the angels, necessarily losing a small portion of its volume …

---

119 Quoted in *The Selected Letters*, 257.
120 'Dialogue between the Intendant des Menus and the abbé Brizel,' in *The Works of Voltaire*, XXXVII, 252ff.
121 Quoted in Julie Sadie, 'Paris and Versailles,' in *The Late Baroque Era* (Englewood Cliffs: Prentice Hall, 1994), 168.

> It is asked, why poetry, being so unnecessary to the world, occupies so high a rank among the fine arts? The same question may be put with regard to music. Poetry is the music of the soul, and above all of great and of feeling souls.[122]

In an article on 'Somnambulists,' Voltaire makes a passing comment worthy of mention. While the French humanists were the most avid contenders for music being written to the poetry, with the words being the most important. Here Voltaire suggests that by the early years of the eighteenth century he was familiar with a practice which was quite the reverse, with the music coming first. Voltaire claims there was a young priest who not only wrote sermons in his sleep, but also music 'notating it with precision, and after preparing his paper with his ruler, placed the words under the notes without the least mistake.'[123]

FUNCTIONAL MUSIC

Voltaire rarely wrote of Catholic church music, although an extraordinary exception is this sarcastic discussion of the relationship of the traditional Latin *Te Deum* with the slaughter of war.

> The most wonderful part of this infernal enterprise is that each chief of the murderers causes his flags to be blessed, and solemnly invokes God before he goes to exterminate his neighbors. If a chief has only the fortune to kill two or three thousand men, he does not thank God for it; but when he has exterminated about ten thousand by fire and sword, and, to complete the work, some town has been leveled with the ground, they then sing a long song in four parts, composed in a language unknown to all who have fought, and moreover replete with barbarism. The same song serves for marriages and births, as well as for murders; which is unpardonable, particularly in a nation the most famous for new songs.[124]

Curiously, a letter to a friend speaks of this form in quite a different light.

> Far be it from me to ask you to reply to me: but while I chant a *De Profundis* with my failing health, I sing aloud *Te Deum laudamus* for you.[125]

---

122 *Philosophical Dictionary*, 'Poets,' in *The Works of Voltaire*, XII, 216.

123 *Philosophical Dictionary*, 'Somnambulists,' in Ibid., XIII, 249ff.

124 *Philosophical Dictionary*, 'War,' in Ibid., XIV, 195ff. When Gossec was commissioned to write a large-scale work for the anniversary of the fall of the Bastille, and elected to write a Te Deum, he was much criticized in the press for this same association of this form with past military exploits.

125 Letter to M. Turgot (July, 1774) in *Voltaire in His Letters*, 240.

ENTERTAINMENT MUSIC

The most interesting discussion of entertainment music by Voltaire is relative to a Comédie-ballet, *Princesse de Navarre* (1745), which he was writing for the Dauphin's wedding, with music by Jean Philippe Rameau.

> Why did you give this entertainment to Rameau? I quite understand that Monsieur de Richelieu would like to have it rehearsed before he leaves for Spain, but if he tries to hurry everything he will spoil everything. He has already done it much harm in compelling me to invent the plot in one day at his house at Versailles ...
>
> There is one more thing I want you to decide: the proportion of [musical] interludes my play ought to have. It must not be stifled by double quavers; the entertainment must be short so that the play does not appear to be long. I don't know whether Rameau will put up with so small a share. Anyway, what a man! He has gone mad. Judge of it by the criticism he has made. And what is worse is that he will be encouraged in his madness by people who take pleasure in sowing discord in the path of pleasure. You ought first of all, my dear angel, to withdraw from Rameau the entertainment I am going to correct, but you should also have someone tell Monsieur de Richelieu that Rameau is not at all fitted for this kind of entertainment, the music of which intermingles all the time with the spoken declamations, that this genre requires as great harmony and union between the author and the composer as there exists between Francoeur and Rebelle. Monsieur de Richelieu ought to have chosen both of them for my interludes, and have given *Prometheus* to Rameau. That would have been in the nature of things. I foresee that it will be impossible to work with Rameau. He is good only to listen to, not to live with. I repeat that his kind of music is not suitable for mixed plays like mine.[126]

Finally, there is this comment on man's generally disinterested taste for entertainment.

> Madam, as you know, all spectacles amuse mankind. We go equally to the marionettes, to the bonfire on the eve of St. John's, to the Comic Opera, to high mass, to a burial.[127]

---

126 Letter to Charles Augustin Feriol, Comte d'Argental (August, 1744), in *Select Letters*, 86ff.
127 Letter to Suzanne Necker (June, 1770), in Ibid., 168.

11 VOLTAIRE, AS PLAYWRIGHT

VOLTAIRE CONSIDERED HIMSELF AN AUTHORITY on dramatic poetry, although the numerous plays of which he was the author are now considered the weakest part of his large literary output. Nevertheless, his prose contains many valuable observations which touch on aesthetics in general in the French Baroque.

On Ancient versus Modern Theater

Voltaire, who considered the theater to be an exalted and noble form of literature, began his discussion of ancient theater with these observations on its origin.

> Buffoon and buffoonery appertain to low comedy ... to all that can amuse the populace. In this it was—to the shame of the human mind, be it spoken—that tragedy had its beginning. Thespis was a buffoon before Sophocles was a great man.
> In the sixteenth and seventeenth centuries, the Spanish and English tragedies were all degraded by disgusting buffooneries. The courts were still more disgraced by buffoons than the stage. So strong was the rust of barbarism, that men had no taste for more refined pleasures.[1]

Voltaire's most extended discussion on the relative virtues of ancient and modern theater is found in a letter to Cardinal Quirini, bishop of Brescia.[2] Here he touches on two of his greatest concerns regarding drama, the court's desire to see plays center on Love and gallantry and the movement toward replacing poetry with prose. While he argues here that contemporary French plays are in many ways superior to those of the ancient Greeks, it is a viewpoint which would attract little sympathy today. We find the tragedies of Racine and Corneille, based on ancient themes, to be rather stilted and lifeless.

> Happily for us, true tragedy appeared before any of our operas, which might have stifled and suppressed it ... By degrees our stage became more and more refined, and shook off that indecency and barbarism which disgraced so many others about this period, and served at the same time for an excuse to those whose unenlightened severity of manners banished all public representations ...

---
1 *Philosophical Dictionary*, 'Low Comedy,' in *The Works of Voltaire*, VI, 289ff.
2 Contained in a letter to cardinal Quirini, bishop of Brescia, quoted in Ibid., XXXVII, 123ff.

Our tragedies were a closer imitation of nature [than the Greeks]: we substituted history instead of Greek fables; politics, ambition, love and jealousy took their turns to animate the scene; while Augustus, Cinna, Caesar, and Cornelia, names far more respectable than the fabulous heroes of antiquity, often made their appearance on our stage, and spoke as they would have done in ancient Rome.

I shall not pretend to assert that the French theater was in all respects superior to the Greek, and ought to bury it in oblivion. Inventors have always held the first place in the memories of men; but whatever respect we may have for the geniuses of former ages, it does not prevent our often receiving much more pleasure from those who succeeded them. We admire Homer, but we read Tasso, and find in him a variety of beauties to which Homer was a stranger. We admire Sophocles also, and yet how many of our good tragic writers have masterstrokes which Sophocles would have been proud to imitate if he had lived after them? The Greeks would have learned from many of our excellent moderns to unravel their plots more naturally, and to link their scenes together in that artful, though imperceptible manner, so as never to leave the stage empty, and to make the actors go in and out with some reason for so doing …

I am satisfied, for example, that Sophocles and Euripides would have considered the first scene of *Bajazet* as a school of instruction … They would have admired the artful method which this conspirator takes in the discovery of his schemes, and the account which he gives of his actions; a merit which was unknown to the ancient writers. That mixture of the passions; that contrast of opposite sentiments; those animated dialogues between rivals of both sexes; those quarrels, reciprocal threats and complaints; those interesting disputes where everything is said that ought to be said; with all those various incidents that are so well managed by modern writers, would have astonished them …

I will even go further, and venture to assert that the ancients, who were so passionately fond of liberty, and have so often said that there could be no dignity of sentiment but in a commonwealth, might learn to speak with energy, even on liberty itself, from some of our tragedies which were written in the bosom of monarchy.

The moderns have moreover succeeded oftener than the ancients in subjects of pure invention. We had many performances of that kind in the time of Cardinal Richelieu: it was indeed his peculiar taste as well as that of the Spaniards; he was fond of forming plots and characters, and afterward giving names to the persons of the drama, as we do in comedy: and in this he frequently amused himself, as an agreeable relief from the fatigue of public business …

I cannot imagine … how Father Brumoy could say, in his account of the Greek theater, that tragedy will not admit of feigned subjects, and that this liberty was never taken at Athens. He then sets himself to work to find out a reason for a thing which never was or could be. 'The reason,' says he, 'I believe may be found, in the nature of the human soul; nothing can move it but probability: now it is not probable that facts so noble as those which must be the subject of tragedy should be absolutely unknown: if, therefore, the poet invents the whole subject, even to the very names, the spectator is shocked; everything appears incredible to him; and the piece can never have its proper effect for want of probability.'

First, I shall beg leave to observe, it is false that the Greeks did not admit this species of tragedy, for Aristotle expressly mentions Agatho as a writer celebrated for it; and, secondly, it is equally false that these subjects never succeed; experience decides against Brumoy in this particular:

in the third place, the reason which he gives for the poor effect which this kind of tragedy must have is no less absurd; he must have little knowledge of the human heart, who thinks it cannot be moved by fiction; in the fourth place, a subject of pure invention, and a true subject not known, are absolutely the same thing to the spectator; and as our stage takes in subjects from every age and nation, a spectator must turn over all the books that ever were written before he can possibly know whether what he sees represented be fable or history; but he will certainly never take that trouble; if the piece is moving and pathetic, he will naturally be affected by it …

To return therefore to the subject in hand, I once more assert that it would be lack of feeling and judgment not to acknowledge that the French stage is infinitely superior to the Greek, in the artful conduct of its plots, in invention, and beauties of diction and sentiment without number; but, at the same time, it would be the height of partiality and injustice not to confess that love and gallantry have almost ruined our stage and deprived us of almost every advantage.

It cannot be denied, that, among four hundred tragedies which have been exhibited on our stage, since the time when it began to flourish, there are scarcely more than ten or twelve which are not founded on some love intrigue, which is certainly much fitter for comedy: the piece indeed is generally the same, the plot formed by jealousy and a rupture, and ended in a marriage; one continued scene of coquetry, in short a downright comedy, wherein princes act the principal parts, and a little blood is shed for form's sake. The greater part of these pieces were so very like comedies, that the actors began at last to recite them in the same tone as they did what we call high or serious comedy, which contributed in a great measure to degrade tragedy, all the pomp and magnificence of declamation being entirely forgotten. The players piqued themselves on the merit of speaking verse exactly in the same manner as prose, without considering that a language above the ordinary language ought to be repeated in a tone above the vulgar and familiar one: and if some actors had not happily corrected this fault, our tragedy would soon have dwindled into a heap of discourses on love and gallantry, repeated without force or spirit, in a cold and lifeless manner …

The French stage has indeed of late years endeavored to wash off this stain, by some tragedies wherein love is represented as a furious and terrible passion, worthy of the theater; and by some others, where even the name of love is not so much as mentioned: never did love cause so many tears to flow as nature has: the heart is generally but slightly touched by the complaints of a lover, but it is deeply affected by the melancholy situation of a mother on the point of losing her son.

In his 'Discourse on Tragedy,' Voltaire mentions again his concern for the emphasis on Love in contemporary theater, stressing his admiration for the ancient Greeks for their handling of this emotion.

The Greeks seldom ventured to bring [love] on the stage of Athens; first, because their tragedies generally turning on subjects of terror, the minds of the spectators were biased, as it were, in favor of that particular species; and, second, because the women at that time led a much more retired life than ours do, and consequently the language of love, not being as it is now the subject of every conversation, the poets had less inducement to treat a passion, which it is most difficult to paint on account of that very delicate management which it requires. Another reason, which

I own weighs greatly with me, was, that they had no actresses, the women's parts being always played by men in masks. Love from their mouths would perhaps have appeared ridiculous.³

On the balance, Voltaire seems to have clearly appreciated the contributions of the ancients to modern theater, and to French culture. In a 'Discourse to the [French],' he observes,

> Be so good as to consider that you have no art or science for the knowledge of which you are not indebted to the Greeks; the very names of those arts and sciences sufficiently prove this.⁴

And, again, in his essay, 'The Ignorant Philosopher,'

> Oh! if we could but imitate; if we could at length do with respect to theological disputes what we have already done, at the end of seventeen hundred years, with respect to the Fine Arts!
> We have returned to the pure taste of antiquity, in regard to literature, after being immersed in the barbarisms of our schools.⁵

In the letter of dedication of his tragedy, *Orestes*, to the Duchess of Maine, Voltaire also summarizes the contributions of Greek drama.

> Nothing but ignorance, and its natural attendant, presumption, can assert that the ancients have nothing worthy of our imitation: there is scarcely one real and essential beauty and perfection, for the foundation of which, at least, we are not indebted to them ...
> Not an art was born among us: everything was transplanted: but the earth that bears these foreign fruits is worn out, and our ancient barbarism, by the help of false taste, would break out again in spite of all our culture and improvement.⁶

On the other hand, he was still thinking here of his arguments for the general superiority of modern theater.

> We should not, I acknowledge, endeavor to imitate what is weak and defective in the ancients: it is most probable that their faults were well known to their contemporaries.

---

3   'A Discourse on Tragedy,' in Ibid., XXXIX, 190.
4   'A Discourse to the Welsh,' in Ibid., XXXVII, 98ff.
5   'The Ignorant Philosopher,' in Ibid., XXXV, 283.
6   Quoted in Ibid., XVII, 65ff.

On the Contemporary French Theater

In Voltaire's discussion of early French drama, we find most interesting his emphasis on the expression of emotions.

> It is true, we have been reproached, and not without reason, that our theater was an eternal school of gallantry, and of a sort of coquetry which has in it nothing of a tragic nature …
>
> We have almost always wanted a degree of warmth; every other quality we possess. The source of this languor, of this weak monotony, was partly that little spirit of gallantry then so dear to the courtiers and to women, which converted tragedy into conversation …
>
> [Formerly] the stage was altogether low and despicable. Comedians had a patent, they bought a tennis-court, they formed a company as merchants form a society. This was not the theater of Pericles … There was a necessity for pieces to consist of long narratives; a dramatic piece was rather a concatenation of conversations than an action. Every performer was desirous of shining in a long soliloquy …
>
> This form excluded all theatrical action, all emphatic expressions of the passions, those striking pictures of human misery, those terrible and affecting strokes which tear the heart; it was only touched by the poet, it should have been torn. Declamation, which, until the time of Mademoiselle Le Couvreur was a measured recitative, a noted song in a manner, obstructed still more those outbursts of nature which are represented by a word, by an attitude, by silence, by a cry which escapes in the anguish of grief. These strokes were first made known to us by Mademoiselle Dumesnil …
>
> Something still superior, if possible, we have seen in Mademoiselle Clairon, and the player who takes the part of Tancred in the third act of the piece of that name, and at the end of the fifth; souls were never agitated by such violent emotions, never were tears shed in greater abundance. The perfection of the player's art showed itself upon those two occasions with a force, of which, till then, we had no idea; and Mademoiselle Clairon must be admitted to have surpassed all the painters in the kingdom.[7]

But the display of emotions will not disguise a poorly written play.

> It is but a few years since players have ventured to be what they should be, that is, living pictures; before they declaimed. We know, and the public knows it better than we do, that poets should not be too lavish of those terrible and shocking actions which make the greatest impression when they are well introduced and properly managed, but are quite impertinent when they have no relation to the subject. A piece badly written, whose plot is badly unraveled, obscure, laden with incredible incidents, which has no other merit but that which pantomime and decorations bestow upon it, is a disgusting monster.[8]

---

7 'Revolutions in the Tragic Art,' in Ibid., XXXIX, 160ff.
8 Ibid., 165.

In thinking of the early period of modern French history, Voltaire also pays tribute to the influence of Italy.

> Among the many obligations which we of later ages are under to the Italians, and particularly to the popes and their ministers, we must not pass over the cultivation and improvement of the Fine Arts, which have softened by degrees the gross and barbarous manners of our northern climates, and to which we are in a great measure indebted for our politeness, our happiness, and our glory.[9]

It seems appropriate to add here, a comment which Voltaire addressed to the French people at large.

> You make it your boast that your language is almost as universal as the Greek and Latin were formerly. To whom are you indebted for this? To about a score of authors of genius; all of whom you neglected, persecuted, and tormented, during their lives. You chiefly owe this triumph of your language in foreign countries, to the multitudes of natives who were obliged to quit their country about 1613.[10]

One of the more interesting discussions of contemporary French drama is one in which Voltaire discusses the manners of the audience. As curious as it seems, such descriptions of theater manners are not rare in the Baroque. He also makes some remarks on the quality of the halls in which drama was presented, and after this passage goes on to make specific recommendations for the building of a proper theater.

> It would be a melancholy consideration to reflect, that after our great masters had surpassed the ancients in almost every part of tragedy, we should fall short of them in our representations of it; but on our stage, one of the greatest obstacles to any grand and pathetic action is the number of spectators that crowd in with the actors; an indecency which caused remarkable confusion on the first night of *Sémiramis*. The first actress from London was present at the representation, and was astonished: she could not conceive how any people in the world could be such enemies to their own pleasures, as to spoil a sight which they might have enjoyed. This abuse was corrected the ensuing night, during the run of *Sémiramis*, and might easily have been terminated. We may think lightly of it if we please, but an inconvenience like this is sufficient to deprive us of a number of excellent productions, which I have no doubt would have appeared, if we had kept our stage free, proper for action, and such as it is in all other parts of Europe.
> But this is most certainly not the only evil which calls for a remedy among us: I cannot sufficiently express my astonishment and concern at the little care which we take in France to make our theaters worthy of the excellent performances represented in them, and of the nation which encourages them: surely *Cinna* and *Athalie* deserve a better place than a tennis-court, with a few vile decorations at the top, in a bad taste, and where the spectators are placed without any order or decorum—some on the stage itself, others below in what they call the parterre, where they are crowded and pressed together in the most indecent manner, throwing themselves sometimes

---

9 Contained in a letter to cardinal Quirini, bishop of Brescia, quoted in Ibid., XXXVII, 115.
10 'A Discourse to the Welsh,' in Ibid., XXXVII, 98ff.

one upon another, as if there were an insurrection of the populace—while as far north as we can well travel, our dramatic works are exhibited in theaters a thousand times more magnificent, and with much more decency and decorum.

But above all, how far do we fall short of that good sense and kind taste, with regard to everything of this kind, which reigns throughout Italy! It reflects shame and disgrace on us to suffer these relics of barbarism to remain in a city so large, so well-peopled, so rich and so polished as Paris is; while, at the same time, a tenth part of what we expend every day in trifles, as costly as they are useless, might enable us to raise public monuments of every kind that should render it as magnificent as it is populous, and one day perhaps place it on a level with Rome itself, which is our model in everything. This was one of the great designs of the immortal Colbert. I flatter myself you will pardon this digression and attribute it to the love I bear to the arts and to my country.[11]

Voltaire, in an essay on earlier writers, calls Molière the best comic poet any nation ever produced.

This article led me to read over the comic poets of antiquity; and it must be confessed, that if we compare the art and regularity of our stage with the loose and unconnected scenes of the ancients, their weak intrigues, and the indelicate custom of making their actors relate, in long, insipid, and improbable soliloquies, either what they had done, or what they were going to do; it must be confessed, I say, that Molière drew comedy from its chaos, as Corneille did tragedy; and that the French are superior, in this respect, to any nation under the sun.[12]

In spite of the above praise for Corneille, in other places Voltaire's appreciation is qualified. Surely the fact that the tragedies of Corneille were in competition with Voltaire's for production had no influence on his judgment!

His sole emulation was to write, when it should have been to write well. His last twelve or thirteen tragedies are not only wretched, but in a very mean style.[13]

Voltaire makes a few observations on the differences between French and English plays, the English after Shakespeare having enjoyed the reputation as the leading nation in this form. He found the primary distinction one between action and language.

It is true we have too much of words, if you have too much action, and perhaps the perfection of the art should consist in a due mixture of the French taste and English energy.[14]

......

---

11 'The Royal Society and Academies,' in Ibid., XXXIX, 102ff.
12 'Notes on Some of the Writers who Lived in the Age of Louis XIV,' in Ibid., XXXVIII, 292.
13 'The Royal Society and Academies,' in Ibid., XXXIX, 102ff.
14 Letter to George Lyttleton (May, 1750), in *The Selected Letters*, 159.

> The English are more fond of action than we are, and speak more to the eye; the French give more attention to elegance, harmony, and the charms of verse. It is certainly more difficult to write well than to bring upon the stage assassinations, wheels, mechanical powers, ghosts, and sorcerers.[15]

In a letter to the English ambassador to Constantinople, Voltaire observes,

> You ought to submit to our rules of the stage, as we submit to your philosophy: we have made as good experiments on the human heart, as you have in physics: the art of pleasing seems to be the art of Frenchmen; the art of thinking is all your own.[16]

Voltaire also makes some enlightening remarks on the contemporary fate of the playwright, thoughts which no doubt reflect his own personal experience. We can understand this busy writer's concern over wasted time, such as he describes in a letter of 1732 regarding the production of his play, *Zaïre*.

> I should have used part of my time writing you and the rest correcting *Zaïre*. But I wasted it completely in Fontainebleau creating squabbles among the actresses over starring roles and between the queen and princesses over the performance of comedies, causing great disputes about trifles and creating dissension in the entire court over trivia.[17]

He also complains of the playwright's treatment by actors and critics.

> It is much worse if you write for the theater. You begin by appearing before an aeropagus of twenty actors, whose profession, though useful and agreeable, is nevertheless stigmatized by the injust and irrevocable cruelty of the public. This unfortunate abasement irritates them; they regard you as a dependent and treat you with all the contempt they themselves receive. You await your first verdict from them; they judge you; in the end they accept your play. And after all this it only needs one practical joker in the pit to make it fail. If succeeds the so-called Italian farce and that of the fairground will parody it, and twenty pamphlets will prove that you should not have succeeded. Scholars who know little Greek, and who do not read what is being written in French, despise you or pretend to do so.
>
> You give your book in trembling to a lady of the Court; she gives it to her chamber-maid, who uses it for hair-curlers.[18]

Last but not least, Voltaire was bothered by the attitude of the court, in particular the courtiers. He specifically mentions this in a letter to the actress, Mdlle Quinault, who retired from the stage at age forty in 1741.

---

15 'A Discourse on Tragedy,' in *The Works of Voltaire*, XXXIX, 188.
16 Letter to Mr. Falkener, in Ibid., X IX, 20ff.
17 Letter to Jean-Baptiste Nicolas de Formont (December, 1732), in *The Selected Letters*, 28.
18 Letter to Le Fèvre (ca. 1740), in *Select Letters*, 71.

No one is better able than you to form an opinion on the profession you adorn. But is not your noble art just as much decried by bigots and equally looked down upon at Court? Is less contempt poured on a business which requires intelligence, education, talent, than on a study and art which teach only morality, decency, and the virtues?

I have always been indignant for both you and myself that work so difficult and so useful as ours should be repaid by so much ingratitude, but now my indignation has turned to despair.[19]

In view of the above, we might imagine a line from Voltaire's *The Tatler* (I, i), spoken by Euphemia in criticism of courtiers, may also reflect Voltaire's reception as a playwright by members of the court.

The perfidious group of courtiers always look on a new-comer with an eye of malevolence, and soon find out all his imperfections: from the first moment they condemn him, without pity or remorse; and, which is still worse, their judgment is irrevocable.

Perhaps these experiences contributed to Voltaire's gradual disillusionment with the theater. He began to question even the lasting contributions of the great playwrights, Corneille and Molière. In the Preface to his play, *Catiline*, Voltaire writes,

What progress those arts may have made in France, those gentlemen of distinguished genius and abilities who have cultivated them among us have not yet imparted true taste to the whole nation. We are not born so happy as the Greeks and Romans, but frequent the theater more out of idleness than from any real regard to literature.[20]

His outlook became increasingly dark. In his dedication of *Orestes* to the Duchess of Maine, Voltaire concludes,

All that I wish for, Madam, is, that some genius may be found to finish what I have but just sketched out; to free the stage from that effeminacy and affectation which it is now sunk into; to render it respectable to the gravest characters.[21]

In a letter to Feriol in 1775, Voltaire sees only a dismal end to French taste in music as well as in the theater.

Nothing is so sacred that it is not abused. We are going to lapse into the extravagant and the gigantic in all things. Farewell to beautiful verse; farewell to feelings of the heart; farewell to everything. Music will soon be nothing more than an Italian din, and theatrical plays nothing more than conjurers' tricks. They wanted to improve everything, but everything has degenerated.[22]

---

19 Letter to Mdlle Quinault (August, 1738) in *Voltaire in His Letters*, 56.
20 Quoted in *The Works of Voltaire*, X IX, 261ff.
21 Quoted in Ibid., XVII, 67ff.
22 Letter to Charles-Augustin Feriol (October, 1769), in *The Selected Letters*, 285.

At the end of his life, reflecting on the decay of theater in Paris, he writes,

> I have seen the end of the reign of reason and taste.[23]

And finally, there was disillusionment with the public, whom Voltaire has Ismenia refer to in his, *Mérope* (IV, v), as,

> … the fickle crowd, still fond of novelty …[24]

On this subject, Voltaire, in the dedication of his *The Orphan of China*, quotes an anonymous Chinese author,

> When you compose any work, show it only to your friends; dread the public, and your brother writers; for they will play false with you, abuse everything you do, and impute to you what you never did: calumny with her hundred trumpets, will sound them all to your destruction; whilst truth, who is dumb, shall remain with you.[25]

The final dissolution with the environment for theater in Paris, for Voltaire, came when his close friend, the actress Adrienne le Couvreur (1692–1730) was denied burial on church property because she was an actress. In a rage, Voltaire wrote his poem, 'La Mort de Mademoiselle Le Couvreur.'

> They deprive of burial,
> Her who in Greece would have had altars.
> I have seen them adoring her, crowding about her;
> Hardly is she dead when she becomes a criminal!

---

23 Letter to Charles Augustin Feriol (July, 1775), in *Select Letters*, 174.

24 It was in a rehearsal of *Mérope*, in 1742, when Voltaire was coaching Mlle. Dumesnil, that she complained she would have to have 'the very devil' in her to simulate the passion he expected. 'Yes,' replied Voltaire, 'you must have the devil to succeed in any of the arts.'

25 Dedication to Richelieu, of *The Orphan of China*, in *The Works of Voltaire*, XV, 180. It is interesting to read, in this same dedication, Voltaire's rather condescending view of the Chinese culture.

> The Chinese, as well as the rest of the Asiatics, have stopped at the first elements of poetry, eloquence, natural philosophy, astronomy, and painting; all practiced by them so long before they were known to us. They began in everything much sooner than us, but made no progress afterwards; like the ancient Egyptians, who first taught the Greeks, and became at last so ignorant, as not even to be capable of receiving instruction from them.

> These people, whom we take so much pains and go so far to visit; from whom, with the utmost difficulty, we have obtained permissions to carry the riches of Europe, and to instruct them, do not to this day know how much we are their superiors; they are not even far enough advanced in knowledge to venture to imitate us, and don't so much as know whether we have any history or not.

On the Purpose of Drama

For Voltaire, the central purpose of serious works written for the theater was to express the emotions, as he makes very clear in answer to a critic of his tragedy, *Mérope*.

> The grand point is to affect and draw tears from the spectators. Tears were shed both at Verona and at Paris. This is the best answer that can be made to the critics. It is impossible to be perfect; but how meritorious it is to move an audience, in spite of our imperfections![26]

In his *Alzire* (II, ii), Voltaire reflects the victory won by the long march of humanism: the expression of the emotions are not a weakness, but the strength of man.

> ZAMOR. Forgive these tears, the memory of past griefs
>   Sits heavy on me.
> ALVAREZ. Let them flow my son,
>   'Tis the best mark of our humanity:
>   The heart that feels not for another's woe
>   Is fit for every crime.

However, since his forte was tragedy, Voltaire was thinking primarily of serious emotions. In this regard, he observes in the Preface to his play, *The Prodigal*,

> I have observed, with regard to the stage, that violent peals of universal laughter seldom rise but from some mistake.[27]

Furthermore, Voltaire correctly understood that the basic emotions are universal, as he expressed in the Preface to *Hérode et Mariamne* (1725), 'the whole depends on passions which are equally felt by all mankind.'[28] He makes this point again in the Preface to his play, *Mariamne*.

> When we are to make the passions speak, all men have pretty nearly the same ideas; but the manner of expressing them, distinguishing the man of wit from him who has none; the man of genius from him who has nothing but wit; and the real poet from him who would be a poet if he could.[29]

Voltaire seems to have been sensitive to the exploitation of Love in both theater and in opera. He appears to have experienced some criticism for not following the fashion, as is suggested in a letter to a friend when he had completed *Zaïre*.

---

26 Letter to M. de la Lindelle, quoted in Ibid., XV, 26.
27 Quoted in Ibid., X IX, 271.
28 Quoted in Clark, *European Theories*, 278.
29 Quoted in *The Works of Voltaire*, X IX, 237ff.

> Everyone here reproaches me that I do not put more love into my pieces. There shall be love enough this time, I swear, and not mere gallantry. My desire is that there may be nothing so Turkish, so Christian, so amorous, so tender, so infuriate, as that which I am now putting into verse for the pleasure of the public.[30]

After *Zaïre* had been performed, Voltaire commented on this subject again in a letter to the English ambassador to Constantinople.

> If my *Zaïre* has met with success, I owe it not so much to the merit of the performance, as to the tenderness of the love scenes, which I was wise enough to execute as well as I possibly could: in this I flattered the taste of my audience; and he is generally sure to succeed, who talks more to the passions of men than to their reason …
>
> If you have not the reputation of being tender, it is not that your stage heroes are not in love, but that they seldom express their passion naturally: our lovers talk like lovers; yours [the English] like poets.[31]

And again, in his 'Discours sur la Tragédie,' (1731), written for the English lord Bolingbroke, Voltaire writes,

> Some judicious critics may ask why I have introduced love into a tragedy which bears the name of Brutus? Why I have mingled that passion with the rigid virtue of a Roman senator, and the political intrigues of an ambassador?
>
> Our nation has been reproached for having enfeebled the tragic stage by too much tenderness; and the English have merited the same accusation for nearly a century; for you have always found our fashions and faults somewhat contagious. But will you allow me to give you my opinion on this matter?
>
> To expect love in every tragedy seems to me to argue an effeminate taste, which always to proscribe it, shows a contemptuous and unreasonable captiousness.
>
> The stage, whether occupied by tragedy or comedy, exhibits a living picture of the human passions …
>
> That love may be deserving of a place in tragedy it must have a necessary connection with the whole piece and not be arbitrarily introduced to fill up gaps, as it does in your tragedies as well as in our own, all of which are too long. It should in reality be a tragic passion, considered as a weakness, and opposed and contrasted by remorse. It should either lead to misfortune and crime, to convince us of its perils; or else virtue should triumph over it, to show that it is not invincible. Treated in any other way, love is of the same nature as that which is the subject of pastorals or comedies.[32]

A few hints reveal that Voltaire was aware, on some level, of the struggle in man between Reason and feeling, or as we would say today, between the left and right hemispheres of the

---

30   Quoted in Ibid., XIX, 4.
31   Letter to Mr. Falkener, in Ibid., XIX, 7, 9.
32   Quoted in Clark, *European Theories*, 283ff.

brain. In the Preface to his play, *The Prodigal*, he correctly recognizes that words (left hemisphere) are ineffective in describing the emotions.

> It would perhaps be agreeable to the present taste for reasoning, and not unsuitable to this occasion, to examine here, what kind of pleasantry that is which makes us laugh in a comedy. The cause of laughter is one of those things easier felt than expressed.[33]

The same deduction is intended when Titus, in *Brutus* (IV, i), observes,

> Urge me no more: I've heard too much already:
> Shame and despair surround me, but begone,
> I am resolved: to, leave me to my sorrows,
> And to my virtue: reason pleads in vain …

Finally, as we have frequently cited references to right-hand preference in these volumes, as an expression of left hemisphere dominance, it is interesting to find this allusion to the right hemisphere's inability to reason in *The Tatler* (I, ii), when Damis asks,

> Did you ever remember such a starched, affected, strained, left-handed understanding?

We should also note two passages where Voltaire speaks specifically of the purpose of comedy. In the Preface to his play, *Nanine*, Voltaire says of comedy in general,

> Comedy, I repeat once more, may be impassioned, may be in transport, or in tears, provided at the same time that it makes the good and virtuous smile … It must be acknowledged that there is no small difficulty in making the spectators pass insensibly from tears to laughter, and yet this transition, hard as it is to manage in a comedy, is not the less natural.[34]

In the Preface to his play, *The Prodigal*, Voltaire provides the more traditional purpose of comedy as 'an exact representation of manners.'[35]

In addition to the purpose of the expression of feelings, Voltaire also gave high importance to the educational value inherent in dramatic plays. His various references to this are invariably interesting, especially in the following where he compares this purpose with that of the expression of feelings.

> I have ever been of the opinion, that tragedy should correct, as well as move the heart. Of what consequence or importance to mankind are the passions or misfortunes of any of the heroes of antiquity, if they do not convey some instruction to us? It is universally acknowledged, that the comedy of 'Tartuffe,' a piece hitherto unequaled, did a great deal of good in the world, by showing

---

33 Quoted in *The Works of Voltaire*, X IX, 271.
34 Quoted in Ibid., X IX, 280.
35 Quoted in Ibid., X IX, 270.

hypocrisy in its proper light; and why therefore should we not endeavor in a tragedy to expose that species of imposture which sets to work the hypocrisy of some, and the madness of others?[36]

He mentions the relative importance of this purpose again in the dedication of his *The Orphan of China*.

I have endeavored to describe the manners of the Tartars and Chinese: the most interesting events are nothing when they do not paint the manners; and this painting, which is one of the greatest secrets of the art, is no more than an idle amusement, when it does not tend to inspire notions of honor and virtue.[37]

Because this value in dramatic literature was so obvious to him, he wonders why this aspect of French theater was so praised by foreigners, and yet had so little impact at home.

I consider tragedy and comedy as so many schools of virtue, reason, and decorum. Corneille, who may really be called an ancient Roman living in France, has founded a school wherein noble sentiments are taught; and Molière an academy wherein are explained the duties of civil life. Those geniuses which they have formed draw strangers from the remotest parts of Europe, who come to receive instructions among us, and who contribute to the opulence of Paris. Our poor are fed by the produce of these works, which have gained us an empire over those very nations who have a natural hatred to us. The whole being well considered, a man must be an enemy to his country to condemn our shows …
But where is the man in Paris who is fired with the smallest spark of love for his country? We game, sup, and like scandal, compose wretched songs, and fall asleep in the hands of stupidity, in order to awake next day to renew the same circle of levity and indifference.[38]

Some of his reflections on the educational potential of the theater are more specifically directed, such as the suggestion for the education of young men found in the Preface of his play, *Catiline*.

I was willing to endeavor once more, by a tragedy without any declarations of love in it, to put an end to the reproaches so often thrown out against us in the learned world, of filling our stage with nothing but gallantry and intrigue, and at the same time to make our young men, who frequent the theater, better acquainted with Cicero.[39]

Similarly, in a letter to Catherine the Great, responding to an earlier letter in which she mentioned the convents for girls in Russia, he offers to personally censor French plays to make them appropriate educational vehicles for young girls in Russia.

---

36 Letter to Frederick the Great, January 20, 1742, in Ibid., XVI, 6.
37 Dedication to Richelieu, of *The Orphan of China*, in Ibid., XV, 180.
38 In a letter 'To a Certain Upper Clerk' (June 20, 1733), in Ibid., XXXVII, 82ff.
39 Quoted in Ibid., X IX, 255ff.

I am extremely interested in your account of your five hundred young ladies. Our St-Cyr has less than two hundred and fifty. I do not know whether you make your girls perform tragedies; but I think that dramatic recitation, of tragedy or comedy, is an excellent form of education. It lends grace to mind and body, and trains the voice, deportment and taste. One remembers a hundred passages which one can later quote as occasion demands. This adds to the pleasures of society and does all the good in the world. It is true that all our plays are concerned with love; it is a passion for which I have the deepest respect, but I agree with your Majesty that it should not be developed too soon. One could, I think, take several selected comedies, and cut out the parts most dangerous to young minds, while retaining the interest of the play.... I shall order tragedies and comedies from Paris in loose-leaf form; I shall have blank sheets of paper sewn between the pages, and on these I shall dictate the changes necessary to preserve the virtue of your fair young ladies.[40]

On Drama as Poetry

Voltaire considered dramatic poetry, works for the stage, the supreme form of poetry itself, a form which stands completely apart from those smaller poetic forms such as epistles and odes.

A good moral epistle teaches us nothing; a well-written ode still less; it may at best amuse those who have a taste for poetry about a quarter of an hour; but to create a subject, to invent an intricate intrigue, and unravel it; to give each person of the drama his proper character, and to support it; to contrive that none of them should enter or make their exits without a reason visible to all the spectators; never to leave the stage empty; to make everyone say what he should say, with elevation but without bombast, with simplicity free from meanness; to compose fine verse which does not discover the poet, but is such as the person who speaks might make if he spoke in verse; this is part of the duty which every author of a tragedy must discharge, upon pain of not succeeding among us ... A poet should, as it were, hold the hearts of spectators in his hand; he should force tears from the most insensible; he should wring the most obdurate hearts: without terror and pity tragedy has no existence; and even though you should excite both pity and terror, if with these advantages you fail in the observance of other laws, if your verse is not excellent, you are only a middling writer.[41]

It was in fact, the art of poetry which, for Voltaire, distinguished the fine playwright. In the Preface to his tragedy, *Hérode et Mariamne* (1725), Voltaire argues,

All poetical performances, though ever so perfect in the other points, must necessarily displease if the lines are not strong and harmonious, and if there does not run through the whole a continued elegance and inexpressible charm of verse, that genius only can inspire, that wit alone can never attain.[42]

---

40 Letter to Catherine of Russia (March, 1772), in *Voltaire and Catherine the Great*, 131ff.
41 'Revolutions in the Tragic Art,' in *The Works of Voltaire*, XXXIX, 170ff.
42 Quoted in Clark, *European Theories*, 277.

And again in his 'Discours sur la Tragédie' (1731), Voltaire explains that it was the quality of the poetry which distinguished Racine.

> It is the minor details which bolster up verse plays, and preserve them for future generations. Often the unusual way of saying ordinary things, and the art of embellishing by literary style what all men think and feel—these are what make great poets. There are neither out-of-the-way sentiments nor romantic adventures in the fourth book of Virgil; everything is natural: it is the great effort of a human mind. M. Racine stands above others not because he has said the same things as he has, but because he has said them better than they.[43]

In view of the above, we can understand how concerned Voltaire was as he viewed the approach of prose, as the replacement for poetry in dramatic works.

> We understand that there exists a rising sect of barbarians, whose doctrine is that no tragedy should henceforward be ever written but in prose. This last blow alone was wanting, in addition to all our previous afflictions. It is the abomination of desolation in the temple of the muses.[44]

MUSIC IN THE PLAYS OF VOLTAIRE

As with the tragedies of Corneille and Racine, there is very little reference to music in Voltaire's plays, either in dialogue or in stage directions, which may be regarded in part, we believe, as an attempt to distinguish drama from the dominant influence of opera. In any case, few though these references may be, there are some worthy of mention. One offers quite a different view of the celebrated salons hosted by the upper class women of Paris. In *The Prude* (I, iv), Collette satirizes, through the nature of its associations, the performances of music in these gatherings.

> … always at her house you will meet with good suppers, new songs, and bonmots, old wines, ice cream, liquors, new ribbons, Saxon monkeys, rich bagatelles …

In only one play does Voltaire comment on the purpose of music, and it is the familiar purpose of offering solace to the listener. In *The Prude* (IV, v), Mme de Burlet offers to Mme Dorfise, 'I have ordered him to get music, to purge your melancholy humors.'

In his *Philosophical Dictionary*, Voltaire makes a dark and curious reference to music as therapy. Here he writes a dramatic scene, from an imaginary play revolving around the cruelty of the Druids, in which Orpheus appears in the tradition of the gods who arrive at the end of plays to solve all the problems and bring about a happy ending.

---

43   Quoted in Ibid., 283.
44   *Philosophical Dictionary*, 'Rhyme,' in *The Works of Voltaire*, XIII, 91.

THE DRUID. I am altogether recovered. Oh, the power of good music! And who are you, divine man, who thus cures wounds, and rejoices hell itself?

ORPHEUS. My friends, I am a priest like yourselves, but I never deceived anyone, nor cut the throat of either boy or girl in my life. When on earth, instead of making the gods hated, I rendered them beloved, and softened the manners of the men whom you made ferocious. I shall exert myself in the like manner in hell. I met, just now, two barbarous priests whom they were scourging beyond measure; one of them formerly hewed a king in pieces before the Lord, and the other cut the throat of his queen and sovereign at the horse gate. I have terminated their punishment, and, having played to them a tune on the violin, they have promised me that when they return into the world they will live like honest men.[45]

The stage direction which follows this morbid dialogue ironically calls for this scene to conclude with 'light and agreeable music.'

The only reference in Voltaire's plays to substantial forces of instrumental or vocal music is a stage direction in *Pandora* (III, i), after Pandora laments,

Hence, ye idle visions; cease,
Discordant sounds,
  [*A Symphony is heard.*]
And give me peace.

Shortly after this, another stage direction calls for the Chorus of Pleasures to 'dance around her and sing.' The lyrics are given for a song in which a solo voice alternates with the chorus.

The only references by Voltaire in his plays to functional music are descriptions of the military trumpet. In *Mérope* (V, v), Narbas says,

Hark! I hear on every side
The trumpets sound, the groans of dying men …

Similarly, in *Zaïre* (I, ii), Osman mentions the 'shrill trumpet heard on every side.'

The sole reference to entertainment music is a curious line in *The Prude* (I, v). Here we encounter Mme Dorfise who finds no joy in the pleasures of the world. When asked even about music and dancing, she answers 'they are the devil's inventions.'

---

45 *Philosophical Dictionary*, 'The Druids,' in Ibid., VIII, 173ff.

12 VOLTAIRE, AS POET

Unlike many earlier poets who had a rather limited range of topics around which their poetry centered, Voltaire's scope is quite broad. This reflects, in part, the fact that Voltaire was very well read in both earlier literature and in current events. We were surprised, for example, to find, in Voltaire's poem 'The Maid of Orleans,' a passage based on a rather obscure work by Chaucer, 'The House of Fame,' in which the allegorical figure of Fame sits in judgment and announces her decisions by the use of one of two trumpets, one of gold and the other of black brass.

> Meanwhile was heard through air the clarion sound
> From one of Fame's two trumpets so renowned …[1]

It would seem that the principal value of poetry, in Voltaire's view, was to confront man with Truth. As he mentions in one of his letters to Frederick the Great, 'Verse that does not teach men new and inspiring truths is hardly worth reading.'[2] One finds this thought again in his poem, 'The Answer.'

> Let others in their lyric lays [songs]
> Say the same thing a thousand ways,
> The world with ancient fables tire,
> I new and striking truths admire.[3]

Regarding the basic elements of poetry, we find interesting this short history of rhyme, which Voltaire provides in his *Philosophical Dictionary*.

> Rhyme was probably invented to assist the memory, and to regulate at the same time the song and the dance. The return of the same sounds served to bring easily and readily to the recollection the intermediate words between the two rhymes. Those rhymes were a guide at once to the singer and the dancer; they indicated the measure. Accordingly, in every country, verse was the language of the gods.
> We may therefore class it among the list of probable, that is, of uncertain, opinions, that rhyme was at first a religious appendage or ceremony; for after all, it is possible that verses and songs

---

1   'The Maid of Orleans,' in *The Works of Voltaire*, XL, Canto VI.
2   Letter to Frederick the Great (September, 1736), in *The Selected Letters*, 58.
3   'The Answer,' in *The Works of Voltaire*, XXXVI, 98.

might be addressed by a man to his mistress before they were addressed by him to his deities; and highly impassioned lovers indeed will say that the cases are precisely the same ...[4]

Some of the learned contend that the Greeks began with rhyming, whether in honor of their gods, their heroes, or their mistresses; but, that afterwards becoming more sensible of the harmony of their language, having acquired a more accurate knowledge of prosody, and refined upon melody, they made those requisite verses without rhyme which have been transmitted down to us, and which the Latins imitated and very often surpassed.

As for us, the miserable descendants of Goths, Vandals, Gauls, Franks, and Burgundians—barbarians who are incapable of attaining either the Greek or Latin melody—we are compelled to rhyme ...

We have observed how French poetry, in rhyme, sweeps all obstacles before it, and that pleasure arose even from the very obstacles themselves. We have been always convinced that rhyme was necessary for the ears, not for the eyes.[5]

From the perspective of a working poet, Voltaire viewed rhyme somewhat differently.

What deterred me more than anything from works of this kind were the severe rules of our poetry, and the slavery of rhyme ... An English poet is a freeman, who can subject his language to his genius; while the Frenchman is a slave to rhyme, obliged sometimes to make four verses to express a sentiment that an Englishman can give you in one. One runs along a large and open field, while the other walks in shackles, through a narrow and slippery road; but, in spite of all these reflections and complaints, we can never shake off the yoke of rhyme; it is absolutely essential to French poetry.[6]

Voltaire offers this advice regarding verse in general,

Shall I give you an infallible little rule for verse? Here it is. When a thought is just and noble something still remains to be done with it: see if the way you have expressed it in verse would be effective in prose: and if your verse, without the swing of the rhyme, seems to you to have a word too many—if there is the least defect in the construction—if a conjunction is forgotten—if, in brief, the right word is not used, or not used in the right place, you must then conclude that the jewel of your thought is not well set. Be quite sure that lines which have any one of these faults will never be learnt by heart, and never re-read: and the only good verses are those which one rereads and remembers, in spite of oneself.[7]

Among the other elements of poetry, we are not surprised to find Voltaire, as a Frenchman, concerned with elegance.

---

[4] We have quoted elsewhere Voltaire's observation that man uses 'adoration' for both God and lovers.
[5] *Philosophical Dictionary*, 'Rhyme,' in Ibid., XIII, 88ff.
[6] 'A Discourse on Tragedy,' in Ibid., XXXIX, 175.
[7] Letter to Helvétius (February, 1739) in *Voltaire in His Letters*, 66.

> The great point in poetry and the oratorical art is that the elegance should never appear forced; and the poet in that, as in other things, has greater difficulties than the orator, for harmony being the base of his art, he must not permit a succession of harsh syllables. He must even sometimes sacrifice a little of the thought to elegance of expression, which is a constraint that the orator never experiences.[8]

In fact, it is under the subject of 'verse,' in Voltaire's *Philosophical Dictionary*, that we find the conclusion,

> It appears to me, that there never existed a truly eloquent man who did not love poetry.[9]

ON THE PHYSIOLOGY OF AESTHETICS

Voltaire's poem, 'The Law of Nature,'[10] deals extensively with Reason. In his publication of this poem, he mentions that it was only intended for Frederick the Great, that it comes from his heart and that it was never intended for the public. His thesis in this poem is that not only Reason, but also conscience are given to man as a basic law of nature. Nature, he says, instructs us more than any philosopher.

> To reason let researches vain give place,
> Let's strive to know if God instructs our race.
> Nature to man has given with bounteous hand
> Whatever his nature's cravings can demand;
> Sense's sure instinct, spirit's varied springs,
> To him each element its tribute brings.
> In the brain's foldings memory is placed,
> And on it nature's lively image traced.
> Ready at every motion of his will,
> His call external objects answer still;
> Sound to his ear is wafted by the air,
> The light he sees without or pains or care.
> ......
> The light of reason heaven gave not in vain
> To man, but added conscience to restrain.
> The springs of sense are moved by her command;
> Who hears her voice is sure to understand.

---

8 *Philosophical Dictionary*, 'Elegance,' in *The Works of Voltaire*, VIII, 192.
9 *Philosophical Dictionary*, 'Verse,' in Ibid., XIV, 156.
10 'The Law of Nature,' in Ibid., XXXVI, 22ff.

And then there is this curious statement, made in a letter to a correspondent, which one can only wish Voltaire had discussed in more detail.

> So be careful not to let yourself be beguiled by imagination. Imagination must be relegated to poetry and banished from physics.[11]

In two places we find reflections which would seem to suggest that Voltaire was aware of the twin intellectual and emotional sides of man, or as we would say, the left and right hemispheres of the brain. In the beginning of Canto VIII of Voltaire's poem, 'The Maid of Orleans,' we find,

> How wise, how interesting proves our page;
> The heart and mind at once formed to engage!

And in a letter which refers to his poem, 'To abbé Chaulieu,' Voltaire mentions in passing, 'But though I distrust my head, I am always sure of my heart.'[12]

On Philosophy

Nothing in Voltaire's life so caused him to question his faith as the Lisbon earthquake of 1 November 1755. This earthquake occurred on a Sunday while the faithful were in church, thus a large number of the victims were those faithful killed in the fall of the churches. If there were a God, reasoned Voltaire, why would he kill his faithful? Voltaire directed his anxiety toward a current philosophy, voiced by Leibnitz, among others, which stated that, since God rules, 'whatever is, is right.' But for Voltaire, it was clear, as he expressed in his poem, 'The Lisbon Earthquake,'

> That man's the victim of unceasing woe,
> And lamentations which inspire my strain,
> Prove that philosophy is false and vain.[13]

And Voltaire could not help but wonder how God choose Lisbon, instead of sinful Paris.

> Was then more vice in fallen Lisbon found,
> Than Paris, where voluptuous joys abound?
> Was less debauchery to London known,
> Where opulence luxurious holds her throne?
> Earth Lisbon swallows; the light sons of France
> Protract the feast, or lead the sprightly dance.
> ......

---

11   Letter to Claude-Nicolas Le Cat (April, 1741), in *The Selected Letters*, 88.
12   Letter to abbé Chaulieu, July 26, 1717, quoted in *The Works of Voltaire*, XXXVI, 283.
13   'The Lisbon Earthquake,' in Ibid., XXXVI, 8ff.

> Say what advantage can result to all,
> From wretched Lisbon's lamentable fall?
> Are you then sure, the power which could create
> The universe and fix the laws of fate,
> Could not have found for man a proper place,
> But earthquakes must destroy the human race?

These questions, of course, have no answers and even Voltaire, in the end, has learned to submit to the unexplainable.

> In youthful prime I sung in strains more gay,
> Soft pleasure's laws which lead mankind astray.
> But times change manners; taught by age and care
> Whilst I mistaken mortals' weakness share,
> The light of truth I seek in this dark state,
> And without murmuring submit to fate.

In a footnote Voltaire published with this poem, he concludes that man lacks the capacity to understand many fundamental questions, save through divine assistance.

> It is self-evident, that man cannot acquire this knowledge without assistance. The human mind derives all its knowledge from experience; no experience can give us an insight into what preceded our existence … In what manner have we received life? What is the spring upon which it depends? How is our brain capable of ideas and memory? In what manner do our limbs obey every motion of the will. Of all this we are entirely ignorant. Is our globe the only one that is inhabited? Was it created after other globes, or at the same instant? … [Man] is utterly at a loss with regard to the first principles of things without supernatural assistance.[14]

ON THE PSYCHOLOGY OF AESTHETICS

There are two references to the emotions in Voltaire's poetry which are particularly interesting. In a poem called, 'Fanaticism,' Voltaire uses the emotions as a means of contrasting humanism with the Church.

> Sometimes we in an atheist's mind
> Humanity's fairest virtues find …
> The man who can compassion show,
> Whose heart can feel another's woe,
> Can by example virtue teach,
> Seems most persuasively to preach.
> The pedant, with overweening pride,

---

14 Ibid., 17.

Intent to argue and decide.
Who blows up persecution's flame,
A vile impostor we should name.[15]

To a correspondent he sends a humorous little poem which suggests that in an older man, Reason at long last rules the emotions.

I'm free from passion, care, and strife;
The muse diversifies my life;
My day begins with joy, and ends
In cheerful suppers with my friends.
I now no more of love complain,
Reason at last has broke my chain;
I follow Cupid now no more,
The happy age of love is over;
With love's flame must I no more burn?[16]

Regarding Pleasure and Pain, in his poem, 'The Nature of Pleasure,' which in part explores the darker, grim side of seventeenth century Christian philosophy, Voltaire makes his case for the inherent orientation of man toward Pleasure.

Man is impelled to act by joy alone,
All other motives are to him unknown …
The taste of friendship, socal tie of hearts,
The love of study, solitude, and arts;
These are my passions, at all time my mind
Could in their charms attractive comfort find.[17]

In his poem, 'Moderation in all Things,' Voltaire repeats the observation mentioned so often by earlier poets and philosophers, that the states of Pleasure and Pain tend to be closely allied.

Pleasure's the God from whom we claim our birth,
Starved 'midst the weeds and brambles of the earth.
Pleasures are various in each varied stage
Of life, and some we taste when chilled by age.
But prudently the soul should feast on joy,
Pleasures are always transient soon they cloy …

Later there is a line, 'Labor with pleasure, joy with pain's combined.'[18]

---

15 'Fanaticism,' in Ibid., XXXVI, 271ff.
16 'Answer to a Lady, or a Person who wrote to Voltaire as such,' in Ibid., XXXVI, 182.
17 'The Nature of Pleasure,' in Ibid., XXXVI, 243ff.
18 'On Moderation in all Things,' in Ibid., I, 304ff.

ON THE PHILOSOPHY OF AESTHETICS

We have quoted above a number of Voltaire's specific observations relating to his ideas on the philosophy of aesthetics in poetry. There are only two other passages which we believe to be a part of his basic views on poetry. First, in his poem, 'The Law of Nature,' Voltaire observes that while the artist shapes his materials, only God can make the material itself.

> Whether in Peru or in China flame
> The golden heaps, their nature is the same:
> From the artist's hands new forms the ingots take,
> But he who shapes unable is to make.[19]

In only one poem does Voltaire raise the ancient question of the relationship between art and nature. In his, 'The Maid of Orleans,' we find,

> And shall I then to every canto stick
> A prosing preface? Moral makes me sick;
> A simple action told without disguise,
> The naked truth depicting to our eyes,
> Narration brief, of tinsel trappings void,
> Neither by wit or affectation cloyed—
> Such are the weapons censure to disarm;
> Then roundly reader, let us court the charm,
> 'Tis my advice: With nature for our aim,
> If we succeed, the picture needs no frame.[20]

A subject which seems to have been much closer to Voltaire's heart was poetry criticism. One poem mentions the most famous critic of poetry of the French Baroque, Nicolas Boileau (1636–1711).

> In Boileau we excuse satiric rage,
> Some beauties please in the malignant page.
> That bee had honey to assuage the grief
> Of those he stung, and give some kind relief.[21]

In another place he adds, 'We are well aware that most of the epistles of Boileau are fine, and that they have truth for their foundation, without which nothing is supportable.'[22]

---

19   'The Law of Nature,' in Ibid., XXXVI, 26.
20   'The Maid of Orleans,' in Ibid., XL, Canto X.
21   'Envy,' in Ibid., XXXVI, 186.
22   'Revolutions in the Tragic Art,' in Ibid., XXXIX, 172.

Voltaire's most interesting comments on critics, expressed in a combination of prose and poetry, are found in the satiric poem, 'The Temple of Taste.' Here he takes aim at a number of his fellow writers and poets. In this Temple he finds,

> a crowd of writers of every rank, age and condition, who scratched at the door and begged of Criticism to permit them to enter. One brought with him a mathematical romance, another a speech made before the Academy; one has just composed a metaphysical comedy; another held in his hand a poetical miscellany long since printed, with a long approbation and a privilege; another presented a mandate written in an affected and over-refined style, and was surprised to find that all present laughed instead of asking his blessing. 'I am the reverend father,' said one: 'Make room for my lord,' said another.
>
> > A prating sir, with voice acute,
> > Cried, 'I'm the judge of each dispute,
> > I argue, contradict and prate,
> > What others like I'm sure to hate.'
> > Then Criticism appearing, cried,
> > 'Your merit is by none denied;
> > But since Taste's godhead you reject,
> > Do not to enter here expect.'
>
> Bardou then cried out, 'The world's in error, and will always continue so; there's no God of Taste, and I'll prove it thus.' Then he laid down a proposition, divided and subdivided it; but nobody listened, and a greater multitude then ever crowded to the gate.[23]

Voltaire then satirizes a number of specific poets, including Jean Baptist Rousseau, La Motte, Fontenelle, Mairan, La Fontane and Quinault. He discovers Leibnitz in the Temple and inquires why he is there.

> I was told that it was because he had written tolerably good Latin verses, though he was versed in both metaphysics and geometry, and that Criticism admitted him into her temple to soften by such an example the austerity of his scientific brethren.

The works of Rabelais are found there, but they have been reduced to less than half of their original content through the corrections of the 'muses.' The same can be said of most Rabelais editions even today!

One poem suggests that Voltaire's own personal experience had left him rather bitter about critics of poetry. In his, 'The Three Manners,' a discourse on Greek drama and modern critics, Voltaire observes that the critics have no heart, and they come from Hell.

---

23 'The Temple of Taste,' in Ibid., XXXVI, 49ff. Voltaire had angered Jean Baptist Rousseau by observing of his poem 'Ode to Posterity,' that it was unlikely to reach its destination. Rousseau responded by attacking Voltaire's recent dramatic work, Zaïre, which in turn prompted Voltaire to write 'The Temple of Taste.'

But of all their inventions that which strikes me the most
Is the stage, of Athenians the pride and the boast;
Whereon heroes renowned, and the chiefs of old times,
Could act over again both their good deeds and crimes.
You see how all nations in this present age
Adopt their example, and would rival their stage.
No folio instruction like the drama conveys,
Perish, perish the wretches who would censure all plays;
When that vile, abject race first existed below,
A heart Nature on them forgot to bestow.[24]

ON THE AESTHETICS OF MUSIC

Regarding the purpose of music, in Voltaire's poetry there are several instances of the familiar reference to music's ability to soothe. In Voltaire's poem, 'The Maid of Orleans,' we find for example,

> Paris felt sorrow at their fate so tragic,
> And was consoled with comic Opera's magic.[25]

Similarly, in the poem, 'The Nature of Pleasure,'

> That man is born to a propitious fate,
> Who to the muse his time can dedicate;
> He from the tuneful art derives repose,
> The Muse his anguish soothes, dispels his woes:
> He laughs at all the follies of mankind,
> And from his lyre a sure relief can find.[26]

And again in Voltaire's epic poem, 'The Henriade,'

> Thy accents too, sweet music, strike mine ear,
> Music, descended from the heavenly sphere.
> 'Tis thine to soothe, to soften, and control
> Each wayward passion of the ruffled soul.[27]

---

24 'The Three Manners,' in Ibid., XXXVI, 141.
25 'The Maid of Orleans,' in Ibid., XL, Canto III.
26 'The Nature of Pleasure,' in Ibid., XXXVI, 246.
27 'The Henriade,' VII, in Ibid., XXXVIII, 109.

In Voltaire's poem, 'The Answer,' there is a reference to the purpose of music to communicate emotions which is especially interesting. He uses a very ancient expression for music, 'harmonious numbers,' as well as an often used metaphor in which the ear, and not the eye, is the passage to the heart.

> Ye boys called Cupids by mankind,
> Who whilst our meadows bloom in spring,
> Inspire men love's soft joys to sing,
> Assist a poet with your skill,
> The charms 'twixt sense and rhyme to fill.
> The enchanting pleasures well I know
> Which from harmonious numbers flow;
> The ear's a passage to the heart,
> Sound can to thought new charms impart.[28]

ART MUSIC

In Voltaire's poem, 'The Maid of Orleans,' we find a description of the type of brief concert performed after banquets, after the tables had been cleared. The music in this case included epic poetry.

> The banquet finished, music played awhile,
> The song Italian, in chromatic style;
> Flutes, hautboys, viols, softly breathed around,
> While three melodious voices swelled the sound;
> They sang in allegory, and the strain
> Told of those heroes mighty love had slain,
> Who fled of sounding glory the career,
> To please the tender fair they loved most dear.
> The concert echoed from concealed alcove,
> Close to the chamber, then the scene of love.
> Thus beauteous Agnes, the discreet and wise,
> Heard all, but was not seen by human eyes.[29]

The most interesting reference to art song in the poems of Voltaire is found in Canto XVI of Voltaire's poem, 'The Maid of Orleans.' Here the poet creates a scene based on the rural singing contest, which was a staple in the works of the ancient lyric poets of Greece. In this case,

---

28 'The Answer,' in Ibid., XXXVI, 98. 'Numbers' was a frequent Scholastic synonym, reflecting the association of music with mathematics, during the latter Middle Ages and Renaissance.

29 'The Maid of Orleans,' in Ibid., XL, Canto I.

St. Peter invites St. George (represented by 'Austin') and St. Denis to compete in composing 'A Hymn in verse, but not an Ode in prose ... [and then] To music set the whole immediately.'

Austin begins with an ode about ancient Egypt and the Hebrews, together with various characters of ancient literature.

> Dull was the litany and somewhat long,
> While interspersed these brilliant traits among,
> Were mighty deeds detailed in sounding [songs],
> Those acts so cherished in remotest days ...

His song was not well received.

> Austin was silent, his Pindaric strain
> Called forth amid the bright empyreal train
> A doubtful murmur—sounds made to infuse
> Ill-favored thoughts on his odaic muse.

Now Denis rose, 'low bent his eyes serene, which straightaway reared, displayed his modest mien.' He sings of the heroes of the Catholic Church, pauses and is encouraged to continue.

> With prudence Denis once more struck the lyre:
> 'Mine adversary may have charmed the choir,
> The arm of vengeance hath he loudly praised;
> Whereas my sounding plaudits shall be raised,
> To honor clemency's bright power with skill,
> Hating is good; but loving's better still.'
>
> Denis more confident in voice and mind,
> Then sang in pleasing verse, the shepherd kind ...

At length, Denis is declared the winner, that is, France over England.

> Hailed was of Denis the odaic treasure,
> The prize it gained, and praises without measure,
> Of England's saint was foiled the boldness dread;
> Austin blushed deep, and skulking, forthwith fled.

In Voltaire's epic poem, 'The Henriade,' there is a reference to a civic victory song.

> Now was all Paris filled with joyful cries,
> And odious songs of triumph rent the skies.[30]

---

30 'The Henriade,' Canoto V, in Ibid., XXXVIII, 81.

In as much as opera was a constant subject of discussion in Baroque France, it is no surprise to find references to it in Voltaire's poetry. It is also no surprise to find him employing his love of satire on this subject in his poem 'The Temple of Taste.' His principal targets here are the cultural pretense of aristocrats and the encroachment of Italian opera on the French language.

> This was a concert given by a gentleman of the long robe, infatuated with music, which he never learned, and chiefly with the Italian music, which he had no knowledge of, but from some indifferent songs which were never heard at Rome, and which are very badly sung in France by some girls belonging to the opera.
>
> They then caused a long French recitative, set to music by an Italian, who did not understand our language, to be performed. It was to no purpose to remonstrate to him, that as this sort of music is nothing more than notated declamation, it is of consequence, subjected to the genius of the language; and that nothing can be as ridiculous as French scenes sung in the Italian taste, except Italian ones sung in the French taste.
>
> > Nature ingenious, fertile, wise,
> > Earth with gifts various beautifies;
> > She speaks to all in language fit,
> > They differ both in tongue and wit;
> > Their tone, their voices suit; each note
> > Is by the hand of nature wrote;
> > And every difference must appear
> > To a refined, judicious ear.
> > Music to charm in France, the tone
> > Of France must imitate alone.
> > Lully could to our taste descend,
> > Not strive to alter but amend.
>
> No sooner were these judicious remarks made, but the pretended connoisseur, shaking his head, cried, 'Come, come, you shall soon see something new.' We could not refuse to enter, and immediately after, the concert began.
>
> > The rivals then of Lully's fame,
> > Their taste and skill in art the same,
> > French verse most dissonantly played
> > With the Italian music's aid:
> > A lady, with distorted eyes,
> > Acted a thousand ecstasies.
> > A coxcomb, of his dress quite vain.
> > Quavered and thrilled a frantic strain,
> > And beat time false, which made them soon
> > All equally play out of tune.[31]

---

31 'The Temple of Taste,' in Ibid., XXXVI, 45ff.

In this same poem there is also a brief exchange between the most famous critic of poetry, Boileau, and the librettist of Lully's operas, Quinault.

> Boileau, at the express command of the God of Taste, was reconciled to Quinault, who may be considered as a poet, formed by the graces, as Boileau was by reason.
>
>> But Boileau, satirist severe,
>> Whilst he embraced could scarce forbear,
>> The lyric poet to revile,
>> Yet Quinault pardoned with a smile.
>
> 'I'll never be reconciled to you,' said Boileau, 'except you acknowledge that there are many insipid lines in those agreeable operas.' 'That's very possible,' answered Quinault, 'but you must at the same time acknowledge that you were never capable of writing *Atys* or *Armida*.'[32]

A particularly negative reference to opera is found in Voltaire's poem, 'The Maid of Orleans,' where the opera dancer is classed together with 'the lover of a brothel's wanton joy.'[33] A less condescending representation of opera reads,

> Each noble art inflamed my breast;
> Painting delights me; oft I've been,
> At the king's or duke's palace, seen
> Gazing on works with raptured eye,
> Where art with nature seems to vie;
> Paul Veronese's noble fire
> And skill divine I much admire;
> Poussin and Raphael, my sight
> Ravish with exquisite delight.
> From those rooms to the opera, I
> Upon the winds of pleasure fly;
> What there gives pleasure, from me draws
> The tribute of deserved applause.
> In music, Mauret's sprightly strain,
> Destouche's grace, my praise obtain,
> Pelissier's art, Le More's fine voice,
> Pleasing by turns, suspend my choice.[34]

In his poem, 'The Worldling,' Voltaire mentions his one high hope for the future of French opera, Rameau.

---

32   'The Temple of Taste,' in Ibid., XXXVI, 67.
33   'The Maid of Orleans,' in Ibid., XL, Canto II.
34   'Answer to a Lady, or a Person who wrote to Voltaire as such,' in Ibid., XXXVI, 180ff.

To the opera house he must repair,
Dance, song and music charm him there.
The painter's art to strike the sight,
Does there with that blest art unite;
The yet more soft, persuasive skill,
Which can the soul with pleasure thrill.
He may to damn an opera go,
And yet perforce admire Rameau.[35]

But in his poem, 'Envy,' there is the suggestion that Rameau fared little better with the critics than Voltaire.

Orpheus alone should dare to hiss Rameau;
Venus to criticize is Psyche's right;
But why should we in censure thus delight?
No beauty she acquires who blames a face …[36]

Finally, in a poem written for Frederick the Great, Voltaire mentions a projected opera which apparently Frederick had planned to compose.

Great Frederick to Berlin with speed shall repair,
And the joy of his triumphs his true subjects shall share;
And by a new opera, of his own writing,
Himself shall exhibit his achievements in fighting.[37]

FUNCTIONAL MUSIC

In Voltaire's poem, 'The Maid of Orleans,' which describes French society at the time of Joan of Arc, contains a number of interesting references to functional music. First, we read of the use of the serpent in the French cathedrals, a practice which would continue until the nineteenth century.

To Heaven's high King, preferred a solemn prayer;
Te Deum sung by Drone from Serpent Bass …[38]

---

35 'The Worldling,' in Ibid., XXXVI, 87.
36 'Envy,' in Ibid., XXXVI, 185.
37 'To the King of Prussia,' in Ibid., XXXVI, 198.
38 'The Maid of Orleans,' in Ibid., XL, Canto XV.

There are also in this poem several references to music used to greet nobles. These vary considerably in tone, from, 'When citizens engaged with wine and dance, Extolled their prince, by songs and couplets graced,'[39] to, 'with joyous hymns, their sire's return they hailed,' and 'twenty trumpets then were heard to sound' in a welcome at a great palace.[40] This same poem also contains a reference to a rabbit 'roused by the echo of the hunting horn.'[41]

In view of the military adventures which characterized the period of Frederick the Great, we are not surprised to find numerous references to military music in Voltaire's poems. Several of these center on the 'shrill' sound of the military trumpet, including, 'To the King of Prussia,' which mentions the military 'trumpet's shrill sound,'[42] and the epic poem, 'The Henriade,' where again we find 'the shrill trumpet.'[43] In this same poem we find,

> The shrillness of the cheering horn provokes
> Their rage, and echoes from the distant rocks.[44]

A somewhat different mood is portrayed where we read,

> Paris, the king, the army, heaven, and hell
> Witnessed the combat—at the trumpets' swell
> On to the field the ready warriors came,
> Conscious of valor, and a thirst for fame ...[45]

Finally, Voltaire uses the trumpet in allegory in 'The Heinriade.'

> Hark! a loud peal comes thundering from afar,
> 'Tis Discord blows afresh the flames of war,
> To thwart the monarch's virtue, with new fires
> His fainting foes the bedlam fiend inspires;
> She blows her fatal trumpet, the woods around
> And mountains tremble at the infernal sound.
> Swift to d'Aumale the baleful notes impart
> Their power, he feels the summons at his heart ...[46]

---

39 Ibid., Canto XV.

40 Ibid., Canto IV.

41 Ibid.

42 'To the King of Prussia,' in *The Works of Voltaire*, XXXVI, 196.

43 'The Henriade,' Canto VIII, in Ibid., XXXVIII, 119.

44 Ibid., Canto VIII, 126.

45 Ibid., Canto X, 147ff.

46 Ibid., Canto VIII, 125ff.

One reference to the military trumpet is included in an allegorical contemplation on the vanity of war.

> The air though roaring cannons rend
> While warriors with fierce rage contend,
> The thoughtless French drink, laugh, and sing,
> And with their mirth the heavens ring ...
> The Phantom, which we Glory name,
> Spurs them to the pursuit of fame;
> With threatening eye, and front all over
> Bedusted, marching still before,
> She holds a trumpet in her hand
> To sound to arms, and cheer the band,
> And loudly sings, with voice sonorous,
> Catches, which they repeat in chorus.
> Oh! people brilliant, gay, and vain,
> Who drag with patience glory's chain,
> 'Tis great, an honorable grave
> To seek, Eugene and death to brave.
> But what will be your mighty prize?[47]

ENTERTAINMENT MUSIC

Voltaire rarely concerns himself with scenes of entertainment, but we particularly noticed in his, 'The Maid of Orleans,' a description of Hell which includes, 'songs in praise of drinking loudly roar.'[48] A resident of Hell observes,

> Cursed and tormented here, why care a jot
> For psalms and praises sung where we are not?

---

47 'In Camp before Philippsburg, July 3, 1734,' in *The Works of Voltaire*, XXXVI, 178ff.
48 'The Maid of Orleans,' in Ibid., XL, Canto V.

13 VOLTAIRE'S FICTION

ALL OF VOLTAIRE'S FICTIONAL ROMANCES are to some degree disguised philosophy, and the most interesting of these today are those which seem to comment on contemporary events. For example, his most famous romance, *Candide*, was written as a direct response to the earthquake in Lisbon, in November 1755, in which 30,000 were killed. The quake hit on All Saints' Day, a very significant church festival day in Europe, and thus it was the fact that so many of the faithful were among the dead that so shook Voltaire's faith. The response by some, such as Rousseau (who said man himself was to blame for being in church) and the followers of Leibniz's philosophy of optimism, astonished Voltaire. In *Candide*, Candide and Professor Pangloss (representing Leibniz) journey to Lisbon in time for the earthquake. Pangloss explains, of the tragedy,

> All this was indispensable for private misfortune makes the general good, so that the more private misfortunes there are, the greater is the general good.

Curiously, as he sometimes did, Voltaire pretended this was not his work.

> What is this brochure entitled *Candide* which people say is being scandalously circulated and is said to come from Lyons? … It is claimed that there are people impertinent enough to impute this work, which I have never seen, to me![1]

The following month, he writes another correspondent,

> I have finally read *Candide*. They must have lost their senses to attribute that filth to me.[2]

Perhaps such statements were made in self-defense, to protect himself against the repetition of earlier unpleasant experiences with the critics. This seems all the more evident in the fact that *Candide* also includes several satirical views of the critics. In a passage which discusses the theater in France, Voltaire comments on those critics ['wits'] who pan a work, even though it is so effective that members of the audience cry.

---

[1] Letter to Gabriel Cramer (February, 1759), in *The Selected Letters*, 198.
[2] Letter to Jacob Vernes (March, 1759), in Ibid., 199.

Candide found himself placed near a cluster of wits: this, however, did not prevent him from shedding tears at some parts of the piece which were most affecting, and best acted. 'You are greatly to blame to shed tears; that actress plays horribly, and the man that plays with her still worse, and the piece itself is still more execrable than the representation. The author does not understand a word of Arabic, and yet he has laid his scene in Arabia, and what is more, he is a fellow who does not believe in innate ideas. Tomorrow I will bring you a score of pamphlets that have been written against him.' 'Pray, sir,' said Candide to the abbé, 'how many theatrical pieces have you in France?' 'Five or six thousand,' replied the abbé. 'Indeed! that is a great number,' said Candide, 'but how many good ones may there be?' 'About fifteen or sixteen.'[3]

Later one of these critics speaks of the 'official rules' of writing drama.

Whoever neglects any one of these rules, though he may write two or three tragedies with tolerable success, will never be reckoned in the number of good authors.[4]

Voltaire provides a picture of another critic in a scene in *Candide* where the latter is touring a great private library. First Candide is shown eighty volumes of memoirs of the Academy of Sciences, a symbol of the Scholastic tradition still alive at the University of Paris. His host observes that these volumes contain not a single article of real utility.[5] Next he is shown volumes comprising three thousand plays, of which scarcely thirty are 'worth anything.' Of huge volumes of sermons, the host admits no one, even himself, ever looks at them. The innocent Candide observes that this must be the happiest man, who owns all these books. His guide responds, no, he dislikes everything he possesses. In an exchanged intended to describe critics, we find,

CANDIDE. But there must certainly be a pleasure in criticizing everything, and in perceiving faults where others think they see beauties.
MARTIN. That is, there is a pleasure in having no pleasure.[6]

Finally, in another work of fiction, 'The World as it Goes,' we find a 'man of letters,' whom we must regard as Voltaire, who speaks of the critics ('pedants') and concludes with a reference to himself.

In all times, in all countries, and in all kinds of literature, the bad swarm and the good are rare. Thou hast received into thy house the very dregs of pedantry. In all professions, those who are least worthy of appearing are always sure to present themselves with the greatest impudence. The truly wise live among themselves in retirement and tranquility.[7]

---

3   *Candide*, in *The Works of Voltaire*, I, 154ff.
4   Ibid., 160.
5   Ibid., 182ff.
6   Ibid., 182ff.
7   'The World as it Goes,' in *The Works of Voltaire*, III, 282.

ON THE PHYSIOLOGY OF AESTHETICS

The few passages among the fictional works of Voltaire which deal with the workings of the mind all involve in some way the dual sides of man, the rational and the emotional. He is almost cynical when he describes this relationship in his 'Memnon the Philosopher.'

> Memnon one day took it into his head to become a great philosopher. 'To be perfectly happy,' said he to himself, 'I have nothing to do but to divest myself entirely of passions, and nothing is more easy, as everybody knows.'[8]

This of course is impossible, for the reason Voltaire submits in his initial description of Candide, 'His face was the true index of his mind.'[9]

In another fictional work, 'The Study of Nature,' Voltaire introduces Sidrac, a 'clever anatomist,' who also reflects the twin sides of man when he distinguishes between 'knowing' and 'feeling.'

> I *feel*, I *know*, that God has endowed me with the faculties of thinking and speaking, but I can neither *feel* nor *know* that God has given me a thing called a soul.[10]

He continues,

> It is, in fact, ridiculous to use words we do not understand, and to admit the existence of beings of whom we cannot have the slightest knowledge.

A character in 'The Chinese Catechism' also reflects on the nature of the emotions and reason.

> We have passions, memory, and reason; but these passions, this memory, and this reason, are surely not separate things; they are not beings existing in us; they are not diminutive persons of particular existence; they are generic words, invented to fix our ideas.[11]

We have, in these volumes, often noted the expression of right hand preference which is mentioned in the literature of all periods since the ancient civilizations. We find a particularly unusual and intriguing example of this in Voltaire's 'Zadig' (1747). This story centers on a Babylonian philosopher and wise man who 'knew as much of metaphysics as hath ever been known in any age, that is, little or nothing at all.' Near the beginning of this story, a young

---

8 'Memnon the Philosoper,' in Ibid., IV, 33.
9 *Candide*, in Ibid., I, 61.
10 'The Study of Nature,' in *The Complete Romances of Voltaire* (New York: Walter Black, 1927), 309
11 'The Chinese Catechism,' in Ibid., 472.

man, Zadig, is wounded in the eye. A messenger is sent to Memphis for the famous physician, Hermes, who came with his large retinue. After his examination of Zadig, the doctor observed,

> Had it been the right eye, I could have cured it; but the wounds of the left eye are incurable.

ON THE PHILOSOPHY OF AESTHETICS

In 'The World as it Goes,' Voltaire suggests that great art does not come without experience. He also takes advantage of the opportunity to make a satirical reference to his contemporaries who are consumed with the art of ancient Greece.

> He entered that immense city by the ancient gate, which was entirely barbarous, and offended the eye by its disagreeable rusticity. All that part of the town savored of the time when it was built; for, notwithstanding the obstinacy of men in praising ancient at the expense of modern times, it must be recognized that the first essays in every art are rude and unfinished.[12]

There are two interesting passages in Voltaire's fictional romances which center on the ancient aesthetic question regarding the relationship between art and nature. The first is found in *Candide*, where we also find a reference to the price of paintings, which had been rapidly increasing since the period of humanism began. Here, the protagonist meets an art collector who has paid a great deal of money for paintings, even though he does not like them.

> 'Pray,' said Candide, 'by what master are the two first of these?' 'They are by Raphael,' answered the senator. 'I gave a great deal of money for them seven years ago, purely out of curiosity, as they were said to be the finest pieces in Italy; but I cannot say they please me: the coloring is dark and heavy; the figures do not swell nor come out enough; and the drapery is bad. In short, notwithstanding the encomiums lavished upon them, they are not, in my opinion, a true representation of nature. I approve of no painting save those wherein I think I behold nature herself.'[13]

The second passage, from 'The Study of Nature,' is no less interesting. Here we find an imaginary dialog between Sidrac, 'a clever anatomist,' and Mr. Goodman, in which the latter questions the relationship of art and nature in a satire largely based on the views of Newton and Descartes.

> I cannot discover any trace of what the world calls nature; on the contrary, everything seems to me to be the result of art. By art the planets are made to revolve around the sun, while the sun revolves on its own axis. I am convinced that some genius has arranged things in such a manner, that the square of the revolutions of the planets is always in proportion to the cubic root from

---

12 'The World as it Goes,' in *The Works of Voltaire*, III, 270.
13 *Candide*, in Ibid., I, 178.

their distance to their center, and one has need to be a magician to find out how this is accomplished. The tides of the sea are the result of art no less profound and no less difficult to explain.

All animals, vegetables and minerals are arranged with due regard to weight and measure, number and motion. All is performed by springs, levers, pullies, hydraulic machines, and chemical combinations, from the insignificant flea to the being called man, from the grass of the field to the far spreading oak, from a grain of sand to a cloud in the firmament of heaven. Assuredly, everything is governed by art, and the word *nature* is but a chimera.[14]

ON THE AESTHETICS OF MUSIC

In his fictional romances, Voltaire offers humorous references to several aspects of contemporary discussion on music and society. 'André Des Touches in Siam,' begins with a concise reflection of Voltaire's opinion of contemporary French music and includes a reference to his favorite composer.

> André Des Touches was a very agreeable musician in the brilliant reign of Louis XIV, before the science of music was perfected by Rameau, and before it was corrupted by those who prefer the art of surmounting difficulties to nature and the real graces of composition.[15]

This same romance includes a passage which reflects the ongoing discussion in France on the relative virtues of ancient and contemporary art. In the course of this story, Des Touches interviews an official from Siam named Croutef. Des Touches wants to discuss the music of Siam, which sounds discordant to him, but Croutef only wants to speak of the 'harmony' of society, in the Platonic sense.

> DES TOUCHES. Tell me, I beseech you, sir, if in Siam you divide the tone major into two commas, or into two semi-commas, and if the progress of the fundamental sounds are made by one, three, and nine?
> CROUTEF. By Sammonocodom, you are laughing at me. You observe no bounds. You have interrogated me on the form of our government, and you speak to me of music!
> DES TOUCHES. Music is everything. It was at the foundation of all the politics of the Greeks. But I beg your pardon; you have not a good ear, and we will return to our subject. You said that in order to produce a perfect harmony —
> CROUTEF. I was telling you that formerly the tonsured Tartar pretended to dispose of all the kingdoms of Asia, which occasioned something very different from perfect harmony.... However, all things go on; people divert themselves, they dance, they play, they dine, they sup, they make love; this makes every man shudder who entertains good intentions.

---

14 'The Study of Nature,' in *The Complete Romances of Voltaire*, 308.
15 'André Des Touches in Siam,' in *The Works of Voltaire*, IV, 5.

DES TOUCHES. And what would you have more? You only lack good music. If you had good music you might call your nation the happiest in the world.[16]

Another reference to the ancient–modern debates is found in 'A Dialogue between Marcus Aurelius and a Recollet Friar.' In the passage in question, the friar is bringing the famous emperor and philosopher up to date on changes in Rome since his death hundreds of years before. Among these, the friar observes,

> Peace and the fine arts flourish here eternally. The ancient masters of the world are now become music-masters. Instead of sending colonies into England, we now send them eunuchs and fiddlers.[17]

Another reference to castrati is found in *Candide*.

> I was born in Naples, he said, where they make eunuchs of thousands of children every year; some die of the operation; some acquire voices far beyond the most tuneful of your ladies; and others are sent to govern states and empires [in the East]. I underwent this operation very successfully, and was one of the singers in the princess of Palestrina's chapel.[18]

In the romance, *Jeannot and Colin*, music is included in a humorous discussion of the limited value of education for a person of high birth. There is a complaint that 'the genius of young persons is smothered under a heap of useless knowledge.'

> A man of quality, like the young marquis, should not rack his brains with useless sciences ... Did anybody ever so much as think of talking of geometry in good company?[19]

It is decided that it would be a virtue if the young marquis would learn to dance, especially as he seemed to have a natural talent for music.

> Nature, which does all, had given him a talent that quickly displayed itself surprisingly; it was that of singing ballads agreeably. The graces of youth, joined to this superior gift, caused him to be looked upon as a young man of the brightest hopes. He was admired by the women; and having his head full of songs he composed some for his mistress. He stole from the song, 'Bacchus and Love,' in one ballad; from that of 'Night and Day' in another; from that of 'Charms and Alarms,' in a third. But as there were always in his verses some superfluous feet, or not enough, he had them corrected for twenty Louis d'or a song.[20]

---

16 Ibid., 11ff.

17 'A Dialogue between Marcus Aurelius and a Recollet Friar,' in Ibid., IV, 68.

18 *Candide*, in Ibid., I, 101.

19 'Jeannot and Colin,' in Ibid., III,10ff.

20 Ibid., 12.

Finally, in 'The Blind as Judges of Color,' Voltaire presents a brief story of the blind in a hospital who pretend to be authorities on color. We take this as a satire on self-proclaimed experts on topics of which they know nothing, as well, perhaps, a reflection of the Scholastic views of the University of Paris, which held that one can only 'know' music in its conceptual form ('speculative music') rather than by the ear. This story concludes with the observation by a deaf man that the 'deaf were the only proper judges of music.'[21]

Is this outrageous? Did the universities really believe this? One recalls that Petrarch, in his 'Remedies for Fortune Fair and Foul' (II, xcvii), wrote this curious contention:

> A deaf person can know the tones and numbers characterizing the intervals of fifth and octave, as well as the other proportions of the musical scale with which musicians work. Although one does not hear the sounds of the human voice, of strings or the organ, he nevertheless may understand in his mind their fundamental canon and, doubtless, will prefer the intellectual pleasure to a mere titillation of the ear.

ART MUSIC

In 'The Princess of Babylon,' Voltaire employs a pastoral scene, so often used in Renaissance and baroque literature, as the setting for the singing of love songs. Here there is an ensemble of birds singing the soprano and alto parts, with shepherds singing the tenor and bass. One listener, with tears flowing from her eyes, calls the resulting music 'consolatory and voluptuous.'[22]

Voltaire included two satiric views of opera in his romances. He was no lover of Italian opera, as is clear in this passage from *Candide*.

> While dinner was being prepared Pococuranté ordered a concert. Candide praised the music to the skies. 'This noise,' said the noble Venetian, 'may amuse one for a little time, but if it were to last more than a half-hour, it would grow tiresome to everybody, though perhaps no one would care to admit it. Music has become the art of executing what is difficult; now, whatever is difficult cannot be long pleasing.
>
> I believe I might take more pleasure in an opera, if they had not made such a monster of that species of dramatic entertainment as perfectly shocks me; and I am amazed how people can bear to see wretched tragedies set to music; where the scenes are contrived for no other purpose than to lug in, as it were by the ears, three or four ridiculous songs, to give a favorite actress an opportunity of exhibiting her vocal-pipes. Let who will die away in raptures at the trills of a eunuch quavering the majestic part of Caesar or Cato, and strutting in a foolish manner upon the

---

21 'The Blind as Judges of Color,' in Ibid., IV, 13ff.
22 'The Princess of Babylon,' in Ibid., III, 206.

stage, but for my part I have long ago renounced these paltry entertainments, which constitute the glory of modern Italy, and are so dearly purchased by crowned heads.'[23]

In 'The Princess of Babylon,' Voltaire satirizes the Church's objections to opera, various excesses of opera itself and the apparent tradition of nobles dating the ladies of the opera after the show, all set in the period of ancient Babylon.

> After dinner he was conducted to a place of public entertainment which was enchanting, but condemned, however, by the Druids, because it deprived them of their auditors, which, therefore, excited their jealousy. The representation here consisted of agreeable verses, delightful songs, dances which expressed the movements of the soul, and perspectives that charmed the eye in deceiving it. This kind of pastime, which included so many kinds, was known only under a foreign name. It was called 'an Opera,' which formerly signified in the language of the Seven Mountains, work, care, occupation, industry, enterprise, business. This exhibition enchanted him. A female singer, in particular, charmed him by her melodious voice and the graces that accompanied her. This child of genius, after the performance, was introduced to him by his new friends. He presented her with a handful of diamonds, for which she was so grateful that she could not leave him all the rest of the day. He supped with her and her companions, and during the delightful repast he forgot his sobriety and became heated and oblivious with wine ... What an instance of human frailty![24]

FUNCTIONAL MUSIC

In 'The Princess of Babylon,' Voltaire presents several views of functional court music, including a master of ceremonies preceded by twenty trumpets and 'a great number' of musicians seated near the buffet table.[25] That this is purely functional dinner music is made clear by the following:

> The music, which continued during the repast, furnished every prince with an opportunity of conversing with his female neighbor.

Voltaire makes several references to Church music. 'The White Bull,' set in the Old Testament time of Nebuchadnezzar, includes the description of a religious procession with a hundred girls playing 'the sacred sistrums' and priests singing in chorus 'with a harmony which ravished the soul, and which melted it.'

---

23   *Candide*, in Ibid., I, 178ff.
24   'The Princess of Babylon,' in Ibid., III, 247ff.
25   Ibid., 169, 182ff.

And at every pause was heard the sound of the sistrums, of cymbals, of tabors, of psalteries, of bagpipes, harps, and sackbuts.[26]

A character in 'The Study of Nature' voices an opinion which was probably near to Voltaire's own.

If God cannot change any of the affairs of the world, what is the use of teasing him with prayers, or of singing hymns to his praise.[27]

A final reference which should be mentioned is found in *Candide*, a work which reflects the deep impression made on Voltaire by the great earthquake in Lisbon. In a typical example of his biting satire, Voltaire writes that the Church arranged for an *auto-da-fé*, a burning of the unfaithful, as 'an infallible preventive of earthquakes.'[28] In his description of this execution he portrays a scene which included the singing of an anthem (which he later identifies as a *Miserere*) accompanied by bagpipes. As odd as this seems, there are other accounts of executions of the Huguenots in Paris being accompanied by lively music.

---

26 'The White Bull,' in Ibid., II, 238ff.
27 'The Study of Nature,' in *The Complete Romances of Voltaire*, 312.
28 *Candide*, in *The Works of Voltaire*, I, 80ff, 89.

BIBLIOGRAPHY

André, Yves Marie, *L'Essai sur le beau* [1741], in Peter le Huray and James Day. *Music and Aesthetics in the Eighteenth and Early-Nineteenth Centuries.* Cambridge: Cambridge University Press, 1981.

Arbeau, Thoitot. *Orchésographie.* [1588]. Translated by Peter Warlock. New York: Dance Horizons, 1966.

Barnes, Clifford, 'Instruments and Instrumental Music at the Théatres de la Foire,' in *Recherches sur la Musique francaise classique.* Paris: A. et J. Picard, 1965.

Batteux, Charles. *Les beaux-arts réduits à un meme principe* [1746], in Peter le Huray and James Day. *Music and Aesthetics in the Eighteenth and Early-Nineteenth Centuries.* Cambridge: Cambridge University Press, 1981.

Benoit, Marcelle, 'Paris, 1661–1687: the Age of Lully,' in *The Early Baroque Era.* Englewood Cliffs: Prentice Hall, 1994.

———. *Versailles et les Musiciens du Roi.* Paris: A. et J. Picard, 1971.

Bergerac, Cyrano de. *Other Worlds.* Translated by Geoffrey Strachan. London: Oxford University Press, 1965.

Bernhard, M. B., 'Notice sur la Confrèrie des Joueurs d'Instruments d'Alsace.' *La Revue historique de la Noblesse* (Paris, 1844).

Bianconi, Lorenzo. *Music in the Seventeenth Century.* Translated by David Bryant. Cambridge: Cambridge University Press, 1989.

Blom, John. *Descartes.* New York: New York University Press, 1978.

Boileau, Nicolas, 'Reflections on Longinus,' in *Selected Criticism.* Translated by Ernest Dilworth. New York: Bobbs-Merrill, 1965.

Bonnet-Bourdelot, Jacques. *Histoire de la musique et de ses effets depuis son origine, et les progrès successifs de cet art jusqu'à present* [1715], in Carol MacClintock. *Readings in the History of Music in Performance.* Bloomington: Indiana University Press, 1979.

Brantôme, Pierre. *Lives of Fair and Gallant Ladies.* Translated by A. R. Allinson. New York: Liverright, 1933.

Brossard, Sébastien de. *Dictionaire de Musique.* Paris: chez Christophe Ballard, 1703.

Brosses, Charles de. *Lettres familières écrites en Italie en 1739 et 1740* [1885], in Carol MacClintock. *Readings in the History of Music in Performance.* Bloomington: Indiana University Press, 1979.

Buelow, George J., 'Music and Society in the Late Baroque Era,' in *The Late Baroque Era.* Englewood Cliffs: Prentice Hall, 1994.

Chambers, Frank. *The History of Taste.* New York: Columbia University Press, 1932.

Chamblain de Marivaux, Pierre Carlet. *The Virtuous Orphan.* Translated by Mary Collyer. Carbondale: Southern Illinois University Press, 1965.

———. *Up From the Country.* Translated by Leonard Tancock. New York: Penguin Books, 1980.

Charlotte-Elisabeth Orléans, duchesse de. *A Woman's Life in the Court of the Sun King.* Translated by Elborg Forster. Baltimore: Johns Hopkins University Press, 1984.

Clark, Barrett. *European Theories of the Drama.* New York: Crown Publishers, 1959.

Cook, Albert. *The Art of Poetry.* Boston: Ginn, 1892.

Corneille, Pierre. *Polyeuctus. The Liar. Nicomedes.* Translated by John Cairncross. Middlesex: Penguin Books, 1980.

Couperin, François. *Concerts royaux*. Paris: Couperin, Boivin, Le Clerc, 1722.

———. *L'Art de tourcher* [Paris, 1717]. Wiesbaden: Breitkoppf & Härtel, 1933, reprint.

———. *Pièces*. Paris, 1722.

Crébillon, fils, Claude Prosper Jolyot de. *Letters from the Marchiness de M*** to the Count de R****. Edited by Josephine Grieder. New York: Garland, 1972.

De Bacilly. *L'Art de bien chanter*. Paris: G. de Luyne, 1671.

Descartes, René. *Descartes Philosophical Letters*. Translated by Anthony Kenny. Oxford: Clarendon Press, 1970.

———. *The Philosophical Writings of Descartes*. Translated by John Cottingham, Robert Stoothoff and Dugald Murdoch. Cambridge: Cambridge University Press, 1985.

———. *Compendium of Music*. Translated by Walter Robert. Rome: American Institution of Musicology, 1961.

Diderot, Denis. *Rameau's Nephew and Other Works*. Translated by Jacques Barzun. Garden City: Doubleday, 1956.

'Documents du Minutier Central,' in *Recherches sur la Musique francaise classique*. Paris: A. et J. Picard, 1968.

Doni, Giovanni Battista. *Compendio del trattato de' generi e de' modi*. Rome: Per A. Fei, 1635.

Donnington, Robert. *The Interpretation of Early Music*. New York:, Farber and Farber, 1964.

Du Bos, Jean-Baptiste. *Réflexions critiques sur la poësie et sur la peinture* [1719], in Peter le Huray and James Day. *Music and Aesthetics in the Eighteenth and Early-Nineteenth Centuries*. Cambridge: Cambridge University Press, 1981.

Duncan, David, 'Persuading the Affections: Rhetorical Theory and Mersenne's Advice to Harmonic Orators,' in *French Musical thought, 1600–1800*. Ann Arbor: UMI Research Press, 1989.

Durant, Will. *The Story of Philosophy*. New York: Simon & Schuster, 1961.

Écorchville, Jules, 'Quelques Documents sur la Musique de la Grand-Écurie du Roi.' *Sammelbande des Internationalen Musikgesellschaft* (1903).

———. *Vignt suites d'orchestre*. Paris, 1906.

Evelyn, John. *The Diary of Jon Evelyn*. Oxford: Clarendon Press, 1955.

Fénelon, François. *The Adventures of Telemachus, Son of Ulysses*. Translated by Patrick Riley. London: Garland Publishing, 1979.

———. *Fénelon's Dialogues on Eloquence*. Translated by Wilbur Howell. Princeton: Princeton University Press, 1951.

———. *Fénelon's Letter to the French Academy* [1746]. Translated by Barbara Warnick. New York: University Press of America, 1984.

———. *Fénelon on Education*. Translated by H. Barnard. Cambridge: University Press, 1966.

Finch, Robert. *Individualism in French Poetry (1686–1760)*. Toronto: University of Toronto Press, 1966.

François, René. *Essay des Merveilles de Nature, et des Plus Nobles Artifices*. Rouen: Osmont, 1626.

Grove, George. *The New Grove Dictionary of Music and Musicians*. Edited by Stanley Sadie. London: Macmillan, 1980.

Harris, Ellen, 'Voices,' in *Performance Practice: Music after 1600*. New York: Norton, 1989.

Hitchcock, H. Wiley, 'The Instrumental Music of Marc-Antoine Charpentier.' *The Musical Quarterly* 47, no. 1 (January 1961): 58–72, http://www.jstor.org/stable/740542.

Kastner, Georges. *Manuel Général de Musique Militaire*. Paris: Didot, 1848.

Kuyper, Jon. 'Marc-Antoine Charpentier's *Règles de Composition*.' Iowa City: University of Iowa, Unpublished Dissertation, 1971.
La Bruyère, Jean de. *Characters*. Translated by Jean Steward. Baltimore: Penguin Books, 1970.
La Font de Saint-Yenne. *Réflexions sur quelques causes de l'État present de la peinture en France*. La Haye: J. Naeulme, 1747.
Le Cerf de la Viéville, 'Traité du bon gout en musique,' in Oliver Strunk. *Source Readings in Music History*. New York: Norton, 1950.
———. *Histoire de la Musique*. Amsterdam: Chez M. Charles Le Cene, 1725.
Lesage, Alain René. *Asmodeus, or The Devil on Two Sticks* [1707]. Translated by Jules Janin. New York: the Bibliophilst Society, 1932.
Lippman, Edward. *Musical Aesthetics: A Historical Reader*. New York: Pendragon Press, 1986.
MacClintock, Carol. *Readings in the History of Music in Performance*. Bloomington: Indiana University Press, 1979.
Maland, David. *Culture and Society in Seventeenth-Century France*. New York: Scribner's, 1970.
Malebranche, Nicolas. *The Search after Truth*, in Malebranche, *Philosophical Selections*. Translated by Thomas Lennon and Paul Olscamp. Indianapolis: Hacket Publishing Company, 1992.
Mallet, Alain. *Les Travaux de Mars ou l'Art de la guerre*. Paris: D. Thierry, 1691.
Marolles, M. de. *Les Mémoires de Michel de Marolles, abbé de Villeloin*. Paris, 1656.
Massip, Catherine, 'Paris, 1600–1661,' in *The Early Baroque Era*. Englewood Cliffs: Prentice Hall, 1994.
Maugars, André, 'Response faite à un curieux sur le Sentiment de la Musique d'Italie, Ecrite à Rome le premier Octobre, 1639,' in Carol MacClintock. *Readings in the History of Music in Performance*. Bloomington: Indiana University Press, 1979.
Ménestrier, Claude. *Des Ballets anciens et modernes, selon les règles du Théâtre*. Paris: R. Guignard, 1682.
———. *Des representations en musique, anciennes et modernes*. Paris: R. Guignard, 1681.
Mercure Galant (Paris, May, 1692).
Mersenne, Marin. *Harmonie Universelle*, II. Translated by John Egan. Bloomington: Indiana University, 1962, unpublished dissertation.
———. *Harmonie Universelle*. Paris, 1636.
———. *Harmonie Universelle*. Translated by Roger Chapman. The Hague: Nijhoff, 1957.
———. *Harmonie Universelle*. 'Fourth Treatise of the Harmonie Universelle.' Edited by Robert Williams. Rochester: Eastman School of Music, 1972, unpublished dissertation.
———. *Harmonie Universelle*. 'Treatise Three, Book One, *Traitez de la Voix, et des Chants*. Translated by Edmund LeRoy. New York: Julliard School, 1978, unpublished dissertation.
———. *Harmonie Universelle*. 'Treatise Three, Book Two (Second Book of Songs) of the *Traitez de la Voix et des Chants*. Translated by Wilbur F. Russell. Princeton: Westminster Choir College, 1952, unpublished dissertation.
Morgenstern, Sam. *Composers on Music*. New York: Pantheon, 1956.
Norman, Gertrude and Miriam Shrifte. *Letters of Composers*. New York: Knopf, 1946.
Ozell, John. *The Works of Mr. de Moliere*. New York: Benjamin Blom, 1967.
Paris, National Archives, MS. 01/715, vol. 171, 173, 179, 181ff.
Paris, National Archives, MS. Bundle 01/2830, Nr. 86, 88.
Pascal, Blaise. *Pensées*. New York: Modern Library, 1941.

Prévost, Pierre Abbé. *Adventures of A Man of Quality*. Translated by Mysie Robertson. London: Routledge & Sons, 1930.
Raguenet, François, 'Parallèle des Italiens et des Français' [1702], in Oliver Strunk. *Source Readings in Music History*. New York: Norton, 1950.
Rameau, Jean-Philippe. *Treatise on Harmony*. Translated by Philip Gossett. New York: Dover, 1971.
Rochefoucauld, François de la. *The Maxims of La Rochefoucauld*. Translated by Louis Kronenberger. New York: Random House, 1959.
Rousseau, Jean-Jacques. *Dictionnaire de Musique*. Paris, Chez la veuve Duchesne, 1768.
Sadie, Julie Anne, 'Paris and Versailles,' in *The Late Baroque Era*. Englewood Cliffs: Prentice Hall, 1994.
Saint-Évremond, Charles de. *The Letters of Saint-Évremond*. Edited by John Hayward. Freeport, NY: Books of Libraries Press, 1971.
Saint-Lambert, Michel de. *Les Principes du Clavecin* [1702], in MacClintock, Carol. *Readings in the History of Music in Performance*. Bloomington: Indiana University Press, 1979.
Saint-Simon. *The Memoirs of the Duke of Saint-Simon*. Translated by Bayle St. John. London: George Allen, 1926.
Saxe, Maurice. *Les Rêveries ou Mémoires sur l'art de guerre*. Hague: Gosse, 1756.
Schmitz, Hans-Peter. *Die Kunst der Verzierung im 18. Jahrhundert*. Kassel: Bärenreiter, 1955.
Secondat, Charles de, Baron de Montesquieu. *The Spirit of Laws* [1748]. Translated by Thomas Nugent, in *Great Books* (XXXVIII). Chicago: Encyclopedia Britannica, 1952.
Secondat, Charles de, Baron de Montesquieu. *The Persian Letters*. London: Athenaeum, 1901.
Sévigné, Françoise Marguerite. *Letters of Madame de Sévigné*. Edited by Richard Aldington. London: Routledge, 1937.
Solomon, Samuel. *Pierre Corneille, Seven Plays*. New York: Random House, 1969.
Trichet, Pierre. *Traité des Instruments de Musique*. Bourdelois, 1631.
Vigneul-Marville [Bonaventure Argonne]. *Mélanges d'Histoire et de Litterature*. Paris: Chez Claude Prudhomme, 1725.
Voltaire. *The Complete Romances of Voltaire*. Translated by George Washington Black. New York: Walter J. Black and Company, 1927.
———. *The Selected Letters of Voltaire*. Translated by Richard Brooks. New York: New York University Press, 1973.
———. *The Works of Voltaire*. New York: St. Hubert Guild, 1901.
———. *Voltaire and Catherine the Great*. Translated by A. Lentin. Cambridge: Oriental Research Partners, 1974.
———. *Voltaire in His Letters*. Translated by S. G. Tallentyre. New York: Putnam, 1919.
———. *Select Letters of Voltaire*. Translated by Theodore Besterman. London: Nelson, 1963.
Walls, Peter, 'Strings,' in *Performance Practice: Music after 1600*. New York: Norton, 1989.
Walther, Johann. *Musikalisches Lexikon*. Leipzig: Deer, 1732.
Weiss, Piero. *Letters of Composers Through Six Centuries*. Philadelphia: Chilton, 1967.
Whitwell, David. *Extraordinary Women*. Northridge: WINDS, 1995.
Yates, Frances. *The French Academies of the Sixteenth Century*. Nendeln: Kraus, 1968.

INDEX

A

Adam, mythical first man, 56
Adrienne le Couvreur, 1692–1730, French actress, 292
Aldorise, Prosper, 17th century French philosopher, 59
Amfrye, Guillaume, Abbé de Chaulieu, 1631–1720, French poet, 118
André, Yves-Marie, 1675–1764, French philosopher, 108, 119ff
Anne of Austria, 1601–1666, queen consort of France, 5
Aquinas, Thomas, 1225–1274, Church philosopher, 80
Arbeau, Thoitot, 16th century French authority on dance, 16
Aristotle, 84, 110, 183, 188, 189, 190, 191, 273, 284
Arnauld, Antoine, 17th century Jansenist theologian, 165
Artin, Guy (perhaps is Guido), 11th century Benedictine music theorist, 40
Auguste Gosselin, Jean Nicolet, 1618–1642, French music critic, 40

B

Bacily, Bénigne de, 17th century French music theorist on singing, 32
Baïf, Jean-Antoine de, 1532–1589, leader of a 16th century French academie, 11, 49, 55, 65, 78
Batteau, Abbé, 1713–1780, important French philosopher, 83ff
Batteux, Charles, 1713–1780, French philosopher on aesthetics, 109ff, 120, 126ff, 131ff, 159
Bergerac, Cyrano de, 1619–1655, French playwright, 219ff
Bergerotti, Anna, soprano, court of Louis XIV, 4
Boileau-Despréaux, Nicolas, 1636–1711, French philosopher, 107ff, 112ff, 272, 307
Bonnet-Bourdelot, Jacques, 1644–1724, French writer on music, 140, 148ff, 155
Brantôme, Pierre, 1540–1614, French historian, 225
Brécourt, 1638–1685, French playwright, 195
Brossard, Sebastien de, 1654–1730, French writer on music, 23, 27, 122
Brosses, Charles de, 1709–1777, French writer, 140ff, 143ff, 146ff, 156ff, 160

C

Calvin, John, Protestant preacher, 253
Cardano, Girolamo, 1501–1576, Italian philosopher, 42
Castel, Louis, 1688–1757, French mathematician, study of optics, 271ff
Catherine the Great, Empress of Russia, 244
Cavalli, Francesco, 1602–1676, Italian composer, 8ff
Caylus, Count, 1692–1765, French painter and critic, 84
Chambonnières, Jacques, harpsichordist under Louis XI, 237
Chanut, Pierre, 17th century French ambassador to Sweden, 176, 178
Chapelain, Jean, 17th century French drama critic, 184ff
Charpentier, Marc-Antoine, 1643–1704, French composer, 14, 19, 24, 30
Chaucer, English poet, 301
Christine of Sweden, 1626–1689, 169
Clairon, Mademoiselle, French actress, 287
Corelli, 146
Corneille, Pierre, 1606–1684, French playwright, 89, 146, 183ff, 187ff, 192, 208, 227, 291ff
Couperin, François, 1668–1733, French composer, 22ff, 24, 25, 26, 27, 28, 30, 31, 32, 34
Crébillon, Claude Prosper Jolyot, fils, 17th century French fiction writer, 215, 222
Créqui, Mareschal, 229

D

Descartes, René, 1596–1650, French philosopher, 163ff, 250, 320
Desjardins, Jean Baptiste, 17th century oboist in the *Les Grands Hautbois*, 2
Diderot, Denis, 1713–1784, French encyclopedist, 28

Doni, Giovanni Battista, 1593–1647, Italian musicologist, 76
Du Bos, Jean-Baptiste, Abbé, 1670–1742, important French philosopher, 84, 110, 116ff, 119, 129ff
Du Bros, 160
Duché, Joseph, 1668–1704, French librettist, 277
Dumesnil, Mademoisele, French actress, 287

E

Elisabeth Charlotte, Duchesse d'Orléans, 1652–1722, 227ff, 238
Elizabeth, 17th century princess of Bohemia, 165ff
Evelyn, John, 17th century English diarist, 13

F

Fénelon, François, 1651–1715, French Church leader, writer, 96ff, 103, 108, 109, 116, 118ff, 135, 193, 213ff, 216, 218ff, 224
Fontenelle, Bernard Le Bovier de, 1657–1757, French philosopher, 117, 308
François I King of France, 1
Frederick II, 'the Great,' 1712–1786, King of Prussia, 2
Frederick the Great of Prussia, 244ff, 301, 303, 315

G

Gillotot, François, 17th century student oboist in Paris, 2
Gossec, François, 1734–1829, French composer, 11
Gresset, Jean-Baptiste, 1709–1777, French poet, 118

H

Handel, Georg, Baroque German composer, 144
Hédelin, François (Abbé d'Aubignac), 1604–1676, French drama critic, 185ff, 190
Henry IV, 1553–1610, King of France, 1
Hesiod, ancient Greek poet, 116
Homer, ancient Greek poet, 116
Houdar de la Motte, Antoine, 1672–1731, French poet, 117, 308
Huygens, Constantin, 1596–1687, Dutch poet, composer, 67

K

Kastner, Georges, 19th century military historian, 15
Kepler, Johann, 1571–1630, astronomer, 40

L

La Barre, Pierre, 1592–1656, organist in Paris, 11
La Borde, Jean Benjamin, 1734–1794, French composer, guillotined in 1794, 272
La Bruyère, Jean de, 1645–1696, French philosophy, 85, 89, 96, 103ff, 107, 118, 134, 150, 160, 161, 186
La Font de Saint Yenne, early 18th century French art critic, 84
La Maupin, 17th century opera singer in Paris, 9
La Mothe-Fénelon, François, 1651–1715, French philosopher, 85
La Rochefoucauld, François de, 1613–1680, French philosopher, 88ff, 102ff, 107, 109, 161

Lambert, Michel, court vocal teacher under Louis XIV, 4, 31, 33
Le Cerf de la Viélle, Jean Laurent, 1674–1707, French noble, 14, 123ff, 141, 142, 146
Le Jeune, Claude, 1528–1600, Franco-Flemish composer, 48
Leibnitz, German philosopher, 83, 308
Lesage, Alain-René, 17th century French playwright, 210, 217, 222, 225
Longius, Cassius, 3rd century author of 'On the Sublime,' 107
Louis XI, 237
Louis XIII, 1491–1548, King of France, 1, 11, 128
Louis XIV, 1638–1715, King of France, 1ff, 8, 16, [on singing in private] 235, 246, [on music of the court] 269, [as a dancer] 279
Louis XV, 1710–1774, King of France, 9, 84
Louis XVI, 246
Lully, Jean-Baptiste, 1632–1687, French composer, 3ff, 8, 145, 149, 260, 269ff, [as a person] 272, 273
Luther, Martin, 253

M

Mahomet, the prophet, 253
Malebranche, Nicolas, 1638–1715, French Church philosopher, 90ff
Mandeville, Bernard, 1670–1733, Dutch philosopher, 261
Marazin, Cardinal, 1602–1661, chief minister under Louis XIII, 1
Marie-Thérèse, b. 1638, queen consort of France, 5

Marivaux, Pierre de, 1688–1763, French novelist and playwright, 194, 200, 205, 209, 214ff, 218, 221
Marolles, Michel de, abbé, 1600–1681, French churchman, 13
Masson, Charles, 17th century French writer, 26
Maugars, André, 128, 138ff, 144, 147ff, 150
Maurice, 17th century Prince of Nassau, 178
Ménestrier, Claude, 1631–1705, French scholar, 16
Mermet, Louis Bollioud de, late Baroque French critic, 32
Mersenne, Marin, 1588–1648, French philosopher, theologian, 15, 37ff, 166ff, 172, 180ff,
Meysonnier, Lazare, 17th century French professor and astrologer at Lyons, 171, 182
Molière (Jean-Baptiste Poquelin), 1622–1673, French playwright, 6ff, 183, 193ff, 233, 264, 291ff
Montesquieu, Secondat, Charles de, Baron de Montesquieu, 1689–1755, French writer, 86ff, 100, 103, 127, 137ff, 213ff, 224

N

Nebuchadnezzar, 324
Newton, 320

O

Ogier, François, 17th century French playwright, 183
Ottoboni, Cardinal, 1667–1740, patron of music in Rome, 141

P

Pascal, Blaise, 1623–1662, French philosopher, 86ff, 101ff, 106ff, 109, 117, 260, 263ff
Philidor, Jacques Danican, d. 1708, member of *Les Grands Hautbois*, 2
Philippe, Duke of Orlénas, Regent under Louis XV, 9
Piles, Roger de, 1635–1709, French painter and critic, 83ff
Pouplinière, Alexandre-Jean-Joseph Le Riche de la, 1693–1762, French financier, 11
Prévost, Pierre Abbé, 1697–1763, French fiction writer, 213
Ptolemy, 85–165, astronomer, 56
Pythagoras, ancient Greek philosopher, 39

Q

Quinault, Philippe, 1635–1688, French librettist, 273, 308, 313
Quirini, 17th century Bishop of Brescia, 283

R

Racine, Jean, 1639–1699, French playwright, 89, 183, 194, 198ff, 200, 207, [accused of murder] 238, 248, 298
Raguenet, François, 1661–1722, French writer, 123, 139, 141, 145ff, 153ff, 159
Rameau, Jean-Philippe, 1683–1764, French composer, 11, 19ff, 25, 29, 35, 267, 273, 281, 313
Raphael, Renaissance painter, 260, 320
Regius, Henricus, 17th century Dutch professor of medicine at Utrecht, 165, 169

Richelieu, Cardinal, 1585–1642, chief minister under Louis XIII, 1, 10, 183, 187, 281, 284
Rivault, David de Flurance, chief tutor to Louis XIII, 11, 128
Rohan-Chabot, Guy Auguste, 1683–1760, French noble, 279
Rousseau, Jean, 17th century French violist, 22, 26
Rousseau, Jean-Jacques, 1712–1778, French philosopher, [as music copyist], 3, 246, 308

S

Saint-Évremond, Charles, 1613–1703, French writer, 89, 151ff, 190ff, 227ff, 237
Saint-Lambert, Michel de, late Baroque French keyboard theorist, 23, 90ff
Saint-Simon (Louis de Rouvroy), Duke of, 1675–1755, 214. 233
Saxe, Maurice de, 1696–1750, French general, 17
Scarron, French poet, 17th century, 12
Schélandre, Jean de, 17th century French playwright, 183
Schuurman, Maria, 1607–1678, Dutch artist and linguist, 164
Segrais, J. R. de, 1624–1701, French philosopher, 117
Seguier, Peter, French Chancellor, 236
Sévigné, Françoise-Margurite, 1646–1705, French noble, 232ff, 236, 238, 241
Silhon, Jean de, 17th century French philosopher, 172
Spinoza, 90
St. Augustine, 4th century, 156

Stamitz, Johann Wenzel Anton, 1717–1759, German composer, 11
Sully, Maximilien, 1560–1641, chief minister under Henry IV, 1

T

Thibault de Courville, Joachim, d. 1581, French musician, 78
Thyard, Pontus de, 1521–1605, French philosopher, poet, 87, 55
Trichet, Pierre, 17th century French writer on string technique, 26

V

Voetius, Gisbertus, 1589–1676, Dutch professor of theology at Utrecht, 164
Voltaire, French philosopher and writer, 243ff, 283, 301ff, 317

ABOUT THE AUTHOR

Dr. David Whitwell is a graduate ('with distinction') of the University of Michigan and the Catholic University of America, Washington DC (PhD, Musicology, Distinguished Alumni Award, 2000) and has studied conducting with Eugene Ormandy and at the Akademie für Musik, Vienna. Prior to coming to Northridge, Dr. Whitwell participated in concerts throughout the United States and Asia as Associate First Horn in the USAF Band and Orchestra in Washington DC, and in recitals throughout South America in cooperation with the United States State Department.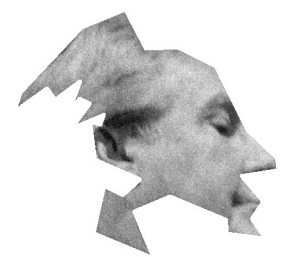

At the California State University, Northridge, which is in Los Angeles, Dr. Whitwell developed the CSUN Wind Ensemble into an ensemble of international reputation, with international tours to Europe in 1981 and 1989 and to Japan in 1984. The CSUN Wind Ensemble has made professional studio recordings for BBC (London), the Köln Westdeutscher Rundfunk (Germany), NOS National Radio (The Netherlands), Zürich Radio (Switzerland), the Television Broadcasting System (Japan) as well as for the United States State Department for broadcast on its 'Voice of America' program. The CSUN Wind Ensemble's recording with the Mirecourt Trio in 1982 was named the 'Record of the Year' by The Village Voice. Composers who have guest conducted Whitwell's ensembles include Aaron Copland, Ernest Krenek, Alan Hovhaness, Morton Gould, Karel Husa, Frank Erickson and Vaclav Nelhybel.

Dr. Whitwell has been a guest professor in 100 different universities and conservatories throughout the United States and in 23 foreign countries (most recently in China, in an elite school housed in the Forbidden City). Guest conducting experiences have included the Philadelphia Orchestra, Seattle Symphony Orchestra, the Czech Radio Orchestras of Brno and Bratislava, The National Youth Orchestra of Israel, as well as resident wind ensembles in Russia, Israel, Austria, Switzerland, Germany, England, Wales, The Netherlands, Portugal, Peru, Korea, Japan, Taiwan, Canada and the United States.

He is a past president of the College Band Directors National Association, a member of the Prasidium of the International Society for the Promotion of Band Music, and was a member of the founding board of directors of the World Association for Symphonic Bands and Ensembles (WASBE). In 1964 he was made an honorary life member of Kappa Kappa Psi, a national professional music fraternity. In September, 2001, he was a delegate to the UNESCO Conference on Global Music in Tokyo. He has been knighted by sovereign organizations in France, Portugal and Scotland and has been awarded the gold medal of Kerkrade, The Netherlands, and the silver medal of Wangen, Germany, the highest honor given wind conductors in the United States, the medal of the Academy of Wind and Percussion Arts (National Band Association) and the highest honor given wind conductors in Austria, the gold medal of the Austrian Band Association. He is a member of the Hall of Fame of the California Music Educators Association.

Dr. Whitwell's publications include more than 127 articles on wind literature including publications in Music and Letters (London), the London Musical Times, the Mozart-Jahrbuch (Salzburg), and 39 books, among which is his 13-volume *History and Literature of the Wind Band and Wind Ensemble* and an 8-volume series on *Aesthetics in Music*. In addition to numerous modern editions of early wind band music his original compositions include 5 symphonies.

David Whitwell was named as one of six men who have determined the course of American bands during the second half of the 20th century, in the definitive history, *The Twentieth Century American Wind Band* (Meredith Music).

A doctoral dissertation by German Gonzales (2007, Arizona State University) is dedicated to the life and conducting career of David Whitwell through the year 1977. David Whitwell is one of nine men described by Paula A. Crider in *The Conductor's Legacy* (Chicago: GIA, 2010) as 'the legendary conductors' of the 20th century.

> 'I can't imagine the 2nd half of the 20th century—without David Whitwell and what he has given to all of the rest of us.' Frederick Fennell (1993)

ABOUT THE EDITOR

CRAIG DABELSTEIN began studying the piano at age seven and took up the saxophone at age twelve. Mr Dabelstein has Bachelor of Arts (Music) and Bachelor of Music degrees from the Queensland Conservatorium of Music, where he majored in the performance of classical saxophone repertoire. He also has a Graduate Diploma of Learning and Teaching and a Graduate Certificate in Editing and Publishing from the University of Southern Queensland.

He has held the principal alto and tenor saxophone chairs in the Australian Wind Orchestra and has been an augmenting member of the Queensland Philharmonic Orchestra, the Queensland Symphony Orchestra, and the Queensland Pops Orchestra. For many years he was also a member of the Queensland Saxophone Quartet.

He has been a casual conductor of the Young Conservatorium Symphonic Winds, and has previously been a saxophone teacher at the Queensland Conservatorium of Music. He is a regular conductor of the Queensland Wind Orchestra, having served as their artistic director and chief conductor from 2004 to 2009.

Craig Dabelstein is a research associate for the *Teaching Music Through Performance in Band* series of books, contributing analyses to volumes 7, 8, 1 (rev. edn), and the *Solos with Wind Band Accompaniment* volume. He served as the copyeditor and layout designer of the *Australian Clarinet and Saxophone Magazine* from 2007 to 2009 and he has written many CD and book reviews for *Music Forum* magazine. He is the editor of the second editions of the books by Dr. David Whitwell including *A Concise History of the Wind Band*, *Foundations of Music Education*, *Music Education of the Future*, *The Sousa Oral History Project*, *Wagner on Bands*, *Berlioz on Bands*, *The Art of Musical Conducting*, and the *Aesthetics of Music* series (8 volumes) and *The History and Literature of the Wind Band and Wind Ensemble* series (13 volumes). From 1994 to 2012 he was a staff member at Brisbane Girls Grammar School. He now teaches woodwinds and conducts bands at St. Joseph's College, Gregory Terrace, Brisbane, Australia.

www.ingramcontent.com/pod-product-compliance
Lightning Source LLC
Chambersburg PA
CBHW080728300426
44114CB00019B/2508